SPACES, SPATIALITY AND TECHNOLOGY

The Kluwer International Series on Computer Supported Cooperative Work

Volume 5

Spaces, Spatiality and Technology

Edited by

Phil Turner
Napier University,
Edinburgh, UK

and

Elisabeth Davenport
Napier University,
Edinburgh, UK

 Springer

A C.I.P. Catalogue record for this book is available from the Library of Congress.

ISBN 978-90-481-6829-3 (PB)
ISBN 978-1-4020-3273-8 (e-book)

Published by Springer,
P.O. Box 17, 3300 AA Dordrecht, The Netherlands.

Printed on acid-free paper

TABLE OF CONTENTS

vi

ACKNOWLEDGEMENTS

Thanks to Fiona Carroll for all of her work in the physical arrangements for the workshop and fielding the queries from the participants.

We would also like to thank the following people who acted as reviewers for both the initial submissions to the workshop and the final chapters.

Prof. Richard Coyne, Edinburgh University
Prof. Blaise Cronin, University of Indiana
Prof. Yvonne Rogers, University of Indiana
Dr. Barry Brown, Glasgow University
Dr. Luigina Ciolfi, Limerick University
Dr. Keith Horton, Napier University
Dr. Susan Turner, Napier University
Dr. Julian Warner, The Queen's University of Belfast
Dr. Luke Zhang, University of Arizona

ACKNOWLEDGEMENTS

1. AN INTRODUCTION TO SPACES, SPATIALITY AND TECHNOLOGY

PHIL TURNER AND ELISABETH DAVENPORT

What are the concerns of those who investigate spatiality across domains and across media? What is significant in these concerns – particularly for the design and evaluation of technology? How are these concerns presented and represented? Can discourse from one domain inform work in another? These are some of the questions addressed in this volume. It is based on a series of papers presented at a research seminar in Edinburgh in December 2004. As the volume shows, the responses to our call for submissions were wide ranging, and the resulting meeting, we believe, opened up new avenues for exploring spatiality, spaces and technology.

THE ORGANIZATION OF THE BOOK

In structuring this volume, we have had to make decisions about clustering the contents. We start with a section on 'Philosophy of Information'. This opens with Coyne's chapter on the 'Digital Uncanny', a paper on the fundamental strangeness of computers that questions many of the prevailing tenets of design and analysis of virtual worlds such as design premised on familiarity and the everyday or the drive to photorealism in visual representation. Coyne suggests that our uneven grasp of virtual worlds is due as much to language as any essential qualities of the medium. This richly textured paper draws on a wide set of sources: phenomenology, psychoanalysis, aesthetics, design. It brings forth themes that are shared with other texts in our volume: the extent to which and ways in which space is socially shaped; the status and nature of our notions of infrastructure.

In the text that follows we explain our decisions in sorting the chapters, while, we hope, mitigating the possible bias in the discussion that ends the chapter of possible cross-links across the sections. We suggest that an important theme is the current re-working of notions of infrastructure - and the emergence of a different lexicon to describe relationships across multiple modalities. The 'new vocabulary' may need to accommodate a spectrum of activities rather than describing them in terms of opposites: ubiquitous computing that surrounds the body with devices or immersive computing that encloses the body; engineering based on artefacts for collaboration or communication for collaboration; Heidegger or Merleau-Ponty. We have, for the nonce, clustered the contents which come after Coyne's paper as follows: 'the social shaping of space'; 'infrastructure'; 'hybrid space'; 'virtual space'.

THE SOCIAL SHAPING OF SPACE

As we note above, a number of the contributors investigate ways in which space may be constituted by social practice, taking elements of the built environment as

P. Turner and E. Davenport (Eds.), Spaces, Spatiality and Technology, 1-4.

technology. Brown and Laurier (chapter 3) discuss ways in which practice makes space in three case studies: the canal network in 19th century USA, the world of mobile workers and the work of a warehouse for storing parts. They call their chapter a 'meditation on Castells', and observe 'the wonder of how people stitch together networks from their own practices'.

Davenport and Buckner (chapter 4) discuss the social shaping of a very large computerised teaching laboratory, and the evolution of rules and norms that allow students and teachers to re-configure elements of classroom presence to accommodate an emerging primary agent - the machine.

Goulding, in contrast, in chapter 5 considers the public library as a Habermasian space where civic presence is nurtured and created. Her discussion is not totally utopian, however, as she expresses some misgivings about the idealistic visions that are summarised in the first part of her chapter in revealing the potential for conflict in multi-modal provision of services. There has been much discussion in the library domain about the civic status of public libraries.

McDougall (chapter 6) discusses the world of the 'new office space' and questions some of the naïve assumptions of planners who have failed to anticipate the effects of social shaping. Buchecker in chapter 7 shows that the local public place fulfils basically the same needs or functions for the local residents as the private home, in particular the regulation of identity, social interaction and social emotions - but on a more social level. This theme of the social shaping of the community or village space is continued by van Dorst in chapter 8 in the context of municipal planning. His focus on the notion of 'hosts' redresses an imbalance in discussions of territory that privilege 'occupation'.

Two chapters consider the shaping of space from the specific perspective of communication in science. Cronin addresses the relationship between intellectual and physical proxemics, an area that has been neglected by information scientists (with some notable exceptions such as Allen), though, as McDougall's paper indicates, it has been the focus of recent work in knowledge management. The technique that is the focus of Cronin's paper (chapter 9) - citation mapping - is one of the oldest applications of social network analysis, and the ways in which such maps impinge on practice are relatively under-explored. A further exploration of the 'transformation of a complex network into a linear sequence' is provided by Warner (chapter 10) in a discussion of writing and text ('surface') and elaborates on ways in which computing can more accurately support the social processes of science (discovery and justification, for example) by allowing us to juxtapose in multiple ways and thus identify consistencies and inconsistencies across related groups.

INFRASTRUCTURE

It is difficult to separate discussion of infrastructure from discussion of the philosophy of space, and it might be better treated as a subset of the latter. Traditionally, design of interface and infrastructure has taken place in separate worlds, as it were, with computerised work evaluated in terms of actors ('users' of 'artefacts') moving across a 'surface' that has been blackboxed as 'infrastructure', separated by the exigencies of the design life cycle into another compartment, that makes invisible the (prior) technical work of engineers that is not directly pertinent to the application work of practitioners. More recently (and notably after the work of Greisemer and Star) the black box has been opened and infrastructure has been discussed in terms of the social relations of an extended group of actors that includes developers. Ethical and political issues are involved (*cf* accountable computing).

Writing broadly within this context, Day (chapter 11) proposes that the concept of 'surface' can assist us to explore space as the product of 'power and the affective and expressive role for materials', rather than the background to this. Surfaces are the 'variously textured...sites for mixtures between bodies', and are thus the 'sites for events'. The notions of 'folding' and 'foldability' and 'unfolding' are discussed at length, as metaphors that account for the interactions of bodies in space across time. Some of the contributors to this volume focus on ways in which we may experience multiple infrastructures. Dix and his colleagues, for example, in chapter 12 explore a complex of models - of spatial context, of 'mixed reality boundaries' and of human spatial understanding across a number of field projects that make up the Equator project to explain the ways in which co-existing multiple spaces are experienced.

HYBRID SPACE

Summerfield and Hayman (chapter 13) present an approach to representing visual context that is based on detailed physiological understanding of the physical role of lighting (as daylight is inherent in our experience of buildings) in what they call veridical synthetic imagery, or VSI, one of a range of simulations that are used to predict the performance of a building in context based on its specifications. Iaccuci and Wagner (chapter 14) discuss the narrative configuration of design ideas within a physical environment, in a presentation of a teaching medium, inspired partly by project techniques from stage lighting, for architecture students. Technology here is part of a distributed cognition system, an approach almost diametrically opposed to that of Summerfield and Hayman. Ciolfi and Bannon (chapter 15) are interested in 'a concept of space that includes the way it is experienced by people' which is their way of defining 'place'. Their concerns are integral to the design of ubiquitous computing environments. Context is different from infrastructure as it is not something to be 'captured' but as something that is constituted by people within their specific activities' and is thus not pre-computable. They have implemented these concepts in museum environments where technology contributes to experience in ways that are radically different from their role in conventional 'informatising' displays. Grasso and her colleagues (chapter 16) discuss technological support for informal communication and *ad-hoc* work in distributed, mobile teams. While these teams necessarily have fewer established opportunities to interact, smart, ubiquitous technology is sufficiently mature to *augment* the physical space to keep distributed groups connected. Smyth's paper (chapter 17) is similarly concerned with people's sense of space on encountering a novel landscape form in an Edinburgh public gallery. He concludes that the body is a 'key element in terms of how it mediates the comprehension of spaces and the layered meanings that transform them into spaces'

- *cf* Whitehead's observations regarding the role of the body in integrating our perceptual experiences.

VIRTUAL SPACE AND PLACE

Zhang and Furnas unapologetically discuss 'virtual space' in chapter 18, and present a new model for design that is based unreservedly on the work of Benford *et al.* on spatial metaphors; Zhang and Furnas propose that multi-scale virtual environments (mVEs) as the 'next space', that will allow users to be 'gigants' or 'nanants' as circumstances require. Users can observe important characteristics of structures at different scales, and act on objects with different sizes easily'. The parameters of avatar design for such environments are described together with the established vocabulary of interaction, namely, *aura, nimbus* and *focus*. Zhang and Furnas make a clear distinction between artefact-oriented and communication-oriented environments, and place their work in the context of collaboration in the former. Turner and his colleagues in the final chapter consider the challenge of recreating real places using virtual reality technology. They begin by discussing some the philosophical and empirical issues regarding relationship with place, focussing in part on the problematic role of the body. The metaphor of tourism is suggested as a means of dealing with the demands of recreating a real place.

CONCLUSION

Can we see the beginnings of an emerging interdisciplinary field of 'spatiality studies' in these contributions? We note above that many of the contributors are participants in the Presence research programme in the which may in itself prove to be a stimulus in the development of an interdisciplinary field. This shared background may explain a group of recurring HCI sources (e.g. Dourish, Dix, Carroll, Rogers, Agostini) that are cited across papers from the relevant contributors. A further group of recurring sources (e.g. Augé, Merleau-Ponty, Heidegger, Tuan and Bachelard) is cited in papers by Presence authors but also by writers with different disciplinary backgrounds. Lewis Carroll is one of this group, as the author of two texts that furnish examples to developers of cyberspaces and to designers of ambient computing devices. Carroll was first invoked in the HCI context by John Walker in a 1988 analysis of interaction 'generations' that exposes, with great prescience, a complex of issues that are highly pertinent to this collection.

REFERENCES

Star, S. and Ruhleder, K. (1994) Steps towards an ecology of infrastructure, *Proceedings of the 1994 ACM conference on CSCW*. New York: ACM, 253-264.
Star, L. (2000) It's infrastructure all the way down. *Proceedings of the Fifth ACM Conference on Digital Libraries*, June 2 – 7, 2000. New York: ACM, 271
Walker, J. (1988) Through the looking glass: beyond user interfaces. http://www.fourmilab.ch/autofile/www/chapter2_69.html

RICHARD COYNE

2. THE DIGITAL UNCANNY

INTRODUCTION

It is common to describe digital systems in spatial terms. In so far as these spaces are configured geometrically, they frequently exhibit properties that present as exaggerated, other-worldly, and disorienting. This can be by design or accident. One thinks of the mysterious and unsettling spaces expertly created through digital effects in films, the 3d environments of computer games, and putative virtual architectures (Lynch, 2002). For all the skill and artistry in such creations these spaces are capable of presenting in a manner that readily identifies as "uncanny." This term was popularised by Freud (1990) in his description of certain unsettling aspects of everyday experience. It was taken up by the surrealists, and also developed independently in the phenomenology of Heidegger (1962). More recently, concepts of the uncanny have been investigated in the realms of spatiality and architecture by Vidler (1995) in his book *The Architectural Uncanny*, Augé on the theme of non-place (1995), Zizek (2002) on surveillance, and by Lovink (2002) and Waldby (1997) in the context of digital media. It seems that with the computer it is easier to create "uncanny environments" than their converse: spaces that are homely and familiar.

THE FAMILIAR AND THE UNFAMILIAR

Designers of 3d environments may actively pursue the uncanny. Arguably, the uncanny as a spatial category provokes and beguiles, and is presented to great effect in film and even mainstream architecture. Spatial representations that excite our curiosity as technically and aesthetically ingenious or spectacular in some sense flit along the boundary between the familiar and the unfamiliar, the calming and the anxious, the safe and the dangerous, conditions that have also been developed in aesthetic theory as pertaining to the sublime (Kant, 2000; Lyotard, 1986).

The tendency to manufacture the uncanny is particularly evident when observing the products of those new to the techniques of 3d computer modelling. Students readily produce scenes populated with platonic shapes hovering and colliding in space, richly patterned, photo-real in their shading, but surreal in the perfection of their edges, the independence of their elements, and resort easily to swirling forms, a strong separation between background and foreground, and arbitrary transparencies, that depict an other-worldly disturbance, the juxtaposition of the familiar with the unfamiliar. The tools seem to prescribe this, and if the effect sought is one of familiarity then it is only achieved against substantial resistance from this tendency towards the uncanny.

P. Turner and E. Davenport (Eds.), Spaces, Spatiality and Technology, 5-18.

Freud (1990) drew attention to the common understanding of the uncanny, as a feeling where something artificial presents to us as living, as in the case of a realistic doll or puppet (p.347). Digital effects in films, photorealistic computer rendering, and three-dimensional computer games can prompt us to remark on the uncanniness of the resemblances they invoke. We commonly describe as uncanny situations in which the imaginary presents to us as real, as in the case where a mechanical object seems to come to life, or in a situation of suspicion, where the innocently inert presents as malevolently living. This applies equally to visual and literary presentations (Kitchin and Kneale, 2001). We will subsequently draw out the role of terms such as "peculiar," "similar," "different," "unfamiliar," "real," "spectacular," and "suspicious." It seems that any representation that relies for its impact on peculiar similarities and differences can be uncanny.

Are other media any more homely? Though childish and naïve art can present as strange, the inexpert and the primitive is not automatically uncanny. Familiar media such as photography, drawing, and modelling in clay have their acceptable amateur manifestations. They are media accessible to most, employing a language and subject matter that is already understood as familiar: family portraits (Rose, 2002), the child's drawing adhered to the refrigerator, sculptures in plasticine, replete with finger prints. Of course, digital media can be used to mimic these, but in so far as computer graphics and modelling copy manual media they come across as even more alien, parodic and unsettling. Bolter and Grusin (2002) refer to these manifestations as re-mediations: one medium of representation informs another. Here my argument is that where this process is not yet absorbed into a well-established and familiar mode of practice then it can produce an outcome that is uncanny. As designers in the new medium of computer spaces it is difficult to resist the tendency to create or represent in ways that are disembodied, distant or surreal, in other words, as presentations of the uncanny.

I have been referring to three-dimensional representations of space on a flat screen or printout, but the same applies to other spaces: the space of interconnections that is the world-wide web, cyberspace as a vastly interconnected network, the social spaces and the implied environments of chat forums, the contracted and distorted telematic spaces of video conferencing, putative telepresence, and the oft times uncanny space of the computer desktop.

We began with a proposition about how an observer or creator might respond to depictions of space in digital media as uncanny. Even more controversial is the proposition that all media participate in the uncanny. Unfamiliarity is a key aspect of the interpretation of images in any case. Interpretation involves negotiation across a distance. The image, computer-generated or otherwise, already has aspects that are alien, unless or until, we become inured to the provocations they pose. Because computer imagery is still new, it helps to highlight the alien aspects of all media.

For Freud, wax museums, doll shops and mechanical experiments were insufficient for revealing the sources of the uncanny. In what follows I demonstrate the extent to which the uncanny aspects of the computer image can be said to reside in mimicry, repetition and suspicion, and how these are related. They are each subject to the workings of interpretation.

CONTROLLABLE SPACES

The current state of computing is often presented as falling short of some ideal (Coyne, 1999). In the future, our interfacing with computers and their environments will be immediate, engaging, seamless and "real." So perhaps the weird, alien and uncanny aspects of computer graphics imagery represent a transient phase, pending more powerful machines, broader bandwidth, and better interfaces. The implication here is that photographic realism is the ideal, and is inhibited only by technical limitations. In the case of digital imagery the realism sought is generally of a mathematical and logical kind. But in so far as digital spaces are devised as exercises in Cartesian geometry they already present as uncanny. (For a discussion on Descartes and the uncanny see McCallum [2003].) It is the quest for reality that is strange. In other words the pursuit of realism inevitably produces an uncanny effect.

The alien character of Cartesian geometry is well presented from the viewpoint of the countervailing phenomenological understanding of space and spatiality. From a phenomenological viewpoint space is always to be understood pragmatically, ahead of any mathematical construction, or at least mathematics as a privileged representation. In fact the various mathematical and logical means for understanding space are pragmatic, but the modes of praxis in which they are developed and appreciated are limited. So it is to particular ends that we think of space in terms of the mathematical constructions of co-ordinate geometry, where everything is related to an origin, and where parallel lines do not converge. Similarly, the Cartesian and logical position presents space in logical or set-theoretic terms, as pertaining to containment, with a series of transitive relationships: if A is in B and B is in C, then A is in C. Or there is the symmetry of: if A is next to B then B is also next to A. The phenomenological position asserts that the spheres of relevance of these logico-mathematical understandings are limited. In any case such constructions are either so self-evident as to be trivial, or they are surpassed even in their own theorising. One thinks of non-Euclidean geometries for example, where basic axioms about space are abrogated (for example, in that parallel lines are allowed cross over one another).

Cartesian geometry also fuels an inflated view of the power of the computer, whose spaces clearly breach the received "rules" of spatiality: in digital spaces several different solid objects can occupy the same coordinates, large objects can be contained by smaller spaces, spaces can be "hyperlinked" in denial of formal spatial relations. But the Euclidean and Cartesian rules are already breached by our experience of space, and by Riemannian, fractal, and other geometries (or mathematical practices), and do not require digital media to effect the disturbance.

A cloud of suspicion also hangs over the privileging of logical and mathematical formulations (Lefebvre, 1991). Perhaps the utility of Cartesian geometry in the control of construction (engineering, architecture) processes is beyond doubt, but it also suggests a degree of control where there is none, a presumption that we can capture and tame the world, by subjecting everything to scrutiny under the same methods (mathematics, logic), the same constituents (objects, measurements, time, space), or rational denominators. Formal geometry excludes other concerns (body, placelessness, the whole social realm), and this scientific imperialism promotes political agendas. One thinks of the role of maps and measuring devices as objective means of delineating claims on space, particularly against those who use different and less acceptably verifiable means of demarcation. The prevalence of CCTV, GPS and other surveillance technologies as a means of collecting objective evidence provides similar grounds for suspicion. So certain representational schemas (particularly the mathematical and the logical) serve the ends of control, within particular realms of practice.

This tendency towards control enables not only the representation of existing spaces, but also spaces of our own invention, possibly recalling the imaginative play of the child, where a cardboard box becomes a rocket ship, a chair is a fort, a cupboard is a house. This sense of control is akin to magic. Objects hover without support, we can penetrate vast and tiny spaces, make objects appear at will, and solid objects appear as if transparent. The creation and manipulation of digital environments brings recollection of a less sophisticated state of mind, where cause and effect were not so well developed. In other words there was an infantile stage when we believed in magic caves, visitations from benevolent beings (Father Christmas, the tooth fairy), spells, ghosts, monsters, and our own omnipotence. Freud links such childhood recollections to the Oedipal condition, which pertains to a longing to return to the primal condition with the mother, and all she comes to represent: comfort, unity, wholeness (against the estrangement of the father). For Freud, the momentary realisation of strange encounters in adult life is the shock that after all, those infantile beliefs were true: you can will objects to move around in space from a distance, fly, make things explode by pointing at them, all the effects of digital media. This is the one aspect of the uncanny for Freud. It is not restricted to watching magic tricks or spectacular digital effects, but is present wherever the familiar turns into the strange. It is abetted by the supposed realism of computer imagery.

THE SPACE OF LANGUAGE

Digital media certainly have the capacity to unsettle the familiar realms of spatial experience. We can fly, control at a distance, and preside over vast spaces and complex structures. But even more remarkable than the degree of control we can exercise over this mathematical space is the fact that we are prepared to describe such widely varied and surreal encounters as spatial at all. In working with, designing for and using computers we are dealing with complex systems, with properties in excess of simple spatial formulations. Yet we are still prepared to use the metaphor of space, even though we entertain the thought that the relations they exhibit can defy the usual mathematical properties (transitivity, co-ordinate geometry). Spaces that fold in on themselves, volumes made up of space-filling curves (fractals), and geometries in the complex number plane, are spatial by virtue of cultural convention, not the innate authority of mathematics.

From a phenomenological point of view our everyday world is basically still intact with these strange formulations of space. The challenge they pose is a linguistic one. Having defined space in mathematical terms we now find that we can still use the term "space" in many contexts where the definitions no longer hold. Whereas this leads some to propose that the computer challenges everything we take for granted about space, a more sophisticated response is to recognise that the computer helps us realise further the nature of language and sign systems: the provisional and contextual nature of terms like "space" and their definitions. For many theorists language needs this loose and jarring function in order to be of use, ie to participate in meaning. So the uncanny character of computer spaces is already subservient to the uncanny, if not the tricky, nature of language (Hyde, 1998).

As exercises in language, the discourses on "virtuality" and "cyberspace" privilege idealist and empiricist views of space. The pragmatic dimension is usurped by the apparent authority of calculation, complexity, interconnectedness, and trajectories of improvement. For some the computer invites projection of hope that technology will rescue us from current social problems. Social progress is equated with technological trajectory. The computer of the future assumes the role of mother (in the sense used by Freud), a welcoming realm that invites us to participate in unity and wholeness, a reconnection with global community, the reconciliation of art, machine, humanity and nature. (The concurrence of digital utopianism and motherhood is not lost in the revival of terms such as "the matrix" in digital discourse.) On the one hand computer spaces challenge what we formerly took for granted, but they are now to be the object of our hope. The shortcoming of any such transcendent philosophy is the neglect of the here and now. People ignore the contingency, the clumsy interface, the uneven access, and project all promise of improvement to the safe distance of the future. Everyone knows that technologies have a habit of letting us down, a flaw that is all the more exasperating as they are the objects of such hope (Hardill and Green, 2003; Coyne, 2002). The digital medium introduces a mismatch between expectation and reality. It brings into sharp relief a particular concept of reality. In fact, reality seems to be a bi-product of the impetus to represent, not the object of representation, and what is representation but an exercise in language!

THE SPACE OF IMITATION

The quest for reality in digital spatiality is also a variant of the theme of mimicry, which receives provocative treatment in Roger Caillois' (1984) study into the adaptive behaviour of insects. Writing in the 1930s, his paper on mimicry and legendary psychasthenia was an acknowledged influence on subsequent interpretations of Freud. For Caillois, mimicry is a propensity found in all of nature, but most peculiarly in insect species that imitate aspects of their environment (other insects, plants, birds and rocks) ostensibly to ward off or escape predators, but apparently with effect in excess of immediate need, and though the ploy seems to be ineffective in some adaptations. It seems that nature's evolutionary, adaptive processes work towards mimicry, opposed to other strategies for survival. There are several important applications of Caillois' curious presentations about mimicry on the quest for spatial realism.

Caillois sees the peculiarities of mimicry in animal species as spatial. The creature is positioned in space, at the edge of a leaf, oriented at just the right angle, inert to just the right degree, in order to effect this camouflage, and in doing so is at the mercy of spatial determinants. Apparently the creature succumbs to "a real temptation by space" (Caillois, 1984: 28).

Caillois sees this mimicry as a disturbance in the perception of space. The creature is dislocated. It is at the mercy of its environment, rather than an agent of choice, with the privileged position of the independent subject. This condition is apparently manifested in human beings in the case of legendary psychasthenia: a psychological disorder characterized by phobias, obsessions, compulsions, or excessive anxiety. It is a disturbance between personality and space. People with this condition say they know where they are but do not feel as though they are there.

By this reading the quest for realism is already an indication of a pathological condition, a strange relationship with our environment. We cannot avoid copying and mimicking other things (our environment, spaces), and this already indicates a lack of control, a subjugation to the dictates of our environment, as though on entering a building we are led to assume a particular posture, move in a certain way, gravitate to certain points. This is not so much an analysis in support of "environmental determinism" as an indication that we, and those who design our environments, are not in control. The propensity to mimic has the upper hand over independent agency and subjectivity, and is already suggestive of disorientation.

Mimicry is also a specula (and spectacular) phenomenon, ie pertaining to reflection and vision. The impulse to mimic privileges the visual field. Clearly, the propensity towards photorealism in computer graphics is of a different order of technical and reflective sophistication than the impulse within insects to mimic their environment. But the strong implication of Caillois' polemic is that the impulse to visual mimicry is ubiquitous, and in excess of the need to reproduce structural, sonic or tactile properties, and already carries within it aspects of the uncanny, for image specialists as for the rudiments of nature. It does not take much to extend Caillois' argument to the other senses (particularly the aural sense), though here the uncanny is primarily given a visual treatment.

Caillois also highlights the bleakness of these environmental spaces, as appropriated by the organism under the spell of mimicry. In so far as the emphasis is on the visual, uncanny spaces are dark spaces, which penetrate and pass through us. For Caillois, dark space envelopes and penetrates deeper than light space. There is also a propensity towards reduced existence, the animate appears as the inanimate. Caillois also relates this reduced experience to magic, which recalls Freud's argument about certain events exorcising infantile beliefs, and further invokes thoughts of the covert, and of night.

In all, by this reading mimicry is a dark practice, beyond the pale of rationality, subject to the exercise of suspicion. Digital spaces are uncanny in so far as they participate in this shady art of mimicry.

THE SPACE OF REPETITION

Freud links reminding and recollection to the processes of repetition. Repetitive situations remind us of the infantile conditions of loss and recovery. Mimicry is also a repetitive operation. The current situation is a repetition of an original situation, or a copy of a copy.

Spaces can repeat. The repetitive sequence of lines in the ubiquitous (Cartesian) planning grid is one conspicuous system of spatial organisation. Repetitive sequences of columns are arrayed on grids. There is the repetition of windows across a façade, and the floors in a multistorey office block. Repetitions are countable and lend themselves to mathematical treatment as constituents of ordered spatiality.

Games too are characterised by repetitive actions. The combatants repeat in order to train for the contest. The footfall of a runner, the roll of the dice, the skipping rope, and the banging of saucepan lids, whatever the game, all speak of the repetition of play. Computer games make conspicuous the repetitive processes of moving, advancing and retreating, aiming and shooting (Kline, 2003; Coyne, 2003). As in computer games the objective is sometimes to retreat from a situation of repetition to a less anxious position, where repetition has ceased, or beginning again with a new object, as in the progression through levels in a game. Repetition is linked to reward.

On the other hand, repetition is the reward. According to Freud we enjoy, or at least indulge, a propensity to repeat, well understood in demonstrations of repetitive behaviour: obsessive hand washing, fidgeting, pacing the floor. In fact to repeat is to re-enact the basic childhood trauma of loss and retrieval, particularly of the mother's company. Apparently, subsequent enactments, voluntary or otherwise, of the repetitive urge, remind us in some way, or are perhaps purgatives, of this primordial condition of loss. The repetitive element of Freud's account is in the company of recovery. The process is of loss and recovery, in succession. The mother leaves the room, but returns, only to depart again, and so on. Irrespective of the source of this propensity, Freud's speculations point out a fascination with repetition, even if we are unconcerned with what it is that is being repeated, or even the first event that is being repeated.

In fact the force of Freud's argument (and that of the tradition that draws on him) is not that there are many sources of the uncanny, but just this one, repetition (Nietzsche, 1961; Deleuze, 1994). Or at least, any other sources can be taken back to repetition. Alienation means what it does by virtue of being a repetition, or by reminding us of repetition.

But then what is reminding, if not mimicry? The current situation is seen as mimicking a previous event. The repetition of the cotton reel game (one of Freud's primary examples of an obsessive game) is a copy of an infantile trauma; subsequent repetitions are copies of previous repetitions.

This is the condition of the uncanny, that peculiar quality we encounter in spaces that are unsettling, where we do not feel at home, and abetted by notions of repetition and mimicry. So being lost in a labyrinth has this character, where we are disturbed by the repeat encounter with the same fork in the path, or pass the same landmark. Spatial experience is not confined to the first spectacular view, but the repeat visit, to habituation, to having already seen (déjà vu). In the film, *The Blair Witch Project,* the young investigators realise they are travelling in circles, though they had set off with the intention of travelling in a straight line. This is surely one of the main determinants of the uncanny in the film, including every other repetition it and other horror films portray: the return of the repressed (Tudor, 1997).

The spatial repetition, of the horror film and the computer game, recalls Freud's (1990) example of his own mundane experience of the uncanny when lost in an Italian town: "I hastened to leave the narrow street at the next turning. But after having wandered for a time without inquiring my way, I suddenly found myself back in the same street, where my presence was now beginning to excite attention. I hurried away once more, only to arrive by another detour at the same place yet a third time. Now however a feeling overcame me which I can only describe as uncanny." (p.359) Lest we are tempted to ascribe the uncanny to extraordinary sources, the radical point of Freud's study is that repetition will suffice.

BENEATH THE SURFACE

We commonly associate the uncanny with suspicion. Uncanny spaces are those in which we find, or suspect, something lurking behind the walls, under the manicured lawn, lurking in the woods. Suspicion as a source of the uncanny also succumbs to an account in terms of repetition.

We may think that the repetitive operation can be tamed and directed, as if in retreat from the uncanny. Deleuze and Guattari (1993) posit the concept of striated space, the successive layering of spaces in a regime of order and control, typical of institutional and bureaucratic modes of organisation, and their spaces. Here, space is controlled and controlling, as in the ideologically-inspired urban spaces of imperial cities: the grand gesture of Versailles, Moscow's Red Square, the Mall of Regency London. Deleuze and Guattari's identification of striated space recalls the suspicion engendered by all adoptions of Cartesian spatial schemas.

Computer systems are no less prone to organising space in this way, as one thinks of hierarchies of menus, access privileges, firewalls, and in computer games, megalomaniacal and imperial architectures, the appeal to levels of engagement, from beginner to advanced, simple to more difficult, or simply progressing through staged environments to some inner sanctum or goal. This is an ordered variation in repetition, a neo-platonic progression to higher planes and positions of power. The progression is often through discrete states and plateaus, and across thresholds.

Arguably, the quest for greater realism also constitutes a progression through levels within the research and development community. Computer graphics is on an upward trajectory to greater and greater realism, transparency and seamlessness.

Progression implies improvement, and greater degrees of sophistication, and advance in a particular direction, up or down, higher or deeper, from which there is no going back. But the process of ascent/descent is already permeated with suspicion. We may be suspicious of the adoption of formal spatial schemas, but there is also suspicion between the various ranks. Hierarchy can present an environment where inferiors and superiors do not trust each other. Any structure based on the rigid separation of roles simply sets up a condition of otherness. Where sociability is confined to rank, level or spatial confines, the other position, stratum or region becomes all the more problematic, either as an object of exclusion, fascination, desire or suspicion. This is one of the manifestations of what Deleuze and Guattari (1993) call "the rhizome": the invading network of discontent and contradiction that surges up from within or amongst the roots of the hierarchical tree, and subverts its ordered connections.

The rite of passage from one level in a hierarchy to another is also a progression through stages of increasing suspicion, as when Alice advances across the chessboard. The movement is from naivete to suspicion, or perhaps greater discrimination of and trust in one's suspicions. By various Freudian readings this is a movement away from the narcissistic phase, away from captivation with one's image, to dealing with anger at parents, finding a substitute object of desire, and so on.

In the computerised Dungeons and Dragons game, the higher levels to which one may progress include the orbit of wizard, the level at which one is entrusted with the design and manipulation of different aspects of the game itself, and the ability to influence the game play of others. Progression to higher levels can imply access to secrets. Of course, the ultimate secret is that there is nothing there after all, or the ultimate progression is to the realisation that there is no higher stratum, ultimate depth or inner core. Whether or not the progression (in the game, story, organisation, or political structure) is carried through to this conclusion, the suspicion may be there. It is sometimes said of organisations that major decisions are made by the most junior staff (Laurence, 1969), as really hard problems so often defy authoritative resolution. In the absence of a decision the outcome defaults to the routine practice of some junior who decides the matter, or acts in her or his own local interest. Irrespective of the generality of this principle the suspicion within organisational structure, bureaucracy, and hierarchy is endemic.

So levels engender suspicion, or at least, suspicion and the problematisation of trust are implicated in such formulations. The concept of surface, or layers, also engenders suspicion of what may be lying beneath. Freud's concept of the unconscious, where the obsessive repetitions are but a surface manifestation of a deeper, underlying cause is already a narrative about suspicion. Repetition is not what it seems, but betrays an underlying condition: a need, a longing, a desire, a first trauma that is being repeated. According to Derrida (1978), what should strike us as remarkable is not the propensity to repeat, but the persistence of our belief in a first time, an original trauma. It is strange to think that there is a first time, a cause to the repetition. The resolution to a primary cause is tantamount to the cessation of the repetition. The repetition unsettles us; so too the thought that it might cease.

We do not require suspicion to induce the uncanny. Repetition will suffice. But is a row of columns, the beat of a drum, or running in circles, sufficient to induce the uncanny. The account that the uncanny resides simply in repetition removes the imperative to look to the dark recesses of cyberspace for its sources, but repetition alone provides an insufficient account of the uncanny. The determination that a space is uncanny is after all a matter of interpretation. It is one aesthetic judgement amongst many possible judgements, dependent on a number of factors. That seasoned film buffs can be indifferent to the cliché of the haunted house or other devices of the horror genre already indicates that we can be inured to situations that might traditionally be described as uncanny, and creative effort needs to be directed at overcoming the cliché, inducing the uncanny effect by progressively more devious and sophisticated means.

PLAY SPACE

Exploring the space of play will further help decipher the relationship between repetition, interpretation and the uncanny. Play strikes us as uncanny when it is used to disguise something distressing, when the torturer in *Reservoir Dogs* "plays" with his victim, or a murder takes place in a circus tent. But play does not need to be coupled with innocence.

Play takes place in a space. One thinks of the arena, the game board, the tabletop, the playground and the playpen. But the space of play is not only a container in which play takes place, or the geometrically ordered checkerboard, but also the space of negotiation, the leeway that protagonists give one another, the distance participants traverse in meeting each other and the objects of the game, the environment of trust that develops, the world of the imagination that is in process, and the possibilities presented. There is a state of play, the space of game states. What is the character of this space? For some theorists of the game (Gadamer, 1975) this space is characterised as the site of a to-and-fro movement, in which the players are absorbed rather than standing back reflectively. It is a non-objectivist realm of engagement. In fact we need not think of the combative game, with its rules, protagonists and spaces, but rather the absorbed actions of a child playing with saucepan lids, animated conversation, the play of waves on the seashore. There is a sense in which play is not played by players, but players are manipulated by the play. By various readings (Huizinga, 1955), play becomes the paradigm for understanding the human-world relationship (commerce, politics, law, war, but also our everyday interactions). In this light, space as understood formally or mathematically is something that emerges as an object when we choose to withdraw from the play, and think in other terms, of containment, measurement, and control. (Perhaps the predator playing with his prey disturbs us because it equates the play element with indifference to (normal) homely modes of human engagement.)

For some theorists this is the nature of interpretation: unselfconscious engagement. It is an engagement with a text in a situation of reading, or of appreciating a performance or admiring a picture. But it also extends to any mode of interaction in which we think of understanding or application as the outcome: diagnosis, deciding a legal case, being a professional, a scientist, computer programmer, creating a work of art, or design (Snodgrass and Coyne, 1997). Designers create spaces, and they may think of spaces (physical or "virtual") intended to inspire and transport us to other realms. They may also take spatial design as the logical manipulation of forms, use measurement, mathematics, computer-aided design and geometrical modellers. But designers also talk about design as a space, and in this participate in the space of play.

What is the relationship between interpretation and repetition? Interpretation invariably involves re-visiting, renewing acquaintance with and re-presenting the object or situation under scrutiny. The computer game is played again, the designer revisits the design task, the audience attends the performance again, the performers offer repeat performances. From a hermeneutical point of view repetition is important, though not just as the duplication of events. Repetition provides an opportunity to exercise difference. Each encounter is potentially different from the last, simply because the performer, designer, viewer, and the user are undergoing transformation. When interpretation is doing its work then every encounter provides a challenge to the interpreter's position, her background, world view, or horizon. In this sense interpretation is a journey, where each step is a moment of starting again. Another way of looking at interpretation is as an excursion, followed by the return home, but the home has changed. We see it in a different light, perhaps a darker light. Until we are inured to the effects of interpretation, and it presents as mere repetition, interpretation presents as a homeward journey to the habitual, but one in which the familiar has become less so. In other words, effective interpretation incorporates the ¥ and narrative, Ricoeur (1999) highlights the different meanings of mimesis, the most typical being where the interpreter enters into the situation of interpretation: the reader's particular background and circumstances impinge on what is being read. An interpretation, at its best, is never just a copy. What about the mimetic behaviour of insects? By this reading perhaps the appearance and posture of an insect is an interpretation. The insect, or perhaps the species, or the process of natural selection, constitutes an environmental interpretation, which is to say an application of response mechanisms or codes to an environmental condition. The response of the predator species presents as a similar mode of interpretation. We do not have access to the interpretive capabilities of insects, but we are intimate with Caillois' interpretive practices as a theorist and writer. He, and we, interpret the situation of the insects as one of mimicry. The spatial disorientation implied takes place within the space of our interpretation. The predator and prey are engaged in the game of life and death, with move and counter-move. Where we find this uncanny it is by virtue of our renewed awareness of the seriousness of play. Play presents to us as other than we expect, as other than innocent.

What is the relationship between interpretation and suspicion? As an alternative to the layering metaphor of knowledge, Ricoeur (1970) investigates the proposition that what we have is never simply a peeling back of layers, as if getting to the truth, but rather various interpretations vying for prominence and authority. Interpretations are not layered, where every repetition should take us closer to some objectively true situation. Interpretations meet resistance. From the point of view of our argument here, resistance is revealed as the uncanny. Is there space for suspicion of play, a suspicion of interpretation? Interpretations are available for scrutiny, which is to say they rub against rival interpretations: play as innocence, play as engagement, play as frivolous, play as life and death.

So interpretation involves distance. According to a slight variation on this reading, the interpreter begins with an expectation. The situation presents as alien in so far as there is a mismatch between our expectations and what is presented to us. Interpretation requires the negotiation of this distance.

The uncanny is everywhere in interpretation, but what prompts us to declare that a particular situation is uncanny, that computer graphics imagery is uncanny in a way that a photograph of a flower, or a child's finger painting, is not. Anything can strike us as uncanny when viewed in a light that makes it so, by being moved to a foreign context: a grandfather clock in a desert, the sound of a steam train on a mountaintop, a building on a cloud, a liquid wall, entomology in a paper about the image. In so far as computer spaces strike us as out of place, or we cannot immediately find our place in them, then they participate in the uncanny.

Freud's characterisation of the uncanny as a situation of reminding is also a story about interpretation. The uncanny is also a situation where we are reminded of the boundaries of interpretive practice, of the inside and the outside, the presence and absence of unreflective engagement; the whole and the parts, the rapture of union and the rupture of articulation and separation. Any situation can remind us of this, though it is not just a reminding, but an ongoing condition, without beginning or end, or perhaps a reminding of a condition that is always with us.

CONCLUSION

The uncanny is a de-privileged category in writing about digital media, giving way to realism or flights of the imagination. The legacies of research and development in digital spatiality privilege sameness, familiarity, realism, correspondence between image and object, or transcendence from these: virtuality, fantasy, other worlds. The philosophical tradition, particularly the phenomenology of Heidegger, Bachelard and others, and the theories of interpretation (hermeneutics) also favour the homely, the importance of being situated in the world, but this is a restless condition. We are also in search of a home, caught in a nomadic condition between the familiar and the alien.

So all media participate in the uncanny. It is a key aspect of interpretation in any case. The image, computer-generated or otherwise, already has aspects that are alien and unhomely. Because computer imagery and the spaces it invokes are still new, they bring the alien aspects of media into sharp relief, and reveal the dark side of interpretation, language and spatiality.

AFFILIATIONS

Professor Richard Coyne
Architecture: School of Arts, Culture and Environment
The University of Edinburgh

REFERENCES

Augé, M. (1995). *Non-places: Introduction to an Anthropology of Supermodernity*. Trans. J. Howe. London: Verso.

Bachelard, Gaston (1964) *The Poetics of Space*, trans. Etienne Gilson, Beacon Press, Boston (first published in French in 1958).

Bolter, Jay D. and Richard Grusin. (2002). *Remediation: Understanding New Media*, Cambridge, Mass.: MIT Press.

Caillois, Roger. (1984). Mimicry and legendary psychasthenia. October, **(31)** Winter, 17-32.

Coyne, Richard (2003). Mindless Repetition: Learning from Computer Games, *Design Studies*, **24**, 199-212.

Coyne, Richard. (1999). *Technoromanticism: Digital Narrative, Holism and the Romance of the Real*, Cambridge, Mass.: MIT Press.

Coyne, Richard. (2002). The cult of the not-yet. In Neil Leach (ed) *Designing for a Digital World*. London: Wiley-Academic, 45-48.

Deleuze, Gilles and Félix Guattari. (1988). *A Thousand Plateaus: Capitalism and Schizophrenia*, trans, Brian Massumi, London: Athlone Press.

Deleuze, Gilles (1994). *Difference and Repetition*, trans. Paul Patton, London: Athlone Press.

Derrida, Jacques (1978). Freud and the scene of writing. In *Writing and Difference*, trans. Alan Bass, Chicago, Ill: Chicago University Press, 196-231.

Freud, Sigmund. 1990. The 'uncanny,' in The Penguin Freud Library, Volume 14: Art and Literature, ed. Albert Dickson, 335-376, Harmondsworth, Middlesex: Penguin. (First published in German in 1919.)

Gadamer, Hans-Georg. 1975. Truth and Method, London: Sheed Ward.

Hardill Irene and Green Anne. 2003. Remote working—altering the spatial contours of work and home in the new economy. New Technology, Work and Employment. 18 (3) 212-222.

Heidegger, Martin. 1962. Being and Time. trans. J. Macquarrie and E. Robinson, London: SCM Press.

Huizinga, Johan. 1955. Homo Ludens: A Study of the Play Element in Culture, Boston: Beacon Press.

Hyde, Lewis. 1998. Trickster Makes This World: Mischief, Myth and Art. New York: North Point Press.

Kant, Immanuel. 2000. Critique of the Power of Judgment. Trans. Paul Guyer and Eric Matthews, Cambridge: Cambridge University Press. First published in 1790.

Kitchin, Rob and James Kneale. 2001. Science fiction or future fact? Exploring imaginative geographies of the new millennium. Progress in Human Geography 25(1) 19–35.

Kline, Stephen, Nick Dyer-Witheford, and Greig de Peuter. 2003. Digital play : the interaction of technology, culture and marketing. Montréal ; London: McGill-Queen's University Press.

Laurence Peter J. 1969. *The Peter Principle*. London: Souvenir Press.

Lovink, Geert (ed.). 2002. Uncanny networks: Dialogues with the virtual intelligentsia. Cambridge, MA: MIT Press.

Leach, Neil (ed.). 2002. Designing for a Digital World. London: Wiley-Academic.

Lefebvre, Henri. 1991. The Production of Space, trans. D. Nicholson-Smith. Oxford, UK: Blackwell. (First published in French in 1974.)

Lyotard, Jean-François. 1986. The Postmodern Condition: A Report on Knowledge. Manchester: Manchester University Press.

McCallum, David. 2003. Encountering and countering the 'uncanny' in Descartes's Méditations. French Studies. 57(2) 135-147.

Nietzsche, Friedrich 1961. Thus Spoke Zarathustra, trans. R. J. Hollingdale, London: Penguin. (First published in German in 1892.)

Ricoeur, Paul. 1970. Freud and Philosophy: An Essay in Interpretation, trans. Denis Savage, New Haven: Yale University Press.

Ricoeur, Paul. 1999. Time and Narrative, Volume I, trans. Kathleen McLaughlin and David Pellauer, Chicago: University of Chicago Press.

Snodgrass, Adrian and Richard Coyne. 1997. Is Designing Hermeneutical? Architectural Theory Review, Journal of the Department of Architecture, The University of Sydney, 1(1) 65-97.

Tudor, Andrew. 1997. Why horror? The peculiar pleasures of a popular genre. Cultural Studies 11(3) 443–463.

Vidler, Anthony. 1995. The Architectural Uncanny: Essays in the Modern Unhomely, Cambridge, Mass.: MIT Press.

Waldby, Catherine. 1997. Revenants: The Visible Human Project and the Digital Uncanny. Body and Society. 3(1): 1–16.

Zizek, Slovoj. 2002. Big brother, or, the Triumph of the gaze over the eye. In T. Y. Levin, U. Frohne, and P. Weibel (eds.), CTRL [SPACE]: Rhetorics of Surveillance from Bentham to Big Brother: 224-227. Cambridge, Mass.: MIT Press.

BARRY BROWN AND ERIC LAURIER

3. EN-SPACING TECHNOLOGY

Some Thoughts On The Geographical Nature Of Technology

INTRODUCTION

Italo Calvino's book "Invisible Cities" is a book of stories about places far away (Calvino, 1997). The explorer Marco Polo visits the court of the Mongolian emperor Kahn. As they sit, resting or smoking opium, Polo tells fantastic stories about the different cities he has visited. Each chapter is about a different – imaginary – city: cities where every travellers memory lives on beyond the life of the city, or the inhabitants worship different gods depending on if they live below or above ground. Calvino's dream like images pass by as Marco Polo tells us of his cities both spectacular and dull. Yet, each chapter is not strictly about a city. Instead they reveal an observation, a comment or description. Calvino describes to us how our memories live on, yet the original observation dies, or that we always wish and dream for what is distant when the monotony of the present seems unbearable.

Indeed, the format of the book – the tales told by Marco Polo – is itself an observation on how we experience and think about places. We have all told stories of places far away, making connections using stories of the distant and the near. The here and now is easily connected, by a comment or an explanation, with somewhere else. "In China, they do this.", the American's story might start, at once connecting himself with supposed events far away. Guidebooks take this to the extreme: stories of different places are arranged together and standardised. You can stay here, you can eat here. A wall of standardised guidebooks tells the story of the world, or the *tourist* world, and stories of the consumption of places (Brown & Perry, 2002; Urry, 1995).

This chapter is about how we make those connections between places and the wonder or 'dazzling' nature of those stories. What Calvino's book retains, even as it focuses on the connections and stories, is the power of specifics. As the world is connected together but we must never lose sight of *who* is connecting *what*. In particular, it is a paper about how the connections which technology supports can lead towards a slight dazzlement towards networked practice. This dazzlement can cause researchers to ignore the more mundane details of technological usage. Although the modern computer networks are something of a *cause celebre,* technology connects and changes in many different less dazzling ways. The number 67 bus, or the frills-free budget airline can also cause innovations in the connections

P. Turner and E. Davenport (Eds.), Spaces, Spatiality and Technology, 19-30.
© 2005 *Springer. Printed in the Netherlands.*

we sustain between places, if without much glamour or 'spectacular' impacts. Yet to truly avoid technological determinism we need to focus on the mundane uses of technology, and how individuals use technology in specific settings, rather than offer generic answers to how technology 'impacts' a specific country, or even the world.

In line with this criticism, this chapter develop a critique of approaches to the 'spaces' of technology which abstract way from the details of what is done in specific places to produce 'generic' accounts of network and technology. While notions such as 'the space of flows' have great impact and drama, they leave much of the work of actual *connecting* unexplicated. To understand that we have to look at more mundane activities such as how mobile workers struggle to make a workable environment in a café, or how a computer database is used to order truck spare parts. Castells talks about "flows", and Latour about "rhizomes", each of them finessing the network as their metaphor of choice for understanding the world (Manuel Castells, 1996; Latour, 1999a). Yet *we* still have Microsoft Powerpoint, text messages and HTML to deal with. Taking a broad approach to connections give great power, yet it end up in a strangely deterministic position, linking together places and events far away, with little understanding of how these connections are actually supported in those places.

CASTELLS AND CANALS

Castells is perhaps the easiest to critique here, although he is not alone in charting a course for a new sociology of networks (with different authors giving very different accounts – e.g. Law, 1994; Law & Urry, 2002; Urry, 2000). In his encyclopaedic treatment of the 'new economy (and much else besides) his three volumes aim high. Yet even though comprehensive much is lost is the overview given by Castells. In particular, we find little in his account which helps us understand how the networks he narrates come into existence. Castells uses the term 'space' to bring out some important *abstract* processes that are involved in the geographic organisation of the world, and how technology changes that organisation. When Castells describes the "space of flows" (Castells, 1996) as the "new industrial space [..] organised around flows of information that bring together and separate at the same time", he is not talking about literal geometric space. He is exploring the abstract processes that contribute to the geographical organisation of the physical world. In this case Castells argues that the world is increasingly organised in the form of flows. These are geographical organisations of work and leisure such that there are flows of material, people, money and information around distributed geographic networks. Or as Castells puts it, flows are "purposeful, repetitive, programmable sequences of exchange and interaction between physically disjointed positions held by social actors in the economic, political and symbolic structures of society". The arrangement of these circuits comes to dominate the organisation of activity in individual places. That is, the site of a place on a network and its relationship with other nodes comes to dominate over the importance of the characteristics of that place itself. The network comes to be more important than the individual place - *space* dominates over *place*.

One example that Castells uses to explain this is the network of narcotics production, distribution and consumption by drug cartels. The raw plants of narcotics are grown in countries like Peru, sent to refineries and management centres in Columbia, precursor chemicals come from production centres in Switzerland and Germany, using money which has passed through financial centres in Miami, Panama, Cayman Islands, distributed through centres such as Tijuana, and finally bought and sold thought-out the western world. For a "space of flows" like the illegal drugs industry it is the ways in which individual places fit into this space – how they fit together for the job of distributing drugs - that is more important than the characteristics of the places themselves. The *network* dominates over the individual nodes.

Castells' use of the word "space" here highlights the abstract features of work, and the ways in which the flows of money and produce across the world effect individual places. There is much power in his account, in particular for how specific activities come to be important not just for what they are in a particular place, but how they interface with actions across the globe – how they fit into the space of flows. Yet what is missing is how these networks and interdependencies between people, technologies and places interact with the situated aspects of action within those places.

The space of flows is not an identifiable place, but rather a concept of how work and action increasingly contribute to abstract and standardised flows across the world, from country to country. Yet this move away from a specific place is at the danger of loosing grip of what is being studied. The notion of space can becomes something of a playground for structures 'behind' the world (in his case the rather devastating sounding "flows", which wash away individual places in dominating networks). This looses sight of the *activities* which make spaces, which connect together the places.

Without knowing about the story itself, knowing that stories of China are told in America is little help. What stories are told? And by who? With talk of 'space' it is easy to become dazzled by the scope of the story. It is indeed impressive – even Latour's scientists in the Boa Vista need to ship soil samples around the world to gain their views (Latour, 1999b). For Castells tables of aggregated statistics take the role of 'actual events'.

To see something of what Castell's descriptions miss out, let us look at a historical example. In 1800s America there were two – famous – transport revolutions right after each other. The advent of canal and railroads changed fundamentally the connections between places in the US, firstly in how long it took to get between places, but in much more besides. Yet understanding the changes in flows needs more than just the network itself: this change was dependent on a change in practice.

Figure one shows some of the changes in terms of how long it took to get between different places in the US. In their textbook of economic history, Attack and Passel argue that the advent of the canals had huge effect on the development of the US (Atack & Passell, 1994). In the 1800s most of the population of the US lived on the eastern seaboard – in cities such as New York and Boston. Before the canal much of the food for these hungry masses came overseas from Europe, or was locally grown in New England. While the canals change the time it takes to get between places, they also change the cost in moving goods. With the canals, the massively fertile lands in the mid-west could now be farmed, and corn shipped along the canals to the eastern seaboard.

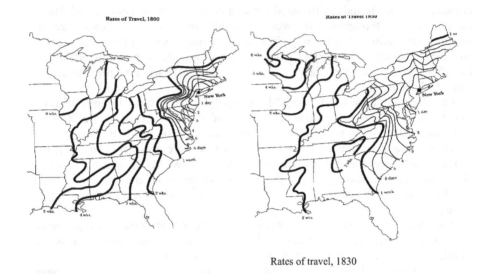

Rates of travel, 1830

FIGURE 1. Time to travel from New York, 1800 and 1830 (Attack and Passel, 1994)

At first appearance this is a very Castellsian story. The 'flows' of grain enabled by canals means that it is the relationship of places to each other (the fertility of the mid-west, the hungry masses in the east) which is more important than the properties of these places *per se*. However, this would neglect a second important element: the mobility of crops depended upon an important change in the practices which took place – a change in how crops themselves were seen. All these flows rely on a second revolution – that of the standardisation of crops and weights.

As it became cheaper to ship food around the US the relationships between buyer and seller change from personal relationship to commoditised relationships through markets, such as the grain markets in Boston and Chicago. Theodore Porter (T. Porter, 1992; T. M. Porter, 1993) points this out when he describes the advent of standardisation in the Chicago and Boston trade markets. The first step in standardisation came from the efforts of the Boston board of trade to enforce the use of a 60-pound bushel of wheat, over the old bushel stack, which was unsuitable for the new grain elevators being introduced. While this standardised weight of wheat was moderately successful, it produced another problem for the Boston board of trade. Since it was the elevator operators who selected what was suitable wheat to be transported, farmers began to mix their wheat with dirt and chaff, since they could receive the same price for it. Soon, the price of wheat from Boston fell to 5 to 8 cents below that of Milwaukee. To prevent this, the Boston board of trade began subdividing its wheat into grades based on quality, eventually training inspectors to certify the grade of each shipment of grain traded on the wheat exchange. To this was added laws against mixing wheat of different grades. Bureaucrats managed to create what had never existed in nature: uniform categories of natural produce.

Now we have a radical change – practice plus technology plus markets. It is with the combination of these three which changes the flows of food around the US – of the commoditisation of food and its movement in massive transport networks. Yet before we are dazzled too much with the changes let us not forget that the networks themselves only exist because of what people do. It is not just the network which is important here, but the changes in practice, in this case how they see food as a standardised object. The flows do not exist without the bureaucrats, it is the bureaucrats counting, tabulating and measuring, who make the flows possible.

SPECIFICS OF NETWORKS

"The highway bridge is tied into the network of long-distance traffic, paced as calculated for maximum yield. Ever differently the bridge escorts the lingering and hastening ways of men to and fro . . . The bridge *gathers* , as a passage that crosses, before the divinities–whether we explicitly think of, and visibly *give thanks for*, their presence, as in the figure of the saint of bridge, or whether that divine presence is hidden or even pushed aside." (Heidegger, 1971)

The argument I am developing here is that by focusing on the networks it is easy to loose sight of the specificities of how connections are made in particular places. While Heidegger was hardly an avid enthusiast for ethnography, as Drefuss points out (Dreyfus & Spinosa, 1997), his comments on technology hint at the tension concerning the details of specific technologies in specific places. The quote above describes a highway bridge 'paced for maximum yield'. Yet Heidegger hints at how this very technological of bridges might do other than simply enframe, or exclude, humanity. In the last line of the quote the highway bridge *gathers together* aspects of our being. This reveal something of how in technology Heidegger saw the possibility of savour as well as danger – not always, not everywhere, but a possibility. In this example it is in how that bridge connects with the history of other bridges which Heidegger uses to hint at its 'saving power'. These sorts of subtleties are lost when one only sees the flows of traffic across the bridge, the bridge as a "network of long-distance traffic" rather than as a "passage that crosses, before the divinities".

So how might we start on studying some of these aspects of technology in the particular? There are two of technology which I have worked on which are perhaps relevant here. Each study looked at a different aspect of network flows in some detail – in the first the focus was the movement of people, in particular mobile workers and their use of paper, laptops and mobile phones. This study looked at how different environments such as trains and cafes would be adopted by mobile workers to be 'workable'(1) (Brown & O'Hara, 2003). Hardly Heidegger's terrain, but an interesting point of departure for those of us interested in how networks of people are supported. With the second study, the focus moved on to the movement of *things* and in particular how the a group of workers at a truck warehouse managed the supply of spare parts distributed in a global network. Here the topic was how *things* moving globally, yet still relied upon what goes on in a specific place.

FLOWS OF PEOPLE

For the first study we interviewed a group of around twenty highly mobile workers about their mobility, and also their experiences with working in new office environments. These workers were interviewed for between one and one and a half hours about their experiences, with half the participants asked to keep a diary of their activities which was used in a second interview. Our focus here as on the effects that places had on their work. For these workers the physical places they could work in become a very important *practical* concern for them. When a mobile worker goes to work, they must decide *where* that work is going to be, under pressures of task and management.

It is important to emphasise that these mobile workers were not simply mobile for the sake of being mobile: they moved around because of the people they needed to work with in each different place. This is the main reason why mobile workers were mobile; so they can meet people face to face. As Boden points out, the face to face meeting is still the paramount means of communication in organisations (Boden, 1995).

This constant movement, connecting places together, has had an impact on many cafés, bars and restaurants. Many of these sites have been augmented with features which turn them into sites of work. As any frequent visitor to a Starbucks café would have noticed, they now have areas available for the use of laptops, and cafés are as much sites for group work now as they are group leisure. To the workers we studied, cafés were useful "semi-offices" where they could meet with colleagues and clients. There mobility meant that they more often than not worked in settings outside their office – café's, cars, airports and such.

However, these places were not merely spaces between places, they were places which themselves had to be skilfully used in managing relations with others. When the world, potentially, becomes a workplace, there are practical and social dilemmas involved in making this happen. Most importantly, the world is *not* literally an office. In attempting to work outside the office much of the artificial construction of the office was made apparent. In the world all manner of noises can interfere with work or conversation. There is also little privacy in public places, and confidential matters can be overheard. Lighting is also a controlled feature of offices, as it is not in the world. Cafés can be too dark to read, or the sun can be too bright while chatting in the park. There can simply be a lack of room in a particular setting, whereas offices are outfitted with ergonomic desks and chairs. Perhaps most serious of all, there is a lack of access to the tools of the office - the records, files, documents, photocopiers and so on, which are important for the process of getting things done.

To some of these problems there are limited solutions. In particular, mobile technologies increasingly support a range of these activities outside the office. The laptop computer, for example, provides a prop that can be used in a variety of settings to re-establish a link with the office. More broadly, technology can *encapsulate* some of the properties of the office into mobile devices. Mobile workers increasingly make use of a range of new mobile technologies, most ubiquitously the mobile telephone (Brown, Green & Harper, 2001), but also an increasing range of more eclectic mobile devices such as PDAs, mobile scanners, text messaging, instant messaging and so on. These devices allow characteristics of places – such as co-presence, informal communication, and such to be supported on the move. They transfer these characteristics of places – such as being able to have a quick chat with a colleague - into a thing (such as a laptop with instant messaging software) which can then be carried around. These mobile devices in turn are objects which can be bought and sold by electronics companies. In this way, some of the characteristics of places become commoditised in the form of consumer electronics.

While non-office places offer challenges to work, they can also be used to present an image; cafés are often settings of informality. This informality can be used as a tool – it can contribute to a friendship with a customer, or emphasise the fashionability of a new media company. The main business of coffee shops – coffee – also already has a strong niche in organisational culture. Yet it cannot be used in settings where flippancy must be avoided, such as a financial meeting. So while the individuals we studied used these "third spaces" between home and work as important workplaces, this was not an automatic or problem free transition. Work had to be done to convert regions that were once demarcated as off-limits from work (or at least explicit work) to be re-interpreted and adopted by their practices. While we have yet to see a pub designed for work, but we have seen people working with laptops and documents in pubs.

So to these highly mobile workers the places they worked in were more, not less, important to them as they moved around. Statistical studies suggest that the flows of mobile workers is increasing (Vilhelmson & Thulin, 2001) - yet these are flows which would not be possible without the activities which take place in each specific environment, activities which make possible work by 'clearing a space'. The 'space of flows', then for mobile workers, relies on a more ordinary transfer of office work to places outside the office. This is some of the work which is done which enables the mobility of workers. Contrary to writers such as Augé we find that non-places *are* places, which very much going on in them (Augé, 1995).

FLOWS OF THINGS

Travelling further on this highway, our second example shows something of how the flows of objects interacts with the places people find themselves in and the work they do. This work comes from some recent fieldwork we[i] conducted looking at how a large Bus and Truck manufacturer managed their spare parts and repairs. In this work the staff we studied were static – at least in the sense of working on one site. Rather than moving between places, it was the things which move around these workers as they controlled the distribution and arrangement of spare parts around their organisation.

We had expected repairs to be a neglected corner of the truck business. Yet we discovered that repairs are at the centre of what this company did: indeed, this truck company only broke even on selling trucks, and make nearly all their money by *fixing* them. In the repair depots where spare parts are sold, and the servicing of trucks done, we found a bunch of friendly yet underpaid store men. Their job was surprisingly difficult – although on paper they simply picked parts from shelves and put them in the hands of company mechanics or customers, finding the *right* part turned out to be a significant daily challenge.

Many of their parts they supplied came from a warehouse in mainland Europe, and were manufactured further a field. Yet the repairs they supplied the parts for needed to be completed as quickly as possible, since a truck off the road could cost a company thousands of pounds an hour. In their work then the logistics of supply interacted with the urgency of repairs. Moreover, each of the trucks or buses they repaired had literally thousands and thousands of standardised parts. In their work, the parts staff needed to work these standardisations to find out what particular parts would be needed to fix a specific truck. These storemen connected together the great flows (in the form of humble part numbers) with the specifics of *this* repair *here*.

For example, the computer system could tell them where each part was stored in the workshop and give extensive details on what that part was. Yet the experienced parts staff knew the workshop very well –they knew themselves where most of the parts were stored. Accordingly, staff could go straight to the correct part of the warehouse, grab the part and hand it to the waiting customer without needing to do any searching on the computer to find the correct part number. With the part in hand that number could be obtained from labels on each part.

Finding parts numbers was cumbersome. So when asked for a part, parts staff would often walk to the correct area of the warehouse and, even if a part was out of stock, look for where the part *should* be. They could then take a note of the part number (written above the empty bay) and use this number to order the part using the computer. So even though the computer told the parts staff where to find parts in the workshop, much of the time they used the arrangement the other way around, exploiting the physical place to find numbers which they could then use on the computer. This practice shows something of how it is that the company's standardised parts numbers (held in the computer system) interacted with the place of the workshop. In using the computer system the partsmen needed to stitch together the information given by their technology with the arrangement of the physical place.

Along with this management of the parts in the warehouse, the parts staff were part of a network of parts distribution worldwide. Through their computer system they could order parts and have them dispatched from warehouses in the UK, and from the main European warehouse. The system even allowed them to put out a 'vehicle off the road" call which would search the whole company worldwide for a part. In this way the parts staff's use of the computer stretched out and could cause goods to be shipped worldwide without any need to directly phone or contact anyone.

Yet, as with our descriptions above, this worldwide network relied upon local connections between offices. Although frowned upon nearly everyday the staff used "half way meets" or "full way meets" to swap parts between local offices. This allowed staff to get hold of parts quicker than waiting for them to be shipped from overseas. Using a 'half way meet', where staff met halfway and exchanged desired parts, they could get parts that day, as opposed to the next day delivery offered for parts from overseas.

So while the computer was at the centre of the distribution of parts – from the ordering and supply of parts coming into the depot, and how parts were found by the staff, this is not to say that the 'space' which the parts occupied and flowed through made the staff themselves irrelevant. There was considerable management of these flows by the parts staff, organising and choosing themselves when and how parts would be supplied, along with local practices such as using locations to find parts numbers, or using "half way meets" to get hold of parts quickly.

In their work the parts staff both managed the flow of parts around the company to their local office, and from that office into the hands of mechanics or customers. These flows were global flows – many of the parts were sourced from beyond Europe, and their ordering of parts had automatic effects on the manufacturing of parts around the world. Yet this flow depended in many ways on their own skills and management. They had to find the right part for a specific customer, without which this *specific* truck would not be repaired. So while this very ordinary of jobs was connected to a networks of goods being ordered, tracked, and distributed worldwide we find that very local concerns were essential in the feasibility of such an arrangement.

CONCLUSIONS

As with the advent of the global postal service at the advent of the 20th century, global networks have a certain mesmerising nature. Be they networks of people, goods, or technology their span and power can make claims of seemingly spectacular power more reasonable than it should. In many ways these networks are amazing, and do have considerable power. Yet we should not forget that they exist only in the actions of individuals in particular places, and that the details of what is done in those specific places is as important as how these places are connected together. For the wonder of the direct dial telephone network, the postal service, mobile work or even just the repair of trucks lies in how people stitch together networks from their own practices.

We started this chapter with the fantastic stories of Calvino's explorer. As this chapter has emphasised, telling stories about places far away is an old tradition, one which connects and networks together without the need for sophisticated technology or 'new economies'. Rather than being dazzled by the scope of such networks, or other networks grander in their telling, it is possible to ask about how particular networks work in detail. We encourage looking at and thinking about specific networks. Calvino's stories are about places far away, but they tell us about how we do things here and now. In this chapter we have travelled through three stories of technology and its connections. While Canals and standardisation, mobile workers and even the supply of spare parts may seem something of a motley combination each one tells us something about how things and people come to distribute and change the places in which they move through and arrive at.

The three examples describe how particular sites network together in details. Our discussion of the advent of canals shows something of how networking relies upon changes in practice – in this case the standardisation of food to enable markets and commoditisation. In turn, our discussion of mobile workers looked at how these workers managed to convert the places they found themselves in to 'workable spaces' using new technology and changes to their cultures of work. Lastly, in looking at the work of the supply of spare parts for trucks we looked at the ways in which a worldwide network of things relies upon the local actions of workshop staff and their manipulation of place.

Our creative opponent in this chapter has been Castell's and his network sociology. Yet we do not seek to simply critique Castells, but rather to move 'network sociology' onto studying specific networks in specific places and times. Our fear is that in moving sociology towards a notion of 'networks', we are starting with concepts as ambiguous as 'society' or 'culture'. The motivations for this chapter then has been to start in a different place, to look at *specific* connections, rather than seeing using these concepts to power generic enquiries.

REFERENCES

Atack, J., & Passell, P. (1994). A New View of Economic History, 2nd Edition : W.W. Norton & Company.

Augé, M. (1995). Non-places: Introduction to an Anthropology of Supermodernity (J. Howe, Trans.): Verso Books.

Boden, D. (1995). The business of talk: organizations in action : Blackwell.

Brown, B., Green, N., & Harper, R. (Eds.). (2001). Wireless world: social, cultural and interactional aspects of wireless technology : Springer Verlag.

Brown, B., & O'hara, K. (2003). Place as a practical concern of mobile workers. Accepted for publication in: Environment and Planning A .

Brown, B., & Perry, M. (2002). Of maps and guidebooks: designing geographical technologies. In Proceedings of Designing Interactive Systems (DIS) 2002 . London, U.K.: ACM Press.

Calvino, I. (1997). Invisible Cities : Cintage.

Castells, M. (1996). The rise of the network society: vol 1. the information age . Oxford, UK: Blackwells.

Castells, M. (1996). The space of flows. In M. Castells (Ed.), The rise of the network society (Vol. 1: The information age, pp. 376-428). Oxford, UK: Blackwell Publishers.

Dreyfus, H. L., & Spinosa, C. (1997). Highway Bridges and Feasts: Heidegger and Borgmann on How to Affirm Technology. In After Post-Modernism Conference . Chicago: University of Chicago.

Heidegger, M. (1971). Building Dwelling Thinking (A. Hofstadter, Trans.). In Poetry, Language, Thought . New York: Harper Colophon Books.

Latour, B. (1999a). On recalling ANT. In J. Law & J. Hassard (Eds.), Actor Network Theory and After (pp. 15-26). Oxford, UK: Blackwell Publishers.

Latour, B. (1999b). Pandora's hope . Boston, Mass.: Harvard university press.

Law, J. (1994). Organising Modernity . Oxford: Blackwell.

Law, J., & Urry, J. (2002). Enacting the social. Lancaster: Center for Science Studies and Sociology Department, Lancaster University.

Perry, M., O'Hara, K., Sellen, A., Brown, B., & Harper, R. (2001). Dealing with Mobility: Understanding access anytime, anywhere. ACM Transactions on computer human interaction, 8 (4), 323-347.

Porter, T. (1992). Quantification and the accounting ideal in science. Social studies of science, 22 , 633-652.

Porter, T. M. (1993). Information, power and the view from nowhere. In L. Bud-Frieman (Ed.), Information acumen: the understanding and use of knowledge in modern business : Routledge.

Urry, J. (1995). Consuming Places . London: Routledge.

Urry, J. (2000). Sociology Beyond Societies: Mobilities for the Twenty First Century . London: Roultedge.

Vilhelmson, B., & Thulin, E. (2001). Is regular work at fixed places fading away? The development of ICT based and travel based modes of work in Sweden. Environment and planning A, 33 , 1015-1029.

ACKNOWLEDGMENTS

Many thanks to Mark Perry, Kenton O'Hara and Henrik Fagrell for their fieldwork, analysis and ideas.

NOTES

1. This work was conducted with Mark Perry and Kenton O'Hara (Perry, O'Hara, Sellen, Brown, & Harper, 2001).
2. This work was conducted with Henrik Fragrell

ELISABETH DAVENPORT AND KATHY BUCKNER

4. SHIFTING PRESENCE IN THE CLASSROOM

THE CASE OF THE OPEN PLAN TEACHING LABORATORY

INTRODUCTION: PRESENCE IN THE CLASSROOM

The chapter explores a specific case of presence, namely a university classroom for teaching computing. By using the term 'presence', we address ways in which actors engage with other actors and artefacts in shared local space. We discuss classroom presence in terms of a 'standard model'. This consists of a complex of people, objects and structures (material and social), in a physical space that is occupied for a period of time. Interaction is choreographed by a lecturer who modulates the focus of attention. This shifts according to a rhythm that reflects established routines (such as turn-taking), and these in turn characterise activity in the classroom. Presence in this context is contingent on points of view, or perspectives, and these, in turn, are contingent on the disposition of actors, artefacts and structures in an occupied space. We suggest that 'presence', defined in terms of owned space or occupancy, and the management of attention is central to the practice of classroom teaching, and that is can be usefully applied to account for aspects of open plan teaching in the case study that is developed in this chapter. Though presence has been used in accounts of 'pure' online learning environments (e.g. Shin, 2002), it is a relatively under-explored concept in discussion of 'hybrid' learning environments of the type discussed here. The layout of a traditional computer laboratory (the norm that the VLCC replaced) provides affordances that shape the learning and teaching behaviours of students and instructors on what may be broadly described as a one to many basis (Tanner, 2000; Emmons and Wilkinson, 2001). These include:

– Clear 'lines of sight' that focus student attention on the lecturer or instructor and that allow the instructor to assess the dynamics of the class at a glance.
– Omni-directional display space (the four walls, floor and ceiling) for support materials on whiteboards, blackboards, posters.
– A clearly defined container that
  o insulates a class against outside distractions and disturbance;
  o encloses and bounds class interactions (peer to peer, and expert to student);

P. Turner and E. Davenport (Eds.), Spaces, Spatiality and Technology, 31-44.
© 2005 *Springer. Printed in the Netherlands.*

o   encourages a sense of identity in the class community by
     providing a recognized and regularly frequented space, or habitat.
–   Mutually understood norms that shape and roles and responsibilities and
    confer authority and legitimacy

In the specific context of teaching with computers in our case study, the
traditional space comprises laboratory or workshop facilities containing between 20
and 50 computers. The computers are normally positioned either around the walls of
the room or in parallel rows. In either case there is a clear 'front' of class from
where the teacher can instruct if they wish; identifiable boundaries (in the form of
classroom walls) and a semi-secure entrance, which can be closed if the instructor
desires. Often there is a computer linked to a dedicated projector from which the
instructor can demonstrate particular activities and other teaching artefacts such as
overhead projectors and whiteboards. Control in this environment works in a
number of ways:

–   Occupation of the space for the duration of the class is ensured at
    institutional level by the timetable, which dedicates a room to a specific
    class for a specific period.
–   Ownership is reinforced by shutting the door, an action that classifies
    entrances and exits within the period of the class as anomalies, for which
    explanations are required.
–   The configuration of artefacts within the space is the responsibility of the
    instructor, and the attention of the students can be gained and held through
    clearly identifiable lines of sight and lines of communication.

Such a room is not a panopticon, however. As we indicate above, classroom
routines allow control to be relaxed to accommodate variations in learning and
teaching – chairs and tables may be moved; students may take the floor at the front
of the class and so on. The space and its activities constitute a well understood
socio-technical pattern (Alexander, 1997). To learn and teach in this environment is
to be familiar with the disposition of materials, technology and people and to
understand what combinations come into play at different times: when to raise the
eyes and check the projected solutions, when to consult the notice boards on the
walls, or when to scan the class for signs of perplexity. There is a local genre
repertory that is as dependent on props and backdrops as any theatre performance
(Orlikowski and Yates, 1994). 'Learning' in this space is shaped by reciprocal (and
at times asymmetric) interaction between teachers and students that allows the latter
to progress towards proficiency. Take the walls away (the case of the open plan
laboratory described here), and the socio-technical order is disrupted. A new set of
micro-level management practices must be developed, and the genre repertoire
refreshed.

Presence in online learning environments differs from that in the standard
classroom in a number of ways. Haythornthwaite and her colleagues (2000; 2001;
2002a; Haythornthwaite & Kazmer, 2002) have undertaken a substantial study of a
distance learning community in Illinois, and identified characteristic patterns of
socio-technical interaction. In this environment, presence is complex as it is
managed across multiple social spaces. Attention is thus shared across different sets
of interactions, and the choreographic role of a teacher is partial at best. Ownership,

or occupation of the learning space emerges from the group's shared identity. In the online environment, 'awareness' is a substitute for attention in the material classroom, defined in terms of availability and responsiveness, articulated in representations (visual and audio cues) that are understood in terms of norms for synchronous and asynchronous action. The focus of attention is artefacts on a screen that singly, or in combination, support dialogue.

As Hardless and Nulden (1999) have shown, maintaining and keeping track of these artefacts is an important duty for instructors, as they support presence in the online classroom. Passwords, for example, 'close the door' and ensure that only legitimate participants engage the instructor's attention. Configuration of the artefacts that are relevant to different parts of a given course needs to be explained, by meta-level menus, concept maps, checklists, FAQ lists, and schedules. A graph showing the social topology of a class may be useful, as may interaction logs of chatroom and discussion list participation. And content needs to be accessible continuously. Learning in this environment is not always visible to the tutor, who may indeed be assigned (by learners) a bit part only (Haythornthwaite and Kazmer, 2002: 440).

Differences in presence can help explain some of the phenomena in the narrative that follows. The HE institution in the case has a robust and established track record in devoting resources to continuous improvement in teaching and learning, and many of the teaching staff in the open plan computer laboratory were fully aware of differences between online learning, and learning in a physical classroom. But issues emerged in the new hybrid environment that were not anticipated. Many of these challenged the legitimacy and authority of teaching staff, issues that are fundamental in maintaining classroom presence.

THE BACKGROUND TO THE EMPIRICAL STUDY

We present the case of a very large multi-user computing centre designed as a high-density open teaching environment for computing students. This consists of 18 clusters of 24 tightly packed machines, back to back on two rows of twelve, with each pair of clusters bounded by a waist high surround, and accessed by means of a system of intersecting aisles.

There are no walls or other form of physical boundaries between clusters although those on upper tiers are separated from those on the lower tiers by height and thus a 'virtual boundary' is formed. The facility is open 24 hours a day, and at full capacity can house 500 individuals.

An efficiency drive in the institution that hosts the VLCC led to a number of modifications in the use of space. The VLCC was set up during the summer of 2001 and was inspired by a vision of economies of scale. The design rationale of the space was industrial rather than pedagogical: the centre was to function as a multi-purpose unit, with high-density seating, high turnover, and low maintenance costs. The affordances for interaction in the space were, by design, minimal, in the interests of adaptability. The rationale was reflected in the local nickname used in the early days to describe the facility, the 'Barn', with its connotations of agribusiness. Though the facility had been designed as an open access IT resource, it was also to serve as the main teaching space for the School of Computing, none of whose staff had been consulted at the design phase. As Bjerrum and Bodker (2003) observe, this is not unusual in 'new' open plan builds, which tend to embed the 'architects' version of 'Anything. Anywhere' (p. 216), rather than the working habits of practitioners. Ambiguity about the status of machines, humans and space in the VLCC raised a number of issues that can be usefully explored by examining shifts in presence.

THE EMPIRICAL STUDY

For the past three years, the authors have been involved in a longitudinal study (ongoing) of evolving practice in the VLCC. To date we have observed three phases of development. Phase One of the project took place during the first semester of teaching in the VLCC (autumn 2001). The space presented a number of challenges, both inside and between the clusters. Lack of walls opened up multiple (and distracting) points of view and sound was difficult to project. Unsurprisingly, attempts were made initially to carry over previous habits, practices and expectations of behaviour. Inspired by Merleau-Ponty's observations of amputees with 'phantom limbs' (1962), we described these efforts as a 'Phantom Wall Syndrome'. Discussion among teaching staff (formal and informal) in the early stages focused on the dislocations produced by the space, rather than on opportunities. Much of the adaptive practice in this phase was a response to ownership and occupancy disputes, defining and identifying the legitimate group in a particular cluster at a given time. Practice was also modified in what we labelled the 'ergonomics of attention', or efforts to engage, and attend to, the members of the class. Discussion among teaching staff in the early stages focused on problem definition rather than problem solution with emphasis on negative aspects of the change.

In Phase Two: 'Adaptive Practice' there was evidence that some practices had been modified to meet some challenges of the new environment. At both individual and organisational level, we observed changes in ownership and occupation strategies, and there were observable changes in the ergonomics of getting, seeking and maintaining attention. The early months of teaching in the VLCC coincided with a national shift in focus in UK Higher Education that emphasised individual learning, rather than classroom instruction. In the VLCC this was evident in moves from whole group interaction to individual or small group interaction with online support. Although some instructors perceived the VLCC as a rather brutal intervention others could see that is would allow them to comply with the national agenda.

In the third year of operation (autumn 2003 to the present), we identified a third phase of the study, and we have called this 'embedding order'. By this stage, the VLCC had become extremely popular with students, to the extent that open conflicts would occur between individual learners and teachers in a given class space over desktop access. In addition, structural changes in the host institution had fragmented the responsibility for management of the facility, which was now shared between the

School of Computing (at the local level of the teaching cluster), the Registry (in charge of scheduling) and the IT service (with overall policing and technical duties). Given our findings in the second phase (summer 2002), we had anticipated that emerging shifts in practice would result in prescriptive organisational intervention in the form of mentoring and/or provision of guidelines for new staff. In fact, there was relatively limited organisational activity of this kind, with a staff survey (a little over half of those involved in VLCC teaching responded) to assess perceptions of the VLCC experience. Though reports on specific problems have been raised in staff meetings since the opening of the VLCC, there was no consolidated attempt to address problems by means of committee work, procedures and so on until the structural change.

PHASE ONE: THE PHANTOM WALL SYNDROME

As we note above, in its early stages, the VLCC presented a number of initial challenges: face to face interaction remained, but lines of sight and sound channels were radically different. Lack of walls opened up multiple (and distracting) points of view; and sound was difficult to project. In addition, the tight and rigid configuration of workstations meant that it was difficult for learners to manage notes, handouts and other paper at their desks, or to re-orient resources for small group activity around the machines. Our fieldwork at this stage took the form of unobtrusive observation (Kathy Buckner enrolled as a student) of two post-graduate modules with a significant teaching component undertaken in the VLCC. Ethical issues relating to observation were discussed at enrolment and due to the unobtrusive nature (i.e. no tape recording or photography of events was used) were not seen to be an issue. Much of the observation was undertaken by note-taking during, and critical reflection after, 'teaching' events. No staff or students were identified individually in any reports on the study. In addition, we gathered data at relevant staff meetings, through informal conversations, and by means of interviews with four 'key informants'.

For both students and teaching staff, ownership and occupation were difficult to assess in the free-for-all of the early weeks of the VLCC. Schedules of legitimate occupation of clusters, based on timetabling of classes, were only displayed part way through the semester. Notices indicating "Class in Progress", were largely ignored by students who started to take ownership of 'their' space in a particular cluster that became their area and had the comforting feel of being 'home', even though there were no walls. Members of faculty also began to identify particular spaces as 'home' - noticeably the preferred clusters were those in the top right hand corner of the VLCC - the 'corner' was a salient and easily recognised feature. The problem of identifying who was the owner of which cluster was compounded in the early stages by lack of traffic control. A dense wave of students arriving for a new session could push smaller pools of students out of a space. Attempts were made to solve emerging traffic flow problems by publishing 'rules' based on pedestrian flow modelling research undertaken by a member of faculty (Kukla and Kerridge 2000).

Members of faculty would attempt to achieve ownership of their allocated 'classroom' on arrival by announcing their presence - usually requesting anyone not in his/her class to log off and vacate the area. However, some found that maintaining 'possession' was a continual challenge with incursions of interlopers (in one reported case this happened 17 times in a one-hour period) threatening to flood their teaching environment. Whilst this was an issue for some staff, others were more relaxed about the situation and happy to accommodate 'other' students in their cluster provided they were not interfering with the learning and teaching experience. Differences in tolerance were confusing to students, but there was no attempt at this stage to design a formal policy on the issue.

As there was no 'front of class', it was difficult to secure the attention of students by establishing lines of sight or other traditional means. Some attempts to use the perimeter walls as teaching artefacts emerged as term progressed. Suspended PC projectors were installed in clusters at the far end of the VLCC, which were pointed towards the boundary walls, but these were not observed in use. No projection or other presentation facility e.g. whiteboards was initially placed in any other of the clusters.

In the first phase, we observed that staff had diverse methods of managing attention in the new open learning space. Tutor 1, for example, established command by identifying who was in the group and asking students to raise their hands if they were 'with him'. To indicate completion of essential tasks students were required to provide a visual signal by putting their hands-up – reinforcing the boundaries of the class group and assuring their attention. With nowhere to write (no walls with whiteboards, for example) the tutor used a paper notepad produced by an assistant to demonstrate a particular task. Tutor 2, in contrast, identified the boundaries of the group by handing out worksheets. These operated like a 'badge' – anyone with the right worksheet being in 'his' class.

Though the acoustics in the VLCC have been designed to absorb sound, noise travels more easily in this open environment than it would between adjacent closed IT workshops. Limitations in lines of sight, coupled with acoustic problems led to some changes in teaching practice. The most significant was a shift away from 'whole group' teaching. Tutor 2, for example, only rarely (e.g. if a mistake needed to be rectified on an instruction sheet) attempted to engage with the whole class in the cluster, and provided support at the individual or paired student level. As we note above, the balance of attention in a traditional classroom shifts throughout the period of contact.. The standard practice involves mixed mode teaching with short periods of time at computer workstations interspersed with 'mini lectures'. These are effective mechanisms for maintaining interest and concentration, for resolving frequently recurring problems and providing students with reassurance on the stage they should have reached. This type of interaction could not be sustained in the VLCC, where students have become more reliant on obtaining support and help from paid student demonstrators rather than teaching staff. They also seek support and advice from their fellow students and collaborative learning has become the norm rather than the exception. They thus resemble the distance learners described by Haythornthwaite (2002b).

We noted some examples of modified practice that seem well aligned with the new hybrid environment. Tutor 1, for example, provided comprehensive, structured materials for each week, which, to a great extent, can be worked on (using supplementary web-based resources) independently by students. He organised his students into small (3 or 4 students in each), collaborative groups whereby he positively encouraged peer-to-peer activity. Each group was seen by either the member of faculty or by 'cherry picked' demonstrators during the course of the one or two hour session with records being maintained to ensure that there was engagement with all the groups each week. Attention was thus distributed across different elements of the hybrid learning environment (co-instructors, artefacts, peers) as happens in distance learning, but the overall environment was choreographed by the instructor in ways that resemble the standard classroom set-up.

PHASE TWO: ADAPTIVE PRACTICE

In Phase Two, observations from the student point of view continued, complemented with observations from the key informants. We observed continuing modifications in presence, most of which were responses to the ongoing challenges of ownership and attention management. Though contests persisted over occupation and ownership, a number of teaching staff had evolved work-arounds. Tutor 3, for example, 'trained' his early arrivals to sit in the 'best seats' in his cluster, knowing that late arrivals would follow the flow and seat themselves nearby. Once this routine was established, he no longer had to arrive in advance to direct students to the positions he preferred them to use. We also observed attempts to routinize lines of sight in the clusters by establishing quasi 'front of class' areas. For some, the 'front' of the class was now seen as being at the entrance to the cluster - from where they could also protect their space. For others, the concept of the 'front' had little relevance in their modified practice. Etiquette was also emerging in this phase to handle disruptions and interruptions due to noise: it was accepted that teachers might ask colleagues in adjacent areas to tone down voice projection, for example.

By the end of the second semester ('Phase Two'), it was clear that some instructors had modified practice to meet the challenges of the new environment. At both individual and organisational level, we observed changes in ownership and occupation strategies at the level of individual learning spaces or clusters, and there were observable changes in the ergonomics of getting, seeking and maintaining attention. These were in many cases unplanned improvisations in the face of management's sluggish response to requests in the early stages of the VLCC for teaching artefacts to be provided. As a result when screens and projectors (familiar props in the old habitat) appeared in the second semester they were under used, as practice had evolved to allow some instructors to cope without them. By the end of the second semester (June 2002) a community of innovators had emerged who exchanged ideas about VLCC teaching practice at coffee, in the corridor and more formally in planning meetings. To help us understand variations in teaching practice (and further explore the concept of presence), we undertook an activity analysis (Engeström, 2000) in the summer of 2003.

We made the assumption that the primary purpose of activity is student transformation by learning. This is shaped by complex interactions between different actors such as learners and instructors who use a number of tools (e.g. computers, projectors; signage, learning resources etc), the community of instructors, students, technical support, and management who occupy and maintain the space according to recognised divisions of labour. The activity analysis led us to identify two main types of instructor, who differ in their management of classroom presence and we called these 'Instructor-Adopters' (I-A) and 'Instructor-Resisters' (I-R). While both are focused on the student, I-As are more focused on the outcome of facilitating effective student learning. There are however two categories of resister, some I-Rs (whom we call I-R/Ls) may be similarly focussed on facilitating student learning but are reluctant to modify practice to meet the demands of the VLCC because they believe that other types of classroom better support student learning, while other I-Rs (whom we call I-R/Ts) are more focused on transforming the student through effective teaching. This fundamental difference has a significant impact on classroom presence, and ways in which it has evolved in the new regime. As we note above, students appear to have embraced the new environment wholeheartedly, and thus an instructor (I-R/L) who believes in student-centred learning is more likely to adapt to the new space.

I-As are most likely to describe as 'useful' those tools that support 'individual' self paced student learning. These may include web-based resources and workbooks, which the student can use either individually or with colleagues in small group activities. I-As do not normally require external props such as whiteboards and PC projectors as their interaction with students is on a one-to-one or small group basis.. I-As allow the student to lead the learning process, and proactively support the student according to individual need. I-R/Ts however prefer to lead the students as a class or group through the learning process and consequently find an environment, which is more conducive to independent learning more difficult. Tensions arise when artefacts such as PC-projectors and whiteboards, previously accepted as standard, are no longer readily available or easily accessible.

Instructors are less visible in the VLCC. This does not indicate (contrary to suggestions by senior management) that they are simply abandoning classes, but that they have altered their mix of visible and invisible work by 'entering' the online learning space and focusing their effort on the development and use of online learning materials. They are thus less likely to be present in the classroom and delegate their presence there to demonstrators who in the labs may assume some of their support role. Adapting the notion of the 'customer in the machine' (Hughes *et al.*, 2002) we think of adaptive teaching staff (I-As and I/R-Ls) as 'lecturers in the machine'. They are, paradoxically, less visible than their resistor colleagues who struggle to sustain a physical presence that is characteristic of traditional up-front 'teachers'. These I-R/Ts favoured a didactic approach in which they set the pace. They were more comfortable if all the students in a class were working on the same problems each week, and found it more difficult to adapt to individual learning styles, speed and approach. They thus preferred to have more exclusive control and ownership of the teaching space – which, as we have observed above, was extremely difficult with regular 'incursions' from students who are not members of the class.

PHASE THREE: EMBEDDING ORDER

In this section of the chapter, we pick up the story in the autumn of 2003. Though there had been some attempt to revise and expand the 'rules' for conduct in the VLCC (http://www.napier.ac.uk/depts/citservices/Documents/acceptable_use_policy.PDF), a number of problems remained unresolved. These were not simply localised difficulties arising from variance in teaching practice, but reflected deeper problems in terms of the shifts in presence that we have commented on in earlier sections. Ongoing problems included:

- The contested status of timetabled space. If it was comparable to a classroom, then teaching staff could invoke the rules and norms of the classroom; if it was not perceived as a classroom (the view of many individual learners), then the jurisdiction of teachers could be challenged.
- An increase in the number of individual students requiring access to computing facilities, and competing with timetabled classes. This was partly the result of a University-wide policy to adopt WebCT as a Virtual Learning Environment.
- The need to provide specialist software for use by School of Computing students, who require access outside timetable class hours.
- Growing concern by teaching staff over the limited teaching mix that could be used in the VLCC clusters, which do not support mixed mode delivery.

To address these issues a working party was formed in November 2003. It was felt that a working party would have more time to focus on relevant issues and that the outcomes from its work would feed into negotiations relating to the School of Computing's use of the VLCC. A number of agencies were now involved in making decisions about the operation of the VLCC. The timetabling issue, formally handled internally, was now the remit of Registry, which was also in charge of user authentication issues. The provision of specialist software was now in the hands of C & IT Services (the central unit for systems management and support), added to their earlier role of technical and facility maintenance. The School of Computing would now have to work across departmental boundaries to address VLCC issues, and compete for attention with other groups in the University.

As we note above, an 'acceptable use policy' had emerged in previous months, but this was difficult to enforce. The major issue was access to empty spaces during class time by non-enrolled students. Staff were on occasion subject to abuse by students, and there was genuine concern that physical violence would erupt. In addition, there was concern from teaching staff that while classroom activities were disrupted by such incidents, seats in non-timetabled spaces might well be occupied by individuals who were engaged in non-academic activity – if anyone should be disrupted, it should be them. The solutions proposed by the working party were both institutional and local. Timetabling should be more prominently displayed, to prevent outsiders from unwittingly entering a time tabled space. Where outsiders are to be admitted, admission would be regulated by a numbering system, with regular class members occupying the lowest numbers in a cluster first to allow the class to start with outsiders arriving at the fringes. The areas filled first by bona fide attendees would become the 'focus of attention' in the classroom space. In addition, it was proposed that student ID cards should be checked by teaching staff to establish legitimate participation (a form of 'closing the door').

To mitigate 'bad temper' in the space, a request was made for increased patrolling by C & IT Services staff, to stop mobile phone use, eating and drinking and trivial use of computers at times when others wished to have access for academic purposes. In addition, the working party proposed that the VLCC should be both 'hard' and 'soft' zoned, with physical partitioning of an area of use by the School of Computing and allocation of other areas (through timetabling) as primarily for teaching purposes. This would facilitate provision of specialist software, clearly identifiable teaching (rather than drop-in) zones, and provide areas where mixed modality teaching (a partial return to the 'standard model') could be undertaken. This request partly arose from concerns about student performance in the new facility. A staff survey re-iterated the view that the clusters in the JKCC were not suitable for the type of teaching regularly undertaken in the School of Computing. As we note above, this often involves short (5-10 minute) whole group briefing/working/demonstration sessions, with students focusing on the lecturer and turned away from PCs. This may be followed by individual, self paced learning or small group activity (often supported with online learning resources). For effective teaching and learning this pattern of interaction may be repeated several times during a timetabled class.

We suggest that the requests emerged from unresolved ambiguities in important management areas, not simply concerns about operational issues. For senior management, the VLCC is simply a collection of time-tabled entities, and is thus in the purview of the Registry. In as much as it is a technical facility it is in the domain of C&IT services. The 'presence' of C & IT staff is ambivalent, however. In as much as the VLCC is a public access utility, they must be visible and accessible (indeed, the C & IT staff were issued with 'branded' sweatshirts to enhance their 'presence'), and from the perspective of the individual undertaking personal tasks in the VLCC, they have a status analogous to teaching staff. But they have a different presence in relation to their role as support for teaching staff (loading software, ensuring that all machines in a cluster are in working order, undertaking patrol work and so on).

DISCUSSION AND CONCLUSION

Our three year study demonstrates clearly that shifts in pedagogic practice involve more than individuals, and it has allowed us to identify questions that need to be addressed when 'new' spaces are introduced into a world of existing work practice (see also studies on University 'space' by Shabha, 2000; Bazillion and Braun, 2001). What kind of social order can support learning and teaching in this parsimonious environment? How is order established and maintained at different levels of organization: the laboratory space, the course, the departmental infrastructure committee, the faculty teaching and learning team? What is the pattern (if any) of impact and diffusion? Are there shifts in the configuration of social and technical elements of interaction?

The case study has also allowed us to chart the emergence of social order in the VLCC. This has evolved from pragmatic strategies for managing highly localised rules and routines, to the formation of a complex institutional infrastructure that shares many of the political dimensions described by Star and Ruhleder (1998) in a ground-breaking account of remote collaboratory work The infrastructure in the VLCC has emerged not through forward planning, but by means of cascading improvisations or situated actions of the sort described by Suchman (1986). The case contributes to a body of work on 'social computing', a corpus of studies that focus on questions of social order and social learning in organizations, and explores how these are achieved and maintained. This body of work brings together work in a number of overlapping domains (Social Informatics, Social Studies of Science, Social Shaping of Technology, Human Computer Interaction, Computer Supported Cooperative Work) that provide a socio-technical account of the workplace.

Dourish, in a recent monograph on embodied interaction (Dourish, 2000), a key factor in social computing, suggests that understanding of this phenomenon demands a 'concern with the mundane aspects of social life, the background of taken-for-granted everyday action'. The focus of attention becomes how orderly social conduct emerges from the detail of each setting in which it is undertaken, and how orderliness is achieved in the face of the endless contingencies to which it is subject' (p. 96). 'Mundane' practice is thus an expression of shared order, articulated in generic activities, ordered by protocols, procedures, documentary genres and other artefacts. Analysis of a growing corpus of micro-level studies reveals a number of 'typical' loci - the helpdesk, the schedule, the classroom (the instance developed in our case study). Ackerman and Halverson (1999), for example, provide a detailed account of a helpdesk in an insurance office, where 'work' is both shaped by what the environment affords, and shapes that environment as novel solutions to caller's problems are embedded in the practice of the group. We suggest that the concept of presence that is developed is a useful (socio-technical) construct for addressing this interplay of environment and practice.

The spatial effects of the new habitat are complex and paradoxical. An effective practitioner in this 'open' teaching environment, must shift her or his point of view, and learn to enact presence in a different way – the line of sight, for example, in the new environment may have the student as the object of the gaze rather than the teacher, who is now a marginal figure, operating at the edge of the space as keeper of the boundaries. The balance of teacher and student 'in the machine' (Hughes *et al.*, n.d.) is also different, as 'old style' material in simple 'depository' mode (teacher-led) is replaced by the learning track record as a primary element (jointly constituted by teachers and learners). Though there are some analogies between what we have observed in the VLCC with accounts of new office spaces (Davenport and Bruce, 2002; Bjerrum and Bødker, 2003) and alternative workspace strategies in the health sector (Gilleard and Tarcisius, 2003), shifts in classroom presence are in many respects specific to the trade, and managerial interventions (such as workshops on best practice) that have successfully contributed to adaptations in new office spaces may not be effective here. Though some teachers engage cheerfully with such a make-over, others cannot accept it. Shifting presence in the VLCC touches on fundamental issues of differences in teaching philosophy and personal sense-making that will take further time to resolve.

ACKNOWLEDGMENTS

We gratefully acknowledge the support of staff and students who have contributed to this study.

NOTES

1. There are affinities between our articulation of 'classroom presence', and the description of 'dwelling' that is offered by Bjerrum and Bodker (2003): a combination of 'place, identity, materials and learning' (p. 204)
2. A fuller version of our findings on this phase was presented at ECCE 2001
3. A fuller of this is provided in Buckner and Davenport (2003).

REFERENCES

Ackerman, M. & Halverson, C. (1998) Considering an organization's memory. In *Proceedings Of The Conference On Computer Supported Cooperative Work*, November 14-18, 1998, Seattle, Washington, United States, 39-48,

Alexander, C. et al. (1997). *A Pattern Language*. Oxford University Press: New York.

Bazillion, R. J. & Braun, C.L. (2001) Classroom, library and campus culture in a networked environment, *Campus-Wide Information Systems*, **18(2)**, 61-67.

Bjerrum, E. and Bødker, S. (2003) Learning and living in the 'new office'. In K. Kuutti et al. (Eds.) *ECSCW 2003: Proceedings of the Eight European Conference on Computer Supported Cooperative Work*, 14 – 18 September 2003, Helsinki, Finland, 199 – 218.

Buckner, K. and Davenport, E. (2002) Teaching and learning in the VLCC: actions, reactions and emerging practice in a very large computing centre. In S. Bagnara, S. Pozzi, A.Rizzo and P. Wright (Eds.) *Proceedings Of The 11th European Conference On Cognitive Ergonomics*. Instituto di Scienze e Tecnologie della Cognizione Consiglio Nazionale delle Ricerche. 355-360.

Buckner, K. and Davenport, E. (2003). Organisational Learning: An investigation of response to rapid change in a traditional environment. In D.Harris, V.Duffy, M.Smith, C. Stephanidis (Eds.), *10th International Conference on Human - Computer Interaction* 4 : Lawrence Erlbaum Associates, 669-673.

Davenport, E. and Bruce, I. (2002) Innovation, knowledge management and the use of space: questioning assumptions about non-traditional office work. *Journal of Information Science*, **28(3)**, 225-230.

Dourish, P. (2000) *Where the action is*. MIT Press.

Emmons, M. & Wilkinson, F. C. (2001). Designing the electronic classroom: applying learning theory and ergonomic design principles. *Library Hi Tech*, **19(1)**, 77-87.

Engeström, Y. (2000). Activity theory as a framework for analysing and redesigning work. *Ergonomics*, **43(7)**, 960-974.

Gilleard, J.D. and Tarcisius, L.C. (2003). Improving the delivery of patient services: alternative workplace strategies in action. *Facilities*. **22 (1/2)**, 22-27.

Hardless C. and Nulden U. (1999) Visualizing Learning Activities to Support Tutors. In *Proceedings of CHI 99*, Extended abstracts. New York: ACM, 312-313

Haythornthwaite, C. (2000). Online personal networks: size, composition and media use among distance learners. *New Media and Society*, **2(2)**, 195-226.

Haythornthwaite, C. (2001). Tie strength and the impact of new media. In *Proceedings of the Hawaii International Conference on System Sciences*, January 3 – 6, 2001, Maui, Hawaii. New York: IEEE. At http://alexia.lis.uiuc.edu/~haythorn/HICSS01_tiestrength.html

Haythornthwaite, C. (2002) Strong, weak and latent ties and the impact of new media. *The Information Society*, **18(5)**, 385-401.

Haythornthwaite, C. and Kazmer, M. (2002) Bringing the Internet home: adult distance learners and their Internet, Home and work worlds. In B. Wellman and C. Haythornthwaite (eds.) *The Internet in Everyday Life*. Oxford: Blackwell Publishing, 431-463.

Hughes, J., Rodden, T., Rouncefield, M. Tolmie, P., Randall, D. and O'Brien, J. Getting to know the 'customer in the machine'. http://www.comp.lancs.ac.uk/sociology/VRbank.html

Kukla R. & Kerridge J. (2000) Developing the Behavioural Rules for an Agent-based Model of Pedestrian Movement, 25th European Transport Congress, 2000, Cambridge, UK, 01/09/2000.

Merleau-Ponty, M. (1962) *Phenomenology Of Mind*. London: Routledge & Kegan Paul.

Orlikowski, W. and Yates, J. Orlikowski, W., & Yates, J. (1994). Genre repertoire: the structuring of communicative practices in organizations. *Administrative Science Quarterly*, **33**, 541-574.

Shabha, G. (2000). Virtual universities in the third millennium: an assessment of the implications of teleworking on university buildings and space planning. *Facilities*, **18(5/6)**, 235-244.

Shin, N. (2002) Beyond interaction: the relational construct of 'transactional presence'. *Open Learning*, **17(2)**, 121-137.

Star, S., & Ruhlehder, K. (1994). Steps towards an ecology of infrastructure: complex problems in design and access for large-scale collaborative systems. In R. Furuta and C. Neuwirth (Eds.) *Proceedings Of The Conference On Computer-Supported Cooperative Work*. New York: ACM, 253-264.

Suchman, L. (1986) *Plans And Situated Actions*. Cambridge: Cambridge University Press.

Wenger, E. (1998). *Communities Of Practice: Learning, Meaning And Identity*. New York: Cambridge University Press.

A. GOULDING

5. THE PUBLIC LIBRARY

A Successful Public Space?

INTRODUCTION

The public library service in the United Kingdom is an enduring and popular institution. A "genuinely successful decentralized cultural institution" (Greenhalgh and Worpole, 1995: 44), there are 4,134 public libraries in the UK, not counting mobile libraries nor facilities in other institutions such as hospitals or prisons[1]. The public library service reaches into just about every community and, as a result, is increasingly recognised as important for neighbourhood renewal in urban areas and as a means of overcoming the isolation of many rural ones. The role that public libraries can play in improving the quality of the daily life of citizens is now being celebrated by both practitioners and policy makers. Lord McIntosh, the Minister responsible for public libraries in the Department for Culture, Media and Sport (DCMS), recently commented that public libraries are, "shared ground in an increasingly diverse society, a place where the whole community can feel a connection" (Cabe, 2003: 3). The physical presence of the public library building in the neighbourhood plays a large part in its ability to promote this kind of community identity and strengthen civil society. Symbols of civic identity like public libraries provide an area with a sense of character and can inspire a mutual sense of satisfaction and common ownership. They also provide space, open to everyone, which can nurture cohesion and solidarity. Without spaces in which social interaction can take place, the links, relationships and networks which make social systems work effectively are unlikely to occur. This chapter will argue that the public library could be a focal point which brings people together and which helps build and sustain a vibrant community culture but there are challenges that need to be confronted before it can be considered a truly successful public space. Although focused on a specific cultural institution, this chapter addresses themes which are of interest to a wide readership, for example, the meaning and importance of public space, how public space can create social capital, the characteristics of successful public space and common obstacles which often prevent public spaces from functioning effectively.

Terminology: the term "the public library" is used in this chapter to indicate a single public library building which provides services to its local community and

P. Turner and E. Davenport (Eds.), Spaces, Spatiality and Technology, 45-66.

also as a more general term referring to the concept and institution of the public library service.

THE IMPORTANCE OF PUBLIC SPACE

An accepted definition or understanding of the term 'public space' is elusive and is becoming even more difficult to pin down as the nature of ownership and management of public space is transformed by government initiatives increasing the involvement of the public sector in both capital projects and the running of public facilities. Definitions have been attempted, nonetheless. Mandipour (1999: 880) defined public space as those areas within towns, cities and the countryside that are physically accessible to everyone, where strangers and citizens can enter with few restrictions while Shonfield's (1998: 11) much wider conception of the term included "everywhere that is neither home nor work". Some definitions acknowledge that public space may be privately owned: "a place to which the public has or is permitted to have access and any place of public resort" (Vasen, 1980: 302) but most, according to Leckie and Hopkins (2002: 328), are united by an understanding of social interaction, social diversity, inclusivity and community.

Although definitions may vary, there does seem to be general acceptance that public space is a common good which should be preserved and nurtured for the benefit of the community and promotion of civic society. The *Project for Public Spaces* (2003a, para 1) in the United States outlines the characteristics of public spaces which work well. These are places where private and public exchanges take place for both social and business reasons and where cultures mix. They are sites for celebration, protest and solidarity which nurture the community, bring the public together and give residents a strong sense of connectivity. Successful public spaces give areas a sense of character, contribute to community health and enhance the civic realm by facilitating public activities and by instilling a sense of pride and ownership among diverse groups. Berman (1986: 482) emphasises the capacity of public space to bring together people from all walks of life and its ability to, "both compel and empower these people to see each other, not through a glass darkly but face to face". Similarly, Besser (2001, para 3) discusses how, even when housing or neighbourhoods have been segregated along class or ethic lines, public spaces have been places where people from different backgrounds and origins are exposed to one another, encouraging them out of their insularity. Good public space, then, is considered essential for citizen involvement and community vitality and the British Government has responded to the realisation of the important role that it plays in people's lives, and concern about its degradation, by making a number of public pronouncements and establishing a variety of initiatives in this policy area.

The policy context

Issues surrounding the provision and use of public space are further up the political agenda now than they have been for many years. A fresh concern for community, inter-connectedness and civic renewal has prompted policy makers to consider the spaces within which individuals and communities operate and how those spaces can contribute to the objective of community regeneration. The British Government has committed itself to neighbourhood renewal, the promotion of stronger local communities and a better local quality of life and the Prime Minister is concerned that the local environment contributes so that it, "fosters rather than alienates a sense of local community and mutual responsibility" (Blair, 2001, para 3). The urban white paper, *Our towns and cities: the future – delivering an urban renaissance*, outlined the results of neglect, poor management, inadequate public services, lack of investment and the culture of short-termism on Britain's urban areas (The Department of the Environment, Transport and the Regions, 2000: 2). It set out the Government's vision of making towns and cities vibrant and successful places, including action to improve parks and open spaces. Similarly one of the Government's seven "cross-cutting" reviews undertaken as part of the 2002 Spending Review focused on "Improving the Public Space" and considered how improvements in the safety and attractiveness of public space could be achieved. The political will to improve public spaces seem to be strong, therefore, although some have questioned whether the desire to improve urban public spaces is prompted more by the need to market localities to businesses and tourists than through concern for the reintegration of fragmented cities (Mandipour, 1999: 886).

Initially, the Government's agenda focused primarily on fighting street crime and tackling anti-social behaviour and also prioritised external public space such as streets, urban parks and green areas. While acknowledging that internal public spaces "such as libraries and town halls" (Office of the Deputy Prime Minister, 2002: 9) are important living places, less attention was paid to the nature and character of public buildings. This relative neglect of public buildings as important public spaces was corrected to a certain extent by the launch of the *Better Public Buildings* initiative in 2000 which aims to "improve the standard of public buildings, spaces and places in Britain" (Better Public Building, n.d). The *Better Public Buildings* report which launched the initiative acknowledged that good design can increase use of public services and community participation but its main focus was the aesthetics and design qualities of public buildings rather than their use (Finch 2000). Similarly, the recent *Better Public Libraries* report considers, almost exclusively, exterior and interior design issues (Cabe, 2003). Design can be an important barrier or, conversely, inspiration to use public buildings of course, but less attention has been paid to the capacity of public buildings like public libraries to act as spaces in which people can meet, interact and participate in a range of educational, cultural and information-related pursuits which promote democratic access, social exchange and participation in civil society. The need to develop and protect space supporting activities like these is considered particularly urgent as public space rapidly disappears.

The crisis in public space

The recent interest in public space as a key neighbourhood and community resource is partly the result of the perception that we live in an increasingly divided society where public facilities are no longer automatically accessible. The issue of privatised public space and its effects has been a key issue for urbanists, geographers and sociologists in recent times. They argue that there has been a shift in emphasis from the public to the private sphere, that there is an increasing trend towards privatisation of the public realm, that modern life has blurred the boundaries between work and home life and that this has led to people being pulled apart from one another and their communities resulting in "a striking diminution of regular contacts with our friends and neighbors" (Putnam, 2000: 115). In particular, informal meeting places are said to be sadly lacking in most towns, cities and villages, public and relaxed "places to be" (Skot-Hansen 2002: 12) which afford citizens the opportunity to "wander, browse, to stand and chat, to sit and watch the world go by" (Greenhalgh & Worpole 1995: 12).

Part of the problem is said to be that the boundary between public and private space has become blurred and shopping centres or malls, for example which, above all else, are held up as examples of the way in which places used by the public are controlled by private interests, are not necessarily as welcoming or inclusive as many definitions of public space suggest. These "pseudo-public" spaces, such as shopping centres, theme parks and sports stadiums, sanitize the environment of certain elements and prohibit activities that do not fit in with their primary objective (Besser, 2001, para 8), laying down rules about access and behaviour which render it sterile and predictable (Day, 1999: 157). Another issue of concern is the impact that private space is having on the vitality of true public space. There has been particular disquiet over the effect that out-of-town shopping centres and retail parks have had on "traditional" town centres which are now often denuded of facilities and used only by those without access to private transport, those with less disposable income or by the less mobile, leading to segregation and exclusion.

In most private space, out of hours access is restricted for everyone, not just the excluded, meaning that many towns have no evening life and people return to their individual homes and families, reinforcing the isolationist tendencies fuelled by private car ownership and patterns of work, among other things. This secluded way of life, most prevalent in North America but increasingly common in Australasia (Newman & Kenworthy, 1992) and the United Kingdom (Williams & Green, 2001:11), is often unfavourably compared with practices in continental Europe where the plazas, passeggiata and café and bar society maintain high levels of sociability and integration. In fact, some would argue that what is lacking from many North American towns and cities now is not *public* space but *civic* space, places where people join together in communal activities, be they cultural, political or ceremonial, which encourage citizen engagement (Lees, 1995: 450). In the latter, the social interaction that takes places is more purposive that that occurring in the former, focused on citizenship engagement and civic practice. In this way, civic space is something akin to the Greek Agora, an arena or forum for community celebration and for interaction with elected officials, professionals and other citizenships on issues and policies affecting the life of the community. In more general public space, on the other hand, the interaction is less focused by and large characterised by more relaxed chatting, meeting others, strolling and observing life. That does not mean that the interaction is less valuable. Indeed, a dearth of social interaction, whether purposive or not, can breed intolerance, prejudice and a narrow-minded outlook which, in cultures increasing in diversity and inequality, are dangerous for social cohesion and established values of democracy. Public space where people from all walks of life can meet and interact is arguably more important than ever, therefore, for social exchange and the strengthening of community bonds but it is clearly under siege in many places (Lees, 1994: 445). The local public library, though, is a place which seems to have retained its ability to act as a public space, both physical and psychological and this aspect of public library use is gaining increasing recognition from commentators, policy makers and practitioners in the field.

Public library space

The idea of the public library as a vital public space has recently been given renewed emphasis, therefore, although recognition of the symbolic nature of public library buildings has a long history. The grandeur of many Victorian municipal libraries testify to the pride with which these institutions were founded and, as Black comments, "In some respects, indeed, it appeared that buildings were more important than they books they contained" (Black, 1996: 225). Similarly, the testimonies of many of those who used public libraries in the 1940s and 1950s suggest that the environment within the public library was the key to its success. Greenhalgh and Worpole (1995: 140) give examples of what they term "the mythology surrounding the public library"; accounts eulogising the quiet of the reading room, the severity of the librarians and even the smell of the fixtures and fittings all of which seemed to have endowed the public library with a quasi-religious aura, giving it mystique and adding to its charm but also perhaps giving it an intimidating air as discussed below. It could be argued that from the 1970s until the 1990s, however, public librarians and their supporters retreated somewhat from celebrating the importance and centrality of the library building. Concerned with "community librarianship" and under ideological and economic attack, public libraries sought to justify their existence by emphasising services provided to the community outside the library walls as well as the importance of the library building as a functional and symbolic institution. Furthermore, advances in ICT and digital resources left many questioning the role of the physical library building now that so many of the materials it housed and made available for use were electronically accessible.

Although the public library building remained an important focus for many, the physical nature of the library and its role as a public place was not celebrated to the extent that it had been previously, therefore. Recently, though, there has been an upsurge in interest in the ability of the public library building to promote and sustain community identity, dialogue and collaboration. In 2003, for example, Re:source (now renamed MLAC – the Museums, Libraries and Archives Council) commissioned the Centre for Public Libraries and Information in Society (CPLIS) to investigate the impact of new library buildings on their communities (Bryson, Usherwood & Proctor, 2003) while the British Government's latest strategy document for public libraries, *Framework for the Future,* asserts that libraries are shared spaces, "public anchors for neighbourhoods and communities" (Department for Culture, Media and Sport, 2003: 9). There has also been considerable attention focused on new public library buildings. In 2003 the new Bournemouth central library won the Prime Minister's *Better Public Buildings* award, Peckham library won the Stirling prize for best new building in Britain in 2000 and others, such as the re-built Norfolk Millennium Library and the Ideas Store in Tower Hamlets, are seen as excellent practice in civic design and a vital element in their areas' regeneration. So despite predications of the death of the library due to the information revolution and the availability of digital resources, new library buildings are attracting renewed attention and, in many cases, increased usage. It has been recognised, then, that public library buildings can make an important contribution to the quality of life of an area. Consideration of how they achieve this leads us to a discussion of the characteristics of successful public space.

SUCCESSFUL PUBLIC SPACE

Public spaces should be centres for public discourse, free speech and diversity, giving a sense of well being and adding to the quality of life of individuals and communities. Some are able to do this better than others. Several attempts have been made to analyse the characteristics of successful public spaces and although most focus on external open spaces (see, for example, Williams & Green, 2001: 3; The Project for Public Spaces, 2003b, paras 8-11), many of the features can be applied to public buildings too. Professor of Sociology Ray Oldenburg's concept of the "third place" is also helpful when considering the attributes of successful public spaces. His book, *The great good place,* describes and analyses the many public places which often act as the heart of the community by providing people with the space to gather away from home and work (their first and second places) and enjoy each others' company (Oldenburg, 1999). These are "social condensers" which enlarge and reinforce civil society by providing a space in which people of a community can meet to interact with others. Drawing on these discussions, we can conclude that a successful public space should be:

- Accessible and identifiable: the space is easily reached, clearly visible and has an established image;
- Receptive: there should be no barriers or obstacles to use whether physical (preventing use by elderly or disabled people, for example), psychological (status or image) or financial (charging an entrance fee or membership charge);
- Comfortable and attractive: people feel safe and want to linger because of the facilities provided which encourage both physical and psychological comfort;
- Versatile: the space supports a range of activities and uses and therefore attracts people from many walks of life who have different reasons for being there;

- Sociable: it is easy to enter conversations with both friends and people encountered on a regular basis in the space as well as those unknown to us who have different backgrounds from those within our usual social circle.

As the *Project for Public Spaces* (2003b, para 1) argues, this last aspect is perhaps the most important of all if public spaces are to successfully reconnect those who have been divided by social polarization and segregation. Within some towns and cities, different communities lead parallel lives with little meaningful exchange or cross cultural social contact between them (Salmon, 2002: 51). This can lead to the breakdown of social cohesion and its consequences: the alienation, maginalisation and disaffection of certain social groups. To overcome these negative consequences for both individuals and communities, governments are promoting initiatives which encourage people to cooperate, understand one another and forge relationships. In the UK, formal mechanisms for citizen participation at community level exist in a variety of forms including parish councils or meetings, community forums and trusts and tenants associations. These formal bodies play an important role in engaging local people and helping them work together for the benefit of their neighbourhoods but services and places which enable members of a community to meet and encounter one another on a regular though informal basis are just as vital in building a dynamic and active civic life and recognition of this has led to increasing concern with public space and its capacity to build social capital.

Popularized by Harvard social policy professor Robert Putnam in his book *Bowling Alone* (Putnam, 2000) which describes the decline of American community life and civic engagement, the term social capital was coined by social scientist James Coleman at the end of the 1980s who used it to describe the relationships among persons, groups and communities which engender trust and/or mutual obligations. These relationships, expectancies and trusting obligations between people function as a kind of social glue enabling them to act more effectively, making society more efficient and making life generally more rewarding. Although there is a danger of social capital being viewed as merely "warm, cuddly feelings or frissons of community pride" (Putnam, 2000: 23), it is also seen as having a range of important desirable policy outcomes, hence government interest in building and maintaining it. Communities high in social capital are said to have lower crime rates, better health, better educational achievement, better child welfare, more effective government and higher economic achievement than those deficient in social capital. This is often summed up by Woolcock's (2001: 12) phrase describing those with strong reserves of social capital as more likely to be "housed, healthy, hired and happy". To achieve these desirable outcomes, communities need spaces in which individuals can come together to build relationships of trust, reciprocity and common values. As suggested above, Britain is not lacking in formal mechanisms through which people engage in civic participation but physical spaces in which people of a community feel happy spending time and which lead to less definable but equally valuable community-based relationships are perhaps less common for all the reasons outlined earlier.

It is this author's contention that this type of space could exist in just about every community in the UK in the shape of the public library. The tentative nature of this assertion is an acknowledgement that many British public libraries do not currently have the capacity to build social capital nor do all act as successful public spaces as defined by the criteria developed above. They are faced with a variety of challenges which limit their ability for either. Nevertheless, public libraries do have a number of attributes which makes them potentially very powerful agents of social capital and which mean they have a strong claim of providing good public space.

THE PUBLIC LIBRARY AS SUCCESSFUL PUBLIC SPACE

The public library has a long, credible history of providing community space (de la Pena McCook, 2000:17) and many commentators have waxed lyrical about its ability to act as the community's "front porch" – a "centering institution, as a place of gathering and as an equalizer" (Cart, 2002: 3). Although de la Pena McCook complains that the role of library services is virtually ignored in the burgeoning literature on civic renewal, many public libraries are beginning to explore their potential for building social capital and to assert their value as a public space that brings together diverse populations into one community space to learn, gather information and reflect. In the UK, public libraries are increasingly being viewed as a vital element of an area's regeneration and their potential for building social capital through the fostering of social links which bind the community together was recently highlighted by Bryson, Usherwood and Proctor (2003: 65). The ability of the public library to act as a dynamic and vital civic space is widely accepted in the library literature then and, clearly, the public library does have many attributes which contribute to the perception that it is a successful public space. Equally, though, there are forces and developments within the library service and beyond which limit its success. These restrictions and the opportunities for the public library to take on the role of a successful public space will be discussed under the criteria developed above.

Accessible and identifiable

The presence of a public library building in communities across the nation have a symbolic as well as a practical role. Ross Shimmon, Secretary General of the International Federation of Library Associations (IFLA), once remarked that the ubiquity of public libraries in local communities is rivalled only by that of refuse disposal services, reminding us that these two disparate facilities are very often the only physical reminder of local government and civic values in areas suffering deprivation or degradation of the public realm. It is of the utmost importance, therefore, that public library services are easily reached and available when needed.

Since 2001, there have been public library standards covering English public libraries, including standards on accessibility relating to location and opening hours with the aim of ensuring that public libraries are accessible to a range of people who may want to use the library at different times of the day and to guarantee that their use is not limited to those with private transport (Department for Culture, Media and Sport, 2001: 8). To date, public libraries have had mixed success in complying with these accessibility standards finding them among the most difficult to meet (Department for Culture, Media and Sport, 2002: 2). National trend statistics also confirm that access to public libraries has become more restrictive. Over the ten year period up to 2002, the number of service points declined overall by 10 per cent and the number of service points open for 60 hours or more fell from 52 in 1992 to 37 in 2002 (Creaser, Maynard & White 2003: 21).

Although opening hours do seem to have contracted, public libraries are still open for longer than many other council or civic buildings and some authorities are now opening for longer on Saturdays and even on Sundays in an acknowledgement that access only during conventional office hours is not convenient for many. Furthermore, studies suggest that a majority of users is satisfied with current arrangements with 71 per cent of users rating their satisfaction with opening hours as good or very good (Cipfa, 2002: 59). This figure has shown a gradual decline over the years, however. In 1997, it stood at 77.5 per cent and there is a perception that the issue of opening hours is a particularly thorny issue for users (see, for example, Proctor, Lee and Reilly, 1998: 38). We should also be aware that user surveys of public libraries are riddled with difficulties. They are said to suffer disproportionately from the halo effect with respondents giving the answers they think the questioner wants to hear and with high satisfaction rates disguising low expectations on the part of users. There is also a perception that users do not complain about public library services for fear of losing them altogether and they are therefore inclined to give very positive responses to satisfaction questionnaires. Surveys of non-users and lapsed users are probably more instructive in obtaining a true picture of how accessible public libraries are, as they may show that location and opening hours have an impact on use of these public spaces. In fact, surveys of non-users of public libraries show that very few of them do not visit public libraries because of access, problem such as inconvenient opening hours or location (Table 1). Lack of need and lack of interest appear to be the main factors keeping people away from public libraries which are perhaps more difficult issues for managers to address. One survey of lapsed users, though, did suggest that for this group access issues such as opening hours had been influential in their decision not to use the library in the previous year (Bohme & Spiller, 1999: 82). Twenty-four per cent of respondents stated that the reason they did not use the library was because the opening hours were not convenient although personal reasons such as a lack of time and a tendency to buy books were more frequently cited reasons for lack of use.

Reason for not using public libraries	All non-visitors (%)	Adults (%)	Children (%)
No need/reason to	39	44	19
Too busy/no time	22	26	5
Buy books/AV instead	17	20	13
Not interested in books/reading	14	17	3
Borrow from friends, family etc.	12	14	5
Not interested in any services	8	9	3
Too young/others borrow on behalf	6	1	30
Use other libraries instead	5	3	14
Get info from elsewhere (e.g. Internet)	5	5	3
Not well/housebound/don't get out	4	5	2
Opening hours inconvenient	4	4	3
No public library convenient to get to	3	3	1
Doesn't have services required	2	2	1
Other	4	3	4
Any reason given	88	90	82

Table 1. Reasons for not visiting public library: adults and children, 1998. Source: Bohme & Spiller 1999: 17.

Non-use does not mean indifference, however, and surveys have shown that awareness of the local library is high, with most passers-by able to identify its location (94.7 per cent) (Cox, 2000: 47) and a majority (85.1 per cent) responding that it is very or quite important to have a library within the community (Cox, 2000: 9). Again, we must be wary of the dangers of the halo effect, but there does seem to be a genuine attachment to the physical presence of the public library in the community, an acknowledgement of its importance for a range of educational and social functions and a widespread knowledge of where the library is located within the local area. The availability for use, rather than actual use, is therefore considered an important characteristic leading local people to feel "a deep sense of place attachment: such places are part of their community, part of their social and cultural fabric" (Leckie & Hopkins, 2002: 5). Studies of the value and impact of public libraries invariably show that they make a large contribution to community identity and social cohesion and that the buildings are identifiable landmarks within the town or city in which people can meet and spend their leisure time (Linley & Usherwood, 1998: 41). Although there are some difficult issues relating to accessibility for libraries to address, then, the public library does seem to be maintaining its distinct identity within communities and is often a source of civic pride (Bryson, Usherwood & Streatfield, 2002: 6), local studies collections and archives adding to the idea that these are centres of community identity. Understood as communal property but not closely associated with the local authority in people's minds, the public library is a symbol of civic culture which provides social moorings (Molz & Dain, 1999: 205).

Receptive

The term 'public' library has a number of connotations attached to it relating to its receptivity. First of all, it is for 'the public', open to everybody who lives or works in the local area irrespective of their standing, background or abilities. Secondly, it is a public service, a civic amenity for the communal use of local people. Finally, there's the notion that the library is public in the sense that it is freely available and has no cost attached to the use of its core services. The second of these interpretations of the term public has been considered to a large extent above; the public library is identified by many as an important community resource and symbol of civic engagement. This section considers how successful the public library is at fulfilling its mission to be 'public' in the other two meanings of the term: how truly free it can be considered in financial terms and, firstly, whether there are any restrictions preventing local people entering and using the library facilities.

Despite the difficulty that some library authorities are clearly having with achieving the levels of accessibility considered acceptable by the DCMS, many do make strenuous efforts to ensure that their libraries are accessible as they can be within resource constraints. For those who cannot easily reach a static service point, the library will often come to them in the shape of a mobile library, housebound service or some form of residential facility. Whether all of these could be said to be acting as a public space is debatable but they do show that the public libraries are concerned that access to their services is as convenient and suitable as possible for people with a wide range of accessibility needs. A study undertaken in 1999 found that the public libraries participating in the research were aware of many of the more obvious physical access needs of disabled people, the need for ramps, lifts etc, and were trying to respond positively to the requirements of the 1995 Disability Discrimination Act (DDA) (McCaskill and Goulding, 2001: 205). Physical access issues that are perhaps less obvious to able-bodied people such as shelving, table and counter proportions, were not consistently addressed, however, but funding the necessary improvements was identified as the key challenge. Once again, though, users seem generally satisfied with physical access. Around 85 per cent of users in one national survey responded that ease of access both entering and within the library were either very good or good (Cipfa, 2002: 14).

The DDA is helping to ensure that physical barriers to public library use by disabled people are being minimised. There are other physiological hurdles, though, which limit the ability of the public library to function as a civic space extending an equal welcome to every member of the community. Commentators acknowledge that the library is not always as unconditionally welcoming as often suggested because of issues surrounding class, race, expectations of appropriate behaviour and the homogeneity of users all of which may discourage certain sections of the local community entering the library. Muddiman (1999) suggests that "a white, middle class, academic culture" alienates disadvantaged people while Durrani asserts that the public library has failed many black people (1999: 270). Although there are undoubtedly issue to address in making the public library more socially inclusive, the perception that public library users are all middle class, middle aged people is not borne out by the statistics. Although it is true that the higher social classes (AB –

professional and managerial) use libraries in excess of their presence within the population as a whole, the data show that all social classes use public libraries and that use is reasonably proportionate (Table 2).

Class	Presence in UK population (%)	Library users (%)
AB	18	22
C1	25	28
C2	27	25
D	15	12
E	15	13
Total	100	100

Table 2. Library use by socio-economic grouping Source: Adapted from: Hawkins, Morris & Sumsion, 2001: 260.

Nevertheless, for some non-users, the perception that the public library is "not for the likes of us" can be an annoyingly enduring one for public library managers despite their best efforts to raise awareness of the diversity of services and facilities provided by public libraries. Linley and Usherwood (1998: 77) suggest that the rules and regulations surrounding library membership and use can intimidate potential users and they can act as another psychological barrier limiting access for some sections of the community. For some, perceptions of culture and atmosphere can be off-putting while others may face practical difficulties. A 1995 study found that 25 per cent of adults tested on their ability to fill out a form could only give very basic information such as name and address (Gregory, 1996: 10). It is vital, therefore, that joining procedures are as simple and accessible as possible to promote equity. Recognizing this, many public library services have addressed the issue either by offering confidential joining schemes through which people can get help filling in forms or by making it standard practice for library staff to fill in the joining form for library users, removing the need for them to ask for assistance. This does not help those without an address, such as travellers or homeless people, not those without the means to prove it, such as a utility bill. Again, though, some library authorities are trying to overcome this obstacle to library use by experimenting with schemes extending membership to groups who have previously been excluded because of their inability to comply with library joining regulations.

One strategy recommended by those seeking to increase the use of public libraries is to locate libraries with other services or facilities. This "co-location", as it is termed, is considered to have multiple benefits for all, engaging groups and individuals perceived as hard to reach (Department for Culture, Media and Sport, 2003, p.41). Public libraries have been sited with a range of other services to this end including other local government services such as housing or social services, with schools, with other leisure and cultural facilities such as museums and within community centres. They have also been placed within shopping centres and retail developments with mutually beneficial outcomes. Although undoubtedly resource efficient, there is some doubt over whether co-located services are as socially inclusive as stand alone library buildings. Housing libraries in the same building as services which are not perceived to be as neutral or welcoming as public libraries, social services for example, could deter those who have had difficult experiences with those services in the past. Similarly, students who have been excluded from school or older adults who did not do well in the formal education system might not want to enter a library on school premises while locating public libraries in shopping developments can give them a consumerist air which does not fit well with their image as free, neutral and accessible to all.

Another factor which could deter potential users from entering the public library space and making use of its facilities is charging for services. Unlike some other European and international public library systems, public library users in the United Kingdom are not charged a joining or membership fee nor or do they have to pay for borrowing books or accessing printed information. The public library is free to enter and there are no charges for using its core services. Public libraries can lever fines for the late return of books, though, and charge for the lending of music CDs, videos and DVDs, for reserving material and for the use of a variety of other facilities including access to specialist databases. Although all library authorities have exemptions for those on low incomes, charges are a potential barrier to use of a library's service at whatever level they are set and will always make some people pause for thought before using a service. Those low income worry about accumulating unmanageable levels of fines and could be reluctant to use services which could lead to them having court action taken against them should they not be able to pay the fines they have amassed.

Comfortable and attractive

The public library building stock in the UK is ageing and not all of it is appropriate for a modern public library service. The financial stringencies of the 1980s and 1990s meant that funds for new buildings or refurbishments were not generous and many libraries became quite run down. More recently, however, rebuilding and refurbishment programmes have been steadily enhancing the building stock in many library authorities. Responses to a recent research questionnaire for a project investigating the role of public libraries in lifelong learning suggested that library managers now generally feel that the quality of their buildings are still variable but improving[2]. Design can impose barriers to use, intimidating some and deterring others through their dull or uninspiring appearance, inflexible layouts and uncomfortable fixtures and fittings (Cabe, 2003: 14) As noted above, the design of public libraries has attracted attention recently with buildings winning awards and plaudits and the *Better Public Libraries* report presenting the diverse range of best practice taking place in the sector (Cabe, 2003: 3). It is now also recognised that buildings need to provide a range of facilities to encourage people to use the library for long periods of time, for study purposes for example, including toilet and refreshment services. Eating and drinking in the library has been a vexed issues for many librarians but more and more new and refurbished libraries are setting aside areas for cafes as well as areas in which more relaxed forms of seating such as armchairs and sofas are provided, perhaps in response to the popularity of these features in many national bookshop chains. Local authorities are taking action to make their library buildings more attractive, therefore, although it could be argued that aesthetic appeal does not lie at the heart of a successful public space. Even the most unprepossessing of places can draw people in and contribute to community identity and dialogue (Project for Public Spaces, 2003b, para 12).

Physical comfort can lead to users feeling welcome and at ease in the library and another important aspect of this kind of psychological comfort is safety. Public libraries are generally considered safe places which are usually self-policing with most users observing unwritten rules of behaviour. An Australian study found that the public library was considered to be a safe place where high levels of trust operate (Cox, 2000:.8). Although the libraries in Cox's study had few formal security measures, they did not have serious problems with behaviour. In fact, she suggests, the lack of overt policing reassures users that the library is safe while heavy security measures such as warnings of thieves and surveillance cameras can make people wary and fear for their possessions and person (Cox, 2000: 29). British social audit research found, though, that crime can be a barrier to public library use especially if the library is located in an area which is considered unsafe and users welcomed the installation of security devices (Linley & Usherwood, 1998: 81). Cox suggests that staff attitude has a big influence on public feelings of safety. Although she does not recommend that problems are swept under the carpet, she asserts that the perception and handling of any incidents directly affect users' perceptions of safety within the library and those taking a more relaxed attitude were more successful in convincing users that the space was safe (Cox, 2000: 30).

Versatile

Social, political, economic and technological developments have meant that the public library service in the UK has had to re-examine its mission and the services it provides at various points over its 154 year history. The number and variety of services it offers have expanded to embrace multiple purposes and multiple constituencies in an attempt to meet the demand of one of the architects of the British public library service that it should be, "catholic and all embracing" (McColvin, 1942: 4). Most modern statements of purpose and role suggest that the public library provides facilities for education, culture, information and leisure and acts as a community focal point although its emphasis will vary according to national and local priorities. Because of its wide remit, public libraries attract a range of users and commentators have drawn attention to the fact that town centre libraries are used by a wider cross-section of the local population than almost any other public, commercial or retail institution (Greenhalgh, 1993: 76). Use and visitor statistics show that people of all ages mix in the public library and it could be said that it is one of the few public places where both old and young are welcome and encounter one another on a regular basis. Use by different age groups is more evenly distributed than often thought, again suggesting that the stereotypical image of the public library user as middle aged or elderly is misplaced (Table 3).

Age group in years	% of users
14 or under	1.8
15-19	4.8
20-24	5.4
25-34	12.6
35-44	17.3
45-54	15.4
55-64	15.6
65-74	17.4
75 or over	9.8

Table 3. Library users by age group. *Source, adapted from Cipfa, 2000:16.*

More women than men use the public library - 58.9 per cent and 41.1 per cent respectively (Cipfa, 2000: 17) – confirming that while many women's access to public space continues to limited by a variety of constraints (Day 1999: 159), the public library remains "one of the few places in a busy centre where people, particularly women, of all ages go alone and spend time without worry" (Greenhalgh & Worpole 1995: 52). Public libraries offer their services to a wide range of people from the local community, therefore, including the retired, students, the unemployed and the homeless. Many have collections in other languages and provide resources in a range of formats for those with disabilities. They also offer space and facilities for groups of people from the local community to meet and undertake a variety of activities meaning that, overall, the public library has been successful in accommodating diverse needs.

Recently, however, there have been concerns that developments in public library services and facilities might be challenging its claims of inclusivity and universality. This has been illustrated most dramatically by the incorporation of ICT facilities in response to the Government's agendas on digital citizenship and lifelong learning. Its community location and neutral and trustworthy public image makes the public library an ideal site for fostering the spread of ICT skills among the population, according to the Government, and for enabling people to access lifelong learning materials and courses via the Internet (Library and Information Commission, 1997: 2). The environment of the public library, specifically, seems to attract many who have never before had the opportunity to use the Internet or online services, one study reporting the comments of one user who felt that the library is an unintimidating place in which to practice ICT skills with encouraging help on hand when needed (Brophy, 2003: 14). Others studies, though, report uncertainty on the part of staff and users of whether the public library is the appropriate place for some of the services facilitated by the Internet (see, for example, Spacey, 2004). Although often supportive of the provision of online learning and electronic information resources, staff can be ambivalent about the use of facilities such as free email which bring quite a different user into the library. Picking up on this uncertainty about the value of some of the services now provided in public libraries, a recent cartoon in *Community Librarian* (see below) illustrates some staff discomfort with the direction in which public libraries seem to be moving, resenting the library being turned into "a glorified Internet café" or an "an amusement arcade" (Spacey, 2004: 108).

This change in the atmosphere of the public library service is difficult for some staff and users to deal with as it may involve a profound and lasting alteration to long-held values and relationships. So while Brophy is enthusiastic about the evidence suggesting that new users from a range of different classes and background are being attracted to libraries by the new facilities, others are less sure about how well the old and the new interact; "the quiet of the reference library and reading areas competing with the clatter of keyboards" (Seered, 2004, The impact upon libraries section). Martin Molloy, responding to author Anne Fine's address at IFLA 2002 which criticised the impact of technology on the public library world, takes issue with the view which seems to suggest that some library users (those avidly reading books) are more worthy users of public library space than other (Molloy, 2003: 21). Nevertheless, service developments have undoubtedly had an impact on the use made of the public library space and, in some cases, have brought different groups into conflict with each other over use of that space. Bryson, Usherwood & Proctor (2003: 53) discuss how some of the new public library buildings they studied alienated the older user because of the emphasis placed on attracting youngsters. As one Head of Services commented, "...it is difficult to serve two groups in very close proximity to each other because of the different expectations..." (Bryson, Usherwood and Proctor, 2003: 68). Similarly, library managers responding to the Biblio.for.mEDA questionnaire suggested that adapting the existing library space for lifelong learners was causing some difficulties and that some of the more traditional library services were being compromised: "We try to balance the needs of our established readers with those of our new learners but with mixed success". In trying to accommodate new uses within the public library space, therefore, there is a danger that the more established will be driven away, restricting its versatility.

Source: 'Through a glass, clearly', Community Librarian, no. 30, Summer 2003, p.14.
Reproduced with kind permission of the cartoonist, Mark Bryant.

Sociable

The public library's versatility and ability to meet a wide range of people's needs means that users will often encounter and interact with those outside their usual social circle. In this, they are considered a "unique place .... within the local townscape" (Greenhalgh & Worpole, 1995, p. 83). Within the public library space, people from the local community and beyond meet, interact and share common interests and in this way the public library plays a social role (Linley and Usherwood, 1998: 32). For the isolated, in particular, the library can play a hugely important role, providing opportunities for member of the community to socialise and make contact. Although users may not, in fact, talk to others, the mere fact of being in other people's company is sufficient for some to appreciate the public library as a community space: "It's just a nice sort of space, you know: plenty of space and no one hassles you or anything. You can sit down and look at books if you want a nice quiet place to sit" (Insight Research, 1999: 29). This aspect of "social reading" is an interesting one, the public library providing social space for "private contemplation in company with others" (Molz & Dain, 1999: 206). Public library users are undertaking personal activities in a public setting surrounded by others from the local community doing the same and individuality is thus combined with communality.

For those who do want to talk to others, there are generally opportunities for interaction within the public library. Regular users get to know one another and the staff and this type of social exchange has been found to be especially important for elderly people, many of whom use static service points rather than the housebound service because of the opportunity to be in company (Linley & Usherwood, 1998, p. 33). The trip to the library is a habitual activity for many who visit on a day and at a time when they know they will meet with other "regulars" and look forward to chatting with them and the staff who often know them by name. Although staffing resources are often stretched to their limit in public libraries, interaction with users is increasingly viewed as a core activity in public libraries. This is in part the result of reader development activities which encourage librarians and library assistants to talk with library users about their reading material in an attempt to persuade them to widen their reading repertoire. The days of the silent public library are most definitely behind us, therefore. As well as this kind of informal social interaction, formal networks of people with similar interests meet in the public library, local history societies, for example, or book clubs which draw their membership from across the local community. These activities strengthen the community's associational life, one of the main factors in building social capital.

The public library is thus a space in which people meet, interact and form relationships, however fleeting. As we have seen, public libraries attract users from across the social spectrum and, in some areas, the public library is the only public space for socialisation, giving people a sense of what it means to be a community (Batt, 2002: 6). The capacity of the public library to provide shared space for a variety of different groups within the community, accommodate diverse needs and enhance social interaction and trust (Cox, 2000: 7) is considered a key attribute by commentators and policy makers and is one of the principal reasons that the public library can be considered a successful public place. Of particular importance is its capacity to give people the opportunity to mingle with those with a different background from their own and although the public library has been criticised frequently for trying to be "all things to all people", the multiplicity of services offered means that it is intergenerational and intercultural, "a center for community, for communing, for co-mingling, for common possession and participation" (Cart, 2002: 5). As public spaces, then, public libraries are conducive to interpersonal relationships and solidarity, encouraging a sense of belonging and community and by providing public space for people to share experiences, views and outlook, libraries can promote and sustain community identity, dialogue and collaboration.

CONCLUSION

There is no doubt that the public library is a valued public institution in the community where it enjoys great support. People are not just attached to the ideals of free access to information and provision of education for everyone but also to the physical presence of the library in the locality. Proctor, Lee and Reilly (1998, p. 62) documented the impact of library closures on local communities and found that familiarity with the local service point led to a strong loyalty and attachment to the familiar surroundings and people they met there. Many of their respondents who stopped going to the library as a result of closures missed the social element of their library visits as well as the physical space of the library and the pleasant atmosphere and environment. Closure, it seems, leaves a physical and social gap in the community and proposals to cut library services are invariably accompanied by campaigns bringing together a range of community groups concerned about the loss of the physical presence of a community space as well as the services provided by the library. The support it enjoys within the community from both users and non-users suggests that the public library is a very popular public space, but is it a successful one?

The analysis above would indicate mixed success. Public libraries are generally perceived as welcoming, accessible and neutral spaces, open to all comers and within which people are treated as citizens rather than consumers. They are not as socially inclusive as they might be, however, and sometimes struggle to meet their aim of being strong community facilities open to all. The "fear of the threshold" common to many cultural institutions (Greenhalgh, 1993: 1) can deter users and is difficult to overcome although publicity, redesign and relocation have been successful for some. Public libraries also need to inspire people to enter them and while many new and refurbished buildings are now state of the art, others are still more state of the ark, struggling to convince potential users that they are comfortable, viable, civic spaces in which they would wish to spend time. To successfully fulfil their symbolic role as public space, public libraries need to reduce some of these barriers to access although the claims for the socialising effect of the public library are extensive in the library literature. It is said to be, "a communal meeting ground for all members of a pluralistic society, a shared site where people of various classes, ethnicities, religions and culture mingle" (Leckie & Hopkins, 2002: 332). Further, "[it] can function as a centre from which to rebuild community and trust, and a forum for civil and collaborative inquiry" (Alstad & Curry, 2003, Conclusion section, para. 1) but there is a dilemma for the public library here. Reading and studying are, in the main, private activities and there is a tension inherent in modern conceptions of public libraries which see them as social centres for regulars while still wanting to preserve their educational or scholarly function. To be successful, public libraries need to meet the individual's need for private space which can be inhabited without confrontation or interference while at the same time supporting group and social activities (Social Inclusion Executive Advisory Group to Cilip, 2002: 16). For those public libraries which have successfully put themselves at the heart of their communities, their major challenge now is to handle the conflicting demands made by their multiple constituencies; solitude versus interaction, quiet versus noise. The solution may lie in zoning (Cabe, 2003: 26) but not all public library buildings have the space or facilities to allow this. Furthermore, some would argue that the strength of public spaces lies in its embrace of plurality and conflict which stimulate debate and dynamism (Berman, 1986: 484). In trying to design out the tensions inherent in any shared space, public libraries may be in danger of destroying the vitality which makes public spaces truly successful.

NOTES

[1] This is the figure for 2001/02 from the latest CIPFA (Chartered Institute of Public Finance Accounting) Public Library Statistics (London: CIPFA, 2004)

[2] The Biblio.for.mEDA project began in January 2004. For more information see: http://www.lboro.ac.uk/departments/ls/disresearch/bibliomeda.html

REFERENCES

Alstad, C. & Curry, A. (2003). Public space, public discourse and public libraries. *LIBRES*, 13 (1). Retrieved August 18, 2003, from http://libres.curtin.edu.au/libres13n1/pub_space.htm

Batt, C. (2000). At the eye of the storm – public libraries and climate change. *Lianza Conference 2000*. Retrieved September 3, 2003, from http://www.confer.co.nz/lianza2002/PDFS/Batt.pdf

Berman, M. (1986). Take it to the streets: conflict and community in public space. *Dissent*, 33, 476-485 quoted in Valentine, G. (2001). *Space and society* (p. 201). Harlow: Pearson.

Besser, H. (2001). *Intellectual property: the attack on public space in cyberspace*. Retrieved February 11, 2004, from http://www.gseis.ucla.edu/~howard/Papers/pw-public-spaces.html.

Better Public Building (n.d.). Retrieved February 23, 2003, from, http://www.betterpublicbuildings.gov.uk/

Black, A. (1996). *A new history of the English public library. Social and intellectual contexts, 1850-1914*. London: Leicester University Press.

Blair, T. (2001). Speech by the Prime Minister: Improving your local environment, 24 April, 2001. Retrieved September 22, 2003, from http://www.number-10.gov.uk/output/page1588.asp.

Bohme, S. & Spiller, D. (1999). *Perspectives of public library use 2. A compendium of survey information*. Loughborough & London: Library and Information Statistics Unit (LISU) & Book Marketing Ltd (BML).

Brophy, P. (2003). *The People's Network: a turning point for public libraries*. London: Re:source.

Bryson, J., Usherwood, B. & Proctor, R. (2003). *Libraries must also be buildings? New library impact study*. Sheffield: CPLIS.

Bryson, J., Usherwood, B. & Streatfield, D. (2002). *Social impact audit for the South West Museums, Libraries and Archives Council*. Sheffield: CPLIS.

Cabe (Commission for Architecture and the Built Environment) (2003). *Better public libraries*. London: Cabe and Resource.

Cart, M. (2002). America's front porch – the public library. *Public Library Quarterly*, 21 (1), 3-21.

Cipfa (2002). *PLUS National Report 2001-02*. Retrieved February 23, 2004, from http://www.ipf.co.uk/plus/plus_nationalreport_200102.pdf

Cox, E. (2000). *"A safe place to go". Libraries and social capital*. Sydney: Public Libraries Branch of the State Library of New South Wales.

Creaser, C., Maynard, S. and White, S. (2003). *LISU Annual Library Statistics 2003*. Loughborough: LISU.

Day, K. (1999). Introducing gender to the critique of privatised public space. *Journal of Urban Design*, 4 (2), 155 – 178.

De la Pena McCook, K. (1999). *A place at the table. Participating in community building*. Chicago: ALA.

Department for Culture, Media and Sport (2001). *Comprehensive, efficient and modern public libraries – standards and assessment*. London: DCMS.

Department for Culture, Media and Sport (2002). *Appraisal of Annual Library Plans 2002. Report on key issues*. Retrieved February 20, 2004, from http://www.libplans.ws/reports/finalreport02.pdf

Department for Culture, Media and Sport (2003). *Framework for the future*. London: DCMS.

Department of the Environment, Transport and the Regions (2000). *Our towns and cities: the future*. Retrieved February 23, 2004, from http://www.odpm.gov.uk/stellent/groups/odpm_urbanpolicy/documents/pdf/odpm_urbpol_pdf_608358.pdf

Durrani, S. (1999). Black communities and information workers in search of social justice. *New Library World*. 100 (1151), 265-279.

Finch, P. (2000). *Better public buildings: a proud legacy*. London: Department for Culture, Media and Sport.

Greenhalgh, L. (1993). *The public library as place*. Gloucestershire: Comedia.

Greenhalgh L. & Worpole K. (1995), *Libraries in a world of cultural change*. London: UCL Press.

Gregory, W. (1996). *Informability: the informability manual. Making information more accessible in the light of the Disability Discrimination Act*. London: Blackstone Press.

Hawkins, M., Morris, A. & Sumsion, J. (2001). Socio-economic features of UK public library users. *Library Management*, 22 (6/7), pp. 258-265.

Insight Research (1999). *Usage of British public libraries: report on an exit survey*. London: Insight Research.

Leckie, G. J. & Hopkins, J. (2002). The public place of central libraries: findings from Toronto and Vancouver. *Library Quarterly*, 72 (3), 326-372.

Lees, L. H. (1994). Urban public space and imagined communities in the 1980s and 1990s. *Journal of Urban History*, 20 (4), 443-465.

Library and Information Commission (1997). *New library: the people's network*. London: Library and Information Commission.

Linley, R. & Usherwood, B. (1998). *New measures for the new library: a social audit of public libraries*. London: British Library Research and Innovation Centre.

Mandipour, A. (1999). Why are the design and development of public spaces significant for cities. *Environment and Planning B: Planning and Design*, 26 (6), 879-891.

McCaskill, K. & Goulding, A. (2001). English public library services and the Disability Discrimination Act. *New Library World*, 102 (1165), 192-206.

McColvin, L. R. (1942). *The public library system of Great Britain : a report on its present condition with proposals for post-war reorganization*. London: Library Association.

MLA (2004). *The disability portfolio*. Retrieved February 28, 2004, from http://www.resource.gov.uk/action/learnacc/00access_03.asp

Molloy M. (2003). Fine words but false ideas. *Library and Information Update*, 2 (1), 21.

Molz, R. K. & Dain, P. (1999). *Civic space/cyberspace*. Cambridge, Mass.: The MIT Press.

Muddiman, D. (1999). *Images of Exclusion: user and community perceptions of the public library*. Leeds: School of Information Management, Leeds Metropolitan University (Public Library Policy and Social Exclusion Working Papers no.9).

Newman, P. & Kenworthy, G. (1992). *Winning back the cities*. Sydney: ACA/Pluto Press.

Office of the Deputy Prime Minister (2002). *Living places: cleaner, safer, greener*. London: Office of the Deputy Prime Minister.

Oldenburg, R. (1999). *The great good place*. New York: Marlowe.

Proctor, R., Lee, H. and Reilly, R. (1998). *Access to public libraries. The impact of opening hours reductions and closure 1986-1997*. London: British Library Research and Innovation Centre (British Library Research and Innovation Report 90).

Project for Public Spaces (2003a). *What is a great civic space?* Retrieved August 18, 2003, from http://www.pps.org/buildings/info/benefits_bb/benefits_public_spaces

Project for Public Spaces (2003b). *Good places*. Retrieved February 11, 2004, from http://pps.org/info/placemakingtools/casesforplaces/goodplaces

Putnam, R. D. (2000). *Bowling alone*. New York: Simon and Schuster.

Salmon, H. (2002). Social capital and neighbourhood renewal. *Renewal*, 10 (2), 49-55.

Seered 2004, *People's network computers – best value or expensive beige elephants*. Retrieved August 30, 2003, from http://www.seered.co.uk/peoples_network_computers.htm

Skot-Hansen, D. (2002). The public library in the service of civic society. *Scandinavian Public Library Quarterly*, 35 (3), 12-13.

Shonfield, K. (1998). *At home with strangers: public space and the new urbanity*. London: Comedia and Demos.

Spacey, R. (2003). The attitudes of public library staff to the Internet and ICT training. (Doctoral thesis, Loughborough University).

Social Inclusion Executive Advisory Group to Cilip (2002). *Making a difference – innovation and diversity*. Retrieved September 10, 2003, from http://www.cilip.org.uk/advocacy/eags/sereport2.pdf

Totterdell, B., Bird, J., Redfern, M. (1976). *The effective library: report of the Hillingdon project on public library effectiveness*. London: British Library.

Vasen, R. S. (1980). *The Canadian law dictionary*. Ontario: Datinder S. Sodhi for Law and Business Publications, Don Mills, quoted in G. J. Leckie & J. Hopkins, (2002). The public place of central libraries: findings from Toronto and Vancouver. *Library Quarterly*, 72 (3), p. 328.

Williams, K. & Green, S. (2001). *Literature review of public space and local environments for the cross cutting review*. London: Department for Transport, Local Government and the Regions.

Woolcock, M.. (2001). The place of social capital in understanding social and economic outcomes. *ISUMA: The Canadian Journal of Policy Research*, 2 (1), 11-17.

LORNA MCDOUGAL

6. UNDERSTANDING SPATIALITY

The Intersection Of Real And Virtual Workspace

SPACE AT WORK

Technology has changed the shape of work organizations and operational space. One of the most obvious effects on the workplace is the growing distance between work and workplace. Distance technologies most recently wireless (see for example Intel 2004), have separated the work we do from the places in which we do it. As workplaces diffuse, we occupy multiple physical and non physical spaces. In addition, the shape of the workplace is changing. Organizations are no longer modelled on HQ with hubs, and radiating subsidiaries. Since the influence of technology in the workplace was first felt in the early 1980s, the physical plant has been progressively affected by each new advance in technology and communications. By 1993, when the Neocon major design exhibition in Chicago took as its theme the notion of 'Breaking the Mold': it was already clear that the design of offices and workspace could no longer be predicated on the principles of hierarchy. Since then the Internet and wireless devices, and the mobile workforce have effectively separated work further from place. In some cases virtual space is as real as space defined by the senses (hard measurable physical space) and that hard space is losing its symbolic significance.

Technology and Hard Space in Office Design

Office space design was until recently effected by applying a pyramid of space standards which mirrored the pyramid of organisational structure. Management at different levels enjoyed different amounts of space. Life in the workplace could no longer be fitted into a model composed of x square feet for CEO's, y for general managers, z for middle management and so on. In addition, the older steeper pyramid with does not easily accommodate organizations with many specialists, with particular space needs or a highly mobile workforce. It does not fit well with highly individualised organisational culture in a way which is appropriate to a specific constellation of operations, activities, management structures and infrastructures. Standardisation is in the process of giving way to diversity in

P. Turner and E. Davenport (Eds.), Spaces, Spatiality and Technology, 67-78.

relation to space allocation which now have to be applied to groups as well as individuals.

New influences in workspace

To contextualize the role of space in organisational life it is helpful to contrast a period in which human labour ran in parallel with production lines and machines with work in contemporary organizations dedicated to knowledge work. The period when Taylor produced his influential work on Principles of Scientific Management (Wood and Wood, 2002b) which argued for the utility and productive capacity of breaking down (and measuring) the tasks within the labour process was characterized by factory layout which favoured a panopticon-like workspace which enabled 'management's disciplinary gaze to be felt throughout the factory' (Miller and O'Leary, 1987)

From a certain point of view the principle of work process determining the size and shape of workspace has not changed. Today's workspace still reflects work processes. What has changed is the nature of work. Taylor's was an age of mass production and standardization and the lay out of the production process reflected the position of the worker in the hierarchy of work. As the hierarchy metaphorically flattens (Cloke and Goldsmith 2003), the allocation of space and in some cases the method by which it is allocated becomes more democratic.

Knowledge work requires performance not of repetitive physical labour, but of diverse intelligence tasks. These are operationalised in 'project work' and may involve forays into the unknown in quest of new products and applications. The level of authoritarianism which informed the earlier command and control has given way to needs for different kinds of control of work. Projects now are frequently based on team work. These developments render steep organisational pyramids with multiple layers of monitoring obsolete and although supervision continues it is more easily consigned to an electronic eye.

As work and the organisational pyramid changed so did the workplace, and the advent of distance technologies dissociated work from a specific place. By the 1990's knowledge workers were spending less of their time in the office. Mobile communications, mobile workers, telecommuting, outsourcing, hotelling, hot desking, job sharing, and other methods of distributed working were fundamentally uncoupling work and a central work location. The net result was desks and offices were often unoccupied and even in the late 80's, there was a mismatch between the extent and actual use of square footage allocated to each employee. Not surprisingly, the need for office space declined, and it was not uncommon for organizations to announce that they would reduce their square footage by half (Johnson, 2001).

A decade later, it was common in space planning to ask do all workers always need a personally dedicated desk? Or are some individuals present infrequently so that others could use the space when they are not on site? By 1998 at Sun Microsystems, a new planning standard had been incorporated into workspace design: for each type of work activity a ratio of use was assigned that related to how space was actually occupied. (Gartner, 2001).

A cynical view of current trends in office space might see the reduction in office size as a simple attempt to reduce overheads and 'squeeze everyone in' as a recent account of PriceWaterhouseCooper's downsizing of their New York office suggested. The reasons for the change in office space consumption have to do with the impact of technology as we have argued, and go beyond efficiency. Consumption of space is ceasing to be one of the most important marks of organisational status; and technology in the shape of workplace equipment is becoming a significant role marker, in an organization in which (as we shall see below) it is not who you are, but what you do that counts.

Access to relevant technologies is a role marker of some importance, which to some extent replaces the role marking function of square footage and positioning. In addition and perhaps more importantly technology is the channel through which life-giving information flows to sustain world-wide systems, which open up new spaces for individuals, groups and offer world wide connections. The World Wide Web is perhaps unintentionally creating a planetary awareness that perhaps nothing else could. Technology connects individual desks with the far reaches of the globe and travel at work includes space travel through different modalities. We turn now to exemplifying some of these spaces, beginning with 'hard' space and the ways in which it is produced.

Knowledge Work

Knowledge workers are concentrated in high-tech/fast growth (HT/FG) companies in the telecommunications, new media, electronics, computer hardware/software, pharmaceuticals, and biotechnology, energy and entertainment industries. From California's Silicon Valley and the Pacific Northwest to Boston's high-tech corridor and New York's Silicon Alley, the phenomenal expansion of this new generation of HT/FG firms is marked by new approaches to organizational management, work styles and non-traditional office layouts that maximize both creativity and productivity

Knowledge Work and Values

Workspace can always be expressed in simple metrics but planning for knowledge work is more like designing ecologically appropriate environments than slots for robots. It is essential to know something of the preferences and habits of the relevant population. For the sake of brevity we can turn to a summary of knowledge worker values, which illuminate the design brief. Some knowledge work characteristics are shared across cultures, and are similar wherever knowledge work communities are found. In the UK where designers also noticed that their models for space management no longer fitted a workforce typified in the new technology companies in which, Thomson (Thomson 1998: 112-123) summarized the new workforce values as follows:

- What you do is more important than who you are
- You don't have to go to work to go to work
- Many individuals do not like to sit in one place for very long
- There is no more 'one person one chair'
- There is extensive group and team work
- There are multiple organisational models
- Effectiveness is more important than efficiency

These beliefs and behaviours are of central importance in creating the new workspace.

The production of space and design briefs

If community values generally included some version of these in the appraisal of how work is carried out, participation by the community in the design process was also becoming more common. The production of space is a complex social phenomenon, which can be interpreted on many levels. What is noteworthy about space production for knowledge work is that the process is becoming user driven, and rather than being a more or less static representation of hierarchy, space allocation presents an opportunity to direct change in workplace dynamics in the environment of rapid development and change associated with technology.

If there had been a gradual 'flattening' of the organisational pyramid during the last decades of the 20th century (Cloke and Goldsmith, 2003) then somewhat participatory space planning was perhaps not unexpected. In accordance with this somewhat democratic trend, space standards generally had been condensed from 8 levels to 4, (Mariot and Eley, 2000:94) More importantly, new designs were predicated not on rank but on functionality – a functionality which in the production of technological break through was defined in terms of the types of mental and social activity were required for the creation of products and services.

Customary corporate standards programs describe a range of work stations and support areas with a floor plan, elevations or isometric drawings, and a list of furniture components. They also prescribe who gets what, including, usually, who has access to which kind of technology, again based on need. At the heart of the planning process, we find now find typologies of intellectual activity, social interaction and their relationships with space. Consumers of work space (whose members come from many disciplines) now call for space design which is, in the first place, aligned with a specific business strategy, and with specific organisational characteristics including distributed locations, varying geographical reach and levels of workforce mobility. The require workspace which is suited to knowledge production. Many who have a say in the design or transformation of workspace hold to the cultural values expressed above. And during a day at work, an individual may experience many spatialities, real and virtual.

The kinds of space through which an individual moves in a work day include some combination of intelligent and psycho-social space. In one high tech workplace, the R&D division of a company involved in the production of computerised medical devices, individuals on a distributed technical support team might for example move into their cubicles, with a space allowance that is the same for the director as for the database administrator, an open 8x8 cube. This space which allows colleagues to approach to within distant to close personal space, allowing the cubicle's resident to keep visitors at arm's length, or to approach into the space of a slightly closer relationship. Individuals on this team might also work from home separated from other members of the team by as much as 3000 miles. He or she might then travel through several kinds of air or communications space. The letter might include e-mail to/from other team members, telephone (landline) to hospitals, telephone (mobile) from the field to other staff or to a supply centre. They might access the intranet to retrieve or perform information updates. Once a week they might 'meet' electronically, and occasionally senior management might engage in a videoconference. From time to time team members assembled in a room at the R&D base to chat with members at remote team locations.

Team members were responsible for maintenance at major hospitals around the country, where cardiac surgeons relied on the devices to function flawlessly during heart surgery. If they did not, team call-outs could be activated by an automatic on line reporting system and automatic initiation of mobile calls to respond to malfunction. Reports on device performance were also transmitted to the software designers in Israel. From time to time the design team visited the California site. The point of this description is not in its detail, but in the observation that any team member in fact moved through the information maze effortlessly, and shifted from real to virtual space without even being aware of it. Technology including intranet and telecommunications as well as physical travel in fact defines workspace, which has expanded far beyond an office base. Technology thus becomes a critical factor in workspace design.

Technology and workspace transformation

Technologies affected workspace in many ways. It was necessary to accommodate increasing numbers of cables and address some of the complexities affecting how often a space was occupied (Duffy *et al.*, 1993; Dechiara *et al.*, 2001). The existence of remote workspace has an impact on office space design. To the extent that the workplace is technologically enabled, that impact is felt across not one but often many sites in ways which reflect activity in many industries. Knowledge work however, has its own requirements in relation to its environment, and it is not surprising that those requirements are defined based on types of functional activity which knowledge work involves.

Sun Microsystems, where Java was created, was initially housed in multiple office buildings in San Francisco, and historically had favoured private offices for its engineers. In 1992 and 1993, Sun undertook development of one million square feet of office space for 3,600 employees in Menlo Park. At Sun there had always been multiple work sites, and Sun Microsystems coined the expression 'network of places,' as a synonym of organisational life and work (Johnson, 2001). Hewlett-Packard's Field Services group created a similarly connected network (ibid).

Sun's functional model of work had three basic categories which were identified as requiring different kinds of space: development, consulting and transaction, (Bakker, 2000). Interestingly, it was the engineer-users who experimented with reduction in individual space allocation when in 1985; they had elected to reduce individual space allocation from 100sq ft to 80 sq ft. in favour of allocating larger square footage to group areas.

In these cases, instead of space planning based being on raw physical requirements, and imposed standards, it was starting to incorporate user input and categories based on technological, social and mental models of functionality (Gartner 2001). The impact of technology was recognised in the mobility index, and social interaction was factored in to collaboration and transactions. Individuals 'rights' to space and square footage remained a priority, with individual allocation at 8'x8'. Sun's mental space types are noteworthy. There were four, with an equal number of subtypes:

Nomadic:	low collaboration and high mobility
Repertory:	high collaboration and high mobility
Huddle:	low mobility and high collaboration
Silo:	low mobility and low collaboration

Johnson, 2001

These categories recognize the several 'spaces' in which knowledge work is facilitated: physical, mental, solitary and connected, and include both isolated quiet spaces for individual seclusion, and spaces for social connectivity. The connectivity takes many forms: planned or serendipitous meetings, casual or more formal interactions to give, check or get information, discuss insights or results, to give or get help, to troubleshoot, to plan, and even to pass the time of day. A typology of office interactions would be interesting, but complex. The Sun approach factors in a technological facilitation of work interactions in space, and it is clear that hard space has several very specific roles in innovative, knowledge intense activity that form the spine of that typology. Workspace is recognised not only as a metric quantity imposed on the environment, but as a location of shared, lived and valued work experience, that is also dependent on office technology.

Sun's users willingness to sacrifice individual space to group needs represents a design situation in an organization with less dedication to territoriality than traditional organizations, where, apocryphal tales suggest, it was not unknown for managers losing territory to measure their new smaller office with a tape measure to ensure that their new space was not an square inch (or centimetre) smaller than that of their peers.

It is one thing to design workspace for a young organization with a willingness to change their space standards and it is a challenge of a different order to transform a long standing industry giant: Nortel, which was a century old when it undertook its space transformation. In 1995 Nortel undertook to re-invent its work environment. The new (downsized) workspace was to create 'cool, creative, energizing places to work' (Roth 1999, cited Johnson 2001) and to reflect Nortel's interest in user well-being and satisfaction.

Like Sun's, Nortel's functional/space categories also included varieties of mental and social activity. There were effectively four broad categories with an equal number of subdivisions. The first was analytical work which needed individual distraction free space. This function was further divided by stage of software development: incubating, emerging, or established. The second was consultative once again reflecting needs for social interaction/ collaboration to resolve problems and monitor progress. Autonomy was also a consideration here. The third space was interactive, where the job required high levels of client contact, and the fourth was process or transaction-based, where the task had certain processual, repetitive features (Johnson 2001).

If each of these organizations was grappling with categories to define knowledge work and to provide liveable appropriate space for it in the right amount, arriving at space solutions was in itself a complex process, and how to implement their models once they had been agreed was also at issue.

Hierarchy, parity and plurality workspace transformation

Experience at organizations such as Sun and Nortel, and many others which had downsized since the late 80's seemed to prove that space redesign was an effective occasion to implement organisational change. Simply announcing that space standards were to be altered and when could raise resistance and barriers to accomplish transformative objectives. While some groups initiated change, others whose space was being downsized regarded the process with horror (Marmot and Eley, 2001) It appeared however that in some instances, the process could be eased by introduction of a parity standard in which every individual regardless of function or rank was allocated equal space. This practice is not new to designers, and is known as a universal standard, but some of the applications were novel.

Famously, or perhaps infamously, Intel adopted this parity standard although the interpretation offered for the practice at Intel is that it is an expression of humility. It is certainly not unimportant that this standard was adopted by Andrew Grove, and that although his cubicle was on a corner of the 5th floor, it was, at 8x8' essentially identical in size to that of entry level staff. (Jackson 1997) Gordon Moore has adopted the same principle at the Betty and Gordon Moore Foundation, where all cubicles are also of equal size and seating at work is random (Betty and Gordon Moore Foundation 2004). As founding fathers of technology, these role models have had widespread influence.

In other instances however, parity is thought to provide an interim period between traditional management hierarchy and plurality, the latter providing a model of organization in which co-existing but different space allocations based on functionality are appropriate. Plurality can be understood as a situation in which in the eyes of the user, one size does not fit all, one model does not fit all, and standards can be redefined to accommodate many different work processes. In the diversity or plurality model space can be allocated based on diverse needs, but can also effectively be negotiated and 'earned', rather than assigned.

This progression hierarchy-parity-plurality (Johnson and McDougall, 2003) is a method of cognitive re-configuration, facilitating transition between one mental model and another. It seems to reiterate the phases of separation and re-integration first observed by Van Gennep with regard to transitions between social stages in the human life cycle: transition from child-to adulthood, single status to married, among many others, where an abrupt social change of status initiates new attitudes and behaviours. It is difficult to conceptualize an individual as a child one day and an adult the next, the change is so gradual. Yet a change in social functioning requires maturity to be recognised. There appears to be a need for a mental and social bridge between the old status (child) and the new (adult). The process initiation into the new role is often carried out in seclusion, away from day to day routine and place. Rites of passage thus involve a period of separation, of liminality, out of which a new role can be fashioned. In the case of space, parity can intervene to cushion the similarly abrupt transition from one space to another when change may in fact have occurred gradually.

KINDS OF SPACE

We have described some of the impact of technology on workspace without addressing the definition of space. Space is characteristically difficult to describe because its meanings are so diffuse. Space has been described as "the hidden dimension" (Hall, 1999). It is so because it is the sine qua non of existence, the medium within which we move more or less automatically, the medium in which we behave, and in which we begin to learn to behave appropriately long before we can speak (Piaget et al., 1968). Our perception of space is culturally conditioned, and we typically occupy more or less standard sized 'space bubbles' which help us to control our distance management with other members of our group. Different sized bubbles are associated with different kinds of relationship. Hall's science of proxemics which studies space as a form of expression and management of social relations is based on proprioception, of which the characteristic dimensions – sight, sound, hearing, thermal awareness and so on operate at the level of the unconscious. There is nothing to suggest that this will change, although other kinds of spatial perception may be added to human capabilities. Eight feet is roughly the limiting distance of what Hall classified as distant personal space. The distance would keep visitors to our space at arm's length. Closer contact could be expressed within the same space if a relationship were to permit closer proximity with comfort. Despite its applicability it has not in fact been firmly incorporated into everyday design methods. However experimentation with different areas has shown that acceptable spatial allocation areas are determined by these hidden dimensions within which we relate to others. Today, although they have not so far as I am aware been recalibrated for present practices, the office environment operates most effectively when space remains within the distance of personal space. This is accommodated by an 8x8 cubicle but not by a smaller space, which would encourage development of more intimate relationships or alternatively might foster negative behaviour due to cramping. Thus the footprint of workspace size has been indelibly, silently and in fact unconsciously stamped on knowledge space. (There are many other aspects of space configuration which Hall's work illuminates, but they are beyond the scope of our present focus.)

Generally, organisational change has modified the social relationships within the workplace in the direction of the less formal. As Edward Hall pointed out (Hall, 1990) less formal relationships translate to diminished spatial requirements: we relate to peers in a smaller space than is required to maintain appropriate social distance with formally defined superiors. In the context of the workplace village which we seem to be creating, it is not unimportant that an important metaphor for social interaction is the water cooler. Sooner or later everyone passes by, and 'water cooler' has become the metaphor for the informal meeting place within organisations where different species come throughout the day to exchange greetings, inquire and inform about current events, chat and gossip, and quench their social as well as their informational and literal thirst.

Other behaviours in workspace are enmeshed in organisational culture. Like space, culture influences behaviour below the level of awareness, and we operate within its values in much the same way as we do in space: without consciously thinking about our every move. Our moves may be associated with patterns of behaviour and structures of belief which we would be hard put to describe objectively.

Members of an organization very often share values and generate their own culture. They look for others like them when they take in new members, and those who will 'fit in'. Becoming more aware of organisational culture can help to make unconscious patterns visible, or more articulate and hence provide a better way to sustain or modify local practices (McDougall 1993; Johnson and McDougall, 2003). Culture encapsulates the largely unconscious cultural frameworks underlying the cognitive and experiential framework described as the 'intangible, cognitive dimension that arises from our experiences and defines our viewpoint' (Gartner 2001). That shared lived organisational knowledge which comes from being in the same space has been recognised as an important factor in innovation and creativity, and central to knowledge work (*ibid*).

Technology, Complexity and Paradox

We have tried to indicate some of the spatial complexity which is implicated in work environments is the result of recent distance technologies, and the influence of the internet. Part of the argument presented here is that technology has not only changed our environments and space use, a change possibly on a par with the change from orality to literacy, it challenges our conventional analytical thinking and presents us with apparent paradoxes. Technology and how it is used has affected our understanding of workspace.

With the telephone it was already possible to collapse distance. With new communications technologies and the new speed at which they operate 'far' can very easily seem like 'near' in present time, at least from a functional point of view. As in our example above, individuals and members of groups pay less attention (if any) to the medium over which it information is transmitted, if the information is relevant and timely for the work process in which they are engaged.

Similarly, Email often modifies our conception of distance in a contrasting way. Rather than collapsing space between distant locations, it can facilitate communications with someone a few feet away where distance can be great if the occupant of a neighbouring workspace is only present intermittently. E-mail obviates the need to co-ordinate availability. Although the impact of the Internet has attracted more public attention, the significance of intranets is at least as important. Intranets have far reaching effects on the organisation of work, and on the nature of communications in the workplace and have had corresponding impact on the meaning we attribute to distance and space. What is distant may be effectively near, while what is near may be effectively distant. In effect, space as a bounded physical entity has not lost its significance, but rather its relevance.

Hybrid Spatiality

Paralleling technological and organisational transformation we now find that workspace implies multi-valent or hybrid conceptions of space: individuals are able to develop an effectively global communications network through technology, and specifically the intranet, and as they do so, a new sense of presence mediated by a different sense of spatiality gradually develops. The old spatiality of 'high modernism' does not vanish, but is augmented by a conception of hyperspace in which space is no longer bounded by Euclidean geometry, but evidences a largely invisible, although electronically traceable, personal presence with a reach bounded only by the extent of its electronic and social infrastructure. It is perhaps not surprising that as a result, the advent of hyperspace has allowed for diminished consumption of physical space, with the approval of space consumers both inside organizations and outside, in online communities. This is especially true when they are participants in the discourses which define space.

UNDERSTANDING THE PROPERTIES OF THE VARIOUS SPATIALITIES

Difficult to find a method to construe the meaning of space since so much of our processing of it is below the level of consciousness. We have mentioned proprioceptive data and tacit knowledge as aspects of space perception in quite different arenas, which co-exist in an individual mind without apparent difficulty. The inarticulate nature of space makes it difficult to subject it to investigation. Jameson recognises that his [by extension our] perceptual habits were formed in that older kind of space he thinks of as the space of high modernism, and in fact:

> 'we as humans who happen into this new space have not kept pace with that evolution—we do not yet possess the conceptual equipment to match this new hyperspace' (*ibid.*)

In his article on the architecture of the Bonaventure Hotel in downtown Los Angeles Frederic Jameson refers to certain kinds of space as those in which it is impossible for us to use the language of volume or volumes any longer. I am proposing, the notion he says 'that we are in the presence of a mutation in built space itself' (Jameson 2003: 242). Jameson believes that [the lobby in the Bonaventure] aspires to being a total space and corresponds 'to a new collective practice, a new mode in which individuals move and congregate: a new and historically original kind of hypercrowd' (ibid. p.243). It does not seem too fanciful to see Jameson wrestling with the perceptual, conceptual and relational challenges which demand a new way to understand space. He seems to recognise the need to make the kind of perceptual shift from the space of modernism to hyper-spatiality which is implicated in the design of office space which we have been describing above. Jameson challenges us to develop new hyperspace influenced conceptual apparatus (and beyond) to understand the nature of hyperspace.

Whether there are consistent patterns which will emerge from process of change in spatial dynamics as evidenced in the new hybrid workspace is not yet known, although there are already hints of the nature of values in the cultures of electronic technologies. The issue of presence as a an aspect of space would appear to be key and empirically it appears that we need to understand space as including both the virtual and physical and as an evolving issue of identity and empowerment, in which identity is not a matter of physical presence but of informational presence and empowerment is measured by its attendant abilities to influence the course of events.

The ability of the individual to exert influence and initiate action as a result of a workplace presence is evident from even the brief descriptions given here. It seems likely that new beliefs and experiences of personal presence, which acquire significance in new technology-based cultures will provide opportunities to surface new understandings of spatiality.

REFERENCES

Bakker, M. 1998, 'Technology drives office design, part II: Sun Microsystems-a case study' ISdesigNET, http://www.isdesignet.com/Magazine/Oct'98/tech.html Retrieved May 27th, 2004.

Berger, P & Luckmann, T. 1966, The social construction of reality, Doubleday& Co, Garden City, New York.

Betty and Gordon Moore Foundation, 'Green Building' http://www.moore.org/stories/08_15/news_story.asp. Retrieved March 3rd 2004

Cloke, K and Goldsmith, J. 2003, The end of management and the growth of organizational democracy, Wiley, Indianapolis.

Dechiara, J, Panero, J, Zelnick, M. 2001, Time saver standards for interior design and space planning [2nd edition] McGraw-Hill, New York and London.

Duffy, F, Laing, A, and Crisp, V. 1993, The re-design of work and offices, Butterworth Heinemann, Oxford.

Duffy, F, Hutton, L. 1998, Architectural knowledge: the idea of a profession, E&FN Spon, London.

Gartner Group and MIT, 2001, 'Workplace Organizational Models,' MIT/Gartner Workplace Forum, August 15 &16, Cambridge, MA.

Greiner, L, 1998, 'Revision: evolution and revolution as organizations grow', Harvard Business Review, May 1st, [1972]

Hall, E.T. 1990, The Hidden Dimension, [1959] Anchor, New York.

Harries, K. 1998, The ethical function of architecture, MIT Press, Cambridge MA

Intel, 2004 'Wireless networking' http://www.intel.com/cd/ids/developer/asmo-na/eng/19336.htm?page=3, Retrieved June 4th 2004.

Jackson, T. 1997, Inside Intel: Andy Grove and the rise of the world's most powerful chip company, Diane Publishing, Collingdale PA.

Jameson, F. 1997, 'The cultural logic of late capitalism' in Leach, N. 1997, Rethinking architecture, pp. 238-246, Rutledge, London.

Johnson,   J,   2001   Designing   for   the   Future   ISdesigNET, http://www.isdesignet.com/Magazine/Sept'01/ceu.html Retrieved December 3rd 2003

Johnson, J. 2000, 'A case study: Nortel reinvents its work environments' ISdesigNET, September, www.isdesignet.com/Magazine/sept02/ceu.htm. Retrieved March 3rd 2004

Johnson, J & McDougall, L. 2002-2003, 'Workplace design and organizational culture' http://www.isdesignet.com/Magazine/sept02/ceu.html.

Marmot, A. and Eley, J. 2000, Office space planning: designing for tomorrow's workspace, McGraw-Hill, New York and London.

McDougall, L. 1993, Ethnographic programming: a method for discerning cultural values relevant to design. Unpublished Ms. Perkins & Will, Chicago and New York

Thomson, Tony 1998, 'Supporting Organisational Change' in Worthington, J. Reinventing the workplace, pp. 112-123. Institute of Advanced Architectural Studies, University of York, Butterworth Heinemann, Oxford.

Van Gennep, A. 1961, Rites of passage, [1908] University of Chicago Press, Chicago

Wood, J and Wood, M. 2002b, Frederick Taylor: Critical evaluation of thinkers in business and management studies. Routledge, London and New York.

Intel: Wireless   networking,   2004,   http://www.intel.com/cd/ids/developer/asmo-na/eng/19336.htm?page=3. Retrieved June 8th 2004

7. PUBLIC PLACE AS A RESOURCE OF SOCIAL INTERACTION

MATTHIAS BUCHECKER

INTRODUCTION

Withdrawal from the public place

Recent studies show that with the increase of urbanization, local residents increasingly stay away from the public and semi-public places within the territory of their residential community. They retreat in their leisure time either into the privacy of their homes or escape into remote recreation areas, which we define as withdrawal from the local <u>public place</u>. The villages or towns thus mutate more and more into "dormitory communities" or "dormitory villages", where the local residents live in the place nearly without interacting with each other and where hardly any public life takes place (Gans, 1969; Krüger, 1987; Brandenburg & Carroll, 1995; Buchecker and Schutz, 2000; Oosterman, 2002; Thorns, 2002).
Fuhrer at al. (1993) found in their empirical study that deficiencies in the need-satisfaction within the private home are compensated by leisure mobility. Accordingly the withdrawal from the local public place also seems to be caused by a loss of need-satisfaction in these areas. But what are the needs that the local public place is supposed to satisfy?

What needs are satisfied by the public place?

We are aware of the symbolic, recreational or aesthetic functions of public place (Kaplan & Kaplan, 1989; Bourassa, 1991; Korpela *et al.*, 2001; Low & Lawrence-Zúñiga, 2003), but what are the (psychological) needs that stand behind them. There are no clear answers to be found in the existing literature. However, there are some sophisticated concepts about the functions of the private home that have been developed in the last decades and these might be transferred to the local public place.

- *The regulation of identity.* Self-identity or the image of the self is constituted by social interactions and thus very susceptive to irritations. At the same time a stable self-identity is a prerogative for autonomous social interactions (Breakwell, 1986). Therefore identity must regularly be restored and developed by reminding the person of positive personal or collective experiences and attributes. Private homes help to stabilize and

79

P. Turner and E. Davenport (Eds.), Spaces, Spatiality and Technology, 79-96.
© 2005 *Springer. Printed in the Netherlands.*

develop the image of the self as the inhabitants are allowed to shape the setting and arrange objects associated with positive experiences, such as photos, souvenirs or handicrafts.

–   *The regulation of social interaction.* Establishing and enhancing social interactions are vital for an individual's need satisfaction and the development of his self identity; at the same time new interactions bring about risks of being misunderstood (Mead, 1934). The private home allows the inhabitants to establish complex interactions because they can control the general set-up (Rapoport, 1982; Fuhrer & Kaiser, 1994).

–   *The regulation of social emotions.* According to the model of social motivation proposed by Bischof (1972) individuals establish social relationships in order to regulate the social emotions of security, autonomy and excitement. The environment of the private home is perceived with the emotional categories security, autonomy and excitement. People feel at ease there, if they can experience the three emotions in a satisfactory amount (Fuhrer and Kaiser, 1994).

But, what has the private home got to do with the public place? We might consider the local public place as the extended home of the residents. When we look back only a few decades, residents of rural regions used to perform typical indoor tasks of home outside in the public place. So we propose that the home functions are not limited to the private home, but are also constitutive for the relation between the residents and their everyday landscape.

Also other recent (theoretical and empirical) studies have pointed out that dwelling and environments of higher scales are closely connected in term of meaning and function (Rapoport, 1982; Lindsey, Buchan & Ducan, 1988; Hollander, 1991; Cuba & Hummon, 1994) - without, however, going into more detail about the nature of their functions. Manzo (2003) and Terkenly (1995) even maintain that home is often interpreted too literal and that this metaphoric expression can in fact span a much higher variety of settings and to much higher scales. Certainly there are gradual differences between the private home and the landscape: Whereas in the private home the personal and intimate aspects dominate, in the landscape the social and collective aspects become more important. Consistently, however, we agree with Terkenly (1995) that the extended home fulfill the home functions better than the private home. Though the private home offers their residents more control for fulfilling its functions, it only allows them limited social interaction and thus the outcomes of the functions (i.e. the regulated identity) are less socially shared and only partly reach social relevance.

The approach of physical setting, which has been developed by Proshansky, Fabian and Kaminoff (1983) from the approach of behaviour setting by Barker (1968; 1987; Fuhrer, 1990), provides a theoretical basis for transferring the functions of home to the public place.

According to this approach, the public place is an entity, which consists of a mosaic of physical settings (see Fig. 1). These settings are on the one hand physical units, with physical delimitations and also with the capacity of representing individual or collective meaning. On the other hand they are behavioral units because within these settings there are determined rules of behavior.

The private home is just one of these physical settings, even though it is a central one, as you can see that on the figure. Every one of these settings fulfils – besides obvious and more superficial purposes – the home functions. The qualities of two pairs of complementary variables of the settings determine how well these functions can be fulfilled.

On the behavioral dimension the variables "behavioral rules" and "behavioral range", on the physical dimension the variables "continuity of the setting" and "shaping range".

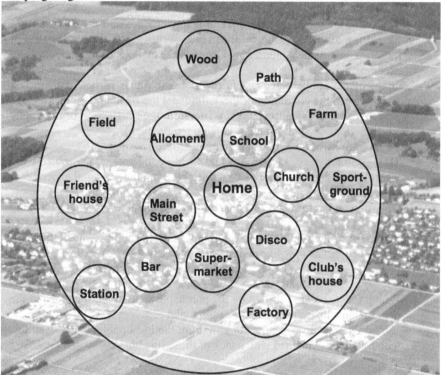

Fig. 1: The physical settings in the everyday landscape (schematical representation)

Behavior rules are social conventions, defining how individuals have to dress, speak or act. For each setting, a characteristic set of behavior rules are defined (Barker, 1967). The smaller this set is and the less stringent the rules are, the more the individual can determine his behavior individually. This means that he or she has a high behavioral range or easier, many opportunities of informal interaction.

The *shaping range* refers to the individuals' or groups' opportunities to change the physical appearance of the setting and leave their *individual or collective traces* in this setting. If on the other hand there is a lack of opportunities to shape the setting, traces once left can be preserved. The mentioned variables of the settings contribute in the following way to fulfill the three home functions:

–   Regulation of identity: The continuity of the setting's physical traces reminding of a person's positive experiences helps to restore his or her identity, and a high shaping range authorizing persons to change the setting and leave new traces allow them to express changes in their personal or collective life.

–   Regulation of social interaction: Clear behavior rules help a person to control social interaction and the remaining (high) behavioral range offers him or her the opportunity to express individuality and deepen social interaction.

–   Regulation of social emotions: Clear behavior rules and the continuity of the setting allow a person to experience security, whereas exhausting or transgressing the behavioral range leads to the experience of autonomy and excitement.

So the settings of the public place can fulfil the home functions best if there is a good balance between the continuity of the setting and the freedom to either change the setting or to vary the default behaviour. Therefore the satisfaction of the public place's home functions depends on the following requirements:

–   The continuity of clear rules in the public place's settings

–   The continuity of the individual and collective traces(objects of identification) in the public place's settings, reminding of good experiences in these settings

–   Opportunities to influence the shape of the public place's settings (shaping range)

–   Sufficient behavioral range in the public place's settings which allow the residents to act as they like and express themselves

Based on these assumptions we started a study trying to answer the following questions:

–   Which functions are fulfilled by the public place? Can the functions of the private home be transferred to the public place?

–   Why do the local residents withdraw from the local public place? Can this withdrawal be explained with a lack of those functions?

METHOD

Methodology

As the aim of the study lay mainly in understanding the investigated phenomenon (the relation between local residents and their public places), an explorative research design and thus the use of flexible methods of qualitative social science research (Gerdes, 1979) was required. The demand for highest flexibility and at the same time the necessity to use existing theoretical approaches to cope with the encompassing topic resulted in the decision to chose the problem-centered interview (Witzel, 1985) as the main technique of data collection. Further techniques applied during the study such as semi-quantitative photo tests, the analysis of school works and the observation of participatory processes in these communities allowed us to triangulate and thus ensure the results.

Research area

To answer the research questions we studied two peri-urban communities in the central plateau of Switzerland as examples. In Switzerland, communities are administrative units of the local level with well defined territories and well defined political rights, and these communities are therefore the place of local public life. According to the qualitative paradigm the comparison of a few extreme case studies allows the researcher to understand a general phenomenon (Oevermann, 1991). In order to achieve a deeper understanding of the phenomenon we were particularly interested in, the withdrawal from the public place, we limited ourselves to a minimum of case studies. So we chose two communities which differed in the degree of urbanization (presence of urban elements, quota of farmers, quota of commuters) – the factor, with which the withdrawal from the public place seems to be linked. The community of Selzach (see Fig. 1), a rather rural community with approximately 4000 inhabitants and the community of Hindelbank, a typical dormitory village in commuting range of the Swiss capital with approximately 2500 inhabitants.

Sample

The interviewees were selected by way of a theoretical sampling (Hunziker, 1995; Flick, 1995). The principle of this strategy is not 'statistical representativity' but rather 'maximum variety' (Morse, 1994). In other words we tried to obtain a sample of local residents with most typical or extreme attitudes concerning their relation to their local public place. As attitudes are normally influenced by factors such as age, gender, profession, origin, club-membership and involvement in public or private initiatives, we strove for a maximum of variety of these factors in our sample (see table 1 at the end of the chapter).

Methods of Data Collection

In the following the main method of data collection, the qualitative interview, will be briefly described.

Out of the range of interview techniques, the problem-centered interview was judged to be the most suited (Witzel, 1985), because it allows induction and deduction to be combined. So this technique offers the chance to examine and modify existing theories on the home functions for the area of the public place and at the same time develop new perspectives.

The basis of our problem-centered interview was a theoretical concept on the relationship between people and places partly described above. A checklist of important questions and issues served as a tool to guarantee that all aspects of the research questions and all the relevant hypotheses were integrated and examined. The interview, however, started with very open questions (e.g. what do you associate with your village/community?), which allowed the interviewees to influence the structure of the talk and to focus on the most relevant issues. We also used a series of photographs for the interview which helped to focus the talk on concrete matters. The interviews, which lasted between 60 and 90 minutes, were recorded on an audio tape and transliterated word by word.

The data were analysed according to the grounded theory using an iterative inductive-deductive procedure.

Analysis

The transliterated interviews, the essays of school classes about their village, the results of various workshops and the recorded observations during the participatory process are the empirical basis of the study. This data was carefully investigated according to the approach of the "Grounded Theory" of Strauss and Corbin (1996), using the software application Filemaker to manage the data.

RESULTS

Preliminary remarks

In a first step we will show on the basis of the inductive findings that the theoretical assumptions for transferring the home functions to the public place have been well anchored in the empirical data. Before presenting the results, we would like to define the most important analytical and empirical terms.

Well integrated and poorly integrated residents:

The analysis revealed two main categories of residents who differed considerably in their relationship to the public place: the majority of residents who described themselves during the interviews as members of the village community and which we thus call well integrated residents, and the minority of residents who delimited themselves from the village community and which we call poorly integrated residents.

Village

When we use the term 'village' for analytical descriptions in this chapter, we refer to the main settlement of the community. During the interviews in the two communities, however, 'village' appeared to be a plurivalent term. For the well integrated residents, this term refers to the main settlement, to the cultivated land of the community as well as to the village community. For the poorly integrated residents village only means the main settlement or even the center of it.

Close to nature areas

This term refers to areas which are at least partly ruled by natural dynamics, such as woods, rivers, mires, but also extensively used agricultural lands (e.g. willows). As some residents, especially farmers, also considered intensively used agricultural lands as natural, this term is not a purely empirical category.

The relevance of the theoretical assumptions for transferring the home functions to the public place

During the inductive analysis, we found evidence that the withdrawal from the public place is an issue in these communities. In both communities the residents expressed that they felt restricted in their freedom within the village and that in their leisure time, they would regularly prefer near-to-nature areas. However we noted a slight difference: whereas the residents of the less urbanized community withdrew into near-to-nature areas within the territory of the community, those of the more urbanized community tended to go to more remote areas.

The inductive analysis could also confirm the assumption that the local public place can be understood as an extended home. In the relationship between the residents and (the public place of) their village, the aspect of attachment – in contrast to the functional aspects - is in the foreground. This is exactly the quality that also makes the difference between a house and a home. As in the context of the private home the residents explain their attachment to their village not with concrete advantages, but with their familiarity with the place and the people. Moreover the significance of the village is described with expressions such as 'having grown up here', 'being rooted here' or 'being at ease here', which are normally applied in the appreciation of the private home. Finally the strong relationship between the residents and their village is often accompanied by a feeling of dependency (i.e. many residents think they could not live elsewhere) and absoluteness which are otherwise characteristic of family ties.

Furthermore the inductive analysis of the data showed that all the (key) categories independently detected in the relationship between the residents and their public place stood in close association with the home functions (see table 2 at the end of the chapter). On the basis of these correspondences the home functions can legitimately be applied also to the public place. The proof of the validity of this transfer, however, can only be made by introducing deductive elements into the analysis.

The relevance of the home functions for the public place

As the functions of home are at the same time very complex and comprehensive, the relevance of these functions for the public place cannot be examined directly, by comparing them with the inductive data. It is, however, possible to prove this relevance by proving the relevance of the requirements of these functions in the public place.

In the inductive-deductive analysis the theoretical categories 'continuity of behavioral rules', 'continuity of individual and collective traces', 'behavioral range' and 'shaping range' recognized as the main requirements for the home functions (see introduction), proved to be not only relevant, but even fundamental in the context of the public place and its physical settings. These categories either form the background of the criteria chosen for valuing the public place or stand behind concrete wishes what the future of the community should be like.

At the same time the analysis made apparent that the home functions are only partially fulfilled in the two communities. For some requirements turned out to be insufficiently available, as we could gather from the content of the wishes, the qualities mentioned in the context of the public place and the criticism voiced regarding the development of the community. Thereby, obvious differences could be observed between the two communities and also between the village and the near-to-nature areas within the communities (see Fig. 2).

Requirements for the home functions	Less urbanised community		More urbanised community	
	Village	Natural areas	Village	Natural areas
Continuity of behavioral rules	+	+	+	+
Continuity of individual traces	-	+	-	+/-
Continuity of collective traces	+	-	+/-	-
Shaping range	-	+	-	-
Behavioral range	-	+	-	-

+   sufficiently available
-   insufficiently available
+/- neither nor

Figure 2: Insufficiency of the home functions in the local public place

In the following we will make explicit in which form and to which extent the home functions respectively its requirements proved to be relevant and fulfilled in the local public place.

Continuity of behavioural rules

The requirement "continuity of behavioural rules" proved to be most relevant and even too dominantly present in the two communities.
Observing the rules is in both communities a key criterion for valuing states and behaviors in the village. If gardens or buildings are not adjusted, if local norms of building are ignored or if adolescents disregard rules of behavior, the residents react with utmost disapproval. The large extent of continuity in the rules is reflected in the feeling of security and restriction the residents experience in their public place.

Continuity of traces

Quite different is the picture with respect to the requirements "continuity of individual traces" and "continuity of individual traces". Both requirements revealed to be relevant only in their abstract form, which can be interpreted as an indicator for a lack of adequate tangible traces reminding of the residents' individual and collective experiences. Interestingly, the traces of individual and collective experiences proved to be spatially separated (village vs. natural areas) which conforms with Augé's assumption of a separate social and individual appropriation of territories (Augé, 1995).

As for the continuity of individual traces, in both communities the residents very rarely mentioned visible traces, which reminded them of personal experiences. Much more often people spoke of places they associated with personal experiences. These places have been appropriated by personal experiences and thus bear invisible personal traces of it. In particular there are four categories of such places:

- Places of regular (volunteer) use: Most of the residents have a closer relationship to some places they regularly frequent. The places mentioned by adult residents are only rarely situated within the settlement (in contrast to children who in general have a strong reference to their way to school and to their playgrounds). In most cases, such places have to do with regularly practiced leisure activities, especially regular walks, and thus preferably lie in the near-to-nature areas. Therefore they are much better represented in the less urbanized community.
- Places of childhood: Many residents feel attached to places where they have left personal traces during their childhood. The loss of such places are most strongly felt. (It is, however, questionable how childhood experiences can contribute to the regulation of identity.)
- Places of friends: Especially poorly integrated residents feel attached to places where persons of personal relation live. They associate these places with experiences of intimate personal interaction.
- Places of admiration. Especially in the near to nature areas most of the residents also refer to places that have little to do with themselves personally but which they perceived as aesthetic or idyllic. As such these abstract traces remind them of personal ideals (Seel, 1996).

Whereas most residents of the less urbanized community have enough places in the near to nature areas of their community which remind them of personal experiences (and thus allow them to regulate their identity there), this is not the case in the other parts of the study area.

What concerns the continuity of collective traces, in both communities only a small part of the inhabitants (farmers, members of traditional clubs) speak in a positive sense of collective traces to which they have contributed by their own activity or by financing. To the numerous collective traces of their ancestors (such as old houses, hedges, old industries) they show a rather ambivalent relationship. On the one hand, they estimate them as elements of their cultural heritage, on the other hand they consider these traditional elements as a burden which inhibits their (economical) activities. Most of the well integrated residents, however, strongly refer to abstract collective traces such as the mere structure of the village - with its center, the absence of building blocks and the separation from the neighboring villages - or the mutual greeting, which symbolize the village community. These traces rather represent mental images than collective qualities and primarily seem to remind them of the existence of the village and especially of their belonging to the village community.

Shaping range

Even more extremely than with the requirement "continuity of traces" the relevance of the requirement "shaping range" for the public place could only confirmed by the frequent complaints of its deficiency and the strong appreciation of the few exceptions.

Corresponding to the lack of concrete, actively influenced traces the residents of the two communities hardly see any possibilities to leave new traces by shaping the public place and do not make use of the few existing ones. They, however, talk very emotionally about the places they had been allowed to shape in their childhood. Within the village strict rules of order do not allow them a creative individual appropriation of places. An often mentioned shortcoming is the lack of flexibility in terms of the building regulations, which inhibit the residents from changing the buildings on their private ground according to their individual taste. At the same time allotment gardens or houses not corresponding with the local standards are widely denounced as a blemish. In the natural area creating huts of collected wood or fireplaces is very popular. Again, such activities are at the same time criticized by strongly integrated residential groups as selfish or even forbidden. A special case are the private gardens: They are often shaped very personally, but mostly they are hidden behind hedges and thus invisible to the public. So they rather serve as a place of private security than of public self-representation. Children and especially the adolescents of the two communities explicitly express the want of opportunities of leaving traces in their public place. They ask for more places to be shaped individually such as former dumps, rivers or a youth center. Furthermore, graffiti activities and vandalism in recent years can be interpreted as the attempt of the adolescents to leave their traces.

The existing opportunities to shape the public place by way of public participation are rarely perceived by the residents and even less used. From the interviews it was evident that most of the residents have their individual ideas how to enhance life in the village, but hardly anybody dares to voice such ideas in public. The fact that such initiatives are even widely condemned as individualistic and urban reveals that public participation breaks hidden collective rules and norms. This seems to apply to individual appropriation of the public place in general, and only children are not inhibited by these real or internalized interdictions in their creative activities.

Behavioural range

The situation with the requirement "bahavioural range" proved to be very similar to the one of "shaping range", but we found a higher diversity of gradations (between highly formal and highly informal interaction, between public and semi-private, between frequented and socially hidden).

In both **villages** only for a small part of the inhabitants - mainly children, sportsmen and politicians - places of informal interaction are available, in which they can act as they like and express themselves. But people even attach high significance to semi-public places that only offer them a slightly raised behavioral range. So quite a number of residents are proud of their club's and society's buildings where they can exhibit their skills. Especially in traditional societies, however, the communication and the behavior are highly ritualized, and therefore the poorly integrated residents describe them as very restricting. Other (semi-public) opportunities for the residents to express themselves in public are guesthouses and political sessions. Our interviewees, however, emphasized that in these places, playing an active role requires a thick skin, for deviating attitudes are sanctioned with personal attacks.

For the children the school and especially the schoolyards offer rather ideal (semi-private) places of informal interaction, and that is why they often consider them as their favorite places.

The *public* places or settings within the village are dedicated to well-defined functions, and the tacit norms only authorize residents pursuing this function to frequent these places. The omnipresent social control makes sure that these rules are observed. The use of the streets offers the best example. The only function of the village streets is the transit, and thus the residents are allowed to pass them (if they follow a corresponding destination) and to have a short chat with residents encountered on their way. But they are not allowed to spend a longer time waiting on the street, sit on a stairway along its side or promenade. Only adolescents dare to break this rule, and in both communities this infringement is considered as a major concern.

In spite of this resistance against the breaking of collective rules, a large number of the residents miss places of informal interaction within the village:

- They lament the loss of places they used to perform their competency such as the former skating rink or the overbuilt sledge tracks,
- the wish for new meeting places within the villages - like parks, swimming pools, tearooms and excessive festivals - are most widely spread, and
- time and again, the residents emphasize the need to regularly escape to places beyond the narrowness of the village, in the city or the natural area.

The **natural areas** in the two communities differ considerably in their supply of places where the residents can express their individuality. Only in the less urbanized community the near to nature areas offer such places - like a river-beach, a ski-lift or a promenade - to a larger part of the local population, which are appropriate to partly *compensate* for the deficiency in the village. The analysis revealed that in the natural areas two kinds of places of informal social interaction can be differentiated:

1. places frequented by the residents in order to perform various activities without worrying about being seen by others
2. places frequented by the residents in order to seek silence and interact solely with nature

1) In the less urbanized community residents report with pride of the many opportunities for leisure activities their natural areas offers them. Thereby they mentioned in particular the riverside and the mountain inns which serve as meeting places and obviously replace the lack of places of informal interaction in the village.

In the more urbanized community the residents speak noticeably seldom of activities in the natural areas of their communities. Few use these areas for sports or just to take the air, but virtual opportunities of social interaction are lacking there respectively do not satisfy. Many residents excused their abstinence from using this area with the omnipresent noise and also with the intensive agriculture. In summer the adolescents meet at a lake for bathing far outside of the territory of their community. Whereas the adult residents accept this shortcoming, the wishes of the children often depicting park-like places seem to express a need for such opportunities.

2) Seeking silence revealed to be an equivalent motive for frequenting the natural areas, whereby this kind of 'social interaction' at least partly seems to substitute (and not really compensate) the lack of satisfying social interactions (for a constitutive effect of social interaction, the reaction of the other, does not take place). In terms of the satisfaction of this need there exist as well considerable differences between the two communities. Whereas the residents of the less urbanized community mentioned plenty of places in the natural areas of their community where they like to enjoy the loneliness, the residents of the more urbanized community already had problems to indicate just one of such a place. Here, even farmers, normally known for their low mobility, increasingly leave the community area in order to recover in silence of nature. To the contrary to the less urbanized community, the desire for more natural elements within their community area ranks high.

The cause for the withdrawal from the public place

The home functions proved to be very relevant and even fundamental for the interaction between the residents and their public place. Especially within the village, however, the requirement for the regulation of individual identity and social interactions are not sufficiently fulfilled, and there is a lack of opportunities to experience the emotions autonomy and excitement. In the natural areas of the less urbanized community, all the requirement for the home functions are sufficiently fulfilled, so that these functions can be compensated within the community area. This, however, is not the case in the more urbanized community. Consequently the insufficiencies of the functions can not only explain, why the residents withdraw from their public place. They also provide an explanation for the higher degree of withdrawal in the more urbanized community reflected in the fact that their residents regularly escape to more distant recreation areas outside of the community area (see Fig. 2).

As the figure shows, the insufficiencies particularly concern the lack of behavioural range and the lack of individual traces. The residents of the two communities try to compensate for these insufficiencies in the near-to-nature areas within the territory of their community (example less urbanized community) – and if they do not find the necessary opportunities, they escape into more distant recreation areas (example more urbanized community). So especially the imbalance between clear rules and behavioural range on the one hand and between collective and individual traces of identification seems to be the source of the withdrawal from the public place.

CONCLUSIONS

In this study we have succeeded in showing that the local public place fulfils basically the same needs or functions for the local residents as the private home, in particular the regulation of identity, social interaction and social emotions - but on a more social level. Whereas fulfilling these functions within the private home allows the residents to cultivate their personal self-image and their intimate relations, the public place has to fulfil these functions in order to maintain the residents' socially shared identity and their social integration. The three functions of home, operationalized by their requirements, did not only prove to be most relevant, but even fundamental for the interaction between the residents and their public place. Thus the transference of the home functions to the everyday surrounding suggested by the approach of physical setting (Proshansky et al., 1983) could be empirically confirmed.

Accordingly the public place can only fulfil its functions, if there is a balance between two pairs of conflicting requirements: a1) Clear behavioural rules within the settings which allow the residents to interact without risking to be misunderstood. a2) sufficient behavioural range (or opportunities of informal interaction) within the settings which allow the residents to express their individuality and to establish a meaningful social exchange. b1) a sufficient continuity of the settings and their traces of former experiences which remind the residents of their personal and social identity, and b2) sufficient scope of shaping (or opportunities to change the settings) which enable the residents to express changes in their personal or collective life. If there is an imbalance of these requirements the residents withdraw from their public place.

Our results confirmed this assumption. In both of the two communities we could observe such a withdrawal, and we could in fact explain this withdrawal (and also the more pronounced withdrawal in the more urbanized community) with a lack of some of these requirements, in particular with the lack of behavioural range within the settings of the villages' public place. Without fulfilling this requirement, the public place cannot perform its function as a resource of social interaction, and therefore it is no wonder that the local residents do no longer make use of it. Social interaction, however, is important for the residents' personal well-being, and therefore they look for a suitable strategy to cope with this deficiency.

A main coping strategy we found was that the residents try to compensate for the unavailable aspects of the home functions in the surrounding close-to-nature areas - a half-way form of withdrawing from the public place. If the close-to-nature areas of the community fulfil the requirements of the home functions (which is to a far extent the case in the less urbanized community), the residents can partly compensate for the home functions within their community. But the lack of social interaction within the village can not be fully made good in the local close-to-nature areas, even if meaningful social interaction takes place in these settings, for the social interaction there is less integrated in the context of everyday socialisation. Accordingly the local residents of both communities were most concerned about the creation of new meeting places within the villages. Most of the settings in the close-to-nature areas which fulfil the functions' requirements, however, do not even offer the residents opportunities for real social interaction, but only for interaction with nature (i.e. projected social interaction). Such settings can only substitute the lack of social interaction and thus just contribute to a momentary psychological well-being (Kaplan and Kaplan, 1989). But they cannot satisfy the residents' need for social recognition (or identity) and social integration within the community, as this takes place only in genuine social interactions (Mead, 1934).

If the close-to-nature areas within the community do not fulfil the requirements of the home functions (which is to a far extent the case in the more urbanised case study), the residents try to compensate for the functions in more distant recreation areas - a stronger form of withdrawal from the public place. This produces increased leisure mobility, and the long journeys deprive the 'withdrawing' persons of their leisure time. But distant recreation areas (even more than in the nearer ones) offer the residents only resources to appease their personal well-being (Kaplan and Kaplan, 1989; Korpela et al., 2001; Hartig, 1993), but not to compensate for the lack of interactive social interaction. Genuine socal interaction, however, is a key factor for the social capital of a community and the social cohesion (Falk and Kilpatrick, 2000), so that a lack of this function has very unfavourable consequences for the future of the community.

Therefore it is important to find measures to reduce the withdrawal from the public place in peri-urban regions. In general, there are two ways to achieve such a reduction. The easier way, however, is rather combating the symptoms: to introduce natural elements around the village and in particular inside. So, the home functions could be fulfilled within the place where the residents spend their everyday life, for natural areas obviously can offer conditions which allow the residents to compensate for the missing aspects of these functions or at least to substitute them. By this measure the withdrawal can probably be reduced, but the success is uncertain and rather moderate, for the deeper cause of the withdrawal process, the lack of genuine social interaction, is not addressed.

The more difficult, but also more profound solution would be to introduce new physical settings (or meeting places) with well defined explicit rules of behaviour in the public place of the village. Such explicit rules allow the residents on the one hand to interact without risking to be misunderstood and leaves them on the other hand in the same way explicit room for expressing individuality. According to our findings, such settings are not only needed for everyday's social exchange, but also for local planning.

The findings of this chapter are based on an exploratory investigation in two case studies and supported by a consistent theoretical framework. In spite of the limited empirical foundation, a cautious generalisation of the findings for peri-urban communities in German speaking regions (or even in regions of Central Europe) seems to be justified, for dormitory communities have spread in all these regions during the last decades, and these processes have generally been accompanied by a loss of traditional forms of living and behaving, without being paralleled by an explicit re-definition of the settings in the public place. None the less more research is needed to fully understand the relation between residents and their public place in an increasingly urbanising world. In a recently started project we are trying to

94 BUCHECKER

enhance our understanding in this field with a more systematic research design (http://www.wsl.ch/land/society/proansprueche-de.ehtml).

REFERENCES

Augé, M. (1995) Non-Places. Introduction to an anthropology of supermodernity. Stanford: Stanford University Press.

Barker, R.G. (1968) Ecological psychology. Standford: Standford University Press.

Barker, R.G. (1987) Prospecting in environmental psychology. In: D. Stokols & I. Altman (Eds.), Handbook of environmental psychology, New York: Wiley, pp. 1413-1432.

Bischof, N. (1972) The biological foundations of the incest taboo. Social Science Information 11 (6), pp. 7-36.

Brandenburg, A.M. and Carroll, M.S. (1995) Your place or mine? The effect of place creation on environmental values and landscape meanings. Society and Natural Resources, Vol. 8, pp. 381-398.

Breakwell, G.M. (1986) Coping With Treatened Identity. London: Methuen.

Buchecker, M., Hunziker, M. and Kienast, F. (2003) Participatory landscape development: Overcoming social barriers to public involvement. Landscape and Urban Planning, 64, 29-46.

Buchecker, M. & Schultz, B. (2000) Lebendiges Dorf, lebendiges Quartier. Birmensdorf: Eidg. Forschungsanstalt WSL.

Cuba, L. and Hummon, D.M. (1993) A place to call home: Identification with dwelling, community and region. The Sociological Quarterly. 34(1), 111-131.

Falk, I. and Kilpatrick S. (2000) What is Social Capital? Sociologia Ruralis, Vol. 40, No. 1, pp. 86-110.

Flick, U. (1995) Handbuch Qualitative Forschung. Weinheim: Psychologie Verlags Union.

Fuhrer, U. & Kaiser F. (1994) Multilokales Wohnen. Bern: Verlag Hans Huber.

Fuhrer, U., Kaiser, F. and Hartig, T. (1993) Place attachment and mobility during leisure time. Journal of Environmental Psychology 13, pp. 309-321.

Fuhrer, U. (1990) Bridging the ecological-psychological gap: Behavior settings as interface'. Environment and Behavior, 22 (4), pp. 518-537.

Gans, H.J. (1969) Die Levitowner: Soziographie einer Schlafstadt. Berlin: Bertelsmann.

Gerdes, K. (1979) Explorative Sozialforschung. Stuttgart: Ferdinand Enke Verlag.

Hartig, T. (1993) Nature experience in transactional perspective. Landscape and Urban Planning, 25 (1993) pp. 17-36.

Hollander, J. (1991) It all depends. Home: a place in the world. Social Research 58: pp. 31-50.

Hunziker, M. (1995) The spontaneous reafforestation in abandoned agricultural lands: perception and aesthetic assessment by locals and tourists. Landscape and Urban Planning 31: pp. 399-410

Kaplan, R. & Kaplan, S. (1989) The Experience of Nature: A Psychological Perspective. Cambridge: Cambridge University Press.

Korpela, K.M., Hartig, T., Kaiser F.G. & Fuhrer U. (2001) Restorative experience and self-regulation in favourite places. Environment and behavior, Vol. 33, No. 4, pp. 572-589.

Krüger, R. (1987) Wie räumlich ist die Heimat? - Oder: Findet sich in Raumstrukturen Lebensqualität?' Geographische Zeitschrift, Jg. 75. Heft 3.

Lamnek, S. (1989) Qualitative Sozialforschung. S. München: Psychologie Verlags-Union.

Lindsey, S., Buchan, R. and Duncan, J.S. (1988) The residential landscape as a system of communication: a semiotic approach. In: M. Herzfeld and L. Melazzo (ed.), Semiotics theory and practice, proceedings of the third international congress of the IASS, Palermo 1984, Mouton de Gruyter, Berlin, Vol. 1, pp. 591-600.

Low, S.M. and Lawrence-Zúñiga, D. (2003) The anthropology of space and place'. Locating culture. Victoria: Blackwell Publishing.

Mead, G. H. (1934) Mind, self and society. Chicago: University of Chicago press.

Morse, J.M. (1994) Designing dunded qualitative research. In: N.K. Denzin, & Y.S. Lincoln, (ed). Handbook of qualitative research, Sage, London, 22o-235.

Oevermann, U. (1991) Genetischer Strukturalismus und das sozialwissenschaftliche Problem der Erklärung der Entstehung des Neuen. In: S. Müller-Doohm 1991, Jenseits der Utopie, Frankfurth a. M.: Suhrkamp.

Oosterman, A. (2002) Green city versus suburban sprawl: the reinvention of Almere. Architecture d'aujourd'hui, 339, 68-75.

Proshansky, H. M., Fabian, A.K. and Kaminoff, R. (1983) Place-Identity: Physical world socialisation of the self. Journal of Environmental Psychology, 3, pp. 57-83.

Rapoport, A. (1982) *The Meaning Of The Built Environment*. Sage, London.

Seel M. (1996) *Eine Aesthetik der Natur*. Frankfurt am Main: Suhrkamp.

Strauss, A. und Corbin, J. (1996) *Grounded Theory: Grundlagen Qualitativer Sozialforschung*. Weinheim: Beltz, Psychologie Verlags Union.

Terkenli, T. S. (1995) Home As A Region. *Geographical Review* **85(3)**, 324-334.

Thorns, D.C. (2002) The transformation of Cities. Urban Theory and Urban Life. New York: Palgrave Macmillan.

Witzel, A. (1985) Das problemzentrierte Interview. In: G. Jüttemann: Qualitative Forschung in der Psychologie. Weinheim.

No.	Sex	Age	Resident Type	*Profession*	Special Features
1	f	28	Newcomer	Religion teacher	Council, mother
2	m	57	Burgher	Traditional farmer	Wood owner
3	f	29	Native resident	Civil servant	Commuter, single parent
4	f	19	Burgher	College student	Commuter
5	m	45	Burgher	Traditional farmer	Pres. of farming cooperative
6	m	67	Old newcomer	Former Worker	Sports club
7	m	54	Burgher	Modern farmer	Former council
8	m	45	Native resident	Farmer & trucker	Council
9	f	55	Old newcomer	Teacher	Culture club
10	m	45	Native resident	Worker	Fisherman and hunter
11	m	32	Newcomer	Computer scientist	Family club
12	m	72	Old newcomer	Farmer	
13	f	43	Burgher	Farmer	Landwomen's club, mother
14	m	45	Burgher	Ecological farmer	Environmental Commission
15	m	52	Native resident	Dentist	Commuter
16	f	36	Old newcomer	Hotel keeper	
17	m	67	Burgher	Restaurant keeper	Former pres. of burghers
18	f	49	Old newcomer	Baker	
19	m	75	Native resident	Former Handcrafter	Former council, Rabbit breed club
20	m	18	Burgher	Apprentice	Leader of youth group
21	f	35	Newcomer	Clerk	amily club, mother
22	f	36	Newcomer	Religion teacher	Single
23	m	46	Burgher	Farmer	Building commission
24	f	90	Old newcomer	Entrepreneur	
25	m	47	Zuzüger	Entrepreneur	Environmental commission
26	m	43	Native resident	Builder	Building commission
27	m	22	Burgher	Industrial farmer	
28	m	35	Burgher	Engineer	Commuter
29	m	45	Burgher	Farmer & Worker	
30	f	68	Old newcomer	Farmer	Landwomen's club
31	f	29	Newcomer	Clerk	Pres. of environmental group
32	m	53	Old newcomer	Teacher	

Table 1: Characterisation of the respondents

Home functions	Key categories
Regulation of identity	Social belonging Need for an individual place Feeling of being accepted Feeling of being supplanted
Regulation of social interaction	Knowing people and places Getting to know people New meeting-places Feeling of restriction
Regulation of social emotions Security Autonomy Excitement	Order, familiarity Independence Surprise, beauty

Table 2: The close association between the key categories detected during the inductive analysis and the home functions.

MACHIEL J. VAN DORST

8. PRIVACY ZONING

The Different Layers Of Public Space

INTRODUCTION

Privacy is conceived of as an interpersonal boundary process in which a person or group regulates interaction with others (Altman 1975: 6). This process can be supported by a physical environment in which territories for residents, visitors and passers-by can be identified. The aim of this chapter is to paint a picture of a territorial space that is just as subtle as the ways in which individuals and groups regulate their privacy. The first section examines the relations between privacy and territorial behaviour. According to Altman there are three territories in space: primary territories, secondary territories and public territories (1975: 112–120). If we look at these not just from the perspective of the individual, but also from the perspective of various groups, we find a complex set of territories embedded within each other. This seems not to agree with Altman's territorial model, but in fact it does fit in with the general concept of privacy and reveals a more complex picture of what we call 'privacy zoning'. The second section discusses a case study of a non-Western residential district: Tunjungan, in Indonesia. In this district we can identify nine zones that are used to regulate privacy. The chapter concludes with conclusions drawn from the Tunjungan case study, which are then translated to the Dutch (or Western) situation. This leads to our final conclusion that the privacy zoning model is a more refined vision of what 'public' space could be.

PRIVACY IN TERRITORIES

Privacy

Altman makes a clear connection between the regulation of social contacts and the physical environment. In doing so he makes use of the concepts of privacy and territoriality. Privacy is 'selective control of access to the self or to one's group' *(Altman 1975: 18)*. This access relates to physical accessibility and access to the available information about yourself. Physical access to individuals relates to visual privacy (the degree to which you can be seen and can see others) and auditive

P. Turner and E. Davenport (Eds.), Spaces, Spatiality and Technology, 97-116.

privacy (the degree to which you can be heard and can hear others). The privacy that relates to information mainly concerns personal details, a form of privacy that is at stake when databases are linked. This definition of privacy is all about *degree* of access. This means that privacy is not just a case of retreating behind closed doors: visiting a busy café in search of social interaction is also a form of privacy regulation. Privacy, therefore, is an important human need and is related to communication (Pedersen, 1997). The built environment is one of the means by which the privacy one is granted can be brought in line with the privacy one desires. The desired level of social interaction depends on personal characteristics, social influences, the physical environment and culture (Gifford 1997: 175). The desired level of social interaction, therefore, can vary per person and over time: a resident on their way to work on Monday morning is less open to social interaction with neighbours than during a walk through the neighbourhood on a Sunday afternoon. The level of desired social interaction may vary, but the need to control social interaction is universal. Control is exercised by setting limits or by actively looking for social contact (or collecting information). The desired result of these actions is a balance between the desired and achieved level of social interaction. If this balance is not achieved, or if it is disturbed, the result is social stress (crowding) or loneliness.

Altman's theory is generally accepted and used (Bell *et al.*, 2001; Gifford 1997). The substance of Altman's theory is supported by research into crowding, in which a person's perceived control over social interaction is an important indicator of stress (Evans and Lepore 1992; Lepore, Evans and Schneider 1992). However, there are differences of opinion about how people behave in situations in which an optimal level of privacy has been achieved. Altman assumes that such an optimum is a temporary situation and that afterwards an individual will again search for a new level, for example the opposite (Altman, Vinsel and Brown 1981). O'Connor and Rosenblood (1996) show in an experiment that this is not the case, that individuals may in fact choose to maintain a certain level of privacy; however, Altman, Vinsel and Brown do not agree with this idea of homeostasis (a 'metabolic' level of desired privacy). Although Altman's theory may not be correct on this point, this does not make the theory unsuitable for use in research into privacy zoning. In this chapter the object of research is not the dynamics of privacy regulation from a social psychological perspective, but the relation between privacy and territories. This concept of territories is, therefore, important in this research.

Territoriality

Territories are geographical areas that are personalised or marked in some way and that are defended from encroachment (Sommer, 1969; Becker, 1973). Altman uses the following definition: territoriality involves the mutually exclusive use of areas and objects by persons or groups (Sundstrom and Altman, 1974). In this definition, people's territorial behaviour is the behaviour and cognition of a person or group, based on the perceptual possession of a physical space (Bell *et al.*, 2001). At the local level, territoriality leads to the building of fences; at the international level to wars. This does not imply that this sort of behaviour is necessarily undesirable; recognisable territories give a clear compartmentalisation to space and make the built environment legible. The garden fence as a physical barrier is easy to overcome, but it is more than a physical barrier. The garden fence imparts a message: this is private territory; enter only with permission from the owner. The built environment contains all sorts of signals of the existence of territories at various scales – entrances, borders and areas – and these signals provide clarity. If this clarity is absent, what is left is a no-man's land; an anonymous terrain. The regulation of social interaction in the living environment, therefore, can be supported by the physical environment. On the one hand, the users must have control over whether they enter into or avoid social interactions. On the other hand, the physical environment must be legible and thus clearly indicate the status and accessibility of the users: Is this person a resident, a visitor or a passer-by? I feel like greeting them, but is that customary or acceptable here?

Altman identifies three types of physical territories: primary territories, secondary territories and public territories (1975: 112–120). Primary territories are easily recognisable private spaces, both physically and legally; the other territories are more diffuse. A courtyard can be seen as a communal territory for all residents, but what about a residential street open to through traffic? Secondary space can take many forms and can consist of communal space in a residential building or a local café. A public space can also change (temporarily) into a secondary territory the moment it is occupied by a group of users (Boomkens, 1998), for example during a demonstration or a rave. The latter example also shows that the function and use of the public space may be contentious. Is public space the space that can be used by anybody and does the possibility of social interaction still play a role (Augé, 1992; Fyfe, 1998)? Although this does not call the division into private, semi-public and public space itself into question, a frequent comment is that semi-public and public territories cannot always be defined with certainty and that their validity depends to a large extent on the use to which they are put (Fyfe, 1998; Boomkens, 1998).

For the immediate living environment, the existence and use of a secondary territory depends on the usability of space or the legibility of the physical territory. Once the public space is no longer legible as the territory of a group of residents, the territory itself will no longer be respected. Solutions currently put forward are the privatisation of these public spaces (for example in shopping centres), surveillance with CCTV cameras and more formal methods of supervision (by police and security companies). This implies a relation between control over social interaction, with the help of legible territories, and the prevention of anonymity and the insecurity that goes with this.

The relation between social cohesion and the usability of space is the subject of a study by Brown and Weber (1985) into neighbourhood attachment. This research suggests that the residents of cul-de-sacs have a stronger affinity with their neighbourhood than residents of through streets. A striking result of this study is that feelings of cohesion and community depended on the attitude the respondents had towards their own home. The front garden plays an important role in this: 70% of all longer-lasting activities in residential streets take place in semi-private *areas* (Gehl, 1986). Cul-de-sacs contain more space for social interaction: the space that people can experience as a context for activities and *interactions* (Skjaeveland and Garling, 1997), for which the usability of space is important. Circulation space (available in excessive amounts in gallery flats, for example) is less suitable or even totally unsuitable for this type of social interaction. A further distinction between cul-de-sacs and through streets is the presence of passers-by: as the amount of through traffic increases, the degree of social contact in the street diminishes (Rogers, 1997). Similar results have been obtained at the level of the individual building: students with rooms on through corridors make fewer social contacts and experience a lower degree of social control than students with rooms on 'dead-end' *corridors* (Baum, Aiello and Calesnick, 1978; Evans *et al.*, 2000).

Altman revisited

The definition of privacy is usually applied from a social psychological perspective that focuses on the perception of the *individual* (Pedersen 1999; O'Connor and Rosenblood 1996). The use of territories involves both a social psychological perspective and a sociological perspective which focuses on the relation between groups and the built environment. The individual is linked to the private territory and their relationship to groups in other territories; groups are linked to the use of the secondary territory and the use of public space. These customary relations do not necessarily follow from Altman's definition of privacy. After all, groups also want to control social interaction, and this forms the basis for the hypothesis that groups can also recognise and own private, semi-private and public territories. It is a fact that an individual can be part of a group, which in turn is part of a larger group: one person is part of a family and the family is part of a religious community or neighbourhood; the religious community and the neighbourhood are in turn part of a city, etc. This means that the private space of a group can at the same time be public space when viewed from a different perspective.

The result is a picture that may come closer to reality. In an urban planning analysis, the territories in the residential environment cannot always be fully described by three categories. Semi-private (or semi-public) space, in particular, is a complex mix of zones with different meanings: a bench on the gallery of a high-rise flat has a different status to the gallery itself; or the lift; or the space in front of the building. According to Altman's definition, the residents of a block of flats or a street should also be able to maintain a collective privacy. The street is a public space for the individual, but at the same time the private space for all the residents of the street as a group. Moreover, group territories are embedded within larger territories in a series of layers because groups are part of larger groups. The complexity of this system is due to the number of different scales of activity and the degree to which residents as a group can be identified. The clarity of this zoning depends on the relation between the legibility of the territory and the distinctiveness of the group. The occupants of a house are clearly a group, but what about all the residents in a busy street? Or all the residents of an urban district? Design plays a part in defining the group and, consequently, the possibilities for social interaction. The model of zones with different meanings for privacy and social interaction is called 'privacy zoning'. In this model, therefore, we abandon the division into private, secondary and public spaces. In the next section we examine a case study in which a more complex form of privacy zoning can be identified.

TUNJUNGAN

In 1989 a joint research proposal was drawn up for the Tunjungan area by the universities of Surabaya and Delft. The initiative for this cooperation was taken by Professor Johan Silas and Dr Josef Priyotomo of the Faculty of Architecture at the Institut Teknoloki Sepuluh Nopember Surabaya (ITS) in Indonesia and Ron Gill of the Faculty of Architecture at Delft University of Technology. The goal of the research was to make a proposal for the restructuring of this city centre residential environment, which was under intense pressure from the surrounding city centre uses (major retail outlets, banks, etc.) and in danger of disappearing altogether. According to Professor Silas, this would not only be a disaster for the residents themselves, but also threaten the vitality of the city centre as a whole. The design was drawn up by H. van de Wahl as a final year project (van de Wal, 1991) after a seven-month research study, three months of which were spent in *Tunjungan* (van Dorst and van der Wal, 1991). The research consisted of a participant observation study, in-depth interviews and a spatial analysis of the *kampongs* of Tunjungan. The researchers took part in the daily life of the *kampong* and lived in Tunjungan. The observation consisted of walking through the *kampongs*, eating and sitting on the street and visiting homes. The behaviour displayed by the residents was observed in relation to the physical environment. During their stay, the researchers conducted 18 in-depth interviews, each interview consisting of three meetings: the first two concentrated on getting to know the interviewee and establishing mutual respect; the third interview covered home life, previous homes and life in the *kampong*. We chose the open interview style to avoid the risk of interviewees simply giving socially acceptable answers: in Indonesia it is 'not done' to answer a question in the negative or to adopt a different viewpoint form the interviewer. We also analysed the form and use of different types of multi-storeyed housing in Surabaya found outside the Tunjungan *kampong*.

Tunjungan

Surabaya is the second largest city in Indonesia with a population of 5.1 million (in 2003). In the middle of this port city, surrounded by all the business, social and leisure activities in the city centre, is the residential area of Tunjungan. The district consists of three kampongs, or neighbourhoods, and its borders are defined by four busy major roads. *Kampongs* are unplanned rural settlements that have subsequently been swallowed up by the expanding city. They are characterised by high densities of homes with ground level access.

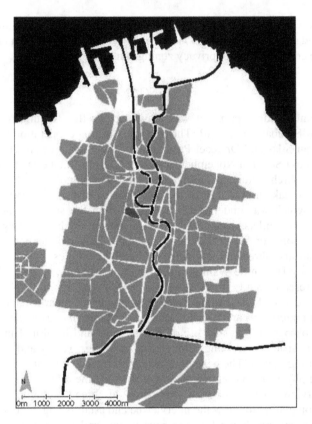

Figure 1: Surabaya, with Tunjungan in the central area

The roads around Tunjungan are main thoroughfares and are part of Surabaya's central business district. The *kampongs*, therefore, are surrounded by shops, businesses, banks and hotels built on a completely different scale. The residential area itself is almost inaccessible by car and the houses are largely hidden from the road. Non-motorised traffic can enter the district in just a few places. About 5000 people live in Tunjungan in 1125 homes of highly variable quality. The houses and housing environment in the Ketanden and Blauran *kampongs* are of reasonable to very good quality and in Kebangsren are poor to reasonable. The residents of the *kampongs* work for the government, in the commercial sector or in the informal economy, which includes street traders, informal shops and kiosks, and letting rooms to workers in the formal sectors of the economy. There is a mutual dependency between the formal and informal sectors. Tunjungan also contains a number of schools and mosques. The dwellings in a *kampong* differ widely in size and quality, the diversity and density evolving over many years as successive generations of the same family add buildings and expand their houses. Poor daylight penetration is not a problem in the tropical climate of Surabaya and many of the plots are completely built up. The houses are built back to back, sometimes with a narrow opening in between. At the front, the houses open onto a *gang*, the Indonesian word for a narrow pedestrian street or alley.

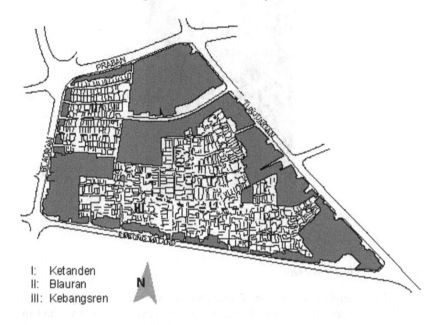

I: Ketanden
II: Blauran
III: Kebangsren

N

Figure 2: Tunjungan consists of three kampongs, enclosed by the backs of public land uses, which are all oriented towards the surrounding main roads.

Figure 3: Traffic around Tunjungan

Figure 4: A kampong street

Quality of life in Tunjungan

Parts of the neighbourhoods in Tunjungan do not meet all hygiene standards. Sufficient light and air cannot always penetrate between the houses and in some places a number of households share the same kitchen and washing area, but the interviews reveal that people are very pleased with their homes. The size and quality of their dwellings has little to do with this satisfaction; the residents judge their homes in terms of the maximum they can get out of the space available. Their satisfaction depends on how they assess the opportunities available to them and they value the existing environment in those terms. These findings resemble those of the study in India by Nathan and Marans *(1998)*, which indicate that the satisfaction of residents depends on their 'housing career': the closer the present dwelling comes to the ideal, the greater the level of satisfaction.

The *kampongs* are centrally located in the city and the social structure is closely knit. Living in Tunjungan means living in a village *and* living in a world city all in the same place. One family head had the idea that, considering his social position and income, he would be better off in a gated area on the edge of the city. Their new house had already been built, but the other members of his family did not want to leave the *kampong*; they preferred not to swap the social structure for more square metres. At first sight, a *kampong* seems to be a community; there is strict social control, both formal and informal. In the formal social structure of a *kampong* there is one or more *Rukun Wargas* (RW) and within a RW a number of *Rukun Tetanggas* (RT), which consist of 30 to 40 houses. RWs and RTs are administrative units governed by three people and serve as a link between government and local residents. RWs and RTs play a role in providing information, organising festivities on official holidays and maintaining outdoor areas. The informal social conventions are experienced by anyone staying in a *kampong*. As a Western resident in the district one is constantly spoken to; in the streets and alleys by other residents from in their own homes; and in the home by other occupants. This seemed to confirm what other 'experts by experience' from the Netherlands have to say: Indonesians are not as individualistic as the Dutch, and have more social contact and less desire for privacy. It is logical, therefore, that building densities in these residential areas can be many times higher than in the Netherlands. Quality of life in these *kampongs* may be determined by the social structure, but this social structure functions to best effect because of an appropriate physical structure; the physical environment supports the way in which individuals can regulate their social contacts. Although there are cultural differences in the degree of privacy and social interaction, the Javanese also want to be able to regulate the degree of privacy they have. During the participant observation study the *kampongs* appeared to function well because of a subtle system of zoning of indoor and outdoor space. This zoning allows individual users to regulate their social interaction, and thus their privacy. We refer to this spatiality that makes it possible to regulate privacy as 'privacy zoning'.

Privacy zoning

Privacy zoning is a system of zones with different meanings for social interaction. The zones are physically identifiable and socially accepted because they make the situation clear to everyone. The following zones were identified in Tunjungan:

Zone 1: The bedroom

This is absolutely private. Only the users of the room are allowed in and no other family members. Sometimes the bedroom is the minimum possible size and in some cases it is just an area cordoned off with a curtain. In all cases, users know that other members of the household will not disturb them in their bedroom.

Zone 2: The family room

This room is shared by those living in the house. Very good friends may occasionally be admitted, but only when invited. The family room, therefore, is more the domain of the family than a Western living room. Here the family consists of the nuclear family, sometimes with the addition of other live-in relatives.

Zone 3: The guest room

This is where family and guests meet. If one family member receives a guest, the rest of the family can stay in the family room. The family room is visible from the *gang*, from where acquaintances can attract the attention of family members, who may then invite them in. The view out onto the *gang* also allows social control over the *gang* from the home.

Zone 4: The veranda

This has a more public function than the guest room because it is not inside the home. The veranda is also visible from the street and therefore more approachable. Occupants may invite passers-by into this space (even strangers).

Zone 5: Front yard or bench in front of the house

A member of the household sitting here may be addressed by any passer-by, whether they know them or not. The initiative for social contact does not lie with the occupant of the house. However, the number of strangers they see is very limited because the *gangs* are used mainly by residents, visitors, food vendors, and seldom by people just passing through.

Zone 6: The gang

The *gang* delineates a social unit. The residents of a *gang* jointly maintain the outside areas. In some cases the *gang* has a washing area which is shared by the residents. Cooperation in a *gang* is formalised in an official administrative unit, the RT (*Rukun Tetangga*). The chair of the RT is the contact person for the *gang* and reminds residents of their neighbourhood duties and obligations. To rent a room in the Ketanden *kampong* we had to visit the chairman of the RT in 'our' *gang* from time to time.

Zone 7: Squares, crossroads and shops in the network of gangs

In these meeting places residents can actively seek social contact and meet people from other parts of the *kampong*. They can easily leave this zone if they want to end the contact. This is also the zone where *kampong* activities organised by the *kampong* leader or a mosque are held. These centres of activity are also used by *kampong* residents who want to meet someone separately from other members of the live-in family. Social control here is exercised by other *kampong* residents.

Zone 8: The entrance to the kampong

This is where the residents of the *kampong* as a group meet people from the outside world. Visitors from outside cannot enter the *kampong* unseen; they are always asked for the purpose of their visit and, if necessary, a *kampong* resident will accompany them to their destination. Residents may pass the time near the entrance out of curiosity. The entrance is also guarded by residents in the evening and at night so that this informal meeting place can function undisturbed for 24 hours a day.

Zone 9: The public spaces in the city

The main public urban spaces are situated directly outside the *kampong*, where strangers form the majority. The *kampong* residents can experience the anonymity of the city just 200 metres from their homes.

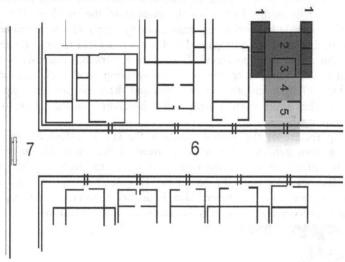

Figure 5: Privacy zoning in Tunjungan

All possible zones have been described here, but not all houses have all possible zones: the family room, guest room and the *gang* are always present; the veranda is sometimes also the front garden; not all residents have a bench outside the front door because they prefer to remain indoors or meet people somewhere else in the *kampong*. Some dwellings may lack certain facilities, such as a bathroom or kitchen, which may be located elsewhere in the *gang*. The very fact that the zoning system is incomplete makes its proper use all the more important. Besides being a spatial structure, the privacy zoning is also a social code that allows people to decide who they do and do not want to meet. All this is possible within a close-knit social structure and a high building density.

Systems of privacy zoning are recognisable in other *kampongs* in Indonesia, but not in the gated areas and high-rise buildings in Surabaya. The gated areas are enclosed suburbs with systems of mainly through roads, without any hierarchy, which are lined with large houses. These houses are set back from the roads and are closed off from the outside world (often with tinted glass windows). These districts are designed along Western lines and suited to car-based mobility; their scale and the absence of pedestrians make informal social contact almost impossible. The gated areas are largely anonymous spaces and no-one walks the streets at night except security guards.

The high-rise districts in Surabaya also have problems that can be explained in part by the lack of privacy zoning. Most dwellings in high-rise buildings are situated along a short and narrow gallery or around a central hall. The spaces in front of the doors and the routes past the dwellings lack usability of space. The consequence is that no co-occupants or visitors regularly walk past the dwellings. Moreover, they do not always have a clear front and back. Even the dwellings in a tall building designed by Professor Silas are situated around a central hall, where no-one passes through, and the dwellings back onto the outside of the building. One woman resident said this made her feel lonely (unpleasantly quiet). Her faith did not allow her to walk in the street unaccompanied and she was unable to regulate her social contacts in the direct neighbourhood. It is quite remarkable that this Indonesian architect set out to build an apartment block, ignoring local social customs. The modernist ideal of light and air was the goal and the residents were expected to adapt to this. They were even issued with a brochure entitled 'How to live in apartment buildings'.

A striking feature of the zoning model is the subtle difference between the function of a front garden and a bench in front of the house for making social contacts. The difference lies in the degree to which the initiative lies with the resident of the house or with the passer-by. Despite this, though, they are still considered to be one zone. The formal clear boundary between private property and public space (or secondary territory) is, in practice, a subtle transition.

Figure 6: Tall building designed by Prof. Silas

CONCLUSIONS AND DISCUSSION

Lessons from Tunjungan

Tunjungan is a residential district where residents have control over their social interaction and are able to change their physical environment. This control is facilitated by the system of privacy zoning described above. For the residents, this privacy zoning is legible as a pattern of territories. The privacy zoning also makes it possible to participate in the social environment, which stimulates social cohesion. Privacy zoning can be described as the materialisation of control over the social environment and social interactions. Although this definition is formulated from a social cultural perspective, it is equally valid to ascribe the privacy zoning to a universal individual need: after all, culture is made by people, not the other way around.

With its emphasis on control and social interaction, the example of Tunjungan gives us a preview of what the physical conditions of social quality might be. At this point it is important to realise that the social and physical environment are not clearly definable entities. The privacy zoning in Tunjungan can be described in purely physical terms, but does not consist solely of physical attributes. The privacy zoning is in itself not directly identifiable in the physical environment and is not easily read by visitors from another culture. But for residents it is implicit and ever present. A consequence of this is that both the residents and the lecturers of the Technical University of Surabaya never mentioned the importance of a physical environment that can support the regulation of social contacts. This was simply too obvious for the residents, while the lecturers may not have thought it sufficiently important to mention – a supposition confirmed by the apartment building designed by Professor Silas. Gibson's ecological psychology (1986) provides an explanation for this by emphasising the meaning of the physical object (physical environment), but this meaning can be interpreted in different ways, depending on the observer: an environment can contain more than one message (affordances) and the same environment can be read differently by different people (users, external experts).

The different meanings and the implicit character of the physical environment does not yet explain the complexity of the observed privacy zoning in Tunjungan. In Tunjungan (as stated above) the division into Altman's three categories of private, semi-private and public space is insufficient. The explanation, paradoxically enough, lies in Altman's theory itself. In his definition of privacy, Altman talks not only about the needs of the individual, but also of the group, implying that groups can also be supported in the regulation of social contacts. Both individuals and groups are recognisable in the housing environments of Tunjungan. The clearest examples are the nuclear family, relatives living in the neighbourhood, the residents of a street, people of the same generation and all the residents of one *kampong*. Altman's private zone is the legally defined private plot, but there is also such a thing as the private zone of one occupant of a house, or the private zone of the residents in a street, or the private zone of the whole *kampong*. This casts doubt on the meaning of the term 'public'. A curious fact to emerge from the Tunjungan example is that the clearest boundary between private areas and public space in legal terms is not the clearest boundary in practice.

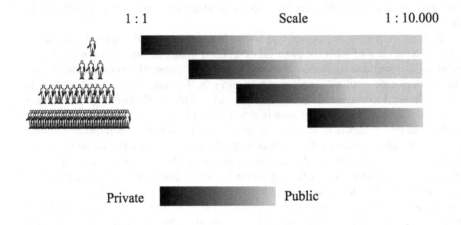

Figure 7: Public space consists of private spaces

At each scale, therefore, a group can be identified that shares the physical environment as a joint private territory (the residents of a city or country). Cultural conventions, as a crystallisation of individual needs, have a part to play in this. Logically, this role becomes more important as the scale increases. On the one hand this can be explained by the size of the group, on the other hand by the greater difficulty of exerting control over a larger territory. Cultural conventions can also take on physical forms: the boundaries in Paris, for example, are not easy to read, whereas the Eiffel Tower is recognisable as a physical cultural icon that represents the territory of Paris.

In Tunjungan, social conventions are not explicit. This may be universal. When do visitors know that they can go in by the back garden when they visit a friend instead of calling at the front door? The advantage of the implicit nature of privacy zoning is that no agreements have to be made about these things, agreements which could then, formally, be broken. The disadvantage of the implicit nature of this privacy zoning is that it remains unspoken. This is probably why privacy zoning does not figure in urban renewal programmes (as in the high-rise developments and gated areas in Surabaya), where there is absolutely no facilitation of social interaction. In Tunjungan the spatial zoning that supports privacy regulation is sustainable in a real sense: it survives many generations of residents *and* dwellings. The fact that the system functions as a whole unit leads one to ask whether just a few zones would suffice. A notable feature of the use of zones in Tunjungan is that they may only function because they are embedded in higher-level zones. The bench in front of the house does not function as a zone if the pedestrian traffic is too heavy or too light (as in the high-rise projects in Surabaya), neither does it function if too many of these people are passers-by, as opposed to residents. This makes privacy zoning an implicit affordance; literally sustainable, but also precarious.

Privacy zoning in the Netherlands

Privacy is a universal need, but the desired balance and the dynamics of social interaction are culture-dependent. Nevertheless, more complex territorial systems can also be discerned in Dutch residential districts. An analysis of a number of post-war districts revealed recognisable territories as well as the groups that could appropriate these territories. For example, a post-war district in Delft with high-rise flats (Poptahof) has the following zones:

1. Dwelling
The zones within the dwelling are less clearly identifiable

2. Gallery
A space shared by 2 or 7 flats

3. Stairwell and lift
Shared by 100 flats, but not all residents use all the areas

4. Entrance area in the building
A private area for all 100 flats

5. Entrance area outside the building
The 'front garden' of the building, where visitors announce their arrival

6. The cul-de-sac where the building is located
Only for use by the residents and a few passers-by

7. The neighbourhood
A clearly legible territory for 1000 flats

This zoning, however, is not recognisable to all residents and contributes little to the regulation of social contacts in the neighbourhood. This limited functionality is due to the fact that various zones have no usability of space, but are only designed for passers-by. This makes the gallery or the stairwell difficult to claim as territories.

Another example is the zoning in a squatted neighbourhood to the west of Amsterdam, the village of Ruigoord. The following zones can be identified in this village:

1. the dwelling
2. the semi-private space, the garden around the dwelling
3. places and access paths for the residents
4. places and paths for residents and visitors (the latter feel welcome here)
5. the through road, the access road and the public space for passers-by

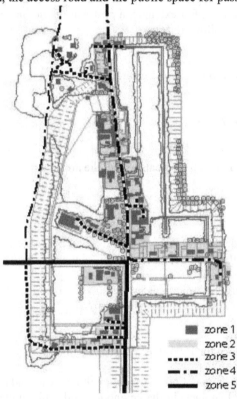

Figure 8: Map of Ruigoord, a squatted village to the west of Amsterdam

Although everywhere outside the private gardens is officially public space, there are varying degrees of 'public'. A longitudinal observation study has shown that the various zones in the public space each display a different relation between private and public (van Dorst *et al.*, 2000), and even differences within zones. This makes it easier for residents to regulate their social interaction and exercise control over their living environment. Both the zoning and the control by residents make the public space more legible for visitors. The visitor is welcome, and although residents can easily retire to their own space there are always some residents available to act as host. This latter role requires a certain intensity of use. The degree of intensity required seems to depend on the physical appearance of the space: in an outdoor space that has the appearance of being a private space the presence on one resident is enough to exercise social control.

Privacy zoning and the design of space

Important factors in the regulation of privacy are personal characteristics (needs, skills, personality) and environmental features, including social factors (the presence and attitude of others) and physical factors (boundaries, distances, sightlines) (Pedersen, 1999). Social pressure and loneliness, therefore, are not generated by the built environment, but the built environment can play a conditional role. Most important, therefore, is the interaction between the individual and the social environment; the physical environment facilitates this interaction. In the subtle process of privacy regulation in the built environment a more detailed zoning of territories would be more useful than just the private, secondary and public zones. The example of Tunjungan makes it reasonable to assume that the space can be divided into many zones. This picture is borne out by observations made in the Netherlands. The differentiation of the public domain can be seen as a critique of Altman's theory, but is in fact based on Altman's privacy theory, which also includes the need for privacy by groups (Altman, 1975). This throws open the very concept of 'public', because public space can also be seen as private space that belongs to a particular group, which can be a neighbourhood or all the residents of a city or country. If outside space as such is legible, this can make a positive contribution to a feeling of citizenship (Steenbergen, 1994).

In non-Western cultures where the immediate living environment is more important than in the West, the desire for privacy is the same, but the social conventions play a greater role (Altman, 1975: 42). Thus we find that in non-Western cultures it is customary to look away when someone is likely to carry out a private act (such as washing in a communal washing area in Tunjungan). The social cultural conventions highlight the two-way traffic in social interaction. Once a privacy zoning is no longer legible or not usable because there is too little open space, social and cultural conventions become important in the regulation of privacy. This can lead to problems in multicultural neighbourhoods, where people do not all share the same conventions. Given that this is an obvious problem in the major cities in Western Europe, these are exactly the places where the legibility and utility of privacy zoning could have a significant effect.

Conclusion

Spaces (indoors and outdoors) belong to residents and users. The first group must be able to manage the available space informally; the second must feel welcome. For this to work, outdoor areas must be legible on various scales and usable as territories: there are many private spaces. The conventional concept of 'public space' assumes one space and is a political concept that does no justice to the possibilities offered by privacy zoning, which allows individual homes, neighbourhoods and cities to function without formal intervention. In Tunjungan, which was built by the residents themselves, the spatial zoning that supports the regulation of privacy is durable. It outlives generations *and* houses.

Town planning as currently practised in the Netherlands restricts discussions about space to the distribution and division of private space and public space; physical conditions which can help residents to regulate their privacy have no place in the design process. To rectify this omission we are currently working on the development of a design process that incorporates privacy zoning. It is to be hoped that this will put the need for privacy on the agenda of urban designers and their clients.

REFERENCES

Altman, I. (1975) *The Environment And Social Behavior: Privacy, Personal Space, Territoriality And Crowding*. Brooks/Cole, Monterey, California.

Altman, I., Vinsel, A. and Brown, B.B. (1981) Dialectic conceptions in social psychology: an application to social penetration and privacy regulation. In L. Berkowitz (ed.), *Advances In Experimental Social Psychology,* Academic press, New York, vol. 14, 107-160.

Augé, M. (1992) *Non-lieux*, Editions du Seuil, Paris. [Non-Paces]

Baum, A, Aiello, J.R. and Calesnick, L.E. (1978) Crowding And Personal Control: Social Density And The Development Of Learning Helplessness, *Journal of Personality and Social Psychology*, **36(9)**, 1000-1011.

Becker, F. D. (1973) Study of spatial markers, *Journal of Personality and Social Psychology*, **26(3)**, 375-381.

Bell, P.A., Green, T.C., Fisher, J.D. and Bauw, A. (2001) *Environmental Psychology*. Harcourt College Publishers, Orlando.

Boomkens, R. (1998) *Een drempelwereld, moderne ervaringen en stedelijke openbaarheid*, NAi Uitgevers, Rotterdam. [A threshold world, modern experience and the urban public domain]

Brown, B.B. and Werner, C.M. (1985) Social Cohesiveness, territoriality, and holiday decorations – the influence of Cul-de-Sacs, *Environment and Behavior*, **17(5)**, 539-565.

Dorst, M.J. van and Wal, H. van de (1991) *The Tunjungan Area Surabaya*. Delft University of Technology, Delft.

Dorst, M.J. van, Heijligers, M., Balvers, E., Timmeren, A. van and Canters, K. 2000, *Ruigoord – Naar een nieuw ecologisch dorp*, DIOC-DGO, Delft [Ruigoord – to a new ecological settlement]

Evans, G.W. and Lepore, S.J. (1992) Conceptual and analytic issues in crowding research, *Journal of Environmental Psychology*, **12**, 163-173.

Evans, G.W., Rhee, E., Forbes, C., Mata Allen, K. and Lepore, S. J. (2000) The meaning and efficacy of social withdrawal as a strategy for coping with chronic residential crowding, *Journal Of Environmental Psychology*, **20**, 335-342.

Fyfe, N.R. (ed.), (1998) *Images Of The Street*, Routledge, London.

Gibson, J. J. (1986) *The Ecological Approach To Visual Perception*. Lawrence Erlbaum, London.

Gifford, R. (1997) *Environmental Psychology,* Allyn and Bacon, Boston.

Gehl, J. (1987) *Life Between Buildings: Using Public Space*, Van Nostrand Reinhold, New York.

Lepore, S.J., Evans, G.W. and Schneider, M.L. (1992) Role of control and social support in explaining the stress of hassles and crowding, *Environment and Behavior*, **24**, 795-811.

Nathan, V. and Marans, R.W. 1998, *An exploration of the evaluative and spatio-cognitive dimensions of environmental assessment,* Paper presented at IAPS 15, Eindhoven.

O'Connor, S.C. and Rosenblood, L.K. (1996) Motivation in Everyday Experience: a theoretical comparison, *Journal of Personality and Social Psychology*, **70(3)**, 513-522.

Pedersen, D.M. (1997) Psychological Functions Of Privacy. *Journal of Environmental Psychology*, **17**, 147-156.

Pedersen, D.M. 1999, 'Model for types of privacy by privacy functions' in *Journal of Environmental Psychology*, 19, pp. 397-405.

Rogers, R. (1997) *Cities for a small planet*, Faber and Faber, London.

Skjaeveland, O and Garling, T. (1997) Effects of interactional space on neighbouring, *Journal of Environmental Psychology,* **17**, 181-199.

Sommer, R. (1969) *Personal space*, Prentice-Hall, Englewood Cliffs N.J.

Steenbergen, B. (ed.) (1994) *The Condition Of Citizenship*. Sage Publications Ltd, London.

Sundstrom, E. and Altman, I. 1974, 'Field study of dominance and territorial behavior' *Journal of Personality and Social Psychology*, **30(1)**, 115-125.

Wal, H. van de (1991) *Surabaya Johnny*, Delft University of Technology, Delft.

BLAISE CRONIN

9. HIGH-FIDELITY MAPPING OF INTELLECTUAL SPACE

INTRODUCTION

In this chapter I revisit some early and also more recent research in information science to show its potential relevance to current thinking on space and spatiality. Unlike other contributors to this volume, I am not concerned with the practicalities and challenges of interaction design, broadly conceived. Rather, my primary focus is intellectual space and its social dimensions. I begin with physical space (how distance influences the degree of informal communication between scientists), move on to intellectual space (conceptual mapping of science) and conclude by suggesting, optimistically it must be said, that hybrid spatial analyses combining social and intellectual components are needed to faithfully capture the multiplex nature of scholarly communication. I raise a number of related questions: (i) How are social relations—forged largely in physical or "real-space" (Dourish, 2001)—reflected in the architecture of intellectual space? (ii) Do co-citation maps of science depict purely intellectual networks or webs of socio-cognitive interactions? How, to put it otherwise and to paraphrase Lucy Suchman (1987), might we represent (socially-) situated semantics? (iii) Are there paratextual indicators, apart from citation and co-authorship data, which can be used to map socio-cognitive ties? (iv) Can social ties be practically captured and visualized, along with or separate from intellectual links? In attempting to answer these questions I draw upon a range of disciplinary literatures.

INFORMATION SPACES

Notions of information space abound. For example, sociologists, urban planners and economists are interested in the geography of the information economy, the emergence of the post-industrial city and the ways in which developments in internetworking have created a new spatial logic, one based on interactions between the space of information flows and the space of places (e.g., Castells, 2000; Hepworth, 1989; Zook, 2003). In a more abstract vein, Max Boisot's (1995, 1999) integrated conceptual framework, the I-Space (Information-Space), creatively explores the relationships between the processes of information codification, abstraction and diffusion in social spaces. The I-Space (instantiated in his ubiquitous, morphing cube) allows him to show how different organizational structures and institutional cultures condition the nature and efficacy of information

P. Turner and E. Davenport (Eds.), Spaces, Spatiality and Technology, 117-128.

exchange—and perceptions of information value—and how those structures, in turn, exert a reciprocal influence on information flows: a process of structuration, in other words (Bosiot, 1995, p. 6).

Within information retrieval, an important sub-field of information science, the vector space model—most closely associated with the work of Gerald Salton—is a well established means of representing the similarity between documents based on weighted term frequency counts: the more topically similar two documents are, the closer they will be located to one another in two-dimensional concept space (e.g., Salton, Wong, and Yang, 1975).

Information science, notably the sub-field of bibliometrics, has long been interested in representing and mapping intellectual space. Recent advances in information visualization techniques and related statistical methods have greatly facilitated the depiction of intellectual spaces and networks of scholarly interaction. The lexicon of information visualization is spatially explicit and metaphor-rich— maps, landscapes, terrain, peaks and cities—and the use of cartographic techniques to show the relationships amongst groups of scholarly publications is well established (e.g., Börner, Chen, and Boyack, 2003; Skupin, 2002). According to Heimeriks and van den Besselaar (2002: 11), bibliometric maps of science "are landscapes of scientific research fields created by quantitative analysis of bibliographic data. In such maps the 'cities' are, for instance, research topics. Topics with a strong cognitive relation are in each other's vicinity and topics with a weak relation are distant from each other." André Skupin (2000,: 91), a geographer by trade, has acknowledged the early contributions of information science—Paul Otlet's in particular—to the use of cartography in the information visualization domain.

> Map metaphors have been associated with the handling of non-geographic information for a long time. They can be traced as far back as the late 19th century when Paul Otlet, regarded by many as the father of information science, made explicit reference to mapping of intellectual domains. Otlet envisioned the use of maps in the exploration of unknown information terrain and even pondered the role of scale in such exploration.

Mapping techniques are now routinely used in information science to reveal the intellectual structure of disciplines (e.g., White and McCain, 1998) and to create real-time, interactive author maps (Lin, White and Buzydlowski, 2003). They have also been used for social network analysis (e.g., Koku, Nazer and Wellman, 2000). Most recently, Howard White (information science) and Barry Wellman (social network analysis) have collaborated to explore the socio-cognitive structure of specialty groups (e.g., White, Wellman and Nazer, 2004). However, there is important prior work to be found in the voluminous literature of bibliometrics and scientometrics, starting with Derek de Solla Price's (1965) landmark article, "Network of scientific papers," one of the earliest attempts to use citation data to reveal the intellectual structure of a scientific sub-field. As it happens, small world theorists have lately come to recognize the importance of the citation network: "...all scientific publications are part of a web of science in which nodes are research publications connected by citations" (Barabási, 2002: 169). The post-WWII Anglo-American information science community clearly grasped the nature and significance of informational spaces, both literal and figurative. However, this fact has sometimes been overlooked.

Thomas Allen carried out groundbreaking studies on the problem solving and communication behaviours of engineers and scientists and the role of the technological gatekeeper in facilitating information flow. Writing more than three decades ago in the *Annual Review of Information Science and Technology* he noted that "[c]ommunication probability decreases with the square of distance and…reaches its asymptotic level within 25 yards" (Allen, 1969: 11). Other kinds of studies have found that there is a strong relationship between distance and the amount of use made of information sources and facilities. The resources—human or documentary, physical or virtual—we routinely use in our work lives are not necessarily the best or most potentially useful for the task in hand; rather (and to oversimplify), we engage in a continual trade-off between factors such as convenience, accessibility, cost and quality (e.g., King *et al.*, 1984). This, of course, has implications for architects, interaction designers, database producers and others. But there are systemic—not just task-level—ramifications. For example, Andrew Odlyzko (2002) maintains that the shift from print-based to digital modes of scholarly communication is ineluctable. He offers the following reasons: (1) the present system is inefficient, expensive and inflexible; (2) scholars are engaged in a "war for the eyeballs," a fact of life in the so-called attention economy; (3) a critical mass of material is available on the Web; and (4) a Web presence translates into more eyeballs. Thus, self-interest dictates that scholars migrate to the Web. Odlyzko's other pertinent observation is that readers will settle for "near substitutes" or "inferior forms of papers" if these can be reached easily.

Odlyzko invokes Clayton Chrisensen's (2000) notion of disruptive technologies to explain the demise of print, but, equally, he could have cited Malcolm Gladwell's (2002) idea of the "tipping point," which has the added merit of foregrounding the role played by opinion shapers (Christensen's framework operates at the level of structural dynamics, not individual influencers). Gladwell identifies and characterizes three kinds of key social actors—mavens, connectors and salesmen (p. 70): "Mavens are data banks. They provide the message. Connectors are the social glue: they spread it." His third category, salesmen, is "a select group of people … with the skills to persuade us when we are unconvinced of what we are hearing." These social pollinators perform a variety of functions, some of which are similar to those carried out by the technological gatekeepers and boundary spanners described by Allen and others in the nineteen sixties and seventies.

PHYSICAL PRESENCE AND PROXIMITY

Contrary to popular belief, the emergence of virtual networks and online communities does not negate the importance of physical proximity in the conduct of research, just as online trading does not mean the dematerialization of commerce or the death of real estate—just think of online trader Amazon.com's giant distribution warehouses. Presence matters in both real and virtual space. Confirmatory evidence comes in a variety of forms and from a variety of contexts. Sylvan Katz (1994: 31) found that the number of intra-national collaborations "decreases rapidly as a function of distance separating research partners," while Mike Thelwall has shown that the "extent of academic web site interlinking between pairs of U.K. universities decreased with geographic distance... neighbouring institutions were very much more likely to interlink than average" (Thelwall, Vaughan and Björneborn, 2005). In her ethnographic account of the culture of high-energy physics, Karin Knorr Cetina (1999, p. 212) notes that "collaborators not continually at CERN ... feel left behind, as if they were chasing after something that is always two steps ahead. In principle, almost everything is accessible to everyone at all times—but in practice, information circulates through local discourse at the centre, which one must be physically plugged into...to be up to date." To be where the action is (if I may appropriate the title of Paul Dourish's book [Dourish, 2001]), counts.

Humans have a penchant for minimizing resistance and economizing on effort. George Kingsley Zipf's "Principle of Least Effort" and Allen's aforementioned "30-Metre Principle" neatly encapsulate such near-universal 'satisficing' behaviours. By way of an aside, Allen went on to note that the architectural profession seems to have ignored the spatial determinants of social interaction (e.g., how distance affects frequency of informal communication). Physical connectivity and degrees of presence matter, even in an age of electronic publication, online fora and digital networks. Geographers recognize that the space of flows and the space of places are co-constitutive: the geography of the Internet is a case of intertwined worlds, the physical and the virtual (e.g., Zook, 2003). In similar vein, media complementarity (not substitution) is a defining feature of contemporary scholarly communication. Email has not displaced other means of information exchange and interaction; in fact, email use correlates positively with most traditional forms of communication (face-to-face, phone, fax and mail):

> Although the Internet helps scholars to maintain ties over great distances, physical proximity still matters. Those scholars who see each other often or work nearer to each other email each other more often. Frequent contact on the internet is a complement for frequent face-to-face contact, not a substitute for it (Koku, Nazer, and Wellman, 2001: 1750).

Social relations are subtly inscribed in the architecture of the scholarly communication system. Many academic domains/specialty groups combine near year-round conference caravanning with intensive electronic communication via email, listserv, chat rooms, etc. Connectivity is a *conditio sine qua non* of professional success, and access, physical or otherwise, to opinion leaders and power brokers matters. Successful scientists will be adept at building, to use Putnam's (2000) terms, bridging social capital (connections across diverse groups) and bonding social capital (connections across homogeneous groups). Virtuality has not diminished the importance of in-group membership. But changes have occurred. The invisible colleges described three decades ago by Diana Crane (1972) are being progressively reconstituted as "visible colleges" (Koku, Nazer and Wellman, 2001). They have been "outed." Today, digital communications media make it much easier to track sociometric stars than in Crane's or Price's day; we can see who posts, and responds; who generates a buzz and attracts attention online. Current efforts to deal with the problems of "teleidentity" and visualize social environments and patterns of interaction, such as those conducted by the Sociable Media Group at MIT (e.g., Boyd, Lee, Ramage and Donath, 2002), may help increase communicative transparency, but the traces left in the ether don't describe the full spectrum of social relations that structure specialty groups, even though they reveal some of the institutional and professional circuitry.

MAPPING CITATION LINKS AND HYPERLINKS

Eugene Garfield's (1955) idea of indexing the literature of science—described in his seminal *Science* paper—by the material which is cited by that literature was elegantly simple. Early developments in automated information retrieval systems made increasingly ambitious bibliometric analyses possible (Cronin and Atkins, 2000). Garfield was interested in the visual representation of citation patterns (the unseen lattices of references implicit in the citation databases). The pioneering work of his ISI (Institute for Scientific Information) colleague Henry Small, an historian of science, stimulated widespread interest in using aggregated citation data to chart the emergence and evolution of scientific specialties. Such visualizations (for instance, the early *Atlas of Science* covering biochemistry and molecular biology) provide users/readers with "a mental image of a domain space" (Williams, *et al.*, 1995:163), without which it would be difficult to make sense of the data, or infer the overall structure of a domain or specialty group.

Hundreds of disciplinary snapshots and maps (using authors and documents) of intellectual spaces have been generated as a result of the foundational work of Price, Garfield and Small, yet, as White and McCain (1997: 116) note, "the principal bibliometricians have never been good, journalistically speaking, at placing what they do in a new, widely intelligible framework." However, ISI's contributions to scientific mapping of knowledge spaces, its "graphical legacy" (Davenport and Cronin, 2000: 528), has not gone unrecognized: the developers of the Google search engine - Sergey Brin and Lawrence Page - acknowledge the similarities between hyperlinking and citation linking. More recently, the parallels between citations and hyperlinks have been explored by Christine Borgman and Jonathan Furner (2002, pp. 13-14):

The success of systems such as Google and Clever is reflected in the extent to which research in Web-based IT is currently dominated by attempts to implement link-analytic techniques at ever-increasing levels of sophistication. It should be recognized (in a manner that Brin and Page, for example, do not) that bibliometricians working on conventional citation analysis have, in their efforts to replace reliance on crude citation counts, produced similar formulations at earlier dates ...

Even though the Web is very different from the controlled document collections that underpin ISI's citation indexes (Page, Brin, Motwani and Winograd, 1998), there are functional equivalents, if one thinks of links (hyper and citation) as being akin to votes, judgments, pointers, recommendations, expressions of trust, or endorsements. [For an early discussion of the potential benefits of hyperlinked citations, see Davenport and Cronin (1990: 177)]. As it happens, those masters of physical space— architects—have not been impervious to the value of mapping intellectual space. William Mitchell noted presciently in his foreword to Juan Pablo Bonto's indexical/citation analysis of American architects and texts (1996: *x*) that, "interest in a subject can be measured by the number of hyperlinks pointing to WWW pages ..."

The rationale underpinning citation mapping has been expressed succinctly by Small (1973: 265): "If it can be assumed that frequently cited papers represent the key concepts, methods, or experiments in a field, then co-citation patterns can be used to map out in great detail the relationships between these key concepts." The reality of science emerges—is constructed—from these representations (Wouters, 1999, p. 129). This, of course, invites the following questions; (a) are the resultant maps reflective of purely ideational interactions, and (b) are citation behaviors normatively governed or idiosyncratic in nature (see Cronin, 1984 for a review of the relevant literature on citer motivation)? More specifically, to what extent do social and psychological factors influence the selection of citations by an author— the citations which become the coordinates of intellectual space? To what extent are social and affective relations inscribed in such maps? To what extent should the intellectual spaces described by citation maps be viewed as *socio*-cognitive spaces?

CAPTURING CITATION IDENTITY AND CITATION IMAGE

Howard White (2001) has undertaken a study of scholars' *recitation* patterns; analyzing the identities of those authors who are cited recurrently by a given author over time. Working with a small sample of information scientists, he attempted to tease out some of the social, collegiate and institutional ties that might influence citation (i.e., intellectual) choices. This kind of authorial exegesis is only possible if one is familiar with both the subject domain and the focal set of authors. White concludes (p. 93) that most members of his sample are "affected by social networks—that is, they cite authors whom they know personally from school, the workplace, or an invisible college (defined as researchers with similar interests who communicate and collaborate although their institutional bases differ and are possibly far apart)." Thus, one's location in intellectual space to some extent reflects one's place in the physical world.

We (Cronin and Shaw, 2001) subsequently employed a variant on White's approach, looking closely at the citation identities (based on 20-years' worth of ISI data) of three information scientists, A, B, C, whom we knew extremely well. We constructed their citation identities (those whom they cited) and their citation images (those who cited them) and looked at the top-25 names on each list. To give a flavor of the findings, A's second most highly cited author was a former doctoral student and faculty colleague. A , in turn, was most frequently cited by this protégé. A knew personally 14 of the 25 names, and had shared an office for two years with one. Among the most frequently cited names by B were four or five former colleagues from another institution; B, in turn, was most highly cited by a former colleague. B's identity included an erstwhile doctoral student. B, to the best of our knowledge, personally knew almost all of those whom he cited, and, in turn, likely knew most of those who cited him. A featured mid-way down B's image-maker list. C most frequently re-cited his doctoral supervisor, who cited him in turn. C's identity list included a former doctoral student. A also featured on C's image-maker list. Late in their careers, A, B and C converged on the same academic department, and the level of mutual referencing increased thereafter. One could go on. The mesh of collegiate and mentor-advisee relationships may typically be imperceptible to most observers, but it is nonetheless real. Physical place and sociality clearly play a role in shaping intellectual spaces, but how might we go about visualizing these social linkages, both weak and strong?

Both these studies suggest that physical presence and professional familiarity are factors that influence citation behavior, though, of course, personal acquaintance is neither a necessary nor sufficient reason to cite an author. That said, the work of one's associates and friends might be more accessible and no less pertinent than the work of others, and thus warrant citation on merit alone. Naturally, we would expect social ties to influence citation behavior. One of the reasons for working together (for setting up collaborations, local or distributed) is to build a common cause, combine talents and resources, energize a collective research agenda, or mobilize a particular paradigm or *Weltanschauung*; in other words, to achieve some kind of multiplier effect, or what economists refer to as returns to specialization. That, of course, is not to say that co-location is synonymous with groupthink. In the illustration above, B, for instance, was part of a widely recognized intellectual group, or "school," but he also had a strong intellectual trajectory of his own. Indeed, B was a boundary spanner/gatekeeper par excellence (more so than either A and C), as we found when we identified the many fields and disciplines from which he harvested citations.

Being together in a shared space, or meeting face-to-face, shapes the intellectual spaces in which scholars' work is located. The central issue has been formulated thus: "Is it primarily *who* citers know (social structure) or *what* they know (intellectual structure)?" (White, Wellman and Nazer, 2004). Of course, things are not quite that simple, as White et al. (2004: 125) concede: "Who you know pays off only if the people you know have something worth knowing—something plainly relevant to your own claims." But unraveling the social dimensions of citation links is still not the whole story. Citations are the most visible part of the influence iceberg; acknowledgments are the part hidden below the water line. Scholastic debts are routinely recorded in a variety of ways; citations just happen to be relatively easy to capture and display. In short, citation-based maps are necessarily partial representations of scholars' interactions and intellectual debts.

TRACKING LOW-VISIBILITY COLLABORATORS

The support networks implicitly described in acknowledgments reinforce the idea that research and scholarship are socially embedded rather than purely individualistic activities. Acknowledgments bear witness to the myriad ties—social, technical, intellectual, affective—that bind scholars together. Indeed, academic writing, as I have argued elsewhere (Cronin, 2004), is a compelling instance of distributed cognition (see Hutchins, 1995), or, to use Andy Clark's (2003: 8) phrase, "an extended cognitive system." The growth in acknowledgments was an important, if underappreciated, development in scholarly publication during the second half of the twentieth century (Cronin, 1995; Cronin, Shaw and La Barre, 2003, 2004). In fields as diverse as astrophysics, chemistry, cell biology and psychology, almost every scientific paper includes (often substantive) expressions of gratitude to a distributed population of peers, informal collaborators and trusted assessors; individuals whose material contributions (technical, instrumental, etc.) and/or conceptual inputs to the work being reported have apparently made a difference to the work being reported. Scientists are connected, socio-technically, and with the progressive "collectivization of academic science" (Etzkowitz and Kemelgor, 1998)—what John Ziman (2000) has termed "post-academic" science—those distributed socio-technical networks will both increase and intensify. As Randall Collins (2003: 150) put it recently: "Rapid-discovery scientists have always owed their reputations, and their ability to make new discoveries, to being connected to evolving generations of equipment...Modern science has always been a cyborg network in this sense."

Collaboration in science is often investigated via co-authorship, yet co-authorship data do not comprehensively capture scholars' functional interdependence. If the intellectual structure of fields is to be mapped with fidelity, then acknowledgment data should, strictly speaking, be taken into account. More specifically, we would want to look at the geographic spread of trusted assessors to further determine the influence of physical space on patterns of both intra- and inter-disciplinary collaboration.

CONCLUSIONS

The conceptual spaces defined by authors' citation behaviors mirror the importance (modest or otherwise) of physical proximity and personal acquaintanceship in shaping patterns of information exchange and knowledge diffusion. It is clear that physical proximity does play some kind of role, direct or indirect, in molding citation behavior, even if the conduits and connections are typically unseen to all but privileged insiders or bibliometric researchers. Of course, it is hardly surprising, to return to our earlier example, that if A, B and C are collocated in the same department, and have cognate or converging research interests, that those latent ties should become manifest, resulting in greater intra-group exchange of resources, ideas and citations over time. A shared physical site (lab, office complex) or virtual space (collaboratory, listserv) can act as an incubator or accelerator of ideas, which, of course, is precisely why we attend professional conferences and engage in computer-mediated communication with our peers. One is not here referring to the forging of purely personal, or "content-neutral" (White et al., 2004, p. 125) ties, but the natural co-development of social and professional relationships and practices in and across work places and work spaces—"epistemic cultures," when aggregated, to use Knorr Cetina's (1999) term.

The physical collocation of scholars and researchers spawns trusting and "knowable communities" (Brown and Duguid, 2000: 169), a phenomenon that has been observed in a variety of contexts. For instance, Eric von Hippel (1987) has described patterns of informal know-how trading between (competing) firms and Robert Allen (1983) has identified a complementary phenomenon, namely, "collective invention." The importance of social networks to innovation is now widely recognized. In recent years, the significance of industry clusters (think of Silicon Valley or Silicon Glen) has been analyzed intensively in the business strategy and economic development literature, most notably by Michael Porter (e.g., Porter, 1998). The evidence shows that geographic concentration of interconnected companies can create local, regional or national comparative advantage. Something similar appears to hold in academia, where the space of place (research sites, science parks) and the space of knowledge flows are tightly linked.

My colleague Katy Börner's (2003) goal is to help create a 'Map of Science' screensaver in the tradition of ISI's prototypical *Atlas of Science*. Such an interface might get close to answering Otlet's question: "How could the intellectual domains be adequately, continuously mapped?" (quoted in Rayward, 1992: 59). Börner envisages an automatically updated, 2-D, layered map based on data fed from all major publication, patent and grant funding databases. Users would be provided with a global overview of topic areas, data on the size and composition of fields, evidence of disciplinary emergence and merging, bird's-eye views of specific knowledge domains, highly-influential papers, funding flows, etc. Such a development would be of practical value not only to career scientists but also science policy analysts, sociologists, and historians of science.

It is an attractive notion, but despite advances in information visualization, present generation toolsets and techniques cannot capture the biographical substrate of scholars' communicative practices, the complex webs of collegiate relationships and "patronage networks" (Baber, 2003: 96) that interleave with the purely cognitive ties to create the double helix of scholarly communication. "Social translucence" (Erickson, et al., 2002) may be attainable within small, clearly bounded work groups, but it is hard to see how such a goal could be achieved in the unbounded world of scholarly communication. The social ties that bind scholars are often implicit, imperceptible and evanescent. In exceptional cases it may be possible to generate "thick description" (Geertz, 1973) of a kind that would faithfully describe the admixture of social, affective and scholastic ties that exist within and between communities of scholars, but, again, scalability remains a seemingly insurmountable obstacle. Indeed, it may well be that the "infrasociality" of science, to borrow Knorr Cetina's (1999: 13) term, is practicably indescribable. Having said that, there is value in recognizing, theoretically, its existence even if it is effectively impossible to separate, observationally, intellectual networks from socio-cognitive interactions.

And even if large-scale socio-cognitive mapping of science were technically feasible, it seems improbable that these forensic tools would reveal, to use White et al.'s (2004: 125) vivid metaphor, "an orgy of back scratching." But that is no reason for not trying to conceptualize and develop innovative tools (e.g., a "social search engine" [Barabási, 2003:. 39]) to harvest and graphically display socio-cognitive influences within and across disciplines. Such visualizations would certainly bring us closer to generating high-fidelity maps of scholarly trade routes and to understanding how social relations, forged in physical space, are reflected in the architecture of intellectual spaces. Whether greater understanding of the social components of scholarly collaboration could ever lead to productive science policy interventions, beyond the known and the simple, is unclear, but the question is at least worth considering.

ACKNOWLEDGMENTS

I am grateful to Katy Börner, Elisabeth Davenport, Yvonne Rogers, Debora Shaw and the anonymous reviewers for their comments on earlier drafts.

REFERENCES

Allen, R. C. (1983). Collective invention. *Journal of Economic Behaviour and Organization*, 4, 1-24.

Allen, T. J. (1969). Information needs and uses. In: Cuadra, C. (Ed.). *Annual Review of Information Science and Technology*, 4. Chicago: Encyclopaedia Britannica, 3-29.

Baber, Z. (2003). The taming of science and technology studies. *Social Epistemology*, 17(2and3), 95-98.

Barabási, A.-L. (2003). *Linked: How Everything is Linked to Everything Else and What It Means for Business, Science, and Everyday Life*. New York: Plume

Boisot, M. H. (1999). *Knowledge Assets: Securing Competitive Advantage in the Information Economy*. Oxford: OUP.

Boisot, M. H. (1995). *Information Space: A Framework for Learning in Organizations, Institutions and Culture*. London: Routledge.

Börner, K. (2003). Towards a cartographic map that shows the evolution of knowledge domains. Paper presented at the *99th Annual Meeting of the Association of American Geographers*.

Börner, K., Chen, C. and Boyack, K. W. (2003). Visualizing knowledge domains. In: Cronin, B. (Ed.). *Annual Review of Information Science and Technology*, 37. Medford, NJ: ASIST/Information Today Inc., 179-255.

Boyd, D., Lee, H.-Y., Ramage, D. and Donath, J. (2002). Developing legible visualizations for online social spaces. In: *Proceedings of the Hawai'i International Conference on System Sciences*, January 7-10, Big Island, Hawaii.

Brown, J. S. and Duguid, P. (2000). *The Social Life of Information*. Boston, MA: Harvard Business School Press.

Castells, M. (2000). *The Rise of the Network Society*. Oxford: Blackwell. 2nd ed.

Christensen, C. M. (2000). *The Innovator's Dilemma: When New Technologies Cause Great Firms to Fail*. Cambridge, MA: Harvard Business School Press.

Clark, A. (2003). *Natural-born Cyborgs*. Oxford: OUP.

Collins, R. (2003). Fuller, Kuhn, and the emergent attention space of reflexive studies of science. *Social Epistemology*, 17 (2and3), 147-152.

Crane, D. (1972). *Invisible Colleges: Diffusion of Knowledge in Scientific Communities*. Chicago: University of Chicago Press.

Cronin, B. (2004). Bowling alone together: Academic writing as distributed cognition. *Journal of the American Society for Information Science and Technology*, 55(6), 557-560.

Cronin, B. (1995). *The Scholar's Courtesy: The Role of Acknowledgement in the Primary Communication Process*. London: Taylor Graham.

Cronin, B. (1984). *The Citation Process: The Role and Significance of Citations in Scientific Communication*. London: Taylor Graham.

Cronin, B. and Atkins, H. B. (Eds.) (2000). *The Web of Knowledge: A Festschrift in Honor of Eugene Garfield*. Medford, NJ: Information Today, Inc. ASIS Monograph Series.

Cronin, B. and Shaw, D. (2001). Identity-creators and image-makers: using citation analysis and thick description to put authors in their place. *Scientometrics*, 54(1), 31-49.

Cronin, B., Shaw, D. and La Barre, K. (2004). Visible, less visible, and invisible work: patterns of collaboration in twentieth century chemistry. *Journal of the American Society for Information Science and Technology*, 55(2), 160-168.

Cronin, B. Shaw, D. and La Barre, K. (2003). A cast of thousands. Co-authorship and sub-authorship collaboration in the twentieth century as manifested in the scholarly literature of psychology and philosophy. *Journal of the American Society for Information Science and Technology*, 54(9), 855-871.

Davenport, E. and Cronin, B. (2000). The citation network as a prototype for representing trust in virtual environments. In: Cronin, B. and Atkins, H. B. (Eds.). *The Web of Knowledge: A Festschrift in Honor of Eugene Garfield*. Medford, NJ: Information Today, Inc. ASIS Monograph Series, 517-534.

Davenport, E. and Cronin, B. (1990). Hypertext and the conduct of science. *Journal of Documentation*, 46(3), 175-192.

Dourish, P. (2001). *Where the Action Is: The Foundations of Embodied Interaction*. Cambridge, MA: MIT Press.

Dourish, P. (2001). Seeking a foundation for context-aware computing. *Human-Computer Interaction*, 16(2-3).

Erickson, T., Halverson, C., Kellogg. W. A., Laff, M. and Wolf, T. (2002). Social translucence: designing social infrastructures that make collective activity visible. Available at: http://www.pliant.org/personal/Tom_Erickson/Soc_Infrastructures.html

Etzkowitz, H. and Kemelgor, C. (1998). The role of research centres in the collectivisation of academic science. *Minerva*, 36(3), 271-288.

Garfield, E. (1955). Citation indexes for science: A new dimension in documentation through association of ideas. *Science*, 122, 108-111.

Geertz, C. (1973). Thick description; Toward an interpretative theory of culture. In: *The Interpretation of Culture*. New York: basic Books.

Gladwell, M. (2002). *The Tipping Point: How Little Things Can Make a Big Difference*. New York: Back Pay Books.

Heimeriks, G. and van den Besselaar, P. (2002). *State of the Art in Bbliometrics and Webometrics*. Available at: http://www.eicstes.org/EICSTES_PDF/Deliverables/

Hepworth, M. (1989). *Geography of the Information Economy*. London: Bellhaven Press.

Hutchins, E. (1995). *Cognition in the Wild*. Cambridge, MA. MIT Press.

Katz, J. S. (1994). Geographic proximity and scientific collaboration. *Scientometrics*, 31(1), 31-43.

King, D. W., Griffiths, J.-M., Sweet, E. A., and Wiederkehr, R. R. V. (1984). *A Study of the Value of Information and the Effect of Value of Intermediary Organizations, Timeliness of Services and Products, and Comprehensiveness of the EDB [Energy Data Base]*. Rockville, MD: King Research Inc. Report submitted to the Office of Scientific and Technical Information, U.S. Department of Energy, Oakridge, Tennessee.

Knorr Cetina, K. (1999). *Epistemic Cultures: How the Sciences Make Knowledge Work*. Cambridge, MA: Harvard University Press.

Koku, E., Nazer, N. and Wellman, B. (2001). Netting scholars: Online and offline. *American Behavioral Scientist*, 44(10), 1750-1772.

Lin, X., White, H. D. and Buzydlowski, J. (2003). Real-time author co-citation mapping for online searching. *Information Processing and Management*, 39(5), 689-706.

Odlyzko, A. (2002). The rapid evolution of scholarly communication. *Learned Publishing*, 15(1), 7-19.

Page, L., Brin, S., Motwani, R. and Winograd, T. (1998) *The PageRank citation ranking: Bringing order to the Web*. Technical report, Stanford Digital Library Technologies Project. Stanford University.

Porter, M. E. (1998, November-December). Clusters: The new economics of competition. *Harvard Business Review*, 77-90.

Price, D. J. de Solla. (1965). Networks of scientific papers. *Science*, 149, 510-515.

Putnam, R. D. (2000). *Bowling Alone: The Collapse and Revival of American Community*. New York: Simon and Schuster.

Rayward, W. B. (1992). Restructuring and mobilizing information in documents: a historical perspective. In; Vakkari, P. and Cronin, B. (Eds.). *Conceptions of Library and Information Science: Historical, Empirical and Theoretical Perspectives*. London: Taylor Graham, 50-68.

Salton, G., Wong, A., and Yang, C.S. (1975). A Vector Space Model for automatic indexing. *Communications of the ACM*, 18(11), 613-620.

Skupin, A. (2002). A cartographic approach to visualizing conference abstracts. *IEEE Computer Graphics and Applications*, 22(1), 50-58.

Skupin, A. (2000). From metaphor to method: cartographic perspectives on information visualization. *Proceedings of the IEEE Symposium on Information Visualization 2000 (InfoVis2000)*. Los Alamitos, CA: IEEE CS Press, 91-97.

Small, H. (1973). Co-citation in the scientific literature: A new measure of the relationship between two documents. *Journal of the American Society for Information Science*, 24(4), 265-269.

Suchman, L. (1987). *Plans and Situated Actions: The Problem of Human-Machine Communication*. Cambridge: Cambridge University Press.

Thelwall, M., Vaughan, L. and Björeborn, L. (2005, in press). Webometrics. In: Cronin, B. (Ed.). *Annual Review of Information Science and Technology*. Medford, NJ: Information Today, Inc.

Von Hippel, E. (1987). Cooperation between rivals: informal know-how trading, *Research Policy*, 16, 291-302

White, H. D. (2001). Authors as citers over time. *Journal of the American Society for Information Science and Technology*, 52(2), 87-108.

White, H. D. and McCain, K. W. (1998). Visualizing a discipline: An author co-citation analysis of information science, 1972-1995. *Journal of the American Society for Information Science*, 49(4), 327-355.

White, H. D. and McCain, K. W. (1997). Visualization of literatures. In: Williams, M. E. (Ed.). *Annual Review of Information Science and Technology*, 32, Medford, NJ: ASIS/Information Today Inc., 99-168.

White, H. D., Wellman, B. and Nazer, N. (2004). Does citation reflect social structure?: Longitudinal evidence from the 'Globenet' interdisciplinary research group. *Journal of the American Society for Information Science and Technology*, 55(2), 111-126.

Williams, J. G., Sochats, K. M. and Morse, E. (1995). Visualization. In: Williams, M. E. (Ed.). *Annual Review of Information Science and Technology*, 30. Medford, NJ: ASIS/Information Today Inc., 161-207.

Wouters, P. (1999). *The Citation Culture*. University of Amsterdam. Ph.D. thesis.

Ziman, J. (2000). *Real Science*. Cambridge: Cambridge University Press.

Zook, M. A. (2003). Underground globalization: mapping the space of flows of the Internet adult industry. *Environment and Planning*, 35, 1261-1286.

AFFILIATIONS

Rudy Professor of Information Science, Indiana University, Bloomington
Visiting Professor, School of Computing, Napier University, Edinburgh.

JULIAN WARNER

10. ESCAPE FROM SURFACE AND LINEARITY

INTRODUCTION

In a passage of English prose whose apparent complexity is only matched by its incisive simplicity once grasped, Samuel Johnson commented on the difficulty for a lexicographer of logically representing etymologies and historical transformations of meaning in linear form: 'When the radical idea branches out into parallel ramifications, how can a consecutive series be formed of senses in their nature collateral?' (Johnson, 1755a: 15). In his own *A Dictionary of the English Language*, the non-linear term *network* is also extravagantly defined, in a manner which has been criticised for being more complex than the term defined:

Network. n.s. [net and work.] Any thing reticulated or decussated, at equal distances, with interstices between the intersections.

Johnson, 1755b: 263

The definition could also be reads as an allusion to the network nature of language, with complex and shifting relations between its constituent semantic entities, such as words and phrases (Johnson, 1755a: 14). At the origin of modern linguistics, Saussure also used the metaphor of a network to characterise a language and its internal semantic relations. In a specific analogy to Johnson's implied contrast between linearity and a network of relations, Saussure distinguished the paradigm, or the associations a term acquires when considered outside its context in discourse, from the syntagm, the stream of speech or line of writing which gives a specific meaning to a word by its proximate context (Saussure, 1916). A further analogue could be drawn from information theory, which distinguished the messages available for selection in a source, broadly comparable to the paradigm, from the message selected in accord with known combinative constraints, more closely comparable to the syntagm (Shannon, 1948). All three procedures, the transformation of etymologies and historical senses into an attempted linear sequence, choice from the paradigm to construct a syntagm, or selection of possible messages from a source to form a specific message, involve the transformation of a complex network into a linear sequence.

In historical experience, the stream of oral speech over time was transformed in to the line of writing arranged across a surface. The activity of language, and more clearly evidenced and understood, the understanding of what a language is, was changed by that transformation. For instance, the idea of a language as a lexicon and

P. Turner and E. Davenport (Eds.), Spaces, Spatiality and Technology, 129-138.

rules for combination emerged. In earlier historical practice, the process of counting extended over time and producing number had been transformed into quantity extended over space and often expressed as a line, but with a less restricted understanding of linearity than for written language (Childe, 1956: 91; Harris, 1986). One effect of the transformation of oral speech into the line of writing was the possibility of verbatim copying of extended passages and precise comparison or collation of the sequences produced.

Late 19th and mid- to late-20th century transitions in methods of communication and data analysis have refocused attention on the transition from primary orality to literacy and have themselves been referred to as secondary orality (Ong, 1982). The 19th century technologies of the telephone and telegraph allowed for the transmission of written messages and then the human voice, rapidly over space. Late 19th and 20th century technologies for data transformation, increasingly concentrated in the computer as a universal information machine (Warner, 2004), have enabled a capacity for collation and comparison beyond that offered by the written or printed document. Different parts of the line of writing can by systematically compared and distributed but formally identical verbal forms recovered from a range of documents.

An epistemological effect associated with the transition from orality to literacy was the possibility of enhanced exactness. An effect of more recent and current transitions is of further exactness, coupled with a revelation of inexactness and inconsistency in the objects subjected to scrutiny (Warner, 2001). The specific mechanisms enabling the enhancement of exactness have not yet been identified, but the possibility offered by the line of writing, and then modern technologies operating on the line of writing, for collation and comparison might be one such mechanism.

Two separately developed discourses, both stimulated by current transitions in information and communication technology (ICT), have isolated a crucial consideration for understanding the epistemological effects of transitions in technology. Similar questions have been explicitly formulated from a historical perspective on communication, specifically the history of writing, and are emerging from a view of ICT as a human construction.

From a historical perspective on communication, the position formulated by Ong (1982; 1986) in relation to orality and literacy, that writing is technology which restructures thought, has been critiqued and transformed, made both more extensive and more precise. Ong's position is regarded as a particular instance of a more general proposition that 'all new intellectual tools restructure thought'. A more precisely formulated and satisfying question is then developed: 'how does *this* innovation make possible or foster forms of thought which were previously difficult or impossible?' (Harris, 1995, p.166). Wittgenstein's remark that, 'without language we cannot ... build roads and machines' (Wittgenstein, 1953, §491), provides a link to considerations derived from studies of technology, rather than directly from a historical perspective on communication.

A view of ICT as a radical human construction, *'organs of the human brain, created by the human hand*; the power of knowledge objectified' (Marx, 1973, p.706), has been developed from a Marxian perspective on productive technologies. ICT is contrasted with productive technology by its concern with the transformation of signals rather than of natural resources into useful goods and services (Warner, 2004). Marx noted that industrial technology did not simply save or substitute for human physical labour, but expanded human powers and activities:

> for, with the help of machinery, human labour performs actions and creates things which without it would be absolutely impossible of accomplishment

Marx, 1973: 389

ICTs need not, then, simply substitute for human mental labour but can extend human mental capacities. A similarly precise question can then be developed, how does this particular information technology extend human mental labour and capacities, in ways which were previously difficult or impossible?

The convergence of considerations between separately developing discourses is indicative of the significance of the issues identified. In an anticipation of the explicit formulation of the question, an enhanced capacity for exactness has been suggested as a crucial feature of though enabled and encouraged by current transitions in ICTs. Exactness is understood as control of complexity and the ability to make precise distinctions, including the comparison of verbal forms through retrieval and for collation and textual analysis. Written language had enabled more exactness than was possible from oral forms alone and modern ICTs, particularly computation on textual objects, enhanced the possibility of exactness, often revealing the inconsistencies of artefacts previously received as self-consistent (Warner, 2001).

In Bacon's original formulation, 'writing [maketh] an exact man' (Bacon, 1597), exactness is understood as a change in the consciousness of the writer, through the process of writing. That change in consciousness may result in more exact and self-consistent verbal products. Surface, on the understanding here, is a given for the process of writing and the line primarily a product rather than a process. Both the surface and the line may reenter the process of writing, as mechanisms with retroactive and reinforcing effects on exactness in consciousness.

Surface, in this context, is primarily understood as a surface for inscription, which can be either naturally given, such as the surface of earth or rock, or humanly constructed from natural materials, such as a clay tablet, vellum, or sheet of paper. The surface of tapestry, produced by weaving lines together, is not the focus of concern. The Euclidean plane is regarded as an abstraction from the natural or humanly created surface, preserving the historical order in which geometry as land-surveying preceded philosophical concerns with ideal geometric forms.

The line is primarily understood as humanly made by purposeful activity on a surface, the line of the plough on the earth or of writing across a surface. Lines inscribed on a plane surface have to conform with certain conditions for intersection (which may be related to the constraints on the possibilities of iconic representation of Boolean logical combinations). The primary concern will be with the line of written language and its epistemological possibilities and constraints.

Line of writing

The line of written language, extended over space and across a surface, offers different epistemological possibilities for investigation to the stream of oral speech, occurring and disappearing over time. Comparisons between different copies of a single text and between occurrences of word forms at different points in a text are enabled. These activities, formalized as bibliographic collation, can in turn enable enhanced exactness, in the sense of isolating differences between texts and attempting to construct an authoritative version. Linearity and fixed extension across a surface, rather than fluid iteration over time, can then be used to increase exactness, reinforcing the exactness associated with writing in human consciousness (Warner, 2001).

Collation can be conducted with the help of an oral reading of a copy text, coupled with attentive listening, and this would have been the case in mid-19th century legal practices:

> It is, of course, an indispensable part of a scrivener's business to verify the accuracy of his copy, word by word. Where there are two or more scriveners in an office, they assist each other in this examination, one reading from the copy, the other holding the original. It is a very dull, wearisome, and lethargic affair. I can readily imagine that, to some sanguine temperaments, it would be altogether intolerable. For example, I cannot credit that the mettlesome poet, Byron, would have contentedly sat down with Bartleby to examine a law document of, say five hundred pages, closely written in a crimpy hand.

> Melville, 1853: 24-25

With more individualistic scholarly work, collation may be conducted by silent and individual comparison. An authority text would characteristically be constructed, both from an oral reading and from silent comparison.

The authority text constructed may still contain errors, some of which may be connected with linearity itself. The length of the line of writing can complicate comparisons between two versions of a verbal text or different parts of a single text. Characteristically a map or index of occurrences of word forms would be constructed as an intermediate step towards a more consistent (either with itself or with other copies) text. The processes of construction of comparisons and of creation of a further line of writing are themselves open to error.

The constraints of the linearity of the printed written form have been sensed, although more prominently with regard to their limited representational possibilities than the difficulties of collation. For instance, the difficulty of connecting senses of words for lexicographic definitions can be more fully recalled from Johnson's prefatory comments:

> In every word of extensive use, it was requisite to mark the progress of its meaning, and show by what gradations of intermediate sense it has passed from its primitive to its remote and accidental signification; so that every foregoing explanation should tend to that which follows, and the series be regularly concatenated from the first notion to the last.

This is specious, but not always practicable; kindred senses may be so interwoven, that the perplexity cannot be disentangled, nor any reason be assigned why one should be ranged before the other. When the radical idea branches out into parallel ramifications, how can a consecutive series be formed of senses in their nature collateral?

Johnson, 1775a: 15

In the conversion of the dictionary to electronic form, the constraints of the linearity of the printed written form were partly reduced, with cross-references are as easily traversed as a linear progression. Cross-referencing from transcription to facsimile is marked by a stylised drawing of a camera, exemplifying the conjunction of written verbal with iconic signs which is becoming increasingly familiar (McDermott, 1996; Warner, 1997).

Darwin's *Origin of Species* is permeated by analogies between the geological record discovered and the page of writing. These analogies are made explicit at one point in Darwin's discussion:

I look at the natural geological record, as a history of the world imperfectly kept, and written in a changing dialect; of this history we possess the last volume alone, relating only to two or three countries. Of this volume, only here and there a short chapter has been preserved; and of each page, only here and there a few lines. Each word of the slowly-changing language, in which the history is supposed to be written, being more or less different in the interrupted succession of chapters, may represent the apparently abruptly changed forms of life, entombed in our consecutive, but widely separated formations.

Darwin, 1859: 316

The comparison is with a written record which cannot be interrogated, not with dialogue with a speaker, and geological record is conceived as series of surfaces or layers arranged over time.

For writing on, rather than reading from, a surface, the difficulty of representing relations between genera and species in a linear fashion is acutely sensed by Darwin:

this natural arrangement is shown, as is possible on paper, in the diagram, but in much too simple a manner. If a branching diagram had not been used, and only the names of the groups had been written in a linear series, it would have been still less possible to have given a natural arrangement; and it is notoriously not possible to represent in a series, on a flat surface, the affinities which we discover in nature amongst the beings of the same group.

Darwin, 1859: 405-406

In the reference to 'much too simple a manner', a danger, sensed in other contexts, can be detected, that the diagram can given too definite an appearance to a description which could be verbally qualified. The reference also intimates the possibility that, while the surface has a greater representational capacity than the line, it may have limitations of its own.

Both Johnson and Darwin, then, sense the constraints of linearity, and, in Darwin's case, make use of the greater representational capacity of the surface. In the complaint of constraints and the use of surface to escape these constraints can be sensed a dialectic development: the line is humanly constructed, imposed upon a surface, offers representational and epistemological possibilities beyond oral discourse extended over time, but then encounters its own epistemological and representational limitations.

Surface

The surface offers a resource whose representational capacity exceeds that of the line. Writing distributed across a surface, rather than restricted to a continuous line, has been recognised as superior to oral speech for the spaced presentation of forms that cannot easily be read aloud, such as lists, tables, branchings, and other graphic configurations. Inscriptions, in the epigraphic sense of marks inscribed upon a hard surface, and handwritten and printed documents, have all made use of these representational techniques and possibilities.

A particularly relevant association can be made between arrangement on a surface and logical symbolism and rationality in consciousness. In the mid- and late-19th century, diagrammatic forms began further to supplement and displace verbal forms of logic. The logic machines concurrently and subsequently constructed, and their descendant in the computer, operate on principles closely related to the diagrammatic representations (Gardner, 1983, pp.78-79). Diagrams, rather than linear presentations, for logical analysis are traceable to the Aristotelian tradition and were noticed by Augustine:

> When I was only about twenty years of age Aristotle's book on the 'Ten Categories' came into my hands. Whenever my teacher at Carthage and others who were reputed to be scholars mentioned this book, their cheeks would swell with self-importance, so that the title alone was enough to make me stand agape, as though I were posed over some wonderful divine mystery. I managed to read it and understand it without help, though I now ask myself what advantage I gained from doing so. Other people told me that they had understood only with difficulty, after the most learned masters had not only explained it to them but also illustrated it with a wealth of diagrams. But when I discussed it with them I found that they could tell me no more about it than I had already discovered by reading it on my own.

Augustine, 398: 87-88; § IV.16

The accompanying use of letters rather than constant words has been considered to give rise to formal logic (Bochenski, 1961, p.69). The surface, like the line, can then be associated with rationality, particularly its more developed logical forms. The surface still has certain representational limitations, not well adapted to the representation of complex networks for instance (allusion has already been made to the known limitations on the iconic representation of Boolean intersections on a surface).

Falling through surface

Escaping the representational limitations of the line and of the surface may involve a fall into a network of less rational, or even irrational, associations. Alice's entry into Wonderland is paradigmatic of this:

when suddenly a White Rabbit with pink eyes ran close by her. There was nothing so *very* remarkable in that; nor did Alice think it so *very* much out of the way to hear the Rabbit say to itself 'Oh dear! Oh dear! I shall be too late' ... In another moment down went Alice after it, never once considering how in the world she was to get out again. The rabbit-hole went straight on like a tunnel for some way, and then dipped suddenly down, so suddenly that Alice had not a moment to think about stopping herself before she found herself falling down what seemed to be a very deep well.

Carroll, 1865: 10

Analogously in *Hard Times*, Stephen Blackpool fall through the forest floor, which can itself be reads as an image for language or texture of the parts of the novel counterposed to the rigid descriptions and categorisations associated with Coketown (Dickens, 1854). Falling through the surface is simultaneously an exit from the novel, an ending, although not a conclusion, to an issue which cannot be resolved by liberal philanthropy.

The process of computation was classically modelled as operations on a line extended across a surface (Warner, 1994). The theoretical conceptualisation of the computational process preceded, and to some extent, may have informed, its practical realisation (Davis, 2000). Greater control of complexity can be enabled by its practical realisation in an appropriately programmed computer. In modern practice, any part of the notional line can be operated on and compared with another part, enabling collation and comparison. The line could extend across a bewildering variety and number of equivalent previous surfaces.

The empirical realisation of the possibility of traversing the line has taken, and may continue to take, different forms, when the line traversed is understood as the line of written language. A search for orthographically identical or related forms across a collection of documents enables comparison of the varying contexts and sense for a word. The skeuomorphism associated with new media, whereby existing media are both inherited and taken as models, has provided a particularly revealing analogue in hypertext. In pursuing hypertext links, we fall through the surface of the document represented on a computer screen into a network of associations. From the perspective developed here, hypertext can be seen as one, but only one, significant realisation of the underlying theoretical possibilities.

Verbal text subject to computer storage and indexing has escaped from the constraints of linearity and of the surface. Identical or similar word forms within or between documents can be collated, regardless of the length of the line of writing.

What are the possible epistemological effects of the escape from linearity and surface? The transition from oral to oral and written communication enabled greater exactness, including the collation of texts. The line and surface functioned as mechanisms, with retroactive effects on human consciousness, for enhancing exactness and enabling the production of more self-consistent products. Current information technologies enable both enhanced exactness, in escaping the constraints of linearity, and greater fluidity, in continually allowing fall through surfaces. One crucial effect is to reveal inexactness in artefacts previously accepted as complete and self-consistent. We could be said to be at the end of the epoch of the illusion of the possibility of exactness.

The significance to be attached to the loss of the illusion of exactness may depend on how deceived we were by the illusion. Significant, if neglected, thinkers have recognised exact methods as an illusion when applied to the process of scientific discovery:

> which of these two roads [inductive or deductive] was reached the most momentous and sublime of all truths – the truth, the fact, of gravitation? Newton deduced it from the laws of Kepler. Kepler admitted that those laws he guessed ... Yes, these vital laws, Kepler guessed, that is to say, he imagined them.

Poe, 1848: 14

The philosophy of science offers an analogous, but more widely diffused, distinction between the context of discovery and the context of justification. The impulse towards exactness in human consciousness, encouraged by writing, may draw upon untidy processes and materials to create exact products. Current instruments of intellectual labour enable an enhanced control of complexity and the creation of self-consistent products. Exerting control over complexity may reveal previously hidden inconsistencies, for instance, disparate terminologies at different points in the line. Products may be made self-consistent more readily on a syntactic or formal than a semantic level, which might involve attempting to ensure consistency of meaning across formally identical, but widely distributed, word forms.

In an allusion to the physical character of the novel as a book, Jane Austen remarked on 'the tell-tale compression of the pages before them, that we are all hastening together to perfect felicity' (Austen, 1817: 250). In an edited collection, the end of an article is intimated more by its length and approaching references.

The line, and then the surface, have been identified as mechanisms, which have both encouraged exactness in human consciousness and enabled its application to semiotic products. The representational limitations of the line for dealing with complexity, particularly hierarchies and networks of relations have been encountered and the greater representational possibilities of the surface explored. In turn, human activity on the surface creates and encounters its own constraints. Escaping the constraints of linearity and surface, through modern information technologies, both enables enhanced control of complexity and revelation of previously unknown inconsistencies.

REFERENCES

Augustine. 398, *Confessions*, 1961, translated by R. S. Pine-Coffin, Penguin Group, London etc..

Austen, J. 1817, *Northanger Abbey*, first published 1817, in J. Austen, *Northanger Abbey and Persuasion* (The Oxford Illustrated Jane Austen), 1989, edited by R. W. Chapman, Oxford University Press, Oxford etc.

Bacon, F. 1597, 'Of studies', in F. Bacon, *The essays*. Edited with an introduction by John Pitcher, 1985. Penguin Books, Harmondsworth, Middlesex and New York.

Bochenski, I.M. 1961, *History of formal logic*, translated by I. Thomas, Notre Dame, Indiana.

Carroll, L. 1865, *Alice's adventures in wonderland*, first published 1865, in L. Carroll, *Alice's adventures in wonderland, and, Through the looking-glass and what Alice found there*, 1998, edited with an introduction and notes by H. Haughton, Penguin Books, London etc..

Childe, V.G. 1956, *Society and Knowledge*, George Allen & Unwin, London.

Darwin, C. 1859, *The origin of species by means of natural selection or The preservation of favoured races in the struggle for life*, first published by John Murray 1859, 1968, edited with an introduction by J.W. Burrow, Penguin Group, London etc..

Davis, M. 2000, *The universal computer: the road from Leibniz to Turing*, W.W. Norton, New York.

Dickens, C. 1854, *Hard Times*, first published 1854, 1989, Oxford University Press, Oxford and New York.

Gardner, M. 1983, *Logic machines and diagrams*, 2nd edition, Harvester, Brighton.

Harris, R. 1986, *The origin of writing*, Duckworth, London.

Harris, R. 1995, *Signs of writing*, Routledge, London and New York.

Johnson, S. 1755a, 'Preface to the Dictionary', in E.L. McAdam and G. Milne (eds), *Johnson's dictionary: a modern selection*, 1982, Macmillan, London and Basingstoke, pp.3-29.

Johnson, S. 1755b, *Johnson's dictionary: a modern selection*, edited by E.L. McAdam and G. Milne, 1982, Macmillan, London and Basingstoke.

Marx, K. 1973, *Grundrisse: foundations of the critique of political economy (Rough draft)*, translation published in Pelican Books, 1973, 1993, translated with a foreword by M. Nicolaus, Penguin Books in association with New Left Review, Harmondsworth.

McDermott, A. (ed), 1996, Samuel Johnson. *A dictionary of the English language on CD-ROM: the first and fourth editions*, Cambridge University Press in association with the University of Birmingham, Cambridge.

Melville, H. 1853, 'Bartleby: a tale of Wall Street', first published 1853, in H. Melville, *The complete shorter fiction*, 1997, New York, Alfred A. Knopf, pp.18-51.

Ong, W.J. 1982, *Orality and literacy: the technologizing of the word*, Methuen, London and New York.

Ong, W.J. 1986, 'Writing is a technology that restructures thought', in G. Baumann (ed.), *The written word: literacy in transition* (Wolfson College Lectures 1985), Clarendon Press, Oxford, pp.23-50.

Poe, E.A. 1848, *Eureka: an essay on the material and spiritual universe*, first published 1848, 2002, Hesperus Press, London.

Saussure, F. 1916, *Course in general linguistics*, first published 1916, 1983, ed. C. Bally and A. Sechehaye with the collaboration of A. Riedlinger, trans. and annotated R. Harris, London, Duckworth.

Shannon, C.E. 1948, 'A mathematical theory of communication', first published 1948, in C.E. Shannon, *Collected papers*, 1993, edited by N.J.A. Sloane & A.D. Wyner, IEEE Press, Piscataway, NJ, pp.5-83

Warner, J. 1994, *From writing to computers*, Routledge, London and New York.

Warner, J. 1997, 'Review of Samuel Johnson. A dictionary of the English language on CD-ROM', *Journal of Documentation*, vol.53, no.5, pp.558-561.

Warner, J. 2001, 'Not the exact words . . . : writing, computing, and exactness', in J. Warner, *Information, knowledge, text*, Scarecrow Press, Lanham, Maryland, pp.33-46.

Warner, J. 2004, 'Organs of the human brain, created by the human hand: toward an understanding of information technology', in J. Warner. *Humanizing information technology*, Scarecrow Press, Lanham, Maryland, pp.5-35.

Wittgenstein, L. 1953, *Philosophical investigations*, first published 1953, 1988, translated by G.E.M. Anscombe. Basil Blackwell, Oxford.

RONALD E. DAY

11. "SURFACE": MATERIAL INFRASTRUCTURE FOR SPACE

INTRODUCTION

Conceptual analyses operating in largely, so-called, "empirical," "quantitative" fields in the social sciences have several functions. They may trace the development of an idea through history or synchronically across different institutional practices. They may critically analyze foundational concepts used in empirical studies. And, finally conceptual analyses may be used toward the deployment of new concepts used for further study. These roles cannot be performed empirically and must be done conceptually. This chapter engages in the last approach and does so with an eye toward developing an ontology and an epistemology of agency following an expressionistic philosophy. It develops a model of agency and structure using the concept of "surface" to articulate the strata through which agency comes to be and structure is created. The notion of "surface" gives a materialist understanding to human agency in space. Surfaces express agency as material events and express structure according to repetitions and folds. Surfaces may be defined as the material grounds through which agencies gain and exhibit expressions in manners appropriate to their potentials. They may also be considered as contributors to the future potential of agencies. "Surface" denotes a materialist, rather than a structuralist, interpretation of "context," which is understood as a constitutive and formal, rather than as a strictly efficient and determinate, cause of expression.

AGENCY

The concept of "surface" is important for considering problems of space, foremost, that of agency, its expressions, and accompanying "internal" and "external" forces and structures. Though the problem of agency in space has lately been exhaustively studied in empirical studies relating users to various technologies and physical structures, a more fundamental exploration of what it means for agency to express itself through corporeal and incorporeal bodies is needed. A topological concept such as "surface" can help us to conceptualize the relation between agency and social structure from the viewpoint of measure and directionality and mediations that both allow and restrict the freedom and expressions of agencies. This chapter falls into two parts: in the first part, I examine the agent's expression and social emergence through incorporeal and corporeal material surfaces; in the second part I look at various qualities of such surfaces. If the first part follows the relation of

P. Turner and E. Davenport (Eds.), Spaces, Spatiality and Technology, 139-150.

agency and emergence, the second part follows the disciplining or control of agency according to various structural surfaces of emergence originating from the relation of one body with another.

In recent memory, the work of the philosopher Gilles Deleuze constitutes a site for discussions of the concept of "surface," but this work also joins with various other philosophical traditions, such as Stoicism, 18th century Scottish philosophy, some parts of Nietzsche's philosophy, and with discussions of emergence and expression from the physical sciences. Though this chapter does not concern itself with Deleuze's work in detail, the concept of "surface" in this analysis owes much to it and thus it is proper to highlight his work, particularly in regard to Deleuze's 1969 book, *The Logic of Sense* (Deleuze, 1988). Some aspects of this work have common ground with other philosophers during the same period, such as the work of Rom Harré (Harré and Madden, 1975; Harré, 2001), with, perhaps, a common thread in the 18th century Scottish philosophical and natural science traditions of emergent powers. This isn't to argue that there are not differences between Deleuze and Harré's writings, of course, but rather, to suggest that the works of these two representatives of different philosophical traditions (one more "continental," the other more "Anglophone") have strong overlaps in terms of thinking about agency in terms of immanent powers of expression and formal events of expression.

The essentially two-part structure to this essay echoes a dualism of human subjectivity that is present in both Deleuze and Harré's works, namely, the difference between a unity of potentiality and intentionality (a primary realm or system) on the one hand, and that of public manifestations and accountability (a secondary realm or system) on the other. In terms of subjectivity, in Deleuze's *The Logic of Sense* (Deleuze, 1988), the primary realm is often (though not consistently I read) associated with the term "person" (Harré's (1989) "self"), and the secondary realm is often associated with the term, "individual" (Harré's (1989), "person"). As I am using it, the concept of "surface" is, thus, meant to convey the area where bodies affectively and effectively intermingle and mix with one another. In Harré's work, and in a more complex way, in Deleuze's work as well, the former realm is inferred through efficient causal relations, in a manner of speaking, read in reverse. In Harré's work, the self, (*pace* Kant's unity of apperception) is a transcendental unified used to explain intentional causality analogous to how hypothetical physical entities are conceptually proposed to explain specific physical effects (for example, the concept of "gravity" used as a causal explanation for the downward force of attraction between the earth and another body). In Deleuze's work, reversed causal inferences are used to propose a state of creative possibility (in Deleuze and Guattari (1983), a "body without organs"). In both cases what is important is that a body is explained, on the one hand as potentialities toward being and, on the other, as an expressed and socially accountable body (a "person" in Harré's terms, an individual in Deleuze's works, or a "molar" (versus "molecular") individual in Deleuze and Guattari's (1987) terms).

Such a dualism differs from the tradition of the Cartesian *cogito* because the self, here, is understood as a conceptual (in Deleuze, "virtual," that is, potential) unity, whereas Descartes and the Platonic tradition before Descartes premised the empirical actuality of material or ideal essences independent of the events that allow their then being "shaped" in different ways (one recalls here Descarte's famous wax metaphor as well as the unresolved problem of the specificity of forms in Plato's dialogues). Both Deleuze and Harre's works argue for the importance of *events* as "releasers" (Harré, 2001) or as moments of becoming in Deleuze that allow expressions to take place and selves to eventually be identified. "Events," in what follows, will be understood as the conceptual site where agency and its structured expression are joined, where potentiality is turned into actualization. "Surfaces" will be seen as the materials, textures, and forms through which expression is given, what after Deleuze, we may call directionality or "sense" (*sens*).

For Deleuze (Deleuze, 1990), surfaces produce sense, and from sense, there may be derived or produced different forms of meaning. Surfaces produce sense because whether they are discursive surfaces or physical surfaces, other surfaces and forces manifest themselves in some manner through their affects and this manifestation may make a difference in terms of physical effects or in terms of thought. Surfaces are the variously textured, relatively porous or non-porous sites of mixtures between bodies, and so affective relations begin at the level of surfaces and may or may not form more substantial bodies with "depth" afterwards. Surfaces are, thus, sites for events—for the expansion or shrinkage of extensions and for the creation of other surfaces and bodies.

Deleuze (1990) illustrates his valorization of surface and sense through the character of Alice in Lewis Carroll's *Alice in Wonderland* and *Through the Looking Glass*. For Deleuze, Carroll's famous double entendres and other rhetorical plays demonstrate the bi-directionality of sense on language's surface. Deleuze is also concerned with the other half of the "double articulation" (Deleuze and Guattari, 1987) of expression, besides the sense of language, the language of physical sense. Alice's extensions and shrinkages and her often playful manners of relating to the other characters in Carroll's tales, and particularly, they to her, help bring her, paradoxically, from a philosophy of "false depth" (Deleuze, 1990:10) embedded in the metaphysical conundrums of language and life to a philosophy of the surface after descending down the rabbit hole or entering through the "other side" of the mirror and encountering the "critical," seemingly mad, philosophical analyses of the other characters.

But, "depth," in Deleuze's work should not be regarded as a negative concept; Deleuze's criticism of depth is directed at the reification of depth in Platonic essences, the cogito, and more recently, in reified notions of mental content, such as has occurred in cognitive psychology and in other social science fields indebted to such (such as some "user" research areas of information science). Depth, for Deleuze, indicates a *puissance* (French), *potenza* (Italian), or *potentia* (Latin) (powers, potentialities, and potencies, in English) of mixtures that are expressed through surfaces: "The question is now about bodies taken in their undifferentiated depth and in their measureless pulsation. This depth acts in an original way, *by means of its power to organize surfaces and to envelope itself within surfaces*" (Deleuze, 1990: 124). Such expressions of potential powers literally *make sense* through linguistic and physical surfaces, and conversely, the notion of "surface" may be characterized through the customs, habits, linguistic, physical, and psychological orders and senses that allow expression to occur in such and such *ways* (i.e., according to directionality or *sens*).

The limits to the production of sense, for Deleuze (1990), lie in surfaces too. Outside of the concept of surface there is the risk of a metaphysics of "false depths"—illusional mental contents and determinative faculties hypothesized and reified from out of verbal descriptions of actions (e.g., "belief," "knowledge," and "artistic creation," from believing, knowing, and creating, respectively)--ideal essences, illusions of matter and form, rather than potentialities, actions, and descriptions. In Deleuze's fantastic, or perhaps, literal, infantile beyond or before of surfaces, the materials of language—sounds—fall back into the meaningless babble of potential mixtures: "When this production [i.e., the production of sense by statements and states of bodies] collapses, or when the surface is rent by explosions and by snags, bodies fall back again into their depth; everything falls back again into the anonymous pulsation wherein words are no longer anything but affections of the body—everything falls back into the primary order which grumbles beneath the secondary organization of sense" (Deleuze, 1990 p.125)[ii]. Surfaces are, thus, not only compositional for the secondary order, but are intrinsic to granting to the primary order a unified field, and, thus, stipulating intentionality and recognitions and self-recognition from such.

The work of the contemporary political philosopher, Antonio Negri, must be mentioned here, in so far as the logic of surfaces that we have presented is expanded to an analysis and theory of political manifestations. For Negri, one of the most primary surfaces for political manifestations is that of language. In language, common nouns or common names (*nome comune*) constitute possible locations for conceptual schemas that both embody certain *ontological powers* (*puissance/potenza*) and give rise to other types of *ontic powers* (*pouvoir/potere*). As such, *nome comune* stand at the junction between the potential and the possible. The common name is, literally, an event, that allows the expression of multiple powers, of multiple "names" in a common name (Negri, 2000: 30-31; Negri 2003b: 156). The notion of *nome comune* is similar to Deleuze's understanding of propositions, namely, that like propositions, *nome comune* refer to states of affairs. The verification of political propositions, for example, as empirically true remains a question of, broadly understood, empirical experimentation (or simply put, experience). (Though the value of such propositions in the realm of social, philosophical, and literary discourses, of course, is not exhausted by, nor reducible to, referential functions, since the future or past histories of concepts have narrative functions in political theory, as well as in political praxis and self-understandings of political identity and agency.) Common names have a symbolic political function, in the sense that they locate conceptual nexuses and directions for thought and physical action. For Negri, politics involves not simply critiques of empirical political events and of concepts, but the imaginative construction and reconstruction of concepts (*nome commune*) toward socially common, that is, political, futures ("The imagination is a linguistic gesture--and thus, common--the gesture of casting a net toward the future, in order to know it, construct it, and organize it, through power (*potenza*)," Negri, 2000 p.31). For Negri, *nome comune* are linguistic and conceptual materials through which not just personal, but also, social powers are stored and released through further linguistic acts or through physical actions. For Negri, one method of political theory is that of critically examining *nome comune* operating in, and as, the public sphere, and conversely, another is that of deploying new terms that may be empirically tested by political events (Negri, 2003a). Here, in a Kantian manner, the reality of political understanding—and with that, self-understanding--is formed by aesthetic and imaginative powers in relation to the possibilities of practical events. This is the Enlightenment (and later, Romantic) idea of the free person as a product and producer of historical risk—that is, risk not only toward the physical or even conceptual continuation of self, but also, more importantly, toward the establishment, critique, or destruction of narratives of history, themselves. The Enlightenment idea of freedom—that is, *freedom as an event*--takes place precisely in the caesura between the imaginative and the practical, judgment and reason, and it is here--in slightly different ways for Enlightenment, Romantic, and even modern reason,--*that in and as risk, history—and the self--are established as the real.*

Just as Deleuze's pre-ontic realm is identified as a realm of pure *potentia*, without strict measure, so Negri's realm of *potenza* is identified as a realm both *smisurato* (immeasurable; boundless) and as *dismisura* (excess; beyond measure) (Negri, 2000). Sometimes Negri (2000) and Hardt and Negri (2001) discuss this ontological realm in terms of "desire" and sometimes, synonymously, in terms of a pre-ontic form of social capital, namely one constituted, in part, by affects (Negri, 1999). As in Deleuze's work, where the realm of the potential is, in a sense, real, so here, social relations in Negri's work form an empirical ground that goes "beyond" traditional empirical claims. It is unclear, however, if in Negri's work the ontological realm is dependent or independent of the ontic and its surfaces or if the ontological realm contains its own powers, independent of the ontic (which in Negri's work often assumes the name of "capital," at least in so far as the ontic commonly appears today in the guise of values dominated by capitalist economic and social relationships (see, for example, Negri, 1999, and for an explication, Day, 2002)). If we were to suppose that the ontological stands as the effect, however different, of a capitalist surface, though, then we would be betraying the very Workerist traditions that Negri's work emerged out of, namely, a tradition of Marxism wherein non-capitalist values of production are taken as real, not simply hypothetical, and "beyond" and excessive to the logic capitalism imposes upon them (Day, 2002).

At this point, let us leave aside Negri's political extension of Deleuze's notion of emergence and expression and return to the epistemological analysis. In certain Anglophone philosophers the problem of potentiality is taken up in terms of dispositions. Harré (2001) has discussed the problem of formal causality in terms of dispositions, challenging the Humean destruction of efficient causality in the physical sciences and challenging the Cartesian reification of the concept of self in terms of mental contents, faculties, and structures. Harré's work follows a philosophical reconstruction of psychological agency from linguistic and anthropological evidence, rather than beginning with psychological categories prior to their linguistic and social construction. We might link Harré's notion of "discursive psychology" (Harré, 1995) to Michel Foucault's understanding of "discourse" in so far as both stress linguistic and social assemblages that construct paths for expression and give the possibilities for structures and identities. Such an account is amenable to a discussion of "surfaces" as we have been using this term.

For Harré (1989), the self, analogous to hypothetical nominal essences in the physical sciences (chemistry, physics), is a *conceptual* (not empirical) unity that explains real events. (On the other hand, "persons," for Harré, are identities within social or moral orders (Harré, 1989).) In a Kantian manner, the concept of "the self" acts as a causal explanation for personal actions even though its own existence is not empirical. Because of selves, we assume a unity of action for an individual, as for ourselves as well (Harré, 1989); if we did not, then causal understandings of our own and others agency (i.e., intentionality) would be meaningless.

Following Wittgenstein's (1958) critique, the grammar of *having* a self is misleading. For Harré, the self is a conceptual notion that allows us to explain personal causal agency in the presence of a restricted range of effects. Premising it as an empirical object is impossible and it is unnecessary for its powers to persist, both theoretically and practically. The self, analogous to physical powers, such as gravity, or other hypothesized physical or chemical existents, is a hypothetical conceptual unity whose existence is premised given certain regular, recognized events understood as effects. These are powers whose expressions are possible in certain allowable conditions ("contexts"), not powers that are free of those conditions or "events" (i.e., certain theological concepts, such as God or the soul, in so far as such are traditionally understood as self-causing essences, are not analogous to Harré's hypothetical conceptual unities). The notion of "disposition" stresses that these "causes" are virtual or potential—in the sense that they may or may not occur—and that their expressions are only relatively variable given certain "releasing" contexts and events (Harré, 2001) that both allow and constitute the character of certain expressions. Such contexts and events may be understood as the "formal" causes for the expression of powers.

Harré's understanding of dispositional powers and his notion of contexts as releasers of these powers is developed from his analysis of dispositional properties in the physical sciences (Harré, 1986), but he then extends these analyses to philosophical and psychological problems of mind and agency (Harré, 1989). Harré's assertion that dispositional properties are to be treated as hypothetical transcendental unities makes no assertion of ontological and ontic realms, whereas, Negri's work, for example, makes a strong claim as to the independence of the ontological, at least in so far as the ontological is to be understood as a realm distinct from--in terms of measure and in terms of limits--to, the ontic. (Deleuze's work, as I have suggested, is more ambivalent in regard to claiming distinct ontological and ontic realms.)

The above dualisms may be understood in terms of potentials on the one hand and actualization and realizations, respectively, on the other (to use Deleuze's (1986) terminology). We have discussed the first realm as a sort of primary realm and the second realm as an organizing, secondary realm, without which, however, the primary would fail to appear or be sensed as unified over time. Whereas the first realm encompasses hypothetical causes as concepts, the latter encompasses simple and complex empirical "effects." We have described this latter realm in terms of material surfaces, because it involves, like commonly understood physical surfaces, affective bodies that interact and that express powers. The manner of such expressions in terms of extension, directionality, intensity, and explicit and implicit manifestations, varies, of course, depending on the actual situation. Raindrops that fall upon a macadam roadway are extended and may have further effects because of the material composition and possibilities given them by that particular surface. Their dispositional and affective powers are manifested in slightly different ways by that surface in comparison to as if they fell upon the sand on a beach. In the same way, human sounds and other gestures are organized in the first years of life by the world, particularly, the world of the parents, allowing the infant to gain a particular identity and expressiveness (Harré, 1989) from a given physical "hardware." Just as the macadam road allows the raindrop to express its molecular dispositions or "powers" in certain manners, so language allows people to express their powers in certain ways, though in the case of socially embedded powers, of course, the social embeds itself in, and as, the potentialities of the powers themselves (i.e., the "self"), as well. The folding of the social into the personal and, conversely, the unfolding of the personal into the social, in this way, makes the social not so much efficiently causal or determinative of the personal, but more, formally constitutive of such.

If we were to visually diagram such a theory of expression and emergence, it might look like a "T" with the vertical bar standing for agency and the horizontal bar standing for the various surfaces that agency emerges through and is expressed by. The point of conjunction of these two bars would constitute an event or events through which both agency is expressed and structure is reaffirmed or is renegotiated. "Surfaces" may be understood as constituting the material properties, textures, and textualities that mediate and express agency toward structure or its renegotiation and that give back to agency its potentials and possibilities for further expression and identity. Surfaces may or may not be folded and or repeated so as to constitute structures that may give agency a "molar" modality. Surfaces may also lead, like a board under the rain, to the "flowing" of agency's power to other or later forms of expression and structuration. "Structure" connotes stability, and in terms of agencies, the self-reflexive repetition and conservation of forces. In the following section, we will survey some of the properties of surfaces that, among other effects, can lead toward or away from structures.

SURFACES

Some qualities of surfaces that may be examined are: 1) texture, 2) durability (hardness and softness in relation to another body, for example), 3) extensions due to repetition, and 4) the foldability of surfaces and certain qualities (such as structure and identity) which are the result of such folds.

Geoffrey Bowker and Susan Leigh Star have suggested that metaphors of texture in regard to infrastructures describe "enabling-constraining patterns over a set of systems (texture) and developmental patterns for an individual operating within a given set (trajectory)" (Bowker and Star, 1999 p.323). The notion of enabling and constraining patterns (broadly, "contexts") leading to developmental processes is a function of the relation of immanent powers and material properties and their "textures." Textures include permeability or impermeability and the ability of one surface to resist, absorb, or to fold into or out of another surface and thus, possibly, to create a third entity, an "in-between" that has the properties of a distinct third or shows itself as an incomplete hybrid (mixing vinegar with baking soda eventually results in a gas, carbon dioxide, with a material residue, whereas vinegar mixed with water results in diluted vinegar). Resistance, absorption, or the ability of one surface to express another or to be more fully expressed by another is a result of material properties and the types, duration, and quality of forces applied.

Brian Massumi's discussion (Massumi, 1992:10-46) of the concept of force in Deleuze and Guattari's two volumes of *Capitalism and Schizophrenia* (Deleuze and Guattari, 1983 and 1987) and other works by Deleuze contains many wonderful illustrations of the different qualities of materials and their relations to different types of forces and subsequent expressions. Massumi's example (1992: 10f.) of the event of a metal plane pushing against a piece of wood and the surface of its blade cutting into and dominating the wood in order to lead to the expression of certain patterns and colors of the wood, the release of moisture, etc., well illustrates the problem of texture as well as the "releasing" nature of contextual events upon the potential expressiveness of materials. When applied to problems of infrastructure, these notions of material qualities, powers, and expression stress that the notion of "*infra*structure" refers to relations of forces that result in expressions, structures, and identities.

Dispositions are oriented toward the past and the future, as well as the present. Organisms and molecules have historically developed in relations with other organisms and molecules and their potentiality lies within mixtures and events in the present, past, and future. Again, Massumi's example of various qualities that lie within the wood, present to the woodworker and his or her tools, well illustrates this point:

> It [a quality of the wood read as a sign] is simultaneously an indicator of a future potential and a symptom of a past. It envelops material processes pointing forward (planing; being a table) and backward (the evolution of the tree's species; the natural conditions governing its individual growth; the cultural actions that brought that particular wood to the workshop for that particular purpose). *Envelopment* is not a metaphor. The wood's individual and phylogenetic past exists as traces in the grain, and its future as qualities to be exploited. On a first, tentative level, meaning is precisely that: a network of enveloped processes.

Massumi, 1992: 11

Even better than Massumi's example, however, may be that of dye entering paper or wood. In the same way as the dye enters into the paper and wood and comes to express both the powers and properties of the dye and the wood, so children grow or "seep" into language and other cultural and social materials (and these material into children) and both their identities and the materials of language become visible through this process. Whereas Massumi's example is that of dominating forces, the example of dye is that of fully positive or expansive forces, which may act as an analogy for the overall progress of growth in life. In children's learning and use of language, language becomes historically concrete and existent, while the identity of each child becomes historically concrete and existent. The hypothetical or "virtual" ideas of "language" or "self" are actualized only through intermixing, existential events and material surfaces and affects. The concept of "language" as a whole is as ideal and as virtual as the concept of the child's self as a whole, yet each is established as a practical, theoretical and regulative *idea* (i.e., as a whole) only through concrete, temporal, and necessarily partial, affective mixtures and expressions.

The notion of "folds" (Massumi, "envelopment," above) is widely developed in Deleuze's work, most of all in his book, *The Fold: Leibniz and the Baroque* (Deleuze, 1993). The concept refers to the affective mixtures of different properties and powers in time and their mutual folding and unfolding in and through each other. Sense is the product of matter affecting other matter at their conjoining surfaces.

Folds occur in relation to materials in and through time. In the folding and unfolding of matter expressing itself as powers and affects, *time itself* comes to be felt as something material with its own affective powers. But, folds also occur as the psychological folding of moments, as occurs in memory for example, and this is the fold of the person. Proust's novel, *Recherche du temps perdu*, constitutes one of the most complex and intensive representations of this process, of course. In that novel, moments are suggested as being folded into the structuration of a person, depicted in the novel as the time of a particular subject (the first person narrator), and this subject, then, unfolds in various turns as a person and as a self through meetings with other persons and objects in the various temporalities that make up public and private life. These foldings and unfoldings trace persons through the forward and backward shuttles of time, and from out of these weavings there emerges public and personal senses of identity.

The concept of repetition is important in regard to public remembrance as well as to the phenomenon of memory, for repetition extends various surfaces in time by means of historical retrieval. Historical retrieval doesn't just bring the past into the present, but casts the present forward in certain manners rather than others, and with this casting, throws the subject into the future as a certain identifiable person. The ability of surfaces to carry a subject into the future varies. Surfaces such as ritual discourses depend on standardized narratives and even upon rhythmical devices for establishing the subject within a certain social space as a person or as a character. Oral literature, and the classical literature that rests upon it, highly depends upon these mnemonic devices. On the other hand, Lyotard (1984) has suggested that genuine scientific discourses implicitly contain methodological strategies for permitting challenges to their truth claims, though it is also true that scientific discourses function within larger social, epistemological, methodological, rhetorical, and cultural frames which bracket in various ways this ideal of scientific practice and position "science," too, within the important modernist surface and sense of progressive historicism.

Along with folds, repetition in its extensionable modality is a device that can be used for creating structures, either in one form or in progressive forms. In Euclidean space, geometrical bodies may be created by the elongation of lines and points.

Traditionally, structures—social, cultural, or even physical—act as sites where expectations and anticipations dwell, recognitions are "made," and where the recognized event can be "discovered" and elongated in, and as, history.

Rom Harré, especially in two books, *Social Being* (1979) and *Personal Being* (1984), has developed the notion of "moral orders" to designate social identities and roles constructed by grammars, narratives, and non-linguistic cultural devices that largely give selves their literal public personas in terms of recognized intentions and responsibilities, but which can also suggest extraordinary, non-prescribed situations for given agents, lying in what deconstruction has more generally identified as an ethical undecidability. The existence of moral orders and surfaces is intrinsic to maintaining stable social relations through matrixes of expectations, responsibilities, and reliance, but the existence of such orders and surfaces also suggests, as Wittgenstein's (1958) pointed out with his discussion of the analogous orders and surfaces of "language games," that the spaces between such surfaces and orders offer generative, creative potential, as well as risk. If governed by the Kantian "ought," for example, moral orders reach into an uncertain future, from an indeterminate present and, at best, a multitude of imaginary pasts, and thus they may exist at the edge of time and at the emergence of surfaces. In this, the moral turns into the ethical, prescription turns into judgment, based on indetermination and causal uncertainty. If surfaces function according to a "social informatics" governed by a logic of recognition, identities and duties, such a social informatics does not exhaust the expressive potentials of individual persons in affective relationships with others in changing situational, radically temporal, conditions. Surfaces change and shift their relations to one another, new surfaces emerge, and old surfaces disappear within such conditions.

Robert Pogue Harrison, in his book on the presence of the dead in the everyday life of the living (Harrison, 2003) points to rituals of grieving as practices that attempt to draw the griever back toward the world of the living, away from the world of the dead and the madness of grief. Consequently, these rituals also help eventually mark for the living the absolute difference between the living and the dead—a difference that must become real lest the griever fail in overcoming grief. Here, not only may surfaces be conceptualized in terms of moral orders, but also in terms of the social order in general and in terms of existence itself. Here, even more than with Harré's concept of "moral orders," we can see that discursive and ritualized social surfaces give the possibility for both personal and social psychological existences.

Along with Proust's work, through Harrison's (2003) example of grief we can see that the most psychologically intensive fold may not be that of the agent "within space," but of space—that is, surfaces--within the agent. The infrastructure of the self is the multitude of surfaces and their relations that make the conceptual unity of the self's potentialities possible and real. The problem with "the dead" as a surface for expression is that the dead are, literally, dead—the person's grief is the expression of powers that have nowhere to go except the imaginary itself. Grieving rituals, on the other hand, attempt to mark the end of death as not just imaginary, but real, through repetitions that have expression itself as their goal. In the act of grieving, the power of life not so ironically reappears, and eventually will reabsorb acts of grief, as markers both of the dead and living persons, into a developing self. Deleuze (1988: 94-123) suggested that the very doubling of the individual--from persons to selves--was an invention of the Ancient Greeks. This claim is not fully satisfactory since no culture lacks some sort of psychology of self. The important point, however, is to see that surfaces are not just materials upon which the self's potentialities may be expressed, but also, that they constitute the very potentialities and unities that we call a "self."

CONCLUSION

The above conceptual schemas attempt to characterize the nature of bodies—structures and identities--in terms of powers, expressions, and the material surfaces that allow those powers to express themselves as personal and collective bodies. It does not attempt to locate those powers in fixed material or formal essences, nor in terms of fully determinate, efficient, social causes. Potential powers and their actualizing surfaces underlie notions of agency, identity, and structure. The events that are composed of actual expressions of powers form the "infrastructure" of bodies and the reality of space. The term "*infrastructure*" must be thought in terms of expressive events through which both bodies and notions of space are arrived at. Conceptions of space that don't account for powers and their expression empty the concept of "space" of any materialist and historical meaning, reducing space to being understood, in a Kantian manner, as a purely formal background or even "structure" for events, instead of as the product of such.

REFERENCES

Bowker, G. and Star, S.L. (1999). *Sorting things out*. Cambridge, Massachusetts, MIT Press.

Day, R. (2002). Social capital, value, and measure: Antonio Negri's challenge to capitalism. *Journal of the American Society for Information Science and Technology*, 53 (12), pp. 1074-1082.

Deleuze, G. (1988). *Foucault*. Minneapolis, University of Minnesota Press.

Deleuze, G. (1990). *The logic of sense*. New York, Columbia University Press.

Deleuze, G. (1993). *The fold: Leibniz and the baroque*. Minneapolis, University of Minnesota Press.

Deleuze, G., and Guattari, F. (1983). *Anti-Oedipus: capitalism and schizophrenia*. Minneapolis, University of Minnesota Press.

Deleuze, G., and Guattari, F. (1987). *A Thousand plateaus: capitalism and schizophrenia*. Minneapolis, University of Minnesota Press.

Hardt, M. and Negri, A. (2000). *Empire*. Cambridge, Massachusetts, Harvard University Press.

Harré, R. (1979). *Social being: a theory for social psychology*. Totowa, NJ, Rowan and Littlefield.

Harré, R. (1984). *Personal being: a theory for individual psychology*. Cambridge, Massachusetts, Harvard University Press.

Harré, R. (1989). The 'self' as a theoretical concept. *IN:* Krausz, M. ed. *Relativism: interpretation and confrontation*. Notre Dame, Indiana, University of Notre Dame Press.

Harré, R. (1995). Discursive psychology. *IN:* Smith, J., Harré, R. and Van Langenhove, L., *Rethinking psychology*. London, Sage Publications.

Harré, R. (2001). Active power and powerful actors. *IN: Philosophy at the new millennium* (supplement to *Philosophy*, No. 48), 91-109.

Harré, R. and Madden, E.H. (1975). *Causal powers: a theory of natural necessity*. Totowa, NJ, Rowman and Littlefield.

Harrison, R. P. (2003). *The dominion of the dead*. Chicago, University of Chicago Press.

Lyotard, J.-F. (1984). *The postmodern condition: a report on knowledge*. Minneapolis, University of Minnesota Press.

Massumi, B. (1992). *A User's Guide to* Capitalism and Schizophrenia: *Deviations from Deleuze and Guattari*. Cambridge, Massachusetts, MIT Press.

Negri, A. (1999). Value and affect. *IN: Boundary 2* **26** (2), pp.77-88

Negri, A. (2000). *Kairòs, alma venus, multitudo: nove lezione impartite a me stesso*. Rome, Manifestolibri.

Negri, A. (2003a). *Cinque lezioni su* Impero *e dintorni*. Milan, Raffaello Cortina Publishing.

Negri, A. (2003b). Kairòs, alma venus, multitudo. *IN: Time for revolution*. London, Continuum.

Wittgenstein, L. (1958). *Philosophical Investigations*. London, Basil Blackwell.

AFFLIATION

Ronald E Day, Wayne State University.

ALAN DIX, ADRIAN FRIDAY, BORIANA KOLEVA, TOM RODDEN, HENK MULLER, CLIFF RANDELL AND ANTHONY STEED

12. MULTIPLE SPACES

SETTING THE SCENE

This chapter is about our experiences of space in the Equator project (www.equator.ac.uk), in particular, the way in which multiple spaces, both virtual and physical, can co-exist. By this we mean that people and objects may have locations in and relationships to both physical space and one or more virtual spaces, and that these different spaces together interact to give an overall system behaviour and user experience. The concepts we develop in this chapter are driven partly by practical experience, and partly by previous theoretical work such as the models and taxonomies of spatial context in (Dix *et al.*, 2000), the models for mixed reality boundaries (Koleva *et al.*, 1999) and capturing human spatial understanding exposed in sources such maps, myths and mathematics (Dix, 2000). We are also building on established work on informal reasoning about space from the AI and GIS communities (Grigni *et al.*, 1995; Papadias *et al.*, 1996) similar to Allen's well known temporal relations (Allen, 1991).

We start by looking at some of the practical experiences in a number of Equator 'experience' projects and how these have each required several kinds of interacting spaces: real and virtual. We then use this as a means to look more abstractly at different kinds of space and the way these overlap and relate to one another. In order to examine some aspects in greater detail we will use two artificial scenarios which each highlight specific problems and issues. Finally, we will discuss how this is contributing to ongoing work including the construction of an Equator 'space infrastructure'.

SPACES WE HAVE KNOWN

Equator is a large multi-site multi-disciplinary project focused on the integration of digital and physical interaction. One of the key methods used in Equator are 'experience projects'. These experiences are focused around the creation of a particular event or outcome, which allow the integration of practical and theoretical work of many kinds. As the focus of Equator as a whole is the confluence of physical and digital life, unsurprisingly the nature of space has been important in many of these sub-projects. We will discuss four of these here: City, CityWide, the

P. Turner and E. Davenport (Eds.), Spaces, Spatiality and Technology, 151-172.

Drift Table and Ambient Wood. In each we will see multiple physical and virtual spaces interacting.

City

The City project allows participants who may be present in person, through virtual reality (VR) or through a simple web interface to all 'share' a visit to the Mackintosh Room at the Lighthouse in Glasgow (Brown *et al.*, 2003). The physical visitor walks around the actual mackintosh room tracked by ultrasound beacons and has a handheld PDA. The VR visitor navigates a desktop VR model of the Mackintosh Room and can see the various exhibits within the rendered world. The web visitor navigates between web pages organised by sections of the Mackintosh room and can see exhibits on the web pages. All three visitors can talk to one another using a microphone and ear-piece and so can discuss what they see. The visitors can also see one another on a map view: shown on the PDA for the physical visitor, and on screen for the VR and web visitors. Also the VR visitor can see avatars representing the physical and web visitors within the VR space.

As well as the physical space of the museum there is a digital reproduction of it for the VR users and a map view used by all. In this virtual map, the VR visitor has a precisely known 'position' within the virtual room. In contrast the web visitor doesn't have an explicitly defined position because they can't actively move themselves around the map. Their position is inferred from their web page browsing: they are implicitly positioned on the map in front of the objects represented in the web pages they are reading. The real visitors of course have a precise position known to them. However, this physical position is sensed using ultrasound, which has limited resolution, varying degrees of accuracy and even coverage black spots within the physical space. Furthermore the ultrasound date then has to be mapped to a physical location lading to further issues.

In fact a detailed analysis revealed seven spaces that impinge directly upon the user not to mention various coordinate spaces used internally within the software (Steed *et al.*, 2004).

Figure 1. Views of the physical, VR and web visitors

CityWide

The CityWide project is using large scale performances that merge artistic performance and game-like activities. One performance called "Can You See Me Now?" allowed online players to be part of a game of virtual tag trying to escape 'runners' in the real world (Flintham *et al.*, 2003). Online players were placed in a virtual model of an urban environment and could see representations of the runners who were chasing them. The 'runners', performers in the real city, were tracked by GPS and had hand-held devices so that they could see and chase the virtual participants. If a runner got within 5 virtual metres of a virtual player they were 'caught'.

'Can You See Me Now?' was staged in Sheffield in December 2001, in Rotterdam in February 2003 and in Oldenberg in July 2003 and attracted over 1500 online players. It was awarded the 2003 Prix Ars Electronica Golden Nica award for Interactive Art (for the Rotterdam performance) and was nominated for a BAFTA in Interactive Entertainment in 2002 (for the initial Sheffield performance).

In 'Can You See Me Now?' the virtual and physical spaces are overlaid as if there were an invisible ghostly realm behind the surface of buildings and streets. Again varying degrees of accuracy of the GPS sensors used to track the physical participants mean that the measured locations available to the virtual participants may not represent truly the actual physical locations. In particular, GPS accuracy was particularly poor in the 'shadow' of buildings as the performances of 'Can You See Me Now?' were always staged in densely packed city spaces where it is hard to get a good GPS fix without multi-path reflections.

Figure 2. Can You See Me Now? runner carrying PDA display

Drift Table

The Drift Table, part of the Equator work on domestic environments, is a coffee table with a small porthole in the middle through which can be viewed an aerial view of the whole UK (Gaver *et al.*, 2004). Weight on different sides of the table makes it drift, like a balloon, over the country. When the table was installed in a real home, the 'owner' augmented the table with a road map and used this to help guide the table to specific locations, thus adding the road map's spatial model to the physical space in the room and the virtual space in the porthole ... which is of course itself a photograph of the real physical space of the UK.

Figure 3. The Drift Table moves across a photographic model of the UK countryside

Although conceptually and physically very simple the Drift Table both hides technical complexity and elicited rich interactions. Within the form factor of the coffee table is a PC, screen and disk array large enough to store over a terrabyte of map data. The table also has weight sensors that are used to determine the direction and speed of travel. At a maximum virtual speed of only a few tens of miles an hour, if the owner of the Drift Table wanted to 'go somewhere' specific he had to place heavy objects on one side of the table and then leave it for several hours before making adjustments.

Ambient Wood

Finally, in Ambient Wood, school children wander around a wood in Sussex on a 'digitally enhanced field trip'. The aim of the experience is to reveal using digital augmentation the features of the natural environment that would otherwise be invisible (Price *et al.* 2003). The children work in pairs and use a humidity and light sensor as they explore the wood. The location of their readings are recorded so that they can be shown later collected together on a map of the wood. As they move through the wood there are zones determined by radio 'pingers'. When the children enter a zone sounds or other events are triggered. For example, in one zone they can listen to the vastly amplified sound of a butterfly sipping nectar.

Deep within the wood the children find a somewhat enigmatic device, the periscope. Atop of a branching metal structure is a cowled screen. As the screen is rotated it shows the wood as it would be under different conditions, for example, if a new organism were introduced. The periscope acts like a magic viewport that overlays a virtual view of the wood over the real one. The sense of connection was so strong that children would stand the other side of the periscope expecting to be visible in the virtual view.

Again we can see multiple spaces: the physical space of the wood, the map used later to plot light and humidity readings, the active zones around the hot spots, and the virtual wood displayed in the periscope.

Figure 4. Activity in the Ambient Wood: moisture reading and periscope

UNDERSTANDING SPACE

As we have seen each of the experience projects has involved multiple spaces some physical some virtual. In this section we will examine at a more abstract level the kinds of spaces involved. First we will look at three levels of virtuality from physical space, through the measured coordinates of real space and objects to virtual spaces. We will then look at three kinds of location systems used for measured space which also correspond to ways in which we envisage real space. Finally in this section we will look at the way overlapping or adjoining spaces map onto one another and how people and computers can manage this intersection.

Three kinds of virtuality

Augmented and mixed reality clearly involves physical space and virtual space. However there are, in fact, three types of space to consider:

- real space – the locations and activities of actual objects and people in physical space
- measured space – the representation of that space in the computer and the representation of locations of objects and people from sensor data, etc.
- virtual space – electronic spaces created to be portrayed to users, but not necessarily representing explicitly the real world

Note that virtual spaces may themselves be models of real world things (e.g. an architect's walk through, the virtual Mackintosh room, aerial photographs in the Drift table), but this differs in intent from a similar representation used to track locations of real objects (measured space).

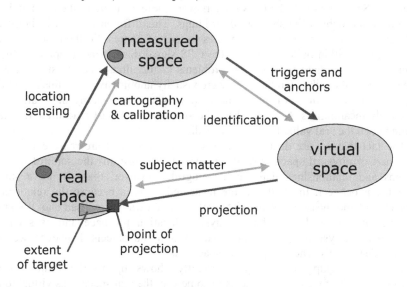

Figure 5. Three kinds of space and relations between them

These three types of space are related in different ways. In each case there is a static relationship between the spaces themselves and a more dynamic relationship about the actual sensing of physical things, the events and behaviours triggered by them in the virtual world and the projection of virtual world back into the physical.

Real – Measured

In order for a measured space to be meaningful it must in some way correspond to aspects of the physical space. This will involve a process of mapping the fixed aspects of the real space using some cartographic measurement of points and their relations, either against a global system (e.g. GPS) or relative to one another (e.g. theodolite or simple tape measure).

This may be a fixed once-and-for-all process but may involve a more dynamic recalibration if the space is not fixed. For example, the variation of air pressure due to weather systems means that the ground can rise or fall by small but measurable amounts. At a slower time scale plate tectonics means that the ocean floor under, for example, the Atlantic is slowly splitting. Measures of longitude therefore change in the order of centimetres from year to year. If location sensing were being done in Iceland then this would even affect relative locations of cities and buildings. Later we will discuss coordinate systems on board moving trains which change even more rapidly.

Given a measured space we then obtain the location of objects within that space using some form of sensing. This sensing may vary in accuracy. For example, in 'Can You See Me Now?' the GPS sensors were more accurate in the open and less accurate when behind the shadow of buildings. This difference is not insignificant and accuracy can vary from a few metres to tens of metres. Furthermore there are areas such as within buildings where the GPS signal disappears completely. In the Mackintosh room there were similar problems as the ultrasound transmitters were placed on top of exhibits (so that they were visually unobtrusive), but this meant that booth-like areas in the room were black-spots where the reading of location was effectively meaningless. Note that here the signal was not just inaccurate (a radius within which the real value lies) but misleading.

The fact that we are dealing with electronic spaces that are representations of some part of physical space is really important. It constrains the sorts of location systems and relationships that are meaningful. However, there is not a simple relationship between the real and the measured. This is because the relationship between real and measured is an existential one not always a realised one. We know that the interior of the car has a physical location in space and as such has constraints of physicality in its coordinate system and objects. However, we may have no idea exactly where in physical space it is!

This relationship to real space actually shows up in the limits on the interrelationship of measured space as in some way the real space is as virtual to the electronic space as the electronic is to the physical.

Measured – Virtual

In the case where the virtual space corresponds to a model of the physical one then there may be a close mapping between measured and virtual spaces. For example, in Ambient Wood location of a moisture or light reading is first derived in a measured space of GPS coordinates. This is then related to the coordinates of a map of the wood on which the readings are later plotted. Similarly in the Mackintosh room ultrasound location is measured to give a coordinates which are then mapped onto the 2D map and 3D virtual room.

We have labelled this 'identification' in figure 5 as this is often a (relatively) straightforward identification of measured coordinates to their corresponding virtual ones. Sometimes the virtual space may not represent the same space as the physical one, but there may still be an identification between the virtual and measured/real:

for example, we may make locations in real space map onto locations in an information space so that we can walk around the real space and navigate the virtual. In the case where there is not a direct mapping between real and virtual this identification between measured and virtual may also be relative rather than absolute. That is a direction of movement in the measured space may give rise to some corresponding movement in the virtual. There is an element of this in the use of weights in the Drift Table although one could imagine having more complex explorations of non-planar spaces.

Whether or not there is a relationship between the measured space and virtual, particular locations or events in the measured space may trigger actions in the virtual space The many tourist and museum information systems are examples of this as is the Stick-e Note infrastructure for location and context-sensitive interaction (Pascoe, 1997). We have also an example of this in the way proximity to a pinger in the Ambient Wood triggers an information source.

Note that as these are triggering electronic world events they will normally (always) be triggered from representations of the objects and space in the measured spaces rather than directly by the physical space. Arguably something like triggering by physical contact or capacitance would be a counter-example. However, even then the event cannot be used to trigger virtual actions unless it is sensed. In this example, the sensing is effectively a relative one "these two objects are near each other" and we'll return to issues of relative location later.

Virtual – Real

The virtual world may in some way represent or be about a particular real space. For example, a web page about London, or a virtual model of the Eiffel Tower. Several of the spaces we have seen are like this: the virtual Mackintosh room, the virtual model of the city streets in CityWide, the aerial photographs of the UK in the Drift Table.

Note that where the virtual space represents a real one this need not be related to the actual space. For example a virtual tourism system allowing you to navigate a mixed reality experience of a distant place or the Drift Table's aerial view.

The Drift Table is interesting in that it is partly corresponding to the real world: if reset it centres itself above the actual location of the table. However, the height and movement of the table means that is more often a view of 'somewhere else'.

Virtual spaces are made available in the real world by being projected, usually visually but also audibly or even by other means such as tactile or haptic devices or even smell (Burdea, G.C. & Coiffet, P. 2003). When the virtual world is made manifest it must be at some particular point in the real world. This has various aspects:

- *point of projection* – The device that embodies the projection is actually in the real space (on a screen, in virtual reality goggles, in the the Ambient Wood periscope, on the Drift Table porthole, on a runner's PDA in 'Can You See Me Now?')

- *range of detection* – There will be a set of locations in the real world where the projection can be seen (or heard, smelt etc.)
- *extent of target* – The projection appears to occupy some part of real space, usually 'behind' the projection surface for visual projections. For example, in a video wall, the space being projected would appear to be 'the other side' of the screen – that is occupying actual space (albeit through a wall!) Again in the Drift Table it appears as though the places in the photographs are somewhere far below and the room floating above. Although the extent is usually 'behind' the point of projection, when viewing a hologram the extent is actually in front of the holographic plate and in an augmented or immersive virtual reality using stereo goggles the extent of projection may appear to be everywhere.

Note that video and audio office shares, CCT video or web cams have similar aspects. When you look at a picture on a cinema screen there is a sense in which the image purports to occupy space behind the screen.

The Interaction Cycle

Note that there is a cycle of interaction here different but reminiscent of the Model–View–Controller (MVC) model for graphical user interfaces (Krasner & Pope, 1988). In fact if one thinks of the location of a puck or mouse being sensed and mapped onto the virtual screen space it seems uncannily close. However, there is a major difference in that (except for specialised devices such as digitising tablets), the physical location of mouse or puck is only important insofar as it controls the virtual space of desktop and screen cursor. In contrast, in mixed and augmented reality experiences, the locations of sensed objects typically have meaning in the real world as well as the virtual.

However, the MVC parallel can teach us something about this mixed reality interaction cycle. One of the tensions of the MVC model is the coupling between the Controller and View. In a simple pipeline interaction model the input (mouse actions or keystrokes) would be processed by the Controller, converted into abstract actions on the Model, leading to changes in the Model state, which are then rendered by the View on the screen. This works for actions such as pressing control-X to cut an object to the clipboard, but not for true graphical actions such as clicking a mouse over an object to select it. To interpret the latter the Controller needs to know what is where on the screen, and so has to 'ask' the View what is rendered at a particular screen location.

Similarly for mixed reality experiences the link between projection and sensing will often be important. For example, torches have been explored as a means to controlling mixed reality experiences (Ghali, *et al.* 2003). Here the exact location of the torch is not so important, what matters is that the location of the torch beam is correctly registered relative to the projected virtual space.

Three Kinds Of Location System

So, when we talked about the measured and virtual spaces as having their own coordinate system, we really mean something more like location system as not all are based on Cartesian coordinates as such. Even physical space has different characteristics depending on perspective: "in this room", as opposed to "near Aunt Mo" or "at 37.32E, 12.56N". Notice also how this location information is of very different kinds:

- *coordinates* – This is where location is in some sort of explicit dimensional representation, not necessarily orthogonal and not necessarily Euclidean (e.g. polar, spherical, UK Ordinance Survey (OS) grid). Note that these coordinate systems will typically only have validity over a finite space (the OS grid is meaningless over North America) and have an even smaller space over which they are expected to have values. For example, a coordinate system based on x, y, z locations in the Mackintosh room would have validity over central Glasgow, but would only be expected to be used within the room. In the case of the Mackintosh room the coordinates are never needed beyond the room, but of there were also sensors in the corridors outside, then the link between the two would be important.
- *zonal* – This is where objects are located within some area. For example the Pepys system used IR-based Active Badges simply to record presence in a room (Newman *et al.*, 1991). Mobile communications typically give some level of zonal information 'for free': a mobile phone can use the current cell to give tourist information or even 'push' advertising and in several systems, notably the early work on the 'GUIDE' tourist system, the current WaveLan base-station is used as a proxy for location (Cheverst *et al.*, 2000).. The simplest form of zonal space is a single proximity sensor such as the pinger in Ambient Wood.
- *relational* – This is where objects report some form of relative location information: device A is close to device B, or device A is about 3 metres north-east of device B. This leads to a space which can be regarded as a graph of all the possible sensors/devices with knowledge of some arcs (approximate distance, possibly direction) and sometimes knowledge between arcs (angle between devices). It is interesting to note that most traditional cartography starts with precisely this information. The simplest form of relational information is also simple proximity, for example, detection of which Bluetooth devices are in range.

Furthermore, measured spaces differ in both accuracy and extent. For example, the ultrasound location in the Mack room only has meaning within the room and even then has voids in information booths that create an ultrasound shadow. In fact, apparently unambiguous cartographic systems such as the OS Grid have limitations as the earth beneath our feet is constantly shifting due to continental drift and even atmospheric conditions.

Note too that these location systems relate principally to the way in which objects are represented within the space. So that even in a zonal space, the zones may have known physical extent within some coordinate system but the objects only known to the granularity of the zone. Also even where detailed coordinates are known they are often converted in zones which represent conceptual regions, for example, around exhibits in the Mackintosh room.

In addition to location, sensors may return orientation, velocity, acceleration or other data that may fit within or relate to a coordinate space. For example, a compass clearly is related to a magnetic map of the earth (in the small Cartesian space), but delivers orientation only. Just as with location this information may be Cartesian (e.g. compass direction), zonal (e.g. facing the window) or relational (e.g. two people facing each other).

Three Kinds Of Relationships

As we saw in the examples earlier, it is not that we have a single measured, real and virtual space, but typically several of each. These multiple spaces are related in various ways. Again these seem to be of three kinds:

-   *topological* – There are a standard set of qualitative relations between regions of space: separate, overlaps, touches, contains etc. (see figure 6) and also relations between lines and regions that are used for qualitative reasoning in AI. For example, Grigni *et al.* (1995) give inference rules for proofs about this type of spatial relation and Papadias *et al.* (1996) uses a richer set that takes into account directions (e.g. to the east of) and hierarchical relations between spaces in spatial databases. There is a similar set of temporal relationships (before, overlaps end, etc.) defined by Allen (1991).These topological relations are usually applied to sub-regions of a universal space. Where we are dealing with spaces in the real worked, this is the case (at least in principle, although measuring may be difficult), but most of the measured and virtual spaces we are dealing with are effectively independent until we define the relationship between them. The second two kinds of relationship are about this.
-   *boundary* – We may have two locational systems that have no substantive overlap, but where there are boundaries that can be traversed. For example, we may have ultrasound sensing in two different rooms and objects may pass from one to the other. As we have already seen when discussing projection, these boundaries can also occur between the real and physical. Koliva *et al.* (1999) discuss in detail the properties of these mixed reality boundaries including the permeability of the boundaries: whether light, sound, objects can traverse them.
-   *mapping* – Where there is a more significant overlap, we need some way to map the locations of one into those of the other. Complications may occur where the location systems differ in kind, for example zonal and coordinate, or where different accuracies or granularities lead to conflicting data.

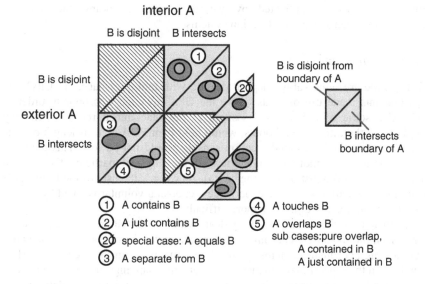

interior A

B is disjoint   B intersects

B is disjoint

exterior A

B intersects

B is disjoint from
boundary of A

B intersects
boundary of A

① A contains B   ④ A touches B
② A just contains B   ⑤ A overlaps B
②Ø special case: A equals B   sub cases:pure overlap,
③ A separate from B   A contained in B
                                    A just contained in B

Figure 6. Qualitative relations between regions of space

For the topological relationships the issue of the extent of the 'normal' area of the space becomes important. We are not talking about the coordinate system intersecting but the natural regions that the spaces represent. That is we have two very distinct ontological categories:

- space as extent within another (perhaps not measured)
- space as potential to measure locations

Topological and existence of boundaries relates primarily to the former. Mapping and mapping at boundaries is largely about the latter. Following the mathematician's habit of always looking for structure-substructure relationships it is clear that there are some here. In coordinate spaces virtually any region may (with some transformation of coordinates) be regarded as a subspace. Similarly the local coordinate space of an individual device in the 'relational' system may be regarded as either a zonal or coordinate space in its own right. There may be some advantage in being clear about this as it stops angst about whether the 'space' is one thing or another. We just say both! Operationally, in any application we need to decide what we represent as spaces (although even then things may be used in different ways at different times), and also what are 'heavy-weight' spaces with permanent representations and what are light-weight ones used when appropriate. The subspace relationship is also complicated by various factors including the dynamic relationship between spaces and location systems.

Managing multiple spaces

In fact, people are remarkably adept at dealing with multiple spaces. In CityWide the participants made use of areas where the GPS coverage was poor in order to 'hide'. Also some of the physical visitors in the Mackintosh room, when they entered one of the information booths, would hold their PDA at arms length outside the booth so that the ultrasound location sensing would not be lost. This gave the remote participants a more accurate view of the physical participant's location (albeit being portrayed just outside the booth). As we saw the user of the Drift Table brought maps and atlases into the experience – choosing voluntarily to add yet more spaces. Computationally things are more difficult!

In mathematics differential geometry deals with spaces that are curved or broken in ways such that no single coordinate system can cover them. Instead a patchwork of overlapping coordinate systems are used with mappings in the areas of overlap. Depending on the type of mathematics being done the mappings are required to have different kinds of properties. for example, to deal with general relativity the mappings are usually required to be 'smooth' – infinitely differentiable.

A more mundane example of this can be seen in a world atlas. The earth is roughly spherical (flattened slightly at the poles) but atlas pages are flat. You can imagine wallpapering a spherical globe with the separate maps. At the overlaps there is a mapping between the local coordinate systems of the individual maps' Cartesian coordinates even though there is no overall 'flat' coordinate system. Note too that the earth is no a series of flat faces, each page of an atlas is a slight morphing of the actual earth's surface. For a small area like a building or town, the approximation form this flattening is insignificant for all but the most accurate measurements, but at the scale of countries the edges tend to become distorted. Different map projections make choices about which areas are most 'true' and which more distorted. For example, the Phillips projection is most 'true' (in the sense of 'flat') at the latitude of Southern Europe whilst the equator is very stretched North South and the poles squashed. In contrast the more common Mercator projection manages to be true (in the sense of flat) everywhere (called a conformable mapping), but at the expense of distorting the relative sizes of countries and not being able to cover the polar regions.

Similar techniques are used in VR systems, often called locale-based models (Barrus *et al.*, 1996). Two rooms may have separate VR models which are linked at the doorway by a local mapping between the coordinate systems. Given these spaces are constructed and Cartesian the mappings are usually well behaved. This may be either a simple scaling and translation of origin or at worst an affine transformation. This boundary mapping means there does not have to be a single super model and so makes the virtual world more computationally tractable and easier to manage. The boundary mapping is then used when objects move between the worlds, or to trace light rays so that one space can be seen from another.

Note however that in all these case the partial spaces are Cartesian and also that the mapping is largely fixed. Unfortunately, neither are necessarily true in the digitally enhanced environments we are considering.

SCENARIOS

In order to explore these issues further we have been using rich scenarios. One advantage of using scenarios is that they are simpler than real life so we can choose to focus on some issues and ignore others, rather than having to deal with every problem at once! For example, the twin doors scenario below deals with only a small number of idealised sensing devices. On the other hand we can use the scenarios to push the extremes of issues that may be exercised to a lesser extent in actual experiments. For example, considering a series of stories about train travel has enabled us to explore issues where a local coordinate system (the location within the train) moves relative another coordinate system (the track and stations) and is not even of constant shape (the train bends).

Twin doors

This scenario is focused on issues that arose due to uncertainty in location sensing when you move between two spaces that are measured using separate technologies. Imagine a building with two doors, as shown in Figure 7. People walk in and out of the building, and are tracked using two types of tracking devices. For outside tracking GPS is used with an accuracy of around 3m, and for inside tracking a more accurate system is used, for example an ultrasonic positioning system with an accuracy of 10cm.

In order to describe this scenario properly, we need at least two spaces. There is the Outside of the building, which is a space that is measured using spherical coordinates obtained from a GPS sensor. We will assume that locally these coordinates are Euclidian. Secondly, there is the Inside of the building, which is at least one space, but there may be one space for each room. The inside-space is described using Cartesian coordinates.

In addition there are two conceptual spaces: the personal spaces of the people who are walking through the doors, and the physical space that these people live in.

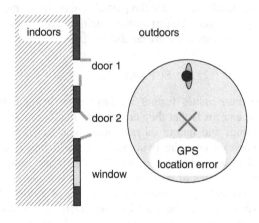

Figure 7. Twin doors – physical situation

Scenario – sudden shifts in positions and walking through walls

Imagine a person, Alison, who is walking towards the building and enters through door 1. While she is outside the building the GPS tracks her position and due to the location error reports a location that leads to door 2, as shown in Figure 8. When she gets inside the building the ultrasonic sensor takes over and reports her correctly as coming through door 1. Although Alison's real path is continuous there is a discontinuity (the sudden jump indicated by the dashed arrow in Figure 8) in the measured location. There is no way to prove that the GPS is wrong and the ultrasonics is right; on average the ultrasonics gives much higher accuracy, but it is possible that the GPS location was right and the ultrasonics system was disturbed by some noise.

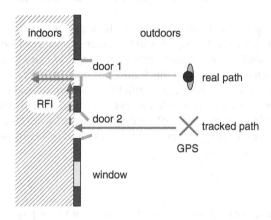

Figure 8. Twin doors – wrong door?

The most important issue to resolve here is how to present this discontinuity outside the location infrastructure. Devices that Alison carry around, devices in the building, or people may need Alison's position. In addition to the position, the path that Alison walked may be requested.

An obvious question is whether the discontinuity should be smoothed out. For example, from GPS and ultrasonics accuracy the system can deduce that the ultrasonics is probably right and the GPS is probably wrong, and the system can hence retroactively alter its representation of the path that Alison walked to gradually go from the red cross to door 1. A problem with smoothing it out retroactively is that applications that request the path twice in a row may get two entirely different answers. On the other hand the position can be smoothed out form door 2 to it correct position, but this knowingly records incorrect positions. This leaves us with the option of not correcting the discontinuity, and leaving the problem to be solved by some other part of the system.

The 'right' answer on how to represent the discontinuity depends on the context, who asks the question, etc. It seems fairly sensible that if we wanted to ask the question the next day "where did Alison start off" then we should use the correction using the ultrasonic location sensing and work out it was opposite door 1. However, if we were looking at an accident enquiry it may be important what other people saw at the time, and to record uncorrected information.

Variant scenarios

We can consider other variants of this. For example, Alison doesn't walk through door 1, but instead meets Brian, who is about to go out from the building. Brian's location is measured as at door 1, Alison's is at door 2. Although they may be talking, and so share a physical space with one another, they are not regarded as having met by the system.

What if Alison and Brian have Bluetooth devices which sense one another's presence (relational space) and report this to the other spaces. How do we deal with conflicting information? If we choose to represent things as a single model of "how things are" in measured space (pretty much how our own brains work), then we are forced to make decisions early between conflicting and partial location information. Alternatively we may simply hold all the evidence (measurements by different systems at different times) and put off dealing with conflicts until decisions are really required. However, this is likely to be both computationally intractable and lead to its own paradoxes.

On the train

We now consider a scenario designed to expose issues of moving spaces. Consider a train that has various forms of location sensing within it. This will clearly make a 'space' of locations within the train, but this space itself both moves and bends within the stationary space of track, buildings etc. (Figure 9).

There are four obvious spaces that need to be represented. First, there is the Outside Space. This space is is fixed and mapped to Ordinance Survey grid or perhaps GPS coordinates. Second there is a Train Space. This space is conceptually linear (in that it consists of a sequence of carriages), but not necessarily straight, as the train may move around a bend in the track. The granularity that is required is low – "I want to get from seat 3F in carriage G to the buffet car". Within a carriage we find the third space, the Carriage Space, which can be represented with a Cartesian system. Finally, there are Seat Spaces requiring fine granularity. For example, to place a paper 'reserved' ticket in the slot in the seat back requires millimetre accuracy.

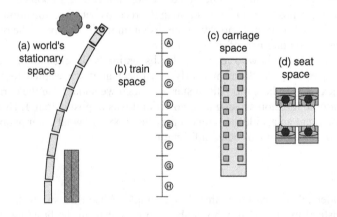

Figure 9. Train spaces

In order to explore the consequences of having those spaces that move relative to each other, we look at three scenarios: getting onto the train, walking through the train, and getting of the train.

Scenario – *Getting onto the train*

Alison is on the train and Brian is on the platform. As the train starts off Brian keeps pace and starts to say something to Alison through the window. Alison cannot hear through window and the noise of the engine, but can see his lips moving. He runs along beside the train until it gets too fast and he is left behind. It is one of those old fashioned trains with open steps and as the open doorway passes he swings himself up into the train.

In this scenario Alison's location is measured relative to the carriage and seat spaces and she is not 'moving' relative to them. The carriage space is also static in the train space, but the train space is moving relative to the world space. Brian's location, as measured in the world-space using GPS is changing. Brian and Alison are staying near to each other because the change in Brian's location, matches the way that the train space is moving relative to the world space.

There are two boundaries between the spaces that are worth discussing. The train window is permeable to vision, but not sound or movement. The window is moves relative to the stationary space, but is stationary relative to the carriage space. The doorway is similar to the train window, but it is permeable to movement. By stepping through this door, Brian stops being in motion relative to the world space, and becomes present, stationary, in the moving train space.

Scenario – *Moving through the train*

Brian is walking quickly down the train to find Alison. Someone's feet are sticking slightly into the gangway and he half trips over them.

"Oops", he says and he turns

"Sorry", says the person sitting at the seat

Then he recognises the person as Clare, another work colleague. After a polite chat with Clare, Brian continues down the train. As he passes the seat of Dave, he meets the ticket collector. Brian does not have a ticket, and he searches for some cash in his pockets to buy a ticket. All this time they stand at Dave's seat.

In this scenario, Brian is moving primarily in the train and carriage spaces. He is not concerned what is happening on the seat space. Only when he trips, his attention shifts from the carriage space to the seat space. This shift in attention was not planned or intentional, and it will be difficult for a system to tell that this shift has happened. If we want to detect that Brian has 'met' Clare, then the best we can do is to use the time of residence within a zone as a measure of focus. However, if time in proximity were used as a heuristic for entering the seat space, Brain would have been regarded computationally as in Dave's seat space when he was buying a ticket, and perhaps a meeting with Dave was logged incorrectly.

Scenario – leaving the train

While the ticket collector is issuing the ticket, the train stops at a station and then starts again. As they finish, Brian looks out through the train only to see Alison slowly moving past the window. She is standing on the platform looking at the information board while the train moves off to the next station. Brian's words are unrecorded.

At the end Alison was stationary relative to the station space, but moving relative to the train space. When she left the door, she traversed from the train space to the world space, which at that moment in time were stationary relative to each other. While looking through the window Brian gets in contact with Alison, but she was not looking at him. A permeable boundary does not imply there is contact, the people on either side need to focus in order to establish contact.

FUTURE WORK – FROM THEORY TO INFRASTRUCTURE

The experience projects described earlier in this chapter were built using a variety of existing and specially constructed mechanisms. Building interactive experiences and applications that exploit space and location requires both low-level underlying infrastructure for linking sensors and managing spatial information and also high-level tools to aid content developers to produce spatially triggered information.

Ongoing work in Equator is addressing several of these issues. At the level of location sensing the deployment of indoor ultrasonic is being made more easy by using automatic calibration instead of requiring accurate measurement of transmitter positions (Duff & Muller, 2003). Also signals from public WiFi access points are being used to give location information in town centres without the need for expensive GPS receivers. At the tools level both designer-controlled methods using 'colouring' of maps and also by-example learning are being used to create semantic zones within continuous coordinate spaces. Finally at the infrastructure level a single spatial infrastructure is currently under construction. For information about this ongoing work on space see:

http://www.hcibook.com/alan/papers/space-chapter-2004/

SUMMARY

In brief, we have seen how experiences with digitally enhanced environments reveal multiple interacting spaces. We distinguished physical, measured and virtual spaces and saw how each can be of several kinds and differ in accuracy and extent. People deal remarkable well with complex special relationships, but it is harder for mere computers! In order to understand the mappings between these complex spaces we have been using scenarios to explore different types of space, complementing our more practical observations.

AFFLIATIONS

Alan Dix, Adrian Friday
Lancaster University
alan@hcibook.com
adrian@comp.lancs.ac.uk

Boriana Koleva, Tom Rodden
Nottingham University
bnk@cs.nott.ac.uk
tom@cs.nott.ac.uk

Henk Muller, Cliff Randell
Bristol University
henkm@cs.bris.ac.uk
cliff@cs.bris.ac.uk

Anthony Steed
University College London
a.steed@cs.ucl.ac.uk

REFERENCES

Allen, J.E. 1991, 'Planning as Temporal Reasoning', in Proc., 2nd Principles of Knowledge Representation and Reasoning, Morgan Kaufmann.

Barrus, J. W., Waters, R. C., & Anderson, D. B. 1996. Locales: supporting large multiuser virtual environments. IEEE Computer Graphics and Applications, 16(6):50–57.

Brown, B., McColl, I., Chalmers, M., Galani, A., Randell, C. and Steed, A. 2003, 'Lessons from the Lighthouse: Collaboration in a Shared Mixed Reality System'. In Proc. of the CHI 2003 Conference on Human Factors in Computing Systems, ACM Press, pp. 577–584.

Burdea, G.C. & Coiffet, P. 2003, Virtual Reality Technology, 2nd Edition, Wiley-Interscience.

Cheverst, K., Davies, N., Mitchell, K., Friday, A. & Efstratiou, C. 2000. 'Developing a Context-aware Electronic Tourist Guide: Some Issues and Experiences'. In Proceedings of CHI 2000, ACM Press, pp. 17–24.

Dix, A., Rodden, T., Davies, N., Trevor, J., Friday, A. & Palfreyman, K. 2000, 'Exploiting space and location as a design framework for interactive mobile systems'. ACM Transactions on Computer-Human Interaction (TOCHI), vol. 7, no. 3, pp. 285–321.

Dix, A. 2000, 'Welsh Mathematician walks in Cyberspace (the cartography of cyberspace)', in Proc. of the Third International Conf. on Collaborative Virtual Environments - CVE2000, ACM Press, pp. 3–7.

Duff, P. & Muller, H. 2003, 'Autocalibration Algorithm for Ultrasonic Location Systems'. In: Proceedings of the Seventh IEEE International Symposium on Wearable Computers, IEEE Computer Society, pp. 62–68.

Flintham, M., Anastasi, R., Benford, S., Hemmings, T., Crabtree, A., Greenhalgh, C., Rodden, T., Tandavanitj, N., Adams, M. & Row-Farr, J. 2003, 'Where on-line meets on-the-streets: experiences with mobile mixed reality games'. In CHI 2003 Conference on Human Factors in Computing Systems, ACM Press Florida, 5-10 April 2003.

Gaver, W., Bowers, J., Boucher, A., Gellerson, H., Pennington, S., Schmidt, A., Steed, A., Villars, N. & Walker, B. 2004, 'The drift table: designing for ludic engagement', In Design expo case studies:

Extended abstracts of the 2004 conference on Human factors and computing systems table of contents, CHI 2004, Vienna, Austria. pp. 885–900

Ghali, A., Boumi, S., Benford, S., Green, J. & Pridmore, T. 2003, 'Visually Tracked Flashlights as Interaction Devices', in Proceedings of Interact 2003, Zurich, Switzerland, IFIP.

Grigni, M., Papadias, D. & Papadimitriou, C. 1995, 'Topological Inference', in Proceedings of the International Joint Conference of Artificial Intelligence (IJCAI), Montreal, Canada, AAAI Press.

Koleva, B., Benford, S. & Greenhalgh, C. 1999, 'The Properties of Mixed Reality Boundaries', in Proceedings of ECSCW'99.

Krasner, G., & Pope, S. 1988. 'A cookbook for using the model-view-controller user interface paradigm in Smalltalk-80'. JOOP, 1(3).

Newman, W., Eldridge, M. & Lamming, M. 1991. 'Pepys: Generating Autobiographies by Automatic Tracking. In Proceedings of the second European conference on computer supported cooperative work – ECSCW '91, 25-27 September 1991, Kluwer.Academic Publishers, Amsterdam. pp 175–188.

Papadias, D., Egenhofer, M. & Sharma, J. 1996, 'Hierarchical Reasoning about Direction Relations', in Proceedings of the 4th ACM-GIS, ACM Press.

Pascoe, J. 1997. 'The stick-e note architecture: extending the interface beyond the user'. In Proceedings of the 2nd international conference on Intelligent user interfaces, ACM Press, pp. 261–264

Price, S., Rogers, Y., Stanton, D. & Smith, H. 2003, 'A new conceptual framework for CSCL: supporting diverse forms of reflection through multiple interactions'. In Wasson, B., Ludvigsen, S. & Hoppe, U. (eds), Designing for Change in Networked Learning Environments. Proceedings of the International Conference on Computer Supported Collaborative Learning 2003.

Steed, A., MacColl, I., Randell, C., Brown, B., Chalmers. M. & Greenhalgh, C. 2004, 'Models of Space in a Mixed-Reality System', in Proceedings of Eighth International Conference on Information Visualisation 2004, 14-16 July 2004, London, England, IEEE Computer Society Press.

A. J. SUMMERFIELD AND S. HAYMAN

13. AN EXISTENTIAL APPROACH TO REPRESENTING VISUAL CONTEXT

Reworking Visualisation Methodology for Architecture

INTRODUCTION

If the use of synthetic images in architecture is to be taken as anything more than a beguiling sham, then their apparent realism poses serious issues for the representation of building proposals. They often implicitly project technological sophistication and scientific authority that derives from underlying associations with lighting analysis. They may seem to be based on photometric data and validated lighting algorithms, but their premises, conditions and limitations are seldom, if ever, explicitly stated. The suspicion arises that their current role is primarily intended to seduce or enchant with technological prowess and thereby sell the proposed project, instead of informing the viewer with accurate information about the proposed design (figure 1).

Figure 1: generated using lighting simulation software, this apparently realistic synthetic image that is entirely whimsical and thus without meaning as a tool for design evaluation.

Rather than have imagery being driven by the priorities of other disciplines or interests, this work is concerned with rethinking visualisation methodology

P. Turner and E. Davenport (Eds.), Spaces, Spatiality and Technology, 173-190.

specifically for architectural evaluation. This means addressing the issue of accurate representation of the context enveloping a building, so that synthetic imagery may provide more reliable predictions for use in robust and critical interrogation of design proposals. The discipline of architecture is often characterised by a lack of consensus and computer graphics by hubris, so it is worthwhile pausing to reflect how uncertainty about the depiction of buildings has arisen and why the representation of rich context is both essential and problematic.

BACKGROUND

Synthetic imagery might be regarded as just the latest technological twist in the long tango between architecture and representation. The ambiguity of the relationship with the earlier technology of photographic imagery remains topical in architectural discourse. In a recent collection of essays edited by Rattenbury (2001), the awkwardness is succinctly captured on the cover with an iconic monochrome image of Mies van der Rohe's Barcelona Pavilion and the subtitle *'this is not architecture'* - echoing Magritte's 1925 ambiguous painting *'ceci n'est pas une pipe'*. The discourse reminds us of Le Corbusier's manipulation of imagery as part of the modernist polemic both in terms of the representation of built forms and in the portrayal of his own work. Outside of the discipline, the history of misrepresentation in architectural projects has been the subject of lengthy criticism in environmental psychology (Appleyard, 1977; Shepperd, 1987; Bosselman, 1998). With synthetic imagery, it might be argued that architects already have *form* in both senses: a long record of manipulation and now the facility to generate and compose virtual geometry into scenes of proposals. But an efficient system for capturing the rich complexity and subtlety of a building interacting within its visual environment has generally remained elusive.

The arrival of virtual environments (VE's) that permit the viewer to look around and in so doing alter and recompose the scene, suddenly reveals the limitations of many previous apparently realistic synthetic images. The active participation of the viewer in a VE, who should more accurately be referred to now as the *reviewer*, has radically altered the degree of control the architect has traditionally had over the presentation of the design proposals. The contrived views of a building proposal floating in space or on the infinite empty plane are glaringly exposed and will no longer suffice.

However, such possibilities lie in stark contrast to the alluring spectacle of the technologically savvy architect as film director - tightly controlling the narrative of design presentation. Hectic animations through building proposals, apparently following the path of some errant winged insect on steroids, are a familiar example. All the more ironic, given current capabilities of accurate lighting simulation and burgeoning courses in architecture on gaining skill with visualisation software, that this appears to coincide with a long-term neglect or failure to fully embrace knowledge about the perceptual and physical role of lighting and particularly from daylight, that is the light of sun, sky, and reflected from the environment (Serra, 1998; Michel 1996).

In one study it has been reported that architects showed little understanding in connecting important features in the design of a passive solar house with well-established design 'rules of thumb' (Donn, 2001). Now more than ever, Donn concludes, building simulation needs tools for quality assurance. Methodological issues, uncertainties, and limitations need to be addressed if VE's even remotely live up to the assertions that '*the realism of computer generated renderings allows the comparative evaluation of design alternatives based on the aesthetics of the visual simulation*' (Bertol, 1997: 50). Or as Decker (1994) has warned '*the potential of this tool will be significantly diminished in point-by-point legal challenges that will at best only create a complex body of misunderstanding.*'

Largely as part of a critique of representation of building proposals, the field of environmental psychology has already established extensive guidelines for visual simulation, which is defined as *visual pictures or images of proposed projects or future conditions, shown in perspective views in the context of actual sites* (Shepperd, 1989: 6). Five principles of simulation have been suggested to determine their comprehension, credibility and bias (Shepperd, 1989: 63):

"Representativeness: portrayal of important and typical views of the project, and under different conditions; Accuracy: similarity in appearance between the simulated and the project post-construction; Visual clarity: ability to distinguish the elements of the scene; Interest: engagement of the reviewer by the simulation; Legitimacy: extent that the correctness of the simulations are demonstrated and defensible."

While Shepperd has expounded these principles as a general protocol for all simulation types that would remain valid as computer simulation developed, they have failed to be adopted by the design community over the intervening years. By claiming all perspective representations as potential candidates of simulation, effectively brings in conceptual sketch drawings within their scope. Such a restriction on creative expression during the early design phase probably made their disregard by architects as inevitable. In the process, the lesser obligation to represent the proposed building on its site, in other words the visual context, has been passed over as well.

One approach that may avoid such objections in the application of VE's in architecture is to redefine their scope as a distinct class of VE's termed *Veri*dical *S*ynthetic *Im*agery, or for brevity *Verisims*. Veridical refers to the notion of correspondence between the attributes perceived in *verisim* and the information provided by other representations, such as plans or sections, or the correspondence of showing the project from different viewpoints or under different conditions. Sufficient veridicality, rather than perfection, underpins the pragmatic aim of informed evaluation. Nevertheless it expresses the objective of having greater methodological rigour than the already diluted terms *realistic* or *photorealistic* imply, both of which may be regarded more as artistic styles of computer graphics in their own right. Moreover *verisims* are not about replicating the characteristics of photographs, but simply to permit the reviewer to make predictions about certain attributes of the designs shown, as based on the specifications given in a project database. They attempt to improve on the reliability of information currently provided by *artistic impressions*, that perennial and convenient let-out clause of many architectural renderings, and specifically to provide definitive answers to a range of evaluative questions about the attributes of the design. Thus verisims should be subject to standards for their validity, in the same way that plans and sections must comply to drawing conventions like constancy of scale.

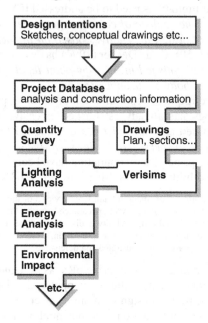

Figure 2: Verisims should be integrated within the wider simulation and analysis structure derived from the project database, but are distinct from representation of design intentions.

Thus the ensemble of imagery that form *verisims* connects far more closely to other simulations used to analyse the project, from plans and sections, to financial costings, to energy efficiency - analyses that are becoming increasingly integrated (Clitherlet & Hand, 2000) - than sketches and other purely presentational drawings. These may now be considered separately as representations of design intentions so that architects can continue to express their conceptual ideas with complete artistic freedom.

Sometimes the suggestion is given that unlike quantitative results, imagery concerns primarily aesthetic and perhaps by implication less consequential issues and so need not be subjected to the same simulation standards (Roy, 2000; Ward Larson & Shakespeare, 1997). For the layperson, images can portray information in a direct way about definitive attributes beyond aesthetics, such as the organisation, relative size, aspect, and clarity of a space, where plans, tables and graphs may remain obtuse. For instance, if the imagery indicates a lack of privacy, excessive direct sunlight or reflections, or just an inappropriate view, then reviewers may indicate their intention to deploy blinds or curtains. Such actions have implications for not only for the aesthetics of the buildings external appearance, but the maintenance cost of the building and its energy consumption.

If this defining *verisims* frames the potential of VE's to inform the reviewer about a design proposal and avoids it being subverted, then it is a worthwhile semantic exercise simply because architecture has serious and enduring consequences. If simulation imagery dealt with just special effects for the cinema or advertising a consumer product - both mainstays of the computer graphics industry - then the individual leaving the theatre or buying a different toaster might mitigated those misleading results. In contrast, architecture powerfully affects the lives and activities of the inhabitants and the community by creating an environment for either an enriched or alternatively an impoverished and dysfunctional existence. For many, such as office or factory workers with minimal control over their workplace, the impact of poor design is unavoidable. The physical permanence and expense of buildings mean their adverse effects may last for a generation or more. Lastly, if sustainable development of the environment is adopted as a high priority in the design process, then the application of *verisims* for reliable prediction and communication of building proposals becomes all the more crucial.

THE PERCEPTION OF ARCHITECTURAL SPACE

Part of the difficulty that has prevented a more predictive role for VE's in architecture, lies in the way the perceived attributes of space in architecture are potentially confounded in systems that simulate architectural space. Specifically two strands of the treatment of space and spatial experience have particular bearing on VE's.

Figure 3: Perspective distortion in the detailed coffering geometry at the Pantheon, Rome (photo by permission Robin Benson, ©2003 R. Benson)

Firstly, the precise consideration of form and material attributes can profoundly alter the spatial experience beyond that which might be implied by less attention to the details of geometry and materials. Such techniques have been practiced since antiquity, for instance the perspective distortion (rather than symmetric arrangement) of coffering geometry detail at the Pantheon at Rome (fig.3).

Holl (1994: 121-124) points to the additional effect of a subtle concavity of the flooring - a detail omitted from many measured drawings. In that environment all such details, along with acoustic and haptic sensations, seem to contribute to an enhanced experience of the space centred beneath the oculus of that vast dome. As Hooper (1978) writes: '*(architecture) is hard and soft, touchable yet illusory. It is inanimate, yet it is the shell for human lives. Ultimately, it exists by these tensions. It is the interaction of physical form and perceptions.* Therefore simplification and abstraction used for efficiency in VE's may project a significantly impoverished experience.

Secondly, without altering the essential geometry or extent of a 'room', spatial properties can be changed via any opening in a wall that connects or extends the perceived space to the realm beyond, to the local environment, or distant view. Again the precise details that mediate the transition can have a profound role in the nature of that spatial experience: the scale, proportions, translucence of the aperture, and the articulation of its boundary (Hooper, 1978). So inevitably this relative and connected notion of space involves the contextual environment beyond the design itself. To ignore the visual context in generating VE's will likely alter the spatial experience.

These issues of spatial perception come together in Le Corbusier's chapel the Notre Dame du Haut at Ronchamp. A key feature of the apparent massiveness of the building is the dark drooping roof form that is in fact an illusion created by lightweight concrete shell construction. Le Corbusier specifically noted that he intended the 10 cm horizontal gap at junction of roof and wall, seen inside as a crack of skylight, to create '*a sense of surprise*' (Millet 1996: 65). The *heavy* roof defies gravity, ironically recalling the levitation of virtual forms. The illusion is created through precisely defined exterior-interior expectations that anticipate a set of perceptions in the viewer. Even in the highly enclosed interior, this crack of skylight creates a specific connection with the open contextual environment, since such an effect would not have worked in a built-up environment that overshadowed the building.

Figure 4: exterior and interior views of Nôtre Dame du Haut at Ronchamp by Le Corbusier (photo by permission Liao Yusheng, ©2004).

It turns out that this building has long acted as an alluring touchstone for computer modelling and lighting simulation, for instance figure 5 (Haines, 1991). The implication being that by representing such a building, the visualisation of architecture has been accomplished. Yet the full illusion of the floating roof is typically missing from synthetic views of the interior. A slippage that is probably due to a combination of substantive differences in geometry, material attributes, and in the external lighting conditions. Typically there are further errors of siting the building on an infinite plane and not approaching it from along a narrow path.

Figure 5: Synthetic image of the chapel interior (image by permission Eric Haines; modeled by Keith Howie and Paul Boudreau, and rendered by Eric Haines. ©1991, The Hewlett-Packard Company; (Haines, 1991).

If such omissions can occur post-construction with numerous photographs available to check the correspondence of the representation, the question arises as to the extent that VE's might compromise and impoverish the design process of architecture? Would Le Corbusier have found the technology of VE's a useful tool for the creative inspiration to include the crack of light in his design or would it have been overlooked due to its absence from the imagery?

The idea of architecture itself as a kind of simulation system, using the attributes of physical elements and the space between them to create the illusion of something else, can be extended to other stages of the design process. For this, a notional equivalence must be assumed between simulation and the imperfect mapping of information from one domain into another. Thus the project brief, through words and site drawings, represents the priorities of the client. From here the architect's response emerges and design intentions are expressed through sketches and conceptual diagrams. If accepted, they are mapped to form a model system of the project via plans, sectional drawings, and material specifications, which in turn can be converted via construction into physical reality. After all these steps of representation, it is hoped that the building remains true to the original intentions. The result is that many aspects of multiple representation systems are deeply enmeshed if not confounded in the design process. Herein lies the fundamental problem in evaluating synthetic imagery: which stage of the design process does a particular VE image attribute reflect, or is it just an artefact of the simulation itself?

Secondly, what attributes of the project have been omitted from the simulation used to generate the VE?

If this were not enough, consider the elemental expression of architecture as the modest building placed in its environment and lit by sun, sky and ground. Daylight is inherent to our experience of buildings. It unavoidably defines the exterior and washes past apertures through the interior space. Heightened interest occurs at the interface between inside and outside - at the entrance, or in the foyer, or atrium. Even in otherwise prosaic buildings, architecture often is afforded in this space a moment of artistic indulgence. Daylight has been part of the metaphysics of architecture, often referred to poetically: '...*natural light is the only light that makes architecture architecture*' (Louis Kahn as quoted by Ronner, 1989: 344). Yet precisely because of all the geographical, temporal variation of sun and sky, with its brilliant intensity and shades that washes with endless subtlety the full expression of a building, this fundamental vision of architecture is probably one of the most difficult scenarios for visual simulation to capture.

Human Visual Perception and the Visual Context

The case for addressing visual context in VE's more generally is supported by the characteristics of human visual perception (HVP) of space in both physical scenes and imagery. For instance stereoscopic vision (primarily through binocular disparity) is particularly effective at detecting the presence of an image surface and so identifying a perspective arrangement of elements as a flat representation. This was even noted by Leonardo Da Vinci: '*And why does a picture seen with one eye give the same effect of relief as the real scene, having the same effect of light and shade?*' (Pirenne, 1975). The counter intuitive notion of enhanced perception by reducing the sensory input can be understood in terms of shifting to a reliance on monocular vision; thereby obviating a key means to detect the image surface. This allows scene perception to be driven by the image content instead, including such perceptual cues as occlusion for depth perception, mutual shadowing, perspective effects, the relative size of elements, inter-reflection, and so on (Ferwerda, 1997; Interrante, 1997).

Selective representation of some cues over others in synthetic imagery, even with subtle effects, risks omitting crucial cues for accurate perception. An elegant demonstration is evident by changing the position of a single shadow in an image to affect greatly the perception of an object depth, height, and size - a fact long recognised by artists in their use of shadows to give perceptual cues (Yonas *et al.*, 1978; Yonas 1979). In architecture it is often the inclusion of such cues that particularly serves to ground visually a building to its site.

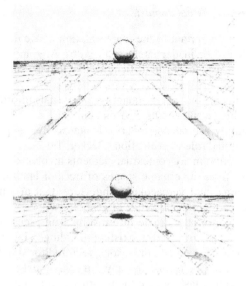

Figure 6: change in a single shadow affecting the perception of depth, height, and size of an object (after Yonas et al. 1978).

A coherent perception of a 3-dimensional scene emerges from imagery in a process that Interrante (1996) suggests should be thought of as an organisation of space: accurate and stable judgements under a range of conditions of global qualitative aspects, combined with good judgement of relative local attributes, such as shape and depth differences. The weight of evidence suggests that with imagery, where the viewer relies on pictorial cues rather than stereoscopic cues, perceptual accuracy benefits from the range of shadowing and shading cues portrayed.

Unfortunately this runs counter to the focus of many simulation systems that under the imperative of rendering speed use lighting models, which simplify the process as far as possible, by for instance assuming that only Lambertian reflection (equal reflectance in all directions) occurs. Such an assumption lies at the core of radiosity lighting algorithms used in many visualisation software packages (Watt & Watt, 1998).

Instead it appears that HVP in applications driven by accurate and reliable evaluations of images a sophisticated lighting model is required, one that as far as possible provides the full range of pictorial cues by accounting for the relative subtleties and details of shadows and shading. In meeting such a challenge the representation of visual context inevitably plays a critical role in the expression of these visual cues. It also reinforces the connection between the methodology used to generate *verisims* and quantitative lighting analysis.

The problematic issue of visual context

If visual context is so important to the representation of architecture, then why is it so frequently neglected or inadequately dealt with? Any approach developed here must confront the intrinsic technical difficulties that may be summarised as follows:

- magnitude: the sheer quantity of visual information involved in describing a site and its environment;
- sensitivity: some contextual elements have a potentially vital and unexpected role in evaluation (Decker, 1997);
- complexity: many contextual elements involve distinctive and complex forms, from the organic shapes of trees or landforms to the details of traditional and vernacular architecture, that are difficult to model in anything more than a crude or generic way;
- lack of information: site information with plans and sections is often unavailable for nearby existing buildings, let alone their material attributes or detailed dimensions, required for simulation;
- relevance: inclusion of any of this 'extra' data burdens the computation task, where the priority is to reduce the database size, as diverting resources away from simulating the project itself.

Thus the importance of visual context in VE's is matched by its complexity in the physical world (in both natural elements and traditional buildings) and to measure and model the context requires scarce resources to be diverted away from modelling the proposal itself. The problem is exacerbated by the software typically used to construct VE's, where simple surface facets from predefined elements that can then be combined to progressively construct more complex components, and then to reproduce as much of the environment as possible. For instance a *solid* object such as a wall may be composed from a series of connected surfaces (that will only appear hollow if observed within the surface) so that every object in the virtual world can be constructed from components in a similar way. But when the same strategy is applied to represent a single distinctive tree, it may require an ensemble of more than a million such facets - more than might be used for the rectilinear building geometry (Ward Larson & Shakespeare, 1998). Thus the proclivity to reduce or impoverish the visual context may be understood as arising from an *ad hoc* need to reduce the computational burden in generating the VE.

Current methods to address visual context in practice often consist of some variation of photomontage, whereby the computer generated image of the project is 'manually' (but using image software) inserted into a digital photograph of the site. One of the key issues is to ensure that the image of the building and photograph have the same viewpoint and lens specifications. The image is then sometimes further retouched manually to 'airbrush' in shadows that might visually connect the synthetic building to its photographic environment. Other interaction between the building and the environment, such as reflection in windows, are far more difficult to reproduce.

The overall lack of rigour and indefensible nature of photomontage has a long record of concerned commentary (Shepperd, 1989; Decker, 1995). Anecdotal evidence from architects and from the author's own experience in practice certainly suggests a widespread manipulation, whereby building size is reduced or expanded to alter its visual impact - as facilitated by the image software - simply to suit the whim of the protagonists as objectors to or supporters of the project. Indeed, this very ease of manipulation in combining images that has allowed photomontage to be used as a provocative and political art form in its own right.

AN EXISTENTIAL APPROACH

An alternative strategy using environment maps extends techniques developed for incorporating synthetic imagery for the cinematic industry (Debevec, 1998; Kerlow, 2000). It can be interpreted as an existential approach where the VE can be structured far more precisely to the specific spatial experience of the individual or *reviewer* from a specific viewpoint. Following Aylward & Turnbull (1978), we suggest a system of visual descriptors that compose a scene and these fall into three groups: form (shape, outline etc.), relation (position, orientation etc.), materiality (shadowing, reflectivity, translucence etc.). The VE can then be structured into three distinct zones:

- *the project*: the part of the VE that the reviewer is intended to directly engage with or inhabits; it presents as complete a set of descriptors as is possible or desired;
- *local environment*: interacts with the project (shadows, reflections etc.), only requires partial or simplified form (outlines and elemental geometry rather than details), and specification of position and materiality;
- *global environment*: only acts upon the project (sun, sky, distant landscape); interpreted as an infinitely distant sphere; it remains constant across the project and local environment and requires only illusion of form, position, materiality.

This approach allocates a level of simulation or representation according to the descriptors required for the zone of the element being rendered.

At each of numerous sample points environment maps are required for the entire visual field available. These need to be pre-selected around the site corresponding to viewpoints that would be most useful for a critical evaluation of the project, including representation from surrounding circulation routes, key vistas and access areas and inside the project. This follows Mitchel (1996) and others who suggest using a series of freeze-frame views in a connected sequence as the basis for evaluation, and supports Shepperd's (1987) principle of *representativeness* for visual simulation. The limitation is that we shall be generating a viewpoint specific scene, and the reviewer jumps from one point to another, but arguably is sufficient for a step-by-step interrogation of the project. Real-time simulation for VE's and animations at 25 frames per second requires considerable computing resources.

For architecture it is arguably sufficient to represent the scene in a series of viewpoints with discussion at each and instead based on the reliance of HVP on image content, focus instead on quality. Nevertheless using QTVR format gives the reviewer the ability to observe the entire context around each viewpoint and to zoom in and out of the scene. The sense of presence at this stage is limited to high quality representations at discrete viewpoints that the reviewer constructs as their own cognitive model of the whole project. In principle a multitude of closely positioned viewpoints can be blended into a fully immersive environment where reviewers may move smoothly around the site (Debevec, 1998).

Overall the measurement process itself must have both simplicity and speed. It requires stable lighting conditions from viewpoint to viewpoint, preferably sunny days with clear skies, or overcast skies with no direct sun. Cloudy conditions, particularly high altitude cloud, can cause problems by partially blocking the solar region and so cause rapid and significant changes in the illuminance levels. On sunny days, changes in the solar angle (and thence shadow angles) during the measurement process may become an important factor, for instance at the equinox the sun advances along its arc by ~5° every 20 minutes.

One rapid way to capture the entire 360° *visual range* available at each viewpoint across a site is by using a digital camera and combining two counter facing fisheye 180° images. However, as distinct from the typical use of environment maps as background images or for reflection mapping, these will be used to describe large area light sources, or illuminants, in the VE. Thus they need to be contain the full range of lighting conditions visible - from the brightest points in the sky to the details hidden in the shadows – that correspond to the luminance of those surfaces. This can be achieved with a series of bracketed exposures at each viewpont, typically three across the range, that when combined form a calibrated luminance map of the entire environment with every existing element visible at that point in time and space. Since direct sunlight is beyond the scale available this source is specified separately (in the same way that sun sources are currently specified via azimuth and altitude angles in standard software).

In validating this stage the global luminance map was projected into the VE about the viewpoint, so it could act as *an equivalent light source around the viewpoint exactly as occurred in the physical environment at that viewpoint.* When the level of lighting was measured in the VE, in terms of the horizontal diffuse illuminance (that is the light received on the horizontal plane from all sources other than sunlight), it was found to agree to within 10% with that measured at that time at the viewpoint on the physical site. The major proportion of the error was systematic and due to the equipment and measuring process rather than the visualization software or mapping procedure itself.

By combining the detailed information of the luminance map with the local and global zone structure constructed in the VE, it is now possible to allocate resources so that the level of modelling of each element is matched to the level of descriptors required in each zone. Thus rather than requiring the complex 3D geometry of a tree in the local environment, it may only need the correct outline form to cast the necessary shadows and to appear correctly shaded according to its appearance from the viewpoint. (Note that when viewed from other positions on the site the shading will appear progressively distorted). No simulation effort is wasted in recreating the lighting of the tree itself, since this information already exists in the information provided by the luminance map. The proposed building - the project - occupies its space in the VE in the usual way, but now it is surrounded by and interacts with a context visually enriched by the information from the luminance map. The result is reminiscent of stage set design with facades and backcloths, but with the environment map projected outwards for the viewpoint, as if constructed for a single member of the audience sitting in the middle of the stage.

Once the scene is correctly generated at the viewpoint any number of perspectives with all manner of camera specification can be generated as imagery. There is in complete contrast with the guesswork associated with traditional photomontage. However QTVR format identifies this as a VE and remains the media closest to the objectives of *verisims*, since the reviewer has the ability to actively engage with and control the composition of the scene. This has been a simplified outline of the process, but the illustrative example in the next section should serve to clarify how the methodology works in practice.

ILLUSTRATIVE EXAMPLE

In a hypothetical building project for a complex contextual site from the University of Sydney it is proposed to replace an existing cottage by a new student centre (figures 7).

Figure 7: Two views of the cottage at the University of Sydney that will be replaced by a hypothetical project for a student study centre.

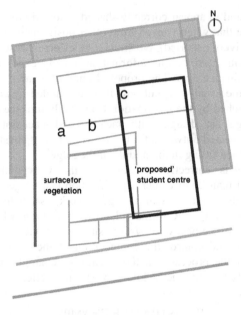

Figure 8: Simplified site plan indicating proposed building and areas of elemental geometry used to model the local context. Global luminance maps are captured at numerous key points ('a', 'b', 'c', etc.) across the site, to be illustrated here by the results for viewpoint 'a'.

Figure 9: proposed building to replace the cottage – without contextual information and then shown sited within the simple local geometry model that contains less than 100 facets.

Figure 10: Fish-eye imagery (calibrated luminance map) for point 'a' and used to project for viewpoint specific simulation onto the local and global zones in the VE.

At numerous points across the site calibrated fisheye images are combined to form global luminance maps and opacity maps at each viewpoint (figure 10). The project is constructed as a detailed virtual model and sited correctly in the VE with respect to the viewpoint. Simple geometric forms are positioned corresponding to the important local buildings and the landscape. Thus far the computer modeling is identical to a conventional virtual model surrounded by a series of block forms. It is important to note that this virtual model is based entirely on the information specified in the project database, a key condition of verisims.

The luminance maps are projected from the viewpoint outwards and mapped onto the local forms to generate a series of shaded outline shapes in a way that preserves their appearance as seen from the viewpoint. The additional opacity maps are used to generate complex outlines at the interface between local and global environments. The remaining elements of the global environment (the sky and distant buildings, trees etc.) are mapped onto the infinite sphere of the global environment.

Six 90° images are generated (that can be conceptualised as looking from the interior at 6 sides of a cube) in order to construct a cubic QTVR for the viewpoint. This gives complete 360° freedom for the reviewer to dynamically choose any orientation about the viewpoint as well as zooming in and out of the scene. Ironically the limitations of printing cannot convey this interaction in the figures generated from the results at point 'a', nevertheless they accurately show the correct occlusion, overshadowing, and reflections automatically generated by this rendering process. In other words the project properly interacts with its site. Not only is this without manual interference, but the representation of the entire local environment of buildings, trees and signage requires less than 100 surfaces. Figure 11 shows three perspective images taken from the QTVR generated at point 'a'.

Figure 11: The project set in the visual context of the VE with the viewpoint information
wrapped onto the simple local geometry and global environment.

The scenes illustrate the projects interaction with the site including shadows cast by trees and nearby buildings as well as reflections of the context in the glazing of the proposed building.

In an initial evaluation of the approach, a series of web-based block design experiments used three distinctive designs on the same site. Participants entered the web site and responded to a questions about QTVR imagery of the projects presented in random order. We compared the participant's perceptions of the project when shown on an empty plane and when shown surrounded by a simple box type model of the context, with those from simulations that used the full contextual model. Evidence was found that participants generally, and to a lesser extent those involved with the design, not only found that full contextual QTVR imagery more useful and easier to understand, but that it significantly (p-value <0.05) affected their evaluations by tending to produce a more favourable response of the project's attributes as well (Summerfield, 2004).

DISCUSSION

We have argued that for VE's to live up to their potential as a useful tool in design evaluation then a rethinking of simulation methodology specific to the requirements of architecture is required. To avoid verisims were defined as conceptually being part of the range of simulations, from plans and sectional drawings to energy consumption, that are used to analyse and predict the performance of building proposals as based on its specifications. They were identified as entirely distinct from the architect's creative use of imagery used to suggest design intentions.

We outlined the crucial role of the visual context in the way architecture and its representations are perceived. To address the problematic issue of complexity in simulating context, an existential approach was developed that is both practical and defensible. It has been illustrated with an example project on a site with typically complex visual context and which would be difficult to represent using standard methods. The structured zones of the virtual environment, combined with the experiential information captured at discrete viewpoints, allows for a more efficient allocation of visualisation resources to where it matters for perceptual interpretation. The results produced complex visual cues between the building and the environment without manual intervention. The methodology presents substantial improvements on both traditional photomontage techniques and standard *ad hoc* methods of simplification and abstraction used in computer simulation of architecture.

While significant advantages of contextual simulation were suggested by the response of the participants in an evaluative study, further validation research is required on the correspondence between attributes in the VE representation of architectural proposals and the eventual buildings. By developing a system of efficient and reliable contextual simulation, numerous paths lie open for extensive testing and critical evaluation of aspects of architectural design proposals. Synthetic imagery generated from VE's may still not fully identify the best possible of all designs, but they may yet help us avoid building mistakes.

AFFILIATIONS

A. J. Summerfield is an Honorary Associate and S. Hayman is a Senior Lecturer at the Faculty of Architecture, University of Sydney, Australia.

REFERENCES

Appleyard, D. (1977). Understanding professional media: Issues, theory and a research agenda. In I. Altman & J. F. Wohlwill (Eds.), *Human Behaviour & Environment* (Vol. 2). New York: Plenum.

Aylward, G., & Turnbull, M. (1978). Visual analysis: the development and use of visual descriptors. *Design Methods and Theories, 12*(2), 72 - 86.

Bertol, D. (1997). *Designing digital space : an architect's guide to virtual reality*. New York: Wiley.

Bosselmann, P. (1998). *Representation of Places: reality and realism in city design*: University of California Press.

Citherlet, S., & Hand, J. (2002). Assessing energy, lighting, room acoustics, occupant comfort and environmental impacts performance of building with a single simulation program. *Building and Environment, 37*, 845 –856.

Debevec, P. (1998). *Rendering Synthetic Objects into Real Scenes: bridging traditional and image-based graphics with global illumination and high dynamic range photography*. Paper presented at the SIGGRAPH 98.

Decker, J. (1994). The validation of computer simulation for design guideline dispute resolution. *Environment and Behaviour, 26*(3), pp 421-443.

Ferwerda, J. A. (1997). *Principles of Visual Perception and their Applications in Computer Graphics*. Paper presented at the SIGGRAPH 97.

Haines, E., Howie, K., & Boudreau, P. (1991). http://www.erichaines.com/

Hochberg, J. (1978). Art and perception. In E. C. Carterette & M. P. Friedman (Eds.), *Handbook of Perception: Volume X, Perceptual Ecology* (pp. 225 - 258). New York: Academic Press.

Holl, S., Pallasmaa, J., & Perez-Gomez, A. (1994). *Questions of Perception: the phenomenology of architecture*. Tokyo: a + u Pub. Co.

Hooper, K. (1978). Perceptual aspects of architecture. In E. C. Carterette & M. P. Friedman (Eds.), *Handbook of Perception: Volume X, Perceptual Ecology*. New York: Academic press.

Interrante, V. (1997). Perceiving and Representing Shape and Depth. In *Principles of Visual Perception and their Applications in Computer Graphics* (pp. 1-27): SIGGRAPH 97.

Kerlow, I. V. (2000). *The Art of 3-D Computer Animation and Imaging*. New York: John Wiley and Sons.

Liao, Y. (2004). http://www.figure-ground.com/travel/image.php?ronchamp

Michel, L. (1996). *Light: the shape of space, designing with space and light*. New York: Van Nostrand Reinhold.

Millet, M. S. (1996). *Light Revealing Architecture*. New York: Van Nostrand Reinhold.

Pirenne, M. (1975). Vision and art. In E. C. Carterette & M. P. Friedman (Eds.), *Handbook of Perception: volume V, seeing*.

Ronner, H. (1987.). *Louis I. Kahn: complete work, 1935-1974 / Heinz Ronner, Sharad Jhaveri*. (2nd rev. and enl. ed. ed.). Basel ; Boston : Birkhauser Verlag,.

Roy, G. G. (2000). *A Comparative Study of Lighting Simulation Packages Suitable for use in Architectural Design*: Murdock University.

Serra, R. (1998). Daylighting. In C. Gallo, M. Sala & S. A. (Eds.), *Rewable and Sustainable Energy Reviews* (Vol. 2, pp. 115-155).

Shepperd, S. R. J. (1989). *Visual Simulation: a user's guide for architects, engineers, and planners*. New York: Van Nostrand Reinhold.

Ward Larson, G., & Shakespeare, B. (1998). *Rendering with Radiance: the art and science of lighting visualisation*. San Francisco: Morgan Kaufmann.

Watt, A., & Watt, M. (1998). *Advanced Animation and Rendering Techniques: theory and practice*. New York: ACM Press.

Yonas, A. (Ed.). (1979). *Attached and Cast Shadows*: Praeger.

Yonas, A., Goldsmith, L. T., & Hallstrom, J. L. (1978). Development of sensitivity to information provided by cast shadows in pictures. *Perception, 7*(3), pp 333-341.

14. PERFORMATIVE USES OF SPACE IN MIXED MEDIA ENVIRONMENTS

INTRODUCTION

Moving computing and interfaces from the virtuality of the screen into the physical environment of space and artefacts not only enables people to interact in an embodied and performative way, it also provides the interfaces with a spatial dimension. As a result, computing becomes embedded in people's physical and social world, opening up possibilities to actively stage their own interaction through creating configurations of interactive artefacts, media and space.

Performative events in interactive and multimedia environments have for some time already been experimented with in the arts. Its potential has been much less explored in everyday environments at work or in domestic settings. This is why in order to argue our case, we use field work material from two different sources: a) an earlier study on the use of programmable light and projections for an artistic performance – the musical 'Kiss of a Spider Woman'; b) a project developing architectures and technologies for inspirational learning environments for an architectural master class.

In the first case we observed how computation was used to create mixed media spaces on the stage of a musical theatre. These observations help us gain a better understanding of how configuring and re-configuring a space (using the principle of collage/montage) affects performative action within the space. It also provides a framework for discussing possible extensions and amplifications of such an environment through, for example, tracking systems and media processing.

The second case deals with a different kind of activity – learning architectural design – and a more advanced technical environment, which offers a variety of input and output components in addition to lighting and multiple projections. We observed interesting similarities between the theatre performance and the ways, in which the architectural students used the technologies for re-creating and re-experiencing aspects of places and situations outside the studio. At the same time, we explored new and additional possibilities of creating connections between spaces (e.g. a field site and the studio), of integrating mixed representations within a space, and of navigating a remote space in ways that are integrated with the physical environment of space and artefacts.

P. Turner and E. Davenport (Eds.), Spaces, Spatiality and Technology, 191-216.

The interest in space

The study of the social organisation of space has its place in social science literature, in particular in urban sociology and in the work of social geographers (Gregory 1994). Their focus is on issues of culture, power, knowledge, and spatiality. As has been argued in particular by Giddens (1990) and Bourdieu (1989), spaces bound and structure activities. A space can be designed to reflect important aspects of context. It may be connected, reflect other places and times. The specific artefacts, symbols, knowledges, and ideologies that inhabit a space are resources, which both, are mobilised in social interactions, and shape these interactions. A sociology of space has "to demonstrate how spatial arrangements construct, sustain, constrain, and, occasionally, transform human practices" (Tellioglu and Wagner 2001: 164).

The social organization of space is at the heart of architectural design. As architect Bernard Tschumi argues, "space is not simply the three-dimensional projection of a mental representation, but it is something that is heard, and is acted upon" (1981, in Nesbitt 1996: 45). Spaces are spaces for something, not things stripped of use. Tschumi critiques the programming of space within architecture in terms of function. He suggests to look at architecture not as an object (or work in structuralist terms), but as an "interaction of space and events" (in Nesbitt 1996, p.162). Tschumi's interest in choreographed movement as creating space – "bodies not only move in but generate spaces produced by and through the movements" (1980, in Nesbitt 1996: 154) – stresses the performative aspect of space. Already in the 1920's Oskar Schlemmer formulated this principle for the theatre. It was commented that in his Bauhaus dance performance in Berlin the moving body is often disappearing „behind the movement, behind moved cloths and forms, behind metal, glass, a system of circles, rods, cubes, etc". Seemingly lifeless objects have "quite intelligently been provided with wings, 'like light on glass' " (Fiebach 1995, p.52). Schlemmer juxtaposed two concepts of space – cubic space with its edges and connecting lines, and the relational network, which results from moving bodies (Lainer and Wagner 2000).

The connection of space with movement introduces the element of time. Michel de Certeau includes the dimension of time into his definition of space (de Certeau 1984, p. 117):

> "A space exists when one takes into consideration vectors of direction, velocities, and time variables. Thus space is composed of intersections of mobile elements. It is in a sense actuated by the ensemble of movements within it. Space occurs as the effect produced by the operations that orient it, situate it, temporalize it, and make it function in a polyvalent unity of conflictual programs or contractual proximities ".

While the interest in space and performance has influenced architectural and artistic practice, few studies investigate the performative aspect of how people actively, flexibly and reflexively stage their actions within space, making use of the resources at hand. To think about the social use of space as 'event' takes a step in this direction, by emphasizing the situated, contextual, evolving, temporary, and performance-like character of activities within space (Lainer and Wagner 1998). One of the few empirical studies in this direction was carried out by Heath *et al.* (2002) in a museum setting. They use the term 'active spectator', pointing to the "relevance of the ecology or setting in which a painting or sculpture is positioned, and to the ways in which the spectator actively 'connects' features of the object to action within the local milieu" (Heath *et al.*, 2002: 11). This study not only stresses the cooperative nature of encountering art work but also looks at how 'active spectators' perform these encounters within physical space.

On the notion of performance

We focus on interpretations of space that emphasize the importance of considering time and performativity as fundamental aspects of its use. We first of all need to make clear how the notion of performance is to be understood in our context, as from an anthropological perspective it can embrace virtually all aspects of our life. In the following we will deal with how it relates to space, to narrativity, and to mixed media, and how it can be applied beyond the theatre in other communicative events where spatial features are consciously created.

"A 'performance' may be defined as all the activity of a given participant on a given occasion which serves to influence in any way any of the other participants", Goffman (1959). Definitions of performance can be taken to include all human acts carried out "with a real or notional spectator in mind, and so with an awareness that they are expressive" (Counsell and Wolf, 2001:157). While anything can be studied "as" performance, something "is" a performance when social context and convention say it is, referring to specific cultural circumstances (Schechner 2002). Performative events differ widely, with respect to the resources that are used and their cultural and spatial framing, as can be seen in familiar examples, such as games (soccer), rituals (church), or theatre performances.

The approach provided by Eugenio Barba contributes with an additional perspective on performance, stressing the importance of skills, energy, and consciousness (thinking) of the performer. Barba (1991) distinguishes between daily and extra daily techniques (p. 9):

> "The way we use our bodies in daily life is substantially different from the way we use them in performance. We are not conscious of our daily techniques: we move, we sit, we carry things, we kiss, we agree and disagree with gestures which we believe to be natural but which are in fact culturally determined… ".

While in our daily techniques we follow the principle of less-effort, that is obtaining the maximum result with the minimum expenditure of energy, "extra daily techniques are based, on-the-contrary, on wasting of energy" (Barba 1995 p. 16). The principle might even be opposite: "The principle of maximum commitment of energy for a minimal result". During the performance, besides investing energy in accomplishing successfully actions on the practical or on the expressive side, we must invest energy in thinking.

Obviously performances are of a varied nature, each commanding a specific context and space: "Culture viewed as speech, gesture, and action is performance; and performance not only requires but commands its own kind of space." (Tuan 1990). Spatial features may be functional, such as walls, but they may also be charged symbolically, resulting in a specific perception of space during a performance. In a theatrical performance, for example, we accomplish:

> "an essentially interpretative act, translating real bodies, words and movements into the objects of another, hypothetical world; ... everything within the defined spatial compass of the stage is to be read differently from the objects seen elsewhere" (Counsell and Wolf 2001, p.155).

The reading of space in performative events, however, does not always imply maintaining a hypothetical world. Spatial features may convey narrative elements to be experienced directly as in some performance art pieces. Particularly interesting to this discussion are artistic movements in the 60ies and 70ies that blurred the boundaries between traditionally separated disciplines. An example is the mixing of art and life in Kaprow's Happenings. As Carlson (1996) notes, Kaprow traced their roots in Cubist collages, which questioned traditional harmonies by introducing irrational juxtapositions and foreign matter into the painting. Kaprow summarising this evolution writes: "The pieces of paper curled up off the canvas, were removed from the surface to exist on their own, became more solid as they grew into other materials and, reaching out further into the room, filled it entirely" (Kaprow 1966 p.185). Carlson, commenting these words, notes how "canvas evolves through collage to assemblage and environments" (1996, p. 97). Happenings emerged out of the evolution in structure and complexity of these environments and of activities of the participants. Kaprow defines his approach to happenings as being through "action collage".

Theatre, installation art and experimental cinema

One of the focal points of this discussion is the use of technology in performative spaces. Already in the 1920s Moholy-Nagy worked with projections of moving light for creating surprising effects on the stage, like in his stage designs for Piscator. Their main element was the interweaving of space with representational functions (Gropius 1934). Much later Richard Kostelanetz took up this tradition in his book "Theater of the Mixed Means", which he elsewhere explains, differs:

> "from conventional drama in de-emphasizing verbal language, if not avoiding words completely, in order to stress such presentational means as sound and light, objects and scenery, and /or the movement of people and props, often in addition to the newer technologies of films, recorded tape, amplification systems, radio, and closed-circuit television" (Kostelanetz 1994).

Other examples of how to make use of digital media for creating spaces can be found in installation art (e.g. Nollert 2003) and experimental cinema (Shaw and Weibel 2003). After decades of pioneering work of artists like Vito Acconci, art installations are increasingly mixing multimedia with architecture and bodily presence. Acconci explains well how performative architecture operates:

> "The viewer activates (operates) an instrument (what the viewer has at hand) that in turn activates (builds) an architecture (what the viewer is in) that in turn activates (carries) a sign (what the viewer shows off): the viewer becomes the victim of a cultural sign which, however stays in existence only as long as the viewer works to keep the instrument going." (Acconci 1981)

In more general terms, performative installations can be considered a "synthesis of art event and art work, of presence and representation, of immateriality and materiality" (Nollert 2003, p.4), with the artist intertwining different levels of presence, temporality, space and experience. An installation is produced in a process of arranging and placing; it is three-dimensional; it relates to the surrounding space, invading it, thereby creating a particular experience of the space. Linked with the materiality of an installation, the solidness or fragility of its physical components, are events or performances. This results in a fusion of presence and representation, ephemeral and static elements, short-term event and duration, immateriality and materiality.

Examples of mixed media installations are provided by Diana Thater who "turn(s) video into architecture, throwing the image up to play over the found space of her installation" (p. 139); or the work of Jennifer Steinkamp where "riots of colour, form, and light blur and reconfigure the place of bodies in space and the relationship of those bodies to the installation, the architectural environment, and one another" (Lunenfeld 2001, p. 11).

While some work focuses on producing dynamic, interactive, non-linear narratives, other work produces installations that explore immersive and technologically innovative environments diverging from the conventional screening formats. An important element of experimental cinema is its move away from a central author – the director. It follows new models like the one of Chilean Filmmaker Raul Ruiz:

> "whereby the autocracy of the director and his subjugating optical apparatus can be shifted towards the notion of a cinema located in the personally discoverable periphery" (Shaw and Weibel 2003, p. 19).

Methodological premises

One of our aims is to inform technology development programs about new opportunities and roles for technology with a view to the performative use of space. Performance refers to interactions as part of an event; it stresses the simultaneousness of action and experience, of presence and presentation. Performance points to how communicative acts are embodied in expressions within the space, the artefacts, and the movement of the body. We also talk of performance insofar as there is a particular consciousness of the act and we have a particular interest in the activities done in preparation of interactions, in actors' configuring or staging the event.

We will use the two field studies to uncover how the roles technology and people may assume in performative events challenge established human-computer interaction frameworks. Moreover we seek to understand, how spatial features participate in the configuration of mixed media environments and the performative aspects of how people interact in them. While our ultimate interest lies in situations of everyday life– in learning, work, and mundane social interactions - we included the case of a theatrical performance. We think that studying artistic performances and the ways these make use of space and technologies helps us identify some of the most salient features of performative interactions. But as we will see, the theatre case also contains some very distinctive features.

THE THEATRICAL PERFORMANCE

"The Kiss of a Spider Woman" is a musical based on a novel of Marcel Puig. The story is based on a dialogue of two men who share a prison cell in a fictitious totalitarian regime. Interwoven into the narrative, is one of the protagonist's memories of movies with his favourite female star, Arora (the leading actress in the musical). She invades the real world of the prison, haunting the dreams, visions and agonies of the captives. As the plot draws to its culmination, the comforting Arora is transformed into the demonic "Spider Woman" and the death of her admirer merges the world of the movie with reality.

The visualization of this concept is based on the interweaving of set, slide projection and lighting into the design of a multi-facetted, lively and quickly changing optical surrounding for the actors that is additionally stimulated by music, songs and dancing. At the core of the set are bars outlining a prison cell. Projected images and the painting of the multicoloured brilliant light beams furnish this basic setting, turning the simple prison cell into a variety of imagined outside worlds.

Our study took place in a Viennese theatre that is specialized in the performing of musicals. The new production in preparation had been bought as a whole from the US production company that originally had designed and implemented it for a stage in New York. The play had already been adapted and performed in London and in Toronto. Our fieldwork focused on the process of adapting the system to the specific environment of the theatre. This was done by a lighting design assistant and a programmer, who both had been working together in the original and in all consecutive productions. Our fieldwork started with the beginning of the lighting rehearsals in the middle of the installing period, covering those and most of the dress rehearsals up to the beginning of the public performances. We observed the work of adjusting the lighting design as well as its effects on the stage.

The technical base of computerized lighting consists of a "VariLite" system, a central controlling and programming unit and a variable number of spot-lights each of which is directly addressable by remote control. The detailed lighting program from the US performance was brought on floppy disks. These pre-designed settings needed to be adapted to the special dimensions of the new stage (and, partially, to changes of the artistic concept). This is basically done in three steps: First, each light setting is adapted to the dimensions and light absorbing and reflecting properties of the stage. Then, the setting is accommodated to scene positions and variations of the set. Finally, it is adjusted to the estimated positions and actions of actors and dancers. All these adaptations are done in real time by the VariLite Programmer who can modify and re-adjust every single parameter (position, intensity, beam, colour, iris etc.) of a single spot or a chosen combination of spots, by turning control knobs or by entering numbers on keypads.

Light has always been a central artistic medium. Light is used for structuring visual fields, for multiplying visual options, and for producing atmospheric qualities.

Light illuminates, shadows, hides, creates sharp or diffuse boundaries; it dims or makes persons and objects glow. Its programmability adds another dimension: as a precise instrument for parametricising a visual field, programmable lighting widens the options for stage design. It is possible to rapidly and synchronously modulate a great number of light sources, their position, movement, colour, intensity, and patterning. Lighting design becomes an integral part of the design of setting and decor; it is used for underlining musical and dance effects and for dramatically accentuating the script. The programmable light allows to implement techniques of representing and visualizing which have been developed in photography and the film: dimming, inserting, cuts, the play of framings, immobilities, still-shots, kaleidoscopic sequences of images can be simulated by rapidly changing lighting arrangements and projections.

We observed, for example, how lighting designer and programmer made small adjustments of the colouring and the intensity of the lighting; how they reprogrammed a fading-out effect; how they frequently consulted their lighting script for checking parameters; how they coordinated the lighting effects with the stage set, adjusting the positioning of spot-lights, actors and decor; how they controlled the positioning and animation of a slide projection.

While watching their work, we observed how the real scene with its fixed spatial dimensions, partitions, walls, openings, vistas, closures, and objects got impregnated with a "space in flux". This space was virtual in the sense of non-tangible, futile and only present as an image of some distant or fantasized place. Light made a thick green jungle with pink orchids fill the prison cell, some image of a movie scene flicker in front of the window, the vista of a bridge appeared and faded out. This virtual space was dynamic. It furnished and re-furnished the here-and-now location of the stage in a rapid sequence of variable light situations, each of which suggested a different arrangement of spatial elements. The modulated shower of light, which swept over the scene, introduced surface equivalents to the spatial dimensions of depth, connectedness and bodily movement (Sobchack 1988).

One of our observations is to do with how the automated, animated lighting affects actors' interaction on the stage. Gliding through beams of light, the actors changed between "light spaces", thereby creating the illusion of bridging large distances and times. Their bodily presence on a real stage in real time was modified in a strange way since the mixed media space they occupied was fluent and multi-layered; it blended a variety of places; it was synchronous and asynchronous at the same time. Paul Virilio talks of 'telepresence' as a mixture of being there and simultaneously at another place (Virilio 1990).

Another observation is to do with the performative qualities of this mixed media space. Already the text of the book works with what art theory coins collage/montage – the assemblage of seemingly unconnected fragments into a new whole. Programmable lighting and projections amplify and perfectionize the collage/montage effect of the textual script, in various ways. One is the sheer speed with which light animations can be varied. This literally pulls the spectator into the unfolding events. Their attention is captured by the rapid display of electronically created sub-spaces.

Art theory argues that collage/montage breaks with the idea of representation. With the cutting out and assembling of material, in this case remote spaces and situations, there is a loss of reference. The projection (houses, bridge) signifies itself and something else (within the new frame into which it has been mounted). It may disrupt, surprise, provoke, irritate, confuse, but it does not offer an unambiguous relation to a "referent". The resulting multi-layered space is both, real in its connection to embodied interaction, and illusionary. Assembling the fragments becomes an integral part of the performance.

A final observation relates to the fact that a performance is a dynamic event, not just a static presentation, intertwined with movement of scene and actors in time. We may look at a theatre (musical) performance as merging a variety of temporal orders: the temporalities that are constituted by actors' movements and speed and flow of speech, the internal rhythm and speed of the accompanying music, the temporal structures of the lighting arrangements, and, finally, the audience's temporalities which may or may not be tuned into time on the stage. The lighting not only dynamizes and virtualizes the stage. It simultaneously serves as a "stage timer" - a predominant temporality, parametrizing the action on stage. In addition to key phrases, stage dimensions, co-actors and music, all persons on the stage had to fine-tune their activities to the rapid light modulations. Even the slightest incorrectness in entering and leaving the stage, in positioning themselves, in the tempering of speech and song became highly visible due to their incongruity with the "blindly acting" light. The granularity of this animated lighting sequence was so fine that the actors had no room for letting the performance evolve as a process.

Since Walter Benjamin (1963) this phenomenon is connected with the notion of reproducibility. The musical was divided into hundreds of small units which are marked by a set of numerical parameters: codes that mark the intensity, colour, speed of the lighting, temporal markers, spot-light numbers. They were used for programming effects and for reading the correctness of a setting. This encoding of sensual categories is necessary for operating the technical equipment. Together with the splitting of the unfolding activities into smallest units, it allowed the directing team to perfectionize each unit and to conserve it, thus ensuring its reproducibility. Once media and interactions have been configured, they form a script, which determines the performance. By storing each unit in a computer, an electronic representation of the performance was created. In this sense, the programmable, animated light is far more than just an additional source. It allows to store the artistic concept in the form of a visual representation of actors' positions and movements, of the duration of actions and their sequencing and temporality, of the properties and dynamics of alternating virtual spaces. This is why the performance can be sold on an ordinary diskette. In combination with a VariLite instalment (which can be rented) and some tailoring of the program, the lighting concept can be implemented on any stage with any team of actors, musicians (which can easily be substituted by an electronically created sound track), and stage personnel.

Our observations of how lighting design created mixed media spaces on a stage influenced the ways in which we experienced the use of technologies and space in the architectural master class, directing our attention to several aspects:
-     the fluent, ephemeral, and rhythmic nature of mixed media spaces

- the role of movement – of the performers but also of the interface (a "space in flux")
- the principle of collage/montage – it resonates with what architects see as an important aspect of their work: the peripheral presence of events or objects, with short-time events, fast, assembled, ad-hoc, such as film, video and fashion photography being important inspirational resources (Wagner 2003)
- the configurability of the space which in the case of the theatre performance becomes fixed in a script.

As we will see, students' mixed media performances in the Atelier project were more informal, less designed and elaborate. At the same time, the more advanced technological environment provided them with additional resources for integrating the environment of space and artefacts into their work.

MIXED MEDIA PERFORMANCES IN THE ATELIER PROJECT

Within this project we explored approaches to mixing physical and digital artefacts and experimented with ways of integrating the physical space into the students' learning activities. The project proceeded in three design circles, starting with an extensive period of fieldwork – video-supported observations and interviews – at the two sites. Based on this material we looked for opportunities for technology-support, developing a set of prototypes and scenarios of use, and designed field trials at both sites (Iacucci and Wagner 2003). Our strategy for these field trials was not to create new and dedicated artefacts and spaces but to enhance existing practices with new technology and to motivate students to integrate the prototypes into ongoing project work.

In the first cycle of field trials we used simple prototypes of physical interfaces and projection set-ups and made extensions to them whilst students were experimenting. Students came up with a wide range of ideas of how to integrate interactivity in physical objects. They used the space as a resource, e.g. by re-creating elements of remote places in the studio with projection surfaces. The experiences of the field trials were used to extend and further evolve the prototypes. The experimental environment we developed consists of input components (sensors, RFID tags, and barcodes), output components (beamers, the Texture painter), an infrastructure providing messaging and registration, configuration applications, a shared hypermedia database, and a configurable spatial set-up (3D Table and Interactive stage). Sensors, tags, and barcodes provide a simple way to associate media files with the environment of space and artefacts. Associations of physical input, digital media and output can be edited and loaded through configuration tables that are stored in the database. The following examples show how the students, through simple configurations of space and technologies, created dynamic representations of their design ideas.

Bodily presence in mixed media spaces

One of the first trials involved simple physical interfaces, such as a barcode scanner interface. The application was used by two architects (also teachers at the Academy of Fine Arts) for associating multimedia files to barcodes. They placed the barcodes on the scale model of one of their designs, a private home and its surrounding garden. Scanning the barcodes triggered the playing of sounds that evoked particular situations and images of the site or of inspiring architectures and interiors were displayed. The architects used this set-up in their presentations to the client. At first they placed the model near the wall, onto which the images where projected (Figure 1), but also other projection arrangements were tried out on different walls and in different scales. For example the architects used the entire wall for a 1:1 projection, creating the feeling of literally "sitting in the garden" (Figure 2).

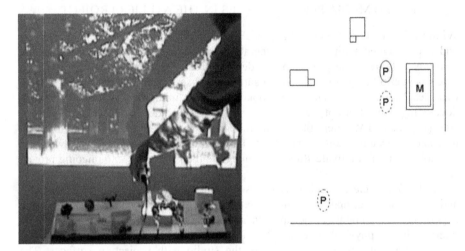

Figure 1. Animating a model barcodes, two performers (P) using two projection set-ups.

As one of the architects commented[1]: "If I want to associate a material with a model, I can use a projection of it in the same space where the model is and get the atmosphere of it or the texture in the right scale and one has to interweave the two representations that help to make a decision." Of Importance for him was not only the multimediality of the emerging amalgams of physical model and large size projections but the fact that the technology enabled him to create and place associative material directly "at the model where I had the association... like having the hyperlink right there where it belongs". He pointed out that adding notes, correction-clouds, and hyperlinks to a document, such as a CAD plan, is already a wide-spread practice in architecture. The barcode application added an important new dimension to this practice, by introducing an expressive element.

---

[1] All the quotes from interviews with students and teaching staff have been put into italics.

More importantly, the technology allowed evoke specific qualities of an environment or an atmosphere in the working space, with the multimediality affecting all the senses. Being *"emotional animals"* we respond to soundscapes and immersive projections. Moods and emotions play an important role in design decisions and the use of sound has recently become more common in architecture, as animations of architectures are created with soundtracks.

The potential of creating atmospheres and playing with them is seen as important, especially as many architects consider their office not only as a place to work in but as a place "to be in". Architects tend to spend more time than other professionals in their studios, which they often furnish with collections of all kinds, from inspirational resources, such as art books, poetry, and music, to samples of materials: *"Many offices store their records and CDs in the office to emotionalize a working night"*. This not only points at immersive multimedia as a source for creating a more pleasurable environment, in line with the tendency of equipping offices with coffee corners, lounges, fitness rooms, recreations areas, bathrooms, music fountains, and magazines. It also shows that immersive and pervasive (integrated in a physical model) multimedia can become an integral aspect of design work.

Figure 2. Animating a model with barcode and projections of different scale.

Our observations of how the Academy's students integrated those first simple prototypes into their work reveal some additional aspects. As part of one of their semester projects - the 'least expensive stadium in the world' - a group of students went on an excursion to London-Lille-Paris, from which they returned with lots of materials in their bags – videos, photos, objets trouvés, their personal diaries. Their task was to use this material for creating a themed presentation of their experiences before they went on to their next assignment, to design an "extreme stadium". We followed the work of three students on these individual stadium projects.

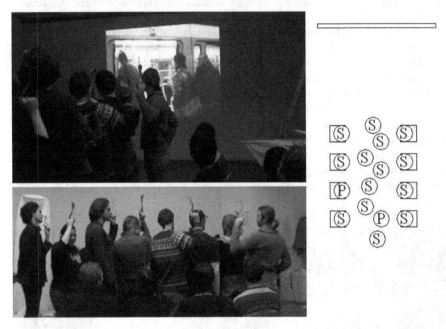

Figure 3. The "train ride" - spectators become passengers sitting and standing in a recreated travelling space

The students used and adapted the space and technologies we provided for re-creating aspects of a <u>remote place</u> – in different ways. One student group decided to present their analysis using the video of a trip to the Stade de France as a structure of their presentation. The *Atelier* space was used by presenters and spectators to perform and thus re-experience this trip with the Parisian métro. Seats were arranged like in the métro and some spectators became passengers. They had to stand and were provided with a handle made from orange plastic. In this configuration they watched the video, which alternated sequences of travelling the métro(which accelerated, growing noisier and more hectic) with the presentation of stills at a calm and slow pace (Figure 3).

Figure 4. A miniature soccer field as an interface to guide the presentation

One student prepared an elaborate presentation of her design ideas for an 'extreme stadium' in the area between Vienna's two large museums. She had prepared a soccer field and two slide shows, with one screen displaying cultural aspects of soccer (images, sound, video) and the second screen displaying her design ideas in the making. The slide show was operated through a sensor that had been fixed underneath the soccer field (Figure 4). The presentation itself was designed as a soccer-game, with the building sites being the teams - stadium versus museums - explaining the design ideas being the team-tactics, and herself as the referee, with a yellow card and a whistle signalling a 'bad idea' and shooting a goal a 'good idea'. In the words of the performer *"it was the idea to have soccer-games or soccer tools like the ball, yellow card as sensor tools. Also the architectural project used soccer terminology instead of common architecture words"*.

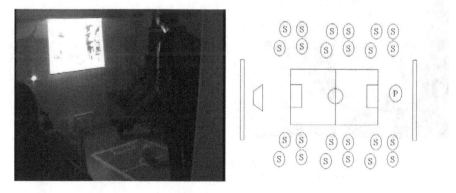

Figure 5. Disposing the spectators as in a noisy stadium

When the ball touched the goal, a sensor triggered off a reporter's voice shouting 'goal, goal' and the cheering of the visitors. The yellow card was also given to members of the teaching staff to interrupt the presentation with questions and comments. Spectators were invited into an arrangement like in a stadium: "*In the presentation them sitting around me, like in a stadium, the whole atmosphere was like in a noisy stadium.*" (Figure 5).

Recreating and performing space

As part of his individual stadium project, a student projected images of two residential buildings with two beamers onto double layers of cloth, which he arranged in the curved shapes of the buildings, with the buildings facing each other so as to recreate the site. During the presentation the two buildings were undergoing changes. He visualized the transformation of the balconies into seating arrangements for viewing a soccer game in the space in-between, performing these changes while the class was watching. (Figure 6).

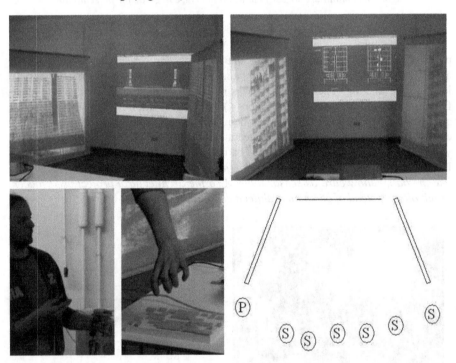

Figure 6. Two back projections on textiles hanging from the ceiling and one front projection on the wall -several artefacts make it possible to direct media in space

The performer held a barcode scanner in one hand, with which he scanned barcodes he had placed on diagrams and plans, a switch in the other hand. This allowed him to direct the display of media onto the three different projection surfaces. A physical model representing his design of bathrooms and other spaces underneath the stadium was augmented with touch sensors. He used this arrangement for projecting detail drawings of this space onto the wall in between the two buildings.

Figure 7. Arranging posters and projection so that they form an enclosed space,

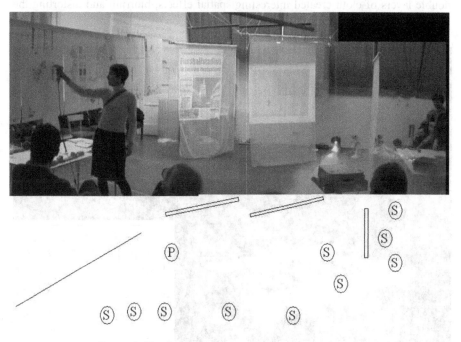

Figure 8. The final arrangement during the presentation

Narrative configurations of design ideas within a physical environment such as these take the bodily presence of spectators into account. This becomes particularly evident in the preparation of another presentation, where a student thought to arrange the posters and projections so that they form an enclosed space, thereby recreating the trapezoid square in the city of Vienna which she had analysed (Figure 7). She later explained: "*First I wanted to create a new space with those hanging posters, a space that can only be experienced, when you walk through the room, change your seat. But the reviewers cannot do that, I mean they could, but you know, they are too lazy maybe. So I arranged the posters and everything so that they could see it from one perspective.*" The new arrangement is shown in Figure 8.

Another group of students reported on their excursion to London-Lille-Parisas well as on their emerging initial ideas for an "extreme stadium", by staging a "poetry game" with a multi projection installation (Figure 9). Their narrative was based on contrasting the memories of those who had participated in the excursion with those who had remained in Vienna. The presentation consisted in the two groups reading short phases capturing their impressions and interpretations in a dialogue, while pictures were shown. This dialogue of experiences and concepts was embodied spatially with four projections: onto a set-up of double layers of transparent cloth facing each other, onto the ground (projected from above), and onto the wall. Te wall was used for projecting enlarged details of street signs (Figure 9). This spatial configuration expressed the contrasting positions of the groups. The double layers of cloth created interesting spatial effects, blurring and distorting the projected images.

Figure 9. The arrangement of four projections in space for the "poetry game".

Reviewers' feedback, which also included some criticism, pointed to important aspects of this conceptual performance. One comment was that *"having these two layers of fabrics, with one and the same image appearing in two different scales, opens up opportunities for simulating a space"*. Another teacher saw in performances of this type a method for conceiving architecture by exploring the *"simultaneity of oppositions or of things that seem unconnected"*. This is again an example of how multimedia installations may become an integral part of design work.

Staging and performing "mixed objects"

These ad-hoc arrangements developed into the *Interactive stage*, a low-tech immersive environment produced by a simple arrangement of a grid, three large-size projection screens, which can be fixed at different angles, and numerous beamers. The grid provides an infrastructure for fixing light-weight, movable projection screens (easy to change projection material) and lighting equipment (Figure 4).

In the *Interactive stage* architecture and technologies can be easily configured for experimenting with immersiveness and scale and for creating mixed spaces. Immersiveness can be obtained with simple means, using several beamers and projection screens, "projecting everywhere". Students may use the space for enacting a design concept in performed scenarios, relating to it with the strong presence of the body. 1:1 scale projections of models and other objects may help them to discover new features of a material or a site, experience how a detail of a model or texture looks like when it is blown up.

Part of the *Interactive stage* is the *3D Table*, a table with an integrated mirror and a semi transparent table-top, which can be used as a surface for placing objects and as a display component. Models placed on the table can be electronically painted with the *Texture painter*. This is a tool for painting virtual overlays – colour, textures, images or video - onto physical objects, such as models, in real time, scaling and rotating them. It provides a fast and highly interactive way of experimenting with scale, colour, background, and social use. The *3D Table* is equipped with integrated plugs for webcams and barcode readers and it has two integrated RFID tag readers. These physical interfaces make it possible to load textures to be used with the *Texture painter*, to load backgrounds on the large projection screens, as well as to save configurations of painted textures and backgrounds. As we discussed in Binder et al. (2004), the use of the *Texture painter* allows create "mixed objects". These have material and digital features and affordances, and they are the product of digital and physical configurations.

This set-up was used in a trial with first semester students whose assignment was to carry out an analysis of one of the 'icons' of modern architecture – Villa Tugendhat/Mies van der Rohe, Ville Savoye/Le Coprbusier, Haus Müller/Adolf Loos, etc. They were required to read texts reflecting original and contemporary views on these buildings. They had to build models in scale 1:50 and 1:20 (of an interesting spatial detail). They used *Interactive stage* and *Texture painter* for exploringing scale, materiality, and context.

Figure 10. Experimenting with scale, materiality and context

The students created "naturalistic" textures, that try to come close to the original ideas about the buildings' interior materials; or they did the opposite, replacing the original function by something completely different, as we can see in the transformations of one model into something like a Las Vegas fuelling station by loading up neon signs and painting them onto their model. They installed a second *Texture painter*, which enabled them to change the appearance of floor and roofs while at the same time 'painting' the façade. They used the projection surfaces for creating different contexts. The students took snapshots of all these variations with a digital camera, thereby continuing the normal architectural practice of documenting change, and projected and viewed these images in the *Interactive stage*.

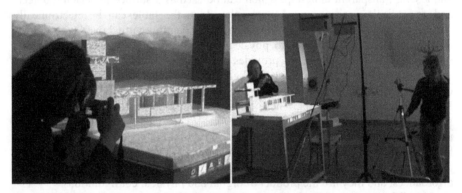

Figure 11. Painting a model with the Texture painter *and taking pictures at different distances and from different directions*

One of the effects of such playful variations was that these iconic architectures became more accessible to the students and open to criticism. The technologies offered them a means of expressing their analysis of the building's design, its strengths and weaknesses.

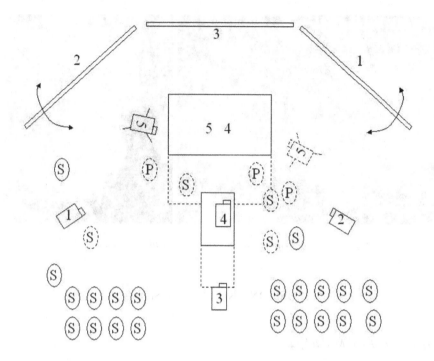

Figure 12. Interactive stage and 3D Table - students' spatial arrangement for painting physical models and for staging them in different scenographies

The textures which students "painted" onto their physical models, together with the background images on large screens, created effects that could be viewed from different distances, and, indeed, the students took pictures from different distances and directions. The three large screens not only served as a background for creating context and landscape, they also supported students in playing with immersiveness and scale, e.g. by "exploding" details of the painted model. For example, students used the webcam (which was attached to the table) for walkthroughs, projecting the video onto one of the screens (Figure 13).

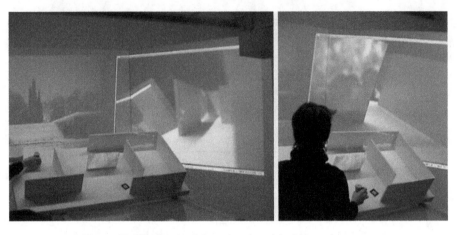

Figure 13. 'Performing' the painted model with a webcamera

DISCUSSION AND CONCLUSIONS

Performing Mixed Media Spaces

The cases we have considered are of a different nature. However, both cases point at the event-like, ephemeral character of mixed media spaces as representations. To communicate and be experienced they first of all need to be "performed".

In the first case, lighting and projections contribute to de-materialising the stage; they fill it with additional meaning by adding dynamic symbolisms (e.g. the blue spot light) and pictorial representations (e.g. slide projections of the Moscow buildings). Agency is distributed to actors and programmed effects, which become virtual actors in the performance, as they contribute actively to the formation of action. The stream of light animations accentuates and amplifies the collage/montage effect of the textual script. Collage/montage breaks with the linearity of a movie. The spatial distribution of lighting and projections results in a spatial collage of physical action and media, where temporality is scripted and programmed. While this particular musical performance maintains the traditional performer-spectator relationship, approaches to the theatre have been developed where "for each production, a new space is designed for the actors and spectators. Thus infinite variation of performer-audience relationship is possible" (Grotowsky 1969:19-20).

The second case reveals additional emerging aspects of mixed media spaces by situating them nearer to everyday life. Architecture students create interactive installations to objectify, present, and discuss their design projects. Installations are inherently different from staged performances, as they engage the spectator bodily, allowing them to turn into co-players (*cf* Suderburg 2000). This is evident in some of the installations the students produced, such as the "train ride" or the "soccer game". The created media space is designed to be inhabited and interacted with, also by spectator-participants. The opportunities for interactivity space and technologies provide invite improvisation. Only part of the performance or presentation is scripted, pre-configured in digital associations of physical inputs and multiple projections. What also distinguishes the students' work from the theatrical performance are some of the functionalities the more advanced technological environment provides. The students were able to integrate physical artefacts in their performance in dynamic ways, through equipping them with barcode and/or sensors or by "painting" them electronically in real time.

The examples from the architecture class also move beyond the traditional 1:1 scale of a staged performance. The examples how the creation of immersive installations resulted from: enlarging a small detail, or scaling a large building down to the size of a person; using multiple projections differently in space resulted . Finally, while in staged performances the represented places may be imaginary and physical location and features of a site secondary, in everyday use it may be important to convey and re-produce specific qualities or features of a site. Students recreated spatial features of remote physical locations.

Based on these observations we single out some features that characterise performative uses of mixed media spaces:

Simultaneousness of *presence and representation, experience and action*: Spectators and presenters in the *Atelier* trials became part of the representation. Bodily presence is important for both, how participants perceive the staged situation and how they contribute to the representation.

Directing digital media in space using interactive artefacts: Before our interventions students used projectors for slide presentations, moving to the next slide with a keyboard key. In the trials a variety of interactive artefacts enabled them to direct digital media in real time on multiple projectors.

Staging and performing mixed objects: Physical artefacts were staged, linking them with digital scenography and providing them with digital costumes. Walkthroughs with a camera through artefacts, such as a physical model, added a performative element to them . This resulted in a , dynamic process, through which students experienced physical representations of their evolving design (rather than a product or static representation).

Roles of participants and authorship: Activating the spatial dimension of media environments and working with them invites people to participate in the performance, either being present in the space or assuming a specific role. This problematises the notion of authorship since spectators can turn into performers.

Scale and immersiveness and site specificity: Scale and immersiveness are important aspects of mixed media spaces. They enable participants to e.g. enact a scene/use situation in a life size environment. Real size is to do with bodily presence. It is not scale in the geometric sense that matters but immersiveness and realism. The possibility of blowing up small details or scaling down pictures of buildings to the size of a person lets objects and their environment mutate in surprising and inspiring ways (Rumpfhuber and Wagner 2004). Another issue is the unusual view onto an object or scene that can be achieved by e.g. using the (web)camera as an artificial eye. This is one of the ways models can be staged.

Temporality and reproducibility: This is a central aspect of a theatrical performance, which enacts a script within a pre-configured environment. In the mixed media examples we described, agency and interactivity are distributed spatially, with a multiplicity of outputs and control points. But also in this case webcams may be used for recording changes made to the space or to an object.

Spatial narrativity: As audio-visual material is configured spatially in a mixed media space, the stage becomes part of a narrative. The story unfolds and can be read in the space architecture as well as in the images and sound that are produced. Spatial features are carefully prepared to co-adapt physical and digital artefacts. The space turns from a passive background into an active element of the performance.

Design Challenges for Human-Computer Interaction

Traditional human-computer interaction approaches, in the attempt to evaluate the usability of products for people, tend to see the person as a "user" and the product as a "tool", where the latter one is used to accomplish a task (cfr. Jordan 2003). The trials we reported on brought the spatiality of interfaces with a multiplicity of inputs and outputs into focus, where all - performer *and* spectators - participate in the interaction. As physical interfaces spread into the environment of space and artefacts, it becomes problematic to reduce applications to a tool. Moreover, complex situations such as the ones we have described, cannot be reduced to a task (*cf* Dourish 2001). The configurability of these physical interfaces potentially turns the user into director, scenographer, and architect. Finally, the fact that in such an environment sensuous experiences, including the body, become central, make use a limited concept.

Experiments with physical interfaces such as ours invite "radical" explorations of the ways space, artefacts, and digital media combine in new experiences, which seek to address our senses more than our analytical thinking. This resonates with Dewey's notion of sense (Dewey 1980/1934 p. 22).:

> ""sense" cover(s)ing a wide range of contents: the sensory, the sensational, the sensitive, the sensible, and the sentimental along with the sensuous. It includes almost everything from bare physical and emotional shock to sense itself – that is, the meaning of things present in immediate experience"

Our findings also move beyond a reflection-in-action perspective (Schön 1983). Performative interactions build upon people configuring, acting in, and perceiving mixed media spaces, in addition to talking with the design material. The performative arrangement of (moving) bodies, projections, and physical artefacts creates a sensual experience of grasping, touching, painting, moving, smelling, hearing, while at the same time being immersed in changing contexts. Spectators are no longer restricted to the role of external observers; their bodily presence makes them part of the performed presentations and representations. As one of the architects pointed out, design work involves playing around with moods and emotions. Students' experiences with staging and perceiving a situation from within open up a new view of computer technologies and of situated action.

The relevance of these elements for ubiquitous computing and other technology development programs is to challenge established imperatives. The notion of user, and the clear distinction between users and designer, is no longer sufficient for explaining the roles people may assume participating in the production and performance of mixed media spaces. While technology, such as in our case the VariLite system or the *Atelier* environment, is still designed by some people, other people configure and reinvent technologies to create interactive spaces, where these and other people perform in social interaction. The notion of user is further problematised by the fact that the system interface no longer is the prime stage of action, since the whole environment becomes included in what traditionally is termed interface. While all these notions are still applicable to the cases we presented, they are distributed and arranged in novel ways. Mixed media spaces, which are composed by a collection of systems, artefacts and infrastructures, are designed, configured, and performed. The interface does not exist singularly. A *multiplicity* characterises actions and reactions, inputs and outputs. Finally space is not merely part of the context of use, a "found space", but is consciously exploited in disposing narrative elements and affordances.

ACKNOWLEDGEMENTS

We are grateful to our co-researchers in the *Atelier* project, which is funded by the EU IST Disappearing Computer program. We are particularly indebted to Martin Kompast for his co-authoring the description and analysis of the case study of the lighting design of the musical 'Kiss of a Spider Woman'. Finally we would like to acknowledge Infotech Oulu for supporting this research at the University of Oulu.

REFERENCES

Acconci, V. (1981). *Some Grounds for art as a political model*. In: Sobel, D., Andera, M., Kwinter, S., Acconci, V. (2001). Vito Acconci: Acts of Architectures, Milwaukee Art Museum.

Antonelli, Paola (ed.), (2001). *Workspheres. Design and Contemporary Work Styles*. New York: The Museum of Modern Art.

Barba, E. (1995, 2002). *The Paper Canoe: a Guide to Theatre Anthropology*. London: Routledge.

Barba, E., & Savarese, N. (1999). *The Secret Art of the Performer, a dictionary of theatre anthropology*. London: Routledge.

Benjamin, W. (1963). *Das Kunstwerk im Zeitalter seiner technischen Reproduzierbarkeit*. Frankfurt: Suhrkamp.

Binder, T., De Michelis, G., Gervautz, M., Iacucci, G., Matkovic, K., Psik, T., Wagner, I., (forthcomming) Supporting Configurability in a Mixed Media Environment for Design Students. *Personal and Ubiquitous Computing Journal*: Springer Verlag, forthcoming.

Bourdieu, P., 1989, Social Space and Symbolic Power. *Sociological Theory* 7(1), 14-25.

Carlson, M. (1996). *Performance, A Critical Introduction*. New York: Routledge.

Certeau, M. de, (1988). *Kunst des Handelns*. Berlin: Merve Verlag.

Certeau, M., de, (1984). *The Practice of Everyday Life*. Berkeley: University of California Press.

Counsell, C., & Wolf, L. (2001). *Performance Analysis: An Introductory Coursebook*. London: Routledge.

Dewey, J., (1980/1934) *Art as Experience*. New York: Perigee Books.

Dourish, P. (2001). *Where the Action is: the Foundations of Embodied Interaction*. London: MIT Press.

Fiebach, J. (1995). Audivisuelle Medien, Warenhäuser und Theateravantgarde. In: Fischer-Lichte. E. (ed.) *TheaterAvantgarde*. Francke, Tübingen/Basel, pp.15-57.

Giddens, A. (1990). *The Consequences of Modernity*, Cambridge/Oxford: Polity Press.

Goffman, E. (1959). *The Presentation of Self in Everyday Life*. New York: Doubleday.

Gropius, W. (1934). Theaterbau. In: Gropius, W. *Apollo in der Demokratie*. Mainz/Berlin: Kupferberg.

Grotowski, J., (1992/1969). *Towards a Poor Theatre*, edited by Eugenio Barba, preface by Peter Brook, Methuen, London.

Heath, C., P. Luff, Lehn, vom, D., Hindmarsh, J., Cleverly, J. 2002, 'Crafting Participation: Designing Ecologies, Configuring Experience', Visual Communication, 1(1), 2002, pp. 9-33.

Iacucci, G., & Wagner, I. (2003). Supporting Collaboration Ubiquitously: An augmented learning environment for architecture students. In: *Proceedings of the 8th European Conference of Computer-supported Cooperative Work*, 14.-18. September 2003, Helsinki, Finland, Kluwer Academic Publishers, Dordrecht, pp. 139-158.

Kaprow, A. (1966). *Assemblage, Environments, & Happenings*, New York: Abrams.

Kostelanetz, R. (1968). *The Theater of Mixed Means*. New York: Dial.

Kostelanetz, R. (1994). *On Innovative Performance's: Three Decades of Recollections on Alternative Theater*. McFarland & Company.

Lainer, R. & Wagner, I. (1998). Connecting Qualities of Social Use with Spatial Qualities. In: *Proceedings of the First International Workshop on Cooperative Buildings*. Springer, Heidelberg, pp. 191-203.

Lainer R., & Wagner, I. (2000). Silent Architecture – Narrative Technology. *Digital Creativity* 11/3, pp. 144-155.

Lunenfeld, P. (2001). *Snap to grid, A user's guide to digital arts, media and cultures*. Cambridge, Massachusetts: The MIT Press.

Nesbitt, K., (Ed.), (1996). *Theorizing a New Agenda for Architecture. An Anthology of Architectural Theory* 1965-1995, New York: Princeton Architectural Press.

Nollert, A., (Ed.), (2003) Performative Installation, Snoeck Verlagsgesellschaft GmbH, Cologne.

Rumpfhuber, A., & Wagner, I., (2004). Sampling 'mixed objects' as part of architectural practice. In: *Proceedings PixelRaiders* 2, 6 - 8 April 2004, Sheffield, UK.

Schechner, R., (2002). *Performance Studies, An Introduction*. New York: Routledge.

Schön, D. (1983, 2000). *The Reflective Practitioner, How Professionals Think in Action*, Burlington USA: Ashgate Arena.

Shaw, J., & Weibel, P., (2003). *Future Cinema: The Cinematic Imaginary after Film.* Cambridge, Massachusetts. The MIT Press.

Sobchack, V. (1988). The Scene of the Screen Beitrag zu einer Phänomenologie der 'Gegenwärtigkeit' im Film und in den elektronischen Medien', in: Gumbrecht, H. U. and Pfeiffer K. L., Eds, *Materialität der Kommunikation.* Frankfurt, Suhrkamp, pp. 416-429.

Suderburg, E. (Ed.). (2000). *Space Site Intervention, Situating Installation Art,* University of Minnesota Press.

Tellioglu, H., & Wagner, I., (2001). Work Practices Surrounding PACS. The Politics of Space in Hospitals. *Computer Supported Cooperative Work (CSCW). An International Journal* 10, 163-188.

Tschumi, B. (1977), The Pleasure of Architecture. *Architectural Design* 47(3), pp. 214-218.

Tuan, Yi-Fu, (1990). Space and Context. In: Schechner, R., & Appel, W., (Eds.) *By Means of Performance, Intercultural Studies of Theater and Ritual.* Cambridge University Press, pp. 236-244.

Virilio, P. (1990). Das dritte Intervall. Ein kritischer Übergang. Vom Verschwinden der Ferne. In: E. Decker and P. Weibel, (eds), *Telekommunikation und Kunst,* Dumont, Köln, pp. 335-346.

Wagner, I. (2003). Open planning: objets persuasifs et fluidité des pratiques. In: F. Seitz & J.-J. Terrin (Eds.), *Architecture des systèmes urbains, Actes de colloque Université de Technologie de Compiègne,* July 5, 2001, L'Harmattan: Paris, pp. 223-237.

NOTES

TECHKUL (Uses of computer systems for architectural practice, film-making, and the theatre), a project supported by the Austrian Science Fund, which was carried out 1993-95 in collaboration with Martin Kompast.
IST-2001-33064 Atelier - Architecture and Technologies for Inspirational Learning Environments http://atelier.k3.mah.se/home/

AFFILIATIONS

Giulio Jacucci
Department of Information Processing Science, University of Oulu, Finland

Ina Wagner
Institute for Technology Assessment & Design, Vienna University of Technology, Austria

LUIGINA CIOLFI AND LIAM J. BANNON

15. SPACE, PLACE AND THE DESIGN OF TECHNOLOGICALLY-ENHANCED PHYSICAL ENVIRONMENTS

BACKGROUND: UBIQUITOUS AND "DISAPPEARING" COMPUTING

The perspective of "Ubiquitous Computing", proposed in the early 1990's by Mark Weiser (Weiser, 1991), is based on technological developments that make it possible to embed powerful computational elements and digital components into everyday objects, portable devices and the built environment. This trend is inducing significant changes not only in the development and implementation of new technology, but also, and more interestingly, on the relationships between interactive systems and their users. Distributing computational power within an environment and its elements means that the design of technology is no longer concerned solely with people's interaction with the standard desktop computer – the 'box' that sits on people's desktops. Design must now concern itself rather with the physical environments that people will experience through their daily lives. People will encounter technologically enhanced spaces and artefacts as they move through a variety of environments. These systems will change the way in which physical spaces are used and shaped by people. The systems will be able to respond and react to their presence and actions. The activities of interacting with the space and its elements and interacting with the computer system will merge into each other. Indeed, recent trends in research on ubiquitous systems involve new paradigms for Human-Computer Interaction such as "invisible" and "disappearing" computing[1].

Such a shift in the understanding of the relationship between people and technologies can also be noted in the labelling of the field, where the term HCI is now being replaced by Interaction Design in many settings. The former is focused on the "mapping" of users' individual traits and preferences to computer functionalities and interface elements, while the latter is concerned not only with this one-to-one relationship but also with the role of social, emotional and contextual factors in influencing human interaction with a computer system. Moreover, researchers have proposed approaches to the design of interactive systems such as, for example, "seductive design" (Agostini, De Michelis and Susani, 2000), that are moving from the design of elements such as graphical user interfaces (GUIs) to a focus on the overall *user experience* of a medium or system.

P. Turner and E. Davenport (Eds.), Spaces, Spatiality and Technology, 217-232.

We believe that this expanded perspective recognises important factors surrounding users and technologies, and is effective in informing and supporting the design and development of novel ubiquitous technologies. Our interest is focused particularly on those distributed systems that enhance and transform the *spaces* where human experience occurs. Bringing technologies beyond the desktop and into the everyday world requires us to pay greater attention to the physical environment where interaction occurs. It also requires us to deepen our understanding of the central concepts of *space* and *place,* as they are used within the Interaction Design field.

RESEARCH ON INTERACTIVE SPACES: TECHNOLOGICAL APPROACHES

Existing technical research in the area of interactive spaces is mainly concerned with three topics:

- The modelling of structural features of the environment in interactive systems (by means of sensors, networks, etc.);
- The introduction into the physical space of elements that carry some sort of computational power (interactive objects, networks, etc.), thus creating an overlapping of different layers of physical and digital information within the physical space;
- The creation of links between different physical and digital spaces, thus redefining the boundaries between local and remote environments.

This work is mainly focused on the physical context of interaction as a setting -a locale within which human actions and behaviours occur, characterised by structural/environmental properties that influence its inhabitants in certain ways. The focus of this body of work is on technological means to augment physical spaces.

Context-aware systems are those that are able to sense features of the physical setting, and to feed a representation of this data into the system itself. The sensing devices can be located both around the physical environment and on the bodies of the inhabitants (Gellersen, Beigl and Schmidt, 2000).

Such systems have been implemented to support spatially-oriented activities such as museum visits. Mobile context-aware devices for museums, such as "Cyberguide" (Abowd et al, 1997) and C-MAP (Sumi et al., 1998) build a model of the user and his or her preferences through recording various forms of data -such as speed of movement and path followed- during a museum visit.

An implicit human-computer interaction framework has emerged from this research, based on the idea that a broad range of sensing devices can capture information that is sufficient for the system to anticipate the user's needs and actions, without the need for explicit interaction between the person and the system (Schmidt, 1999). The computational elements within interactive spaces can be either part of the setting, i.e. embedded within the structure of the space (walls, floors, ceilings) or they can be embedded in entities within the setting, such as furniture or everyday objects. Examples of this kind of research include the "Community

Portals" project (Sawhney, Wheeler and Schmandt, 2000). This project consists of technology integrated into the environment with the intention of ensuring community awareness of the behaviour and activities of other inhabitants, in a variety of social settings and at different times of the day. The application consists of several shared community appliances, mainly digital walls containing sensors and displays. The interaction with the system takes place in a public context, in particular, in peripheral and transitional spaces such as corridors and halls. The system can sense the presence and identity of a person in the vicinity of the interactive display, thus allowing for information tailored for the specific person to be promptly displayed

Another example of enhanced spaces is that of "Narrative Spaces" (Sparacino, 2002), where users are able to produce "augmented" performances on an interactive stage with the support of sensors and gesture modeling tools: the performers' physical movements trigger the production of sounds and computer-generated images on large display screens.

The work being conducted by Streitz and his colleagues, on the other hand, focuses on technologically augmented "Roomware": chairs, tables and displays that are enhanced with interactive capabilities (Streitz, Geißler and Holmer, 1998). This vision aims to create new architectural features and structures within rooms and buildings that are designed to support sociability and collaboration (Streitz et al. 2003).

While these approaches are technically sophisticated, their underlying assumptions are open to question. Specifically, many of these approaches view "context" as something that is 'out there', and relatively easy to 'capture', given sufficient sensors and computational power. We believe that such an approach is problematic, as context is, in our view, something that is constituted by people within their specific activities, and is not amenable to pre-computation (see Bannon, 2003; Dourish, 2004). Sensors only detect a series of quantitative variables that are not able to cover all the relevant aspects of human activities: beyond measuring task performance and quantitative variables related to movement, gesture, etc., we believe that to fully understand users' interaction with a system it is essential to focus on dimensions such as social interaction, emotional and affective responses etc.

BEYOND TECHNICAL CONCERNS: REFLECTING ON SPACE AND PLACE

Our focus is on the relationship between physical spaces and their inhabitants, on the connections between the properties of an environment and the patterns of action and behaviour occurring within them.

The first question to ask is "what is space?" The easy answer to this question identifies space only just as the physical context of interaction, as the "backdrop" – the physical setting where action occurs. But, according to our everyday experience, we know that the physical environments we inhabit contribute to shaping our experiences and activities in many ways. We also actively re-arrange and modify the space and its elements, we organize our activities around it, we encounter and interact with other people in it. We even become attached to particular environments, they *mean* something to us, and evoke feelings and emotions.

From these simple, everyday life examples it is evident that space is not a mere setting, a "container" for our experiences. The relationship between the physical locale and the events occurring within it is much more complex.

The concept of space has been explored occasionally in earlier HCI literature. For example attention to the importance of space and spatial metaphors for supporting social interaction is evident in some for the research within Virtual and Augmented Reality, with respect to the design of Collaborative Virtual Environments (Benford, 2001).

In an early paper, Erickson observed how physical space structures and enriches human interaction, suggesting that spatial environments and their structures might work as effective metaphors for interface design (Erickson, 1993). Subsequently, Erickson adopted Alexander's architectural theory of Patterns[2] as a possible framework to support the design of spatially-based systems (Erickson, 2000). Lainer and Wagner (1998) note the relationship between the qualities of built spaces (as envisioned by architects and planners) and the activities and events that take place within them. In particular, they discuss how specific qualities of social use can be supported through the design of appropriate spaces and places, whether physical or digital. This vision is based on an assumed direct connection between physical qualities of spaces and the patterns of social activities occurring within them. Thus, this work suggests that it is possible to support and even trigger particular uses and behaviour within the space through the features of its physical design.

In both Erickson's and Lainer and Wagner's work, space is not seen as simply a "stage" anymore, but rather as the "substrate" for human interaction: space thus supports and engenders individual and social activities and behaviours. While this research is suggestive, we believe that it merely scratches the surface of the relationship between people and space. Earlier, we mentioned how we become attached to certain environments, how they convey meaning to us.

Erickson (1993) notes how one of the most important attributes of space is that people read meaning into it. He suggests that "place", rather than space, should be the term to describe environments that people invest with understandings, meanings, and memories.

Fitzpatrick (2003) is another author who proposes place, and not space, as the foundational metaphor for her "Locales Framework", a perspective on the analysis and design of collaborative systems, as place represents a lived relationship, with the structures and resources that support communication and interaction within a group. Work on what has been termed Media Spaces - physical spaces connected by various media - has been ongoing for two decades, begun by researchers at Xerox PARC and –subsequently- EuroPARC (Bly, Harrison and Irwin, 1993). Within this body of work, research has also focused on place as concept of reference, and provided a definition of it as the notion of space inextricably linked with the wealth of human experiences and use occurring within it.

In an influential and oft-cited paper, Harrison and Dourish (1996) propose that the notion of place, and not that of space, is central to the understanding of human behaviour, and thus should inform the design of interactive systems. They note:

"Place is a space which is *invested with understandings* of behavioural appropriateness, cultural expectations and so forth. We are *located* in 'space', but we *act* in 'place' " (Harrison and Dourish, 1996). This theme of place has figured more prominently in the Interaction Design literature in recent years. For example, Munro, Höök and Benyon (1999) discuss several conceptions of place noting how the concept of place in architecture can inform the design of information spaces.

Brown and Perry (2002) present some geographical perspectives on the concept of place and its relevance for the design of a different kind of technologies – spatially-oriented interactive systems such as electronic tourist guides.

Turner and Turner (2003) use a phenomenological approach to place, and show how it can inform the design of virtual models of real places.

These examples from the literature show that the concept of place has become of more central concern to the broad human-computer interaction field, but there is a need for a more analytic treatment of the concept. Also, it should be noted that, to date, the notion of place has been dealt with almost exclusively in a very abstract way, with no reference to actual geographical locations. The potential utility of the notion of place for design has been discussed with reference to "virtual spaces", systems that create digital environments for communication and collaboration. We believe that an understanding of the concepts of space and place can be beneficial for the design and development of actual *physical* spaces enhanced by technology. This is the topic for the subsequent sections of the Chapter.

PLACE AND INTERACTIVE PHYSICAL ENVIRONMENTS

Our research aims to apply the concept of place to a particular set of ubiquitous systems: technologically-enhanced physical spaces.

With ubiquitous technologies becoming more reliable and widespread, we are now dealing with fully interactive physical spaces, containing tangible elements acting as interfaces to access features of the digital domain. We believe the concept of place can assist interaction designers to understand interaction dynamics in this context, and to propose effective design concepts: place goes beyond the vision of space just as a physical setting, a container, and includes many dimensions of human experience within an environment.

To make our perspective clear, we will provide a brief overview of some conceptualisations of place, in order to highlight their key aspects. Although the concepts of space and place have been used and discussed in classical philosophy, a refined conceptual distinction between the two was developed only in the 20th century.

Trying to analyse the constituent elements of human experience, many philosophers dealt with *space* as a fundamental dimension of our being and acting in the world, and they realised that, to properly understand space and its connection with human feelings and actions, it is necessary to overcome the vision of it as pure structure, and to view it as dimension for interaction and experience, dynamically shaped by such events.

Merleau-Ponty's concept of *anthropological space*, as opposed to geometric space, is one of the first philosophical concepts of place (even if the actual word 'place' is not used by Merleau-Ponty): anthropological space is irreducible to physicality and transcends its structural dimensions to encompass human activity as constituent of the identity of the space itself (Merleau-Ponty, 1945).

Gaston Bachelard offers a related concept of space in his definition of *localised experience* (Bachelard, 1958). In his book "The Poetics of Space" Bachelard is interested in exploring the psychology of human experience of intimate spaces. His vision of space consists of a blend of experience and physical structure, or, in other words, place[3].

Theorists in the field of Geography have translated this twofold nature of the physical environment into the concepts of space and place. Where space refers to abstract geometrical extension and location, place describes our experience of being in the world and investing a physical location or setting with meaning, memories and feelings. Place has, of course, an existential significance as places are entities which "incarnate the experience and aspirations of people" (Tuan, 1971, p.281).

Particularly influenced by phenomenology and existentialism, Humanistic Geography is the first discipline to extensively explore the concept of place not only theoretically, but from a pragmatic perspective (Ley and Samuels, 1978). They suggest that we stop considering space as a mere container or location and start looking at it as a setting for action, experiences, communication. If we take this perspective, our studies of human interaction with the environment will be richer, more thorough and effective. As Peet notes: "Humanistic Geography looks at environment and sees place - that is, a series of locales in which people find themselves, live, have experiences, interpret, understand, and find meaning" (Peet, 1998, p. 48)

Place is more than just a location - a spot on a map - and it is more than just a landscape. Place is inextricably linked to people and the things that happen in that location that are meaningful to them.

Also there is a complex relationship between place and human action. When actions take place, the particular places in which they occur make a difference. Places both constrain and enable us: they offer us structural, cultural, social clues that shape our conduct; and our actions and interactions within that place add to its meaning and value.

> "Place constrains and enables our actions and our actions construct and maintain places"
> (Sack, 1997: 13)

In order to make place the perspective from which human interaction with the environment is studied, humanistic geographers have explored the many facets of place as an instance of space and experience.

For example, in "Place and Placelessness" (Relph, 1976), Edward Relph identified what he called the "raw materials" for the identity of places: physical appearance (e.g. topography), activities, and meanings (e.g. particular significance deriving from past events and present situations)

The geographer Yi-Fu Tuan discusses in further detail the elements that merge to build a place through his lifelong work (see for example Tuan, 1977 and Tuan,

1998). He stresses the importance of the physicality of place, the primacy of its structural and material features, and discusses the many layers of human experience that contribute to making a space into a place: *sensory perception, memories, feelings, social connections and the presence of others, cultural rules and conventions.* We wish to infuse our design work on interactive spaces with the rich conceptualizations of place evident in this body of work, in an effort to produce more habitable and meaningful interactive spaces. In the remainder of this chapter, we describe how we are approaching this issue, firstly describing how our design concepts are influenced by this approach, and then illustrating our approach through a brief outline of a recent interactive exhibition we have designed, which was informed by this approach.

ARTICULATING THE CONCEPT OF PLACE FOR DESIGN

The concept of place we wish to adopt in our interaction design research is one that has been developed within the field of Humanistic Geography. This perspective on place is rich and articulated, and includes an experiential perspective which we find of use. Yi-Fu Tuan's vision of place is grounded on what he calls the "experiential perspective" (Tuan, 1977): human beings and their lived experience of a locale create, shape and make place exist. At the same time, place can only be grounded in the physical, material reality of the world. We make places of spaces through physically sensing, exploring and inhabiting them. Thus, the first dimension of the geographical concept of place is the physical, structural one.

Apart from the physical aspect (related to materials, structures and environmental features), what other dimensions constitute the experience of place? In Tuan's view the other three dimensions of place are:

- Personal: related to the feelings and emotions we associate with a place, with the memories related to or evoked by it, with the personal knowledge and background we invest in the place while making sense of it.
- Social: related to social interaction and communication within the place, to the sharing of resources and memories, to social co-ordination and ethics, etc.
- Cultural: related to the rules, conventions and cultural identity of a place.

Each dimension is present at any moment of one's experience of a place, and the experience is shaped by the dynamic interconnections among these dimensions. We provide an outline visual representation of Tuan's conceptual structure, gleaned from his writings, in Figure 1 below.

DIMENSIONS

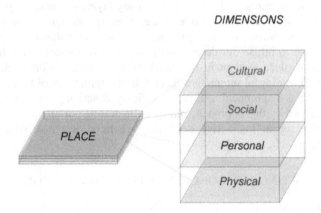

Figure 1. A representation of Tuan's conceptualization of Place

Each particular experience of place is individual and unique, although it is influenced by the presence of, and interaction with, others, captured by the social dimension.

These dimensions do not exist *a priori*, as a series of abstract categories, but emerge through people's actions and activities, practice and experience.

In order to understand a place and its inhabitants, all these dimensions and their interplay with each other have to be taken into account.

On the basis of Tuan's conceptualisations, we propose a visual articulation of the concept of place that highlights the different dimensions as interconnected aspects of the individual's experience. Each dimension is inter-related with the others. Together, they lead to and are shaped by actions and activities.

The articulation of the four dimensions shows how this notion of place might be useful for the design of interactive spaces: it brings together aspects of individual traits and preferences, social interaction, and cultural influences with the physical features of the space. Also this notion of place is oriented to individual experience, to one's actions and activities that occur within an environment.

The importance of this becomes clear when we ask ourselves what does it mean to "augment" a space through technology? It means changing its physical features by means of new materials for handling, for visual and auditory information displays. It means affecting one's personal experience through providing the possibility for new activities and modifying existing ones, evoking individual responses. It means engendering and supporting new possibilities for social interaction, communication and collaboration. Finally, it means that the new system will impact the culturally influenced qualities of an environment or even change them to some extent.

Yet another aspect of the notion of place according to Humanistic Geography is that it has, importantly, strong methodological implications: in order to understand people's experiences of a place in all its richness, qualitative methods of enquiry should be employed to study individuals' activities within a space and to highlight the emergence of the four dimensions. Geographer Graham Rowles calls this approach "experiential field work" (Rowles, 1978). Facing the complexity of data collected, the four dimensions provide a flexible, non-prescriptive and broad framework for analysis and reflection.

Experiential fieldwork implies participant observation by the researcher. Thus the perspective that we take over the study of space and place is not a top-down, detached view of our domain of investigation, an exercise in "mapping" activities to environmental qualities, but a bottom-up one, focused on understanding the lived experience of a place by its inhabitants.

Going back to the literature we mentioned earlier, although motivated by similar concerns, our perspective differs from Harrison and Dourish's in two fundamental ways. First of all, the notion of place we adopt implies that what the two authors refer to as "*spaceless place*" (Harrison and Dourish, 1996, p. 71) cannot exist, as sense of place can only emerge through physical immersion within a space. Thus, we are not looking at how placeness can emerge in spatially organised virtual systems, but in physical spaces enriched by technology. However, we share their vision of the role of place as a sensitizing notion for design: "Placeness is created and sustained by patterns of use; it's not something we can design in. On the other hand, placeness is what we want to support; we can design *for* it." (Harrison and Dourish, 1996; p. 70).

In the following section we will briefly illustrate an example of interaction design to support place-making within a technologically-enhanced physical environment, namely an interactive museum exhibition.

A DESIGN EXAMPLE: "RE-TRACING THE PAST"

"Re-Tracing the Past: Exploring Objects, Stories, Mysteries" was an interactive museum exhibition developed within the EU SHAPE Project[4].

The project focus is on creating *hybrid* environments that allow users to actively interact with features of both physical and digital spaces. SHAPE is specifically investigating issues of *hybridity* (augmenting everyday objects with technologies) and *assembly,* in the context of public spaces such as museums and exploratoria. "Living Exhibitions", where the project's explorations were exhibited for public experimentation, took place at three selected European museums (Fraser et al., 2003; Taxén *et al.*, 2003). "Re-Tracing the Past" was hosted by the Hunt Museum in Limerick, Ireland during June 2003 (Ferris *et al.*, 2004).

As our focus was the creation of a fully interactive space that would co-exist alongside the existing museum galleries, we aimed at designing an exhibition that would build on and extend the Museum's identity, philosophy and material qualities.

Thus we conducted an extensive series of field studies aimed at understanding the museum as a specific place and at designing an exhibition that would both share some of these place-related features and, at the same time, offer new ones through its material qualities, interactive components and content. The articulation of the concept of place into the four dimensions discussed above guided us through the phases of field studies, design and evaluation of the exhibition.

The museum's exhibition and access policies, and its educational approach were studied (Ciolfi and Bannon, 2002; Hall *et al.*, 2002). We also examined the wealth of information regarding the history of the collection and of the Hunt family patrons, in order to inform the scenarios and design concepts that we developed. We wished to ensure that whatever we designed would fit into the ethos of the Museum. Thus the "Re-Tracing the Past" exhibition is a *site-specific intervention* and its rationale is deeply grounded in the fabric of the museum We conducted surveys of the museum spaces in order to appreciate not only the Hunt Collection in its entirety, but also the features of the space, the exhibition layout and the information made available to the public. Through this phase of fieldwork we became familiar with the objects on display and with the history of the Hunt family, as the two are interwoven in the Museum. Our main concern, however, was to understand how the museum is experienced as a place not only by visitors, but also by curators and staff, educators and docents (the volunteers that informally support the visitors' exploration of the museum). We collected stories and anecdotes, observed hands-on activities such as educational workshops and handling sessions, and participated in walking tours of the museum, accompanying docents and visitors, to collect data related to their lived experience as they explored the galleries.

The insights we gained from this phase informed the design of "Re-Tracing the Past". The exhibition, organised into two connected physical spaces, was focused around four particular objects from the Hunt collection that have never been fully interpreted. Visitors were encouraged to explore these mysterious objects and to propose an interpretation of them. Their opinion on the objects were archived so that they, and future visitors, could hear the variety of opinions.

We envisaged the interactive exhibition as an environment where the visitors' experience would follow a narrative form, arranged around four main activities: exploration of objects, investigation of informative material, reflection on their nature and use, and expression of an opinion.

Trying to outline the structural features that the physical space of the exhibition should present, we identified a study room space as ideal to support the first three activities (See Figures 1, 2 and 3).

In the first space, the Study Room, a number of interactive elements provided certain information about the objects. An old trunk (Fig. 2) revealed where the object was found. A painting on the wall showed a detailed 3-D model of the objects that could also be virtually "tapped" to hear the sound it would make in reality. A map spread over an antique desk (Fig.3) would reveal the provenance of the objects.

Fig. 2: The trunk in the Study Room

Fig. 3: The interactive desk in the Study Room.

Finally, visitors could browse the channels (each object was assigned a channel) on an old radio and hear other people's opinions and theories about the mysterious artefacts (Fig. 4).

Fig. 4: The radio in the Study Room

The ambience of the study room – intimate, comfortable, period design - reflects the ambience of the Hunt Museum itself. The room also connects to the history of the collection and of the Hunt family (apparently, John Hunt himself used to work in a similarly decorated study room, which also had access to a "secret room"). The study room also presented itself as a space for investigation and exploration without the constraints that a museum gallery evokes in the visitors (fixed labels, prescriptive information, artefacts locked behind screens etc.).

On the other hand, the second space, the Room of Opinion (Fig. 5), presents very different features. The "feel" and material quality of the two spaces had to be designed so as to offer two different localised experiences, even though they are interconnected. The idea of visitors navigating and exploring existing knowledge about an object is supported by the design of the Study Room. Leaving one's own interpretation and a trace of one's presence call for a very different setting. In our final design, the Study Room contained information sources as well as props and elements that would contribute to its homely feeling. The Room of Opinion would have to be less crowded, immersive, without being cluttered, containing only minimal elements. We decided that it should support the visitors in examining the objects closely, through the use of replica objects that could be picked up, handled, and that it would contain a means for the visitors to leave their opinion, in a manner that would be easy to use and non-threatening, i.e. visitors should not feel intimidated by complex recording equipment. Thus the Room of Opinion was simply decorated in black and white. The "recording station" had the appearance of a normal telephone. Visitors could record their opinions through speaking into the handset, and then store them by simply putting down the receiver. Once their opinion was recorded it would appear as another mark that was added to a graphical representation of the existing body of opinions projected in the room (see screen in Figure 5), and stored as a new "station" on the radio in the Study Room. In this way, visitors had the opportunity of leaving their own imprint on the exhibition, making it available to other visitors.

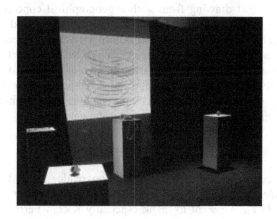

Fig 5: The Room of Opinion

Reflecting on the visitors' experience of "Re-Tracing the Past", the four dimensions of the experience of place noted earlier appear to emerge from our analysis of video data of visitors collected during the life of the exhibition.

The corpus of data offers numerous significant episodes of interaction involving visitors, museum personnel and exhibition designers around the interactive components of "Re-Tracing the Past" and around the replica objects. From the conversations that accompanied the physical exploration of the exhibition, the four dimensions of the experience of place emerge clearly showing how the design of "Re-Tracing the Past" supported people's experience of making a 'place' of the exhibition spaces and its features.

A thorough analysis of the data collected during the exhibition's life is currently underway[5].

CONCLUSIONS

This chapter has outlined a perspective on the design of interactive environments that articulates a nuanced appreciation of the dimensions of place, originating from work within humanistic geography. We have shown how this concept assisted us in the design of a specific interactive environment, helping us to focus on its experiential quality and the primacy of its material constituents.

As this geographical concept of place is by definition pragmatically oriented and is expressed as a dynamic interconnection of structural, personal, social and cultural elements, we believe it could be successfully applied in the field of interaction design for ubiquitous technologies. Its introduction would have theoretical and methodological implications: it would influence the range of concerns involved in field studies, and the range of methods used to gain data related to the users' experience of a place.

We believe that drawing from such a geographical concept of place could be beneficial for improving the conceptual development and implementation of ubiquitous technologies. In the case of both newly created "reactive" environments as well as existing ones being enhanced through technology, it is important for the effectiveness of the design to understand human experience of place and the way novel interactive elements could change and shape people's conception of place. We are currently exploring these issues in a number of ongoing research projects involving human activity in interactive environments.

ACKNOWLEDGEMENTS

We acknowledge the significant contribution made by all the members of the Interaction Design Centre at the University of Limerick for their work on "Re-Tracing the Past". We want to thank especially Kieran Ferris, Paul Gallagher and Tony Hall.

We also acknowledge the contribution to the exhibition by members of the SHAPE consortium, particularly John Bowers and Sten-Olof Hellström for their work on the auditory environment in the Room of Opinion, and Gustav Taxén, who created the graphical display of the visitors' opinions. Support for the preparation of this chapter from the Science Foundation Ireland for the Shared Worlds project is gratefully acknowledged.

AFFILIATION

Interaction Design Centre, University of Limerick, Ireland

NOTES

[1] See notably the recent EU Future and Emerging Technologies initiative "The Disappearing Computer" (http://www.disappearing-computer.net).
[2] Patterns are structures that associate architectural features to actions and episodes of behaviour.
[3] The concept of place appears in the work of many other philosophers. A thorough discussion of the history of the concept of place in philosophical thought is presented in (Casey, 1997).
[4] SHAPE (Situating Hybrid Assemblies in Public Environments) is funded by the EU FET IST "Disappearing Computer" Initiative. Partners in the SHAPE Consortium are: The Royal Institute of Technology in Stockholm (Sweden, Coordinating partner), the University of Nottingham (UK), King's College London (UK) and the University of Limerick (Ireland).
[5] The complete analysis of "Re-Tracing the Past" through the geographical notion of place is a major part of the first author's doctoral dissertation.

REFERENCES

Abowd, G., Atkeson, C. G., Hong, J., Long, S., Kooper, R. and M. Pinkerton (1997). "Cyberguide: A mobile context-aware tour guide", *Wireless Networks*, 3(5):421-433.

Agostini, A., De Michelis, G. and M. Susani,, 2000. "From user participation to user seduction in the design of innovative user-centered systems", *Proceedings of the Fourth International Conference on the Design of Cooperative Systems*, Sophia Antipolis, France, 23-26 May 2000.

Bachelard, G., 1958. *The Poetics of Space*, Boston: Beacon Press.

Bannon, L.J., 2003. "Creating New Design Spaces. Conceptualising Human Activities in Context", Tales of the Disappearing Computer, Santorini, June 2003.

Benford, S., Greenhalgh, C., Rodden, T. and J. Pycock , 2001. "Collaborative Virtual Environments", in *Communications of the ACM*, Volume 44 Issue 7 , July 2001.

Bly, S., Harrison, S. and S. Irwin, 1993. "Media Spaces: bringing people together in a video, audio, and computing environment", in *Communications of the ACM*, Vol 36, Issue 1, January 1993.

Brown, B. and M. Perry, 2002. "Of Maps and Guidebooks: designing geographical technologies", in *Proceedings of the conference on Designing interactive systems: processes, practices, methods, and techniques*, New York: ACM.

Casey, E.S., 1997. *The Fate of Place. A Philosophical History*. Berkeley: University of California Press.

Ciolfi, L. and L.J Bannon, 2002. "Designing Interactive Museum Exhibits: Enhancing visitor curiosity through augmented artefacts", in Bagnara, S., Pozzi, S., Rizzo, A. & Wright, P. (Eds.), *Proceedings of ECCE11, European Conference on Cognitive Ergonomics*, Catania (Italy) September 2002.

Dourish, P., 2004. "What We Talk About When We Talk About Context", to appear in *Personal and Ubiquitous Computing*.

Erickson, T., 1993. "From Interface to Interplace: the Spatial Environment as Medium for Interaction". *Proceedings of the Conference on Spatial Information Theory*. Heidelberg: Springer-Verlag.

Erickson, T., 2000. "Towards a Pattern Language for Interaction Design", in Luff, P., J. Hindmarsh and C. Heath (eds) *Workplace Studies: Recovering Work Practice and Informing Systems Design*. Cambridge: Cambridge University Press.

Ferris, K., Bannon, L., Ciolfi, L., Gallagher, P., Hall, T. and M. Lennon (2004), "Shaping Experiences in the Hunt Museum: A Design Case Study", to appear in *Proceedings of DIS04*.

Fitzpatrick, G. (2003). *The Locales Framework. Unserstanding and Designing for Wicked Problems*. Dodrecht: Kluwer.

Fraser, M, Stanton, D., Ng, K.H., Benford, S., O'Malley, C., Bowers, J., Taxén, G., Ferris, K. and J. Hindmarsh, 2003. "Assembling History: Achieving Coherent Experiences with Diverse Technologies", in Kuutti, K. et Al (Eds). *ECSCW2003*, London: Kluwer, 2003.

Gellersen, H-W., M. Beigl and A. Schmidt, 2000. "Sensor-based Context-Awareness for Situated Computing", *Proceedings of the Workshop on Software Engineering for Wearable and Pervasive Computing SEWPC00*, ICSE 2000, Limerick (Ireland), June 2000.

Hall, T., Ciolfi, L, Hickey, N., Bannon, L., "From hands-on to minds-on: toward the design of interaction and technology to enhance children's learning in a museum", *Proceedings of ICLS02, International Conference of Learning Sciences*, Seattle (WA) October 2002.

Harrison, S. and P. Dourish, 1996. "Re-Place-ing Space: the Roles of Place and Space in Collaborative Systems", in *Proceedings of CSCW 1996*. New York: ACM.

Ley, D. and M. Samuels (eds), 1978. *Humanistic Geography. Prospects & Problems*. London: Croom Helm.

Merleau-Ponty, M., 1945. *Phenomenology of Perception*. London: Routledge

Munro, A., Höök, K. and D. Benyon (eds.), 1999. *Social Navigation of Information Space*. London: Springer-Verlag.

Peet, R., 1998. *Modern Geographical Thought*. Oxford: Blackwell.

Relph, E., 1976. *Place and Placelessness*. London: Pion.

Rowles, G., 1978. "Reflections on Experiential Field Work", in Ley, D. and M. Samuels (eds), *Humanistic Geography. Prospects & Problems*, London: Croom Helm.

Sack, R. D., 1997. *Homo Geographicus. A Framework for Action, Awareness and Moral Concern*. Baltimore: Johns Hopkins University Press.

Sawhney, N., S. Wheeler and C. Schmandt, 2000. "Aware Community Portals: Shared Information Appliances for Transitional Spaces", in *Proceedings of CHI2000, Workshop on Situated Interaction in Ubiquitous Computing*. New York: ACM.

Schmidt, A., 1999. "Implicit Human-Computer Interaction Through Context", *Proceedings of 2nd Workshop on Human-Computer Interaction with Mobile Devices*, Edinburgh 1999.

Sparacino, F. (2002). "Narrative Spaces: bridging architecture and entertainment wia interactive technology". *Proceedings of the 6th International Conference on Generative Art*, Politecnico di Milano (Italy), December 2002.

Streitz, N., J. Geißler and T. Holmer, 1998. "Roomware for Cooperative Buildings: Integrated Design of Architectural Spaces and Information Spaces", in Streitz, N., S. Konomi and H. Burkhardt (eds), *Proceedings of CoBuild98*, Berlin: Springer.

N. A. Streitz, Th. Prante, C. Röcker, D. van Alphen, C. Magerkurth, R. Stenzel, D. A. Plewe (2003). "Ambient Displays and Mobile Devices for the Creation of Social Architectural Spaces: Supporting informal communication and social awareness in organizations". In K. O'Hara, M. Perry, E. Churchill, D. Russell (Eds.), *Public and Situated Displays: Social and Interactional Aspects of Shared Display Technologies*. London: Kluwer Publishers.

Sumi, Y., T. Etani, S. Fels, N. Simone, K. Kobayashi and K. Mase. "C-MAP: Building a Context-Aware Mobile Assistant for Exhibition Tours". *Social Interaction and Communityware*, Japan, June 1998.

Taxén, G., Hellström, S. O., Tobiasson, H., Bowers J. and M. Back, 2003. "The Well of Inventions – Learning, Interaction and Participatory Design in Museum Installations", *Proceedings of ICHIM2003*, Paris, September 2003.

Tuan, Yi-Fu, 1971. "Geography, Phenomenology and the Study of Human Nature", *The Canadian Geographer*, 15, 181-92.

Tuan, Yi-Fu, 1977. *Space and Place. The Perspective of Experience*. Minneapolis: University of Minnesota Press.

Tuan, Yi-Fu, 1998. *Escapism*. Baltimore & London: Johns Hopkins.

Turner, P. and S. Turner, 2003. "Two Phenomenological Studies of Place", in O'Neill, E., Palanque, P. and P. Johnson (eds), *People and Computers XVII- Designing for Society*, London: Springer.

Weiser, M, 1991. "The Computer for the Twenty-First Century", *Scientific American*, pp. 94-10, September 1991.

SARA ALBOLINO, ANTONIETTA GRASSO AND FREDERIC
ROULLAND

16. AUGMENTING COMMUNAL OFFICE SPACES WITH LARGE SCREENS TO SUPPORT INFORMAL COMMUNICATION

INTRODUCTION

The role of space in support of work practices has been highlighted in a number of studies of knowledge workers, especially because different space layouts can facilitate or on the contrary make informal communication among colleagues more difficult. Recently renewed attention has been paid to these issues because the way work is organized is changing toward more distributed groups which are not co-located and are more mobile, with less opportunity to interact, making communication exchange more difficult. On the other hand ubiquitous computing technology (smartphones, large interactive screens, white boards, cameras, and so on) is becoming mature and opens new possibilities to *augment* the physical space to keep distributed groups more connected. In this chapter we present a system that augments physical spaces in an organization in order to promote informal communication and ad-hoc work in distributed teams. We start by recalling how informal interaction articulates and why it is an important element in the support of work. Then we present the incremental and multidisciplinary methodology of the prototype design (which is part of a larger system developed in the EU project Multimedia Interaction for Learning and Knowing). Finally we describe in detail the features of the prototype.

The relevancy of informal communication

A number of ethnographic studies in the last decade have examined in a closer way how interpersonal communication articulates in the work place (for example how it is initiated), what is its nature (for example the length and frequency of interactions) and how activities can be supported and with what relevance. First of all, reported studies highlight that the vast majority of interactions in the workplace do not happen in a pre-planned manner. In particular a number of studies of work organization collectively report that:
- Between 25% and 70% of time was spent in face-to-face interactions.
- Meetings and other interactions were primarily unscheduled (~80% for professionals and ~60% for managers) and were dyadic (~80% for professionals, lower for managers).

P. Turner and E. Davenport (Eds.), Spaces, Spatiality and Technology, 233-248.

- The unplanned conversations were brief (between 1.9 minutes and 15 minutes) – see Isaacs *et al.* (1997).

These kinds of interaction occur in support of a variety of work needs. According to their purpose they have been classified as *planned, intended, opportunistic,* and *spontaneous.* Planned interactions are the ones that occur in prescheduled meetings, with formal agenda and minutes circulated among participants; intended interactions are the ones where there is a need for certain information in order to continue to carry on with the work and another person is actively sought out; opportunistic exchanges are those where some communication occurs because a person is encountered and a previous information need comes back to mind; and finally spontaneous interactions are the ones that happen among peers with similar background, but not in response to a specific immediate information need.

In all but the planned interactions, space is highlighted as relevant in facilitating these informal exchanges. In particular the same body of ethnographic studies reports that:

- The exchanges are dependent on the physical location (the closer the offices are the more people tend to interact).
- Being able to determine presence and interruptibility of the other person *at a glance* is a key enabler for the intended interactions where there is a specific need to fulfil.
- *Serendipitous encounters* are a key enabler of spontaneous interactions (such as the ones carried on in communities of practices - Lave and Wenger, 1991).
- The awareness of the social rhythms of public places facilitates the creation of opportunities for encounters.

However, when organisations start to operate across distributed sites and people are more mobile, many collaborative tasks are carried on across a space that is no longer co-located and sometimes spans even different time zones. The natural support to informal communication given by the possibility of at a glance noticing and using visual cues, or even just bumping into each other, is no longer available.

If informal communication is so important, how can technology and especially ubiquitous computing technology support it? Is it possible to create an *augmented* space where some of the affordances of a shared physical space can be brought back? What can be used to replace visual physical clues about peoples availability and the scope of current activities?

In answering these questions we have restricted our scope especially to supporting either opportunistic exchanges inside projects or communities of peers (i.e. those exchanges that are triggered by a specific need, where people happen to have the opportunity to talk) and spontaneous exchanges (i.e. those exchanges where there is a mutual exchange of useful information, but it was not triggered by a specific immediate need).

With respect to these two categories of exchange, less pressed in time and more due to the occasion and possibility of exchange, a number of proposals for facilitating them have been made especially around media spaces (Dourish *et al.,* 1996) and more recently Instant Messaging tools (Isaacs *et al.,* 2002). The work present here shares some similarity with both. From media spaces we have taken the idea of using video connections to link physically distributed spaces and from IM systems we have taken the idea of capturing and displaying information about people's current activity.

Moreover, while not denying the benefit of having this information on the desktop, in our work we have investigated how to augment also the physical communal places of an organization, in order to expand the possibility of benefiting from the collected information. In particular we have been studying how large screens can augment and connect distributed sites and support informal unplanned exchanges, either synchronously or asynchronously.

Characteristic of the target organizations

The work organization that MILK addresses is typically characterised by large knowledge bases, where people store and crystallize the outcomes of highly knowledge intensive processes. Most of such knowledge bases are built into document management systems (DMS) as a shared space where activities performed by knowledge workers, or inside communities of practice, leave a trace because the repository is used in support of the collaborative work that the organization carries out. Due to this daily use of knowledge, many companies have tried to develop more comprehensive portals, where the shared DMS becomes more globally a place for promoting communication, networking and exchange. The attempts to foster exchange across projects and inside communities of practice starting from on-line forums and directories of experts have been numerous. In our experience they are, however, not as successful as they could be. At best they attract a core set of people, but are considered too costly and too detached for the rest of the work population, even when there could be an interest and desire to have this kind of exchange (Snowdon and Grasso, 2002).

In MILK our objective has been to place interactive boards where the activities going on in the organization, as inferred from DMS logs of use, are automatically published. The boards are in semi-public places (like the printer room, the entrance hall, the library, etc.); in figure 1 one of the two installations at one of the user sites of MILK are shown, where a service area with printer and a leisure area with magazines are augmented with the interactive large screens. In this way our objective is to create attractive information points that can be used to see at a glance what is currently going on inside units of work (business processes, projects, task forces, etc.) and inside professional communities. Additionally, these information points are connected by video and audio links. In this way we aim at recreating a virtual common space where people have the opportunity to meet as if they were in the same physical space. The design idea that we had was of an attractive broadcasting space that could support communication whenever needed, e.g. when some information found on the screen triggers the need to know more from the author, or when we want or need to talk to other people who are reading news on the other site.

Figure 1. One of the site installations.

In summary, we have been interested in supporting both opportunistic and spontaneous informal communication, by creating public information points that provide features that can be enablers of informal communication as depicted in table 1. In order to do so we started our investigation by mapping some of the possible functionality to the types of exchange we aimed at promoting and supporting. Following this preliminary design phase we moved to an iterative design phase where we tested our assumptions and designed the actual system functionality and appearance, as described in the next sections.

Possible functionality	*Opportunistic*	*Spontaneous*
Public news and information from ongoing projects		People read this information in public places and information can trigger or support discussion with local or remote peers
Public information about current location of people	People passing by can glance at the current location of colleagues and use this information to contact them more easily	
Video connection among sites		

Table 1: Addressed informal communication types.

CO-DEVELOPING WITH USERS

In the design of our system we have adopted an incremental and multi-disciplinary approach. Very few systems of this kind have already been designed and deployed; a survey of these can be found in O'Hara *et al.* (2003) and many issues are still not clearly understood, including:

- – type of information to provide on the interactive public large screen;
- – appearance of information appropriate for quick interaction and visibility from far;
- – interconnection with the physical places where the screens are placed.

We decided therefore to rely not only on technology design expertise, but also to involve typical users to better understand if a system like this could provide facilitation of informal communication. We also worked with interaction designers regarding the aspect of how to present information in public spaces, relying on their expertise in the industrial design field, especially to address issues related to attractiveness and readability of a public display. The design aspects will be presented in the section about the prototype design, while in the following we present the user studies and the organizational context where we have collected feedback to be used in the prototype design.

The organizational context

The analysis of communities and their main knowledge management requirements have been conducted through a combination of ethnographic methods and an action learning approach, where the focus has been on the observation of the working practices and their analysis (Barley, 1996). Our approach has been interactive and aimed at activating user participation on system design as building a mutual understanding among observers and observed workers. The field analysis mainly focused on: the identification of the main knowledge exchanges among people (i.e., identification of a knowledge network among experts in different business sectors) and the study of the social usage of the physical space (Holland and Leinhardt, 1979; Wellman, 1988).

Moreover, during the case study, representations of typical working scenarios (i.e. scenario-based design analysis – Carroll, 1995) have been used to support our work. The idea that knowledge management and learning processes are not managed at formal organizational level but happen spontaneously within daily work activities has been our guideline. The actors in these processes are people who work in teams and participate in communities; the analyzed units belong to two different organizations: an Italian consultancy firm and a German software-house, both very dynamic and performing knowledge intensive activities.

The Italian consultancy firm is active, over more than thirty years, in providing professional services to major enterprises and government agencies in the fields of change management, organization, HR, Knowledge Management and Customer Relationship Management. The firm's approach to consultancy is based on working in partnership with the client to build a "tailor made" solution that lasts in time. Therefore, each project requires specific, in-depth understanding of the clients' organization and needs, aimed at devising specific solutions to maximize effectiveness and the quality of working life. The firm employs 50 consultants and 9 staff, located in Milan and Rome, and has had 50% growth in personnel in the last two years, mainly young and just graduated from University.

The German software house has developed a complete Digital Asset Management (DAM) solution under a single roof: software development, MSP – Managed Service Provider, Hotline and support and consulting services. The company was founded in 1992 and it is in a growing phase. It employs 60 people, located in 3 offices at two sites: Hanover and Hamburg. In comparison with the consultancy company, the software house has a more heterogeneous population of workers. Due to the nature of its business, there are: technicians that are in charge of developing system functionality; support staff who are responsible for system maintenance and user assistance; and, finally, project managers and sales people both working in direct contact with the clients. The latter are responsible for developing new business while the former are in charge of user requirement analysis and of developing the required solutions.

Even if the two organizations work in very different business areas, they seem to be very similar concerning both social practices and knowledge management issues. Moreover both of them have core processes based on project structures and relying on document production and processing, along the lines presented in the section before. Every employee usually works on different projects, with different customers located in different sites and all the working activities are characterized by knowledge intensive exchanges in highly mobile contexts.

TYPICAL WORKING PRACTICES, KNOWLEDGE NEEDS AND REQUIREMENTS

The analysis has been realized through the identification of some typical daily working scenarios illustrating some main issues. A longer description of those is available in Agostini *et al.* (2003). As part of the observations we found some interactions of interest to us, as illustrated in the following example:

"Giovanni prints some documents and goes to the printer where he meets Paola, project manager of the CRM area; they start a conversation about ongoing work. When Paola looks at the documents printed by Giovanni, she tells him that Carlo of the CRM area has also worked with that client the year before. Paola tells Giovanni that Carlo is in the office in Milan so he can immediately call him and collect useful information. In particular, Carlo informed him that in the company server there are some interesting documents about that client and at the end of the conversation sends their coordinates to Giovanni via email." These informal discussions represent a key cross-fertilization path for knowledge sharing. Another occasion for cross-fertilization that has been observed occurs when people join new projects; however it has also been observed that in this case knowledge flow is particularly slow.

However, as a result of the observations, a general conclusion has been also that, due to the frequent travel associated with a fast growing business, the chances for casual encounters and conversations are strongly reduced. Therefore, the conditions for knowledge exchange such as the one reported above, are missing. Moreover, knowledge shared within informal meetings cannot be recorded in any of the repositories of the company, and therefore remains private.

From the analysis of the users' practices, some main knowledge needs arose that have to be taken into account in the design of the MILK system. Of these, the one that we have aimed at addressing relates to the observation that innovation occurs through cross-fertilization and communication and it should be supported as well among people located in different places and who are highly mobile.

On the base of the observation that cross-fertilization is important when it happens, but it is not promoted by the environment, we elaborated a proposal for a knowledge sharing set of functionalities. We developed some possible scenarios of use and then tested them on a "low-tech" early prototype to both obtain early feedback on our proposal and to start to familiarize the user about what the future system could be. This early prototype was named CWall, where the C stands for Community. The scenarios support both spontaneous and opportunist interactions, both synchronous and asynchronous.

Scenario 1: Promoting asynchronous spontaneous communication

"Lucilla passes in front of the Cwall and she needs to get information about new activities and projects concerning her area of practice: CRM (Customer Relationship Management). First of all, she reads the news about CRM issues and finds a number of items, but one item especially draws her attention: it is news about a new paper done by a colleague concerning CRM Case Studies. In the article there is the location of the document on the server, so she decides to connect to the server and to have a look at this document. It is very interesting, so Lucilla saves it in her folder "in transito", in order to download it to her PC. After that she comes back to the news section and adds a comment to the news about the document "CRM Case Studies" and rates it, informing people that this is a very good document and inviting people to read it!"

Scenario 2: Supporting synchronous opportunistic communication

"Annalisa is in the Milan office and passes by the CWall. She needs to prepare a commercial presentation about training (her area of practice), so she decides to have a look on the server for existing materials and documents on this subject. Through the video connection she sees Sofia in the Rome office. Annalisa greets her and explains to Sofia what she is doing. Sofia knows that there is a very interesting commercial presentation concerning training, so she helps Annalisa to find it on the server. Annalisa saves it in her "in transito" in order to download it to her PC. Sofia gives Annalisa a lot of good ideas and suggestions in order to prepare her presentation about training. Furthermore, Sofia tells Annalisa that Patrizia Cinti can probably also help her. Through the people finder function they see that Patrizia is not in the office, so Annalisa sends her an-email from the Cwall asking for help to get materials. Waiting for Patrizia's reply, Annalisa comes back to her PC and starts to prepare her presentation following Sofia's suggestions."

Scenario 3: Supporting synchronous opportunistic communication

"Roberta from the Rome office goes for her morning coffee break. On the way to the break room she passes by CWall and sees on the video picture that Thomas is just involved in a chat with Maurizio in front of the CWall in Milan. From the CWall she opens an audio connection request to Thomas and asks if he has time to quickly schedule his commitments in a new project for which she is currently doing the planning. Thomas agrees and Roberta picks up her project planning document from the company server and puts it into the application sharing program (NetMeeting) such that Thomas can see it. She then opens the page with the resource planning and starts to fix the commitment dates and locations with Thomas. In 15 minutes she is finished, stores the document back on the server and leaves for her well deserved cappuccino. CWall has just saved her a lot of time as she did not have to wait for Thomas to give her a slot in his busy agenda".

Early deployment

In order to test these scenarios an early version of the system was deployed at the Italian consultancy firm, having offices in Milan and Rome. A low tech user interface was put together on the basis of a previous system; however it was augmented with the functionality we had seen as important for supporting multiple interconnected sites. Figure 2 is a picture of the prototype. Three main categories of functionality were provided:

- automatic broadcast of company related information (news function);
- automatic sensing of the presence of people in one of the company offices (availability function);
- video-audio connection (meeting function).

Figure 2. An early deployment of the system.

The system was then left in use and feedback about it was collected in interactive sessions with users. A total of 5 sessions (1 with each individual without video connection, 1 collective without video connection, 3 collective with video connection) were recorded covering a user sample of 12 people (4 analysts, 3 consultants, 3 senior consultants, 2 partners). A summary of the main findings and some samples of feedback are presented in Table 2. From this early deployment we draw a number of conclusions that reinforced our belief in the value of the system. In particular we found that:

- It was perceived as enlarging the opportunities to exchange opinions and ideas among colleagues.
- CWall was evaluated as providing functionalites that could be included on a desktop, but people reported a different approach to using them. The desktop is used for task focused activities and the CWall was perceived as an enabler of useful unplanned interactions.
- It could not take the place of other office tools and systems (Intranet, PC, server, and so on), but it can positively integrate their functionalities and add new ones.

Functionality	Feedback	Sample remarks
Displaying dynamic news.	Displaying materials related to projects drawn from the Intranet and speaking with people passing by has provided evidence that many are unaware of the projects that other colleagues are engaged in.	*"The true added-value of this tool concerns the possibility to create a social environment to interact with people, for instance, if I am going to the bathroom, I pass by the CWall, I see a news item and stop a colleague to show him the news, it can start a conversation and a discussion about it"* *"The news must be about projects in which I'm working, and it must indicate who I can address to have more information, where I must look for, etc."*
Displaying where colleagues currently are (location).	Availability window is considered very useful to enlarge organizational awareness.	*"It can happen that if a colleague is not in the office, I think that he is with a client or in a meeting, so I hesitate to contact him, but if I know that he is just working in the other office I can contact him without hesitation"* *"This functionality should not be like a Big-Brother?! I do not want to inform everyone about every daily movement and action"*

Connecting different sites with audio/video conferencing tools.	The video connection is considered the most value-added functionality for seeing and speaking with colleagues.	*"It is important to place the Cwall in a public place for the news and spontaneous hello to colleagues passing by in Rome. However the location should also be chosen in order not to disturb offices nearby. It is not a stimulating factor to use the video connection knowing that using it you are disturbing other people that are working."*

Table 2: Users' feedback.

Applying Interaction Design Principles

From the early deployment of a system presenting the main functionality to the users, we got a positive sense that the high level services we were planning were actually bringing value to the users. However, on the basis of that installation, we could not collect fine grained feedback about the appearance of the services and the detail about how we were going to provide them in the final prototype. We therefore worked them out with a group of interaction designers, specialized in new user interface for ubiquitous computing devices, like our large interactive screens. They had access to the user feedback, which also influenced the work on the user interface, even if an inspirational way, rather than an analytical one. First of all we refined together what content to display and how to display it. In terms of content, the main guidelines that were defined were:

–   The content has to be automatically broadcast in order to keep the cost of updating minimal.
–   The content has to be related to the current organisational activities in order to be meaningful.
–   The content has to be very clear to be quickly glimpsed at, and therefore articulated into specialised broadcasting channels.
–   The content has to also serve wide organizational communication purposes, with the broadcasting of edited news.
–   The content has to highlight information about people (who is doing what, where he or she is, contact details, etc.).

Because of the public appearance of the screens, visual attributes were also worked out. In terms of layout and interaction modes, the main guidelines were:

–   Different content has to be displayed at different moments during the day, e.g. information about people presence early in the morning.
–   Information can be navigated according to personal needs.
–   Information has to be presented in a very attractive way, appropriate for public spaces, in order to be eye-catching.
–   The system should facilitate interaction, e.g. by sensing identity instead of requiring explicit authentication or by facilitating the moving of information

from personal devices to the screen and to the other connected sites and vice versa.

THE FULL SYSTEM

The interactive large screen application that we describe here is part of a bigger system that is aimed at supporting people's activity around documents in a variety of working situations, in particular when at the desktop, when mobile and finally, which is our focus, during informal interactions that can happen and are promoted in the shared spaces of the organization. The full system is based on a shared repository of the documents manipulated by the organization on top of which sits a Knowledge Management engine in charge of extracting meta-data required by each different visualization in the different working situations that are supported.

Let us describe the basis of the KM Engine. From the user observations a requirement was derived that the system should capture, organize and make available both informal and formal knowledge to team members. Therefore knowledge organization in MILK is based on a profiling mechanism that associates a common knowledge description with objects of a different nature. Practically a profile is associated with any MILK element and an element can be any piece of information from formal reports to more informal e-mail messages. Moreover, projects, communities, people and their activities are considered part of the knowledge too. Integrating the knowledge associated with any kind of element, we are able to compare and contrast elements to compute various kinds of relationships. Profiles are based on three main metadata categories. *Generic metadata* contains information such as the author and creation date for documents. *Content metadata* allows correlating elements on the basis of the topics; e.g., interests and expertise for people. Finally, *Qualifying metadata* attempts to capture the evolution of the relevance of an element over time and use. User actions on elements like rating, accessing, etc., together with the age of an element, help to better qualify and relate each element and provide users with the most accurate response from the system.

In order to promote and support circulation of knowledge among people, MILK supports both organizational projects and communities of practice [0]. Both project and community workspaces can contain (other than people) any kind of knowledge ranging from formal documents to informal annotations. Projects and their members are defined by the organization. On the other hand people are free to create or join one or more communities for publishing information, discussing topics, recommending elements; and so on. Whilst the composition of project teams has to deal with contingent aspects (e.g., client issues, budget issues), communities in MILK reflect people's interests and support the natural exchange of knowledge around topics, which are independent of actual organizational projects. Communities and projects in MILK are two complementary and transverse views on knowledge. They allow knowledge shaping, stressing the focus either on the organization of the work or on interesting topics.

In addition to document services, other services supporting awareness of people's availability are provided. An availability server is connected to the KM engine to provide dynamic information about current location of people (e.g. in front of the large screen, sitting at the desktop). Users can also specify the preferred set of communication means to reach them in each given situation (e.g. "when in a meeting just send me sms"). These services are used and rendered in different ways in the three user interfaces addressed by the whole MILK project (Office, Mobile, Social). In the next section we focus on the Social environment.

Social Environment

Public displays in MILK are designed to be put in public and semi-public spaces (cafeterias, halls, meeting rooms...) inside working areas. The public displays, based on what we have defined as a *broadcast* model, work as information pushing devices when nobody is interacting with them, mixing the different channels. As soon as somebody starts interacting with the system it switches to pull mode, and the user gets access to any information he or she needs. The broadcasting mode in the social environment is designed to give both hints of what's going on inside the company to non-interacting onlookers, and to urge them to start interacting with the screen (switching then to pull mode), to go deeper inside the items they find more relevant, or to browse by organizational theme exploring the system content. The alternation between the channels in the broadcasting mode depends on a set of rules based on time of the day and users' activities, controlled and modified by the system administrator to push certain kinds of data and promote specific information to all fellow workers. As mentioned before, information to be broadcast has been clustered in channels. Each channel represents a specific view on the knowledge present in the organisation and is relevant for different communities. In the following the various broadcasting channels are described.

Thematic channel

The Thematic channel (fig. 3) is the channel providing information about current units of work, i.e., projects and community forums. It is the channel from where new and interesting information can be accessed, read, bookmarked, and also enriched with comments and personal notes. Moreover, using this channel it is possible to access information across different sites in support of synchronous video contacts.

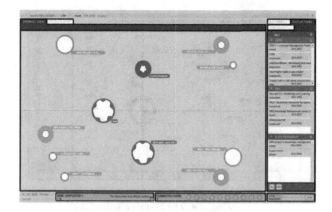

Figure 3. The Thematic channel layout.

In order to retrieve its content, it monitors the activity in the DMS and prioritises it in order to provide only live information. It utilizes some layout rules in order to represent activity parameters:

- Colour: Membership of an organisational area of activity.
- Distance from the centre and colour fading: the overall amount of recent activity.
- Size: overall amount of activity.
- Thickness: degree of novelty.
- Shape: to differentiate among projects and communities.

People channel

The People channel (figure 4) is the channel providing information about people in the organization, the means to contact each person and their current location and availability. The channel dynamically updates the information about the current location of the users. The granularity of the information is kept at the level of the different organizational locations or not being in the office. The system integrates functionality from an availability service that can also register at each moment the preferred channels for interactions (e.g. SMS while attending a meeting).

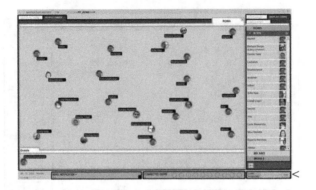

Figure 4. The People channel.

A number of layout rules are used in order to facilitate quick overview:

- Location tabs: each tab represents a site showing the people who have that reference location.
- Colours: identify a location, people currently detected in a location are represented with the colour of the site where they are.
- Guest area: People visiting the site.
- Grey Colour: Mobile people.

News channel

The news channel is used to broadcast information that the organization wants to transmit to everyone on a site or across all sites.

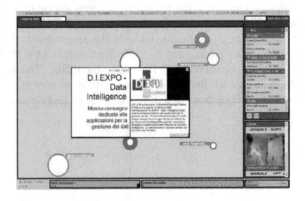

Figure 5: The News channel (overlaid).

The news has its own channel, but is also overlaid to whatever current channel is displayed if no one is interacting with the screen. It is displayed using a style borrowed from newspapers and is meant to attract attention even from afar.

Video channel

The video channel is a channel devoted to support synchronous communication. It provides the visualization of the connected sites (figure 5) and supports the possibility of unplanned video-audio sessions. It also includes some light support for collaboration, i.e. it is possible to share content on the fly across the various sites in order to support the discussion. This feature is however not meant to be a fully synchronized access to the documents (as in NetMeeting, for example).

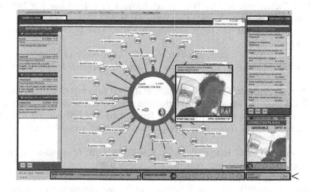

Figure 6: The Video channel (bottom right and overlaid windows).

SUMMARY

Research on media space in the past has already shown the benefits of connecting multiple sites in order to maintain and provide occasions for unplanned interactions and developing a common rhythm that can in turn facilitate informal interactions.

With our research we have explored the concept of enriching communal work spaces with information points showing current organizational activities. We have articulated activities in terms of community, project, people and locations and developed overview visualization in order to promote knowledge sharing and unplanned interactions, both asynchronously and synchronously. Our preliminary observations and feedback collected from our user settings are encouraging about the appropriateness and benefit of augmenting office space with such interactive information points. We are now testing the fully working version of the system and collecting feedback both in a qualitative and quantitative way.

AFFILIATIONS

Sara Albolino
Irso
Piazza Giovine Italia, 3
Milan, Italy
ALBOLINO@IRSO-BEP.IT

Antonietta Grasso, Frederic Roulland
Xerox Research Centre Europe
6, Chemin de Maupertuis
Meylan, France
<name.surname>@xrce.xerox.com

REFERENCES

Agostini, A., Albolino, S., Boselli, R., De Michelis, G., De Paoli, F. & Dondi, R. (2003) Stimulating Knowledge Discovery and Sharing. *Proceedings of Group 2003*, ACM Press, 248-257.

Barley, S.R. (1996) Technicians In The Workplace: Ethnographic Evidence For Bringing Work Into Organization Studies. *Administrative Science Quarterly*, **41(3)**, 404-441.

Carroll, J.M. (1995) *Scenario-Based Design: Envisioning Work and Technology*. In Carroll, J.M. (Ed), System *Development*.

Dourish, P., Adler, A., Bellotti, V. & Henderson, A. 1996 Your Place or Mine? Learning from Long-Term Use of Audio-Video Communication. *Journal of Computer Supported Cooperative Work*, **5 (1)**, 33-62

Isaacs, E., Whittaker, S., Frohlich, D., and O'Conaill, B. (1997) Informal Communication Re-Examined: New Functions For Video In Supporting Opportunistic Encounters. *Video-Mediated Communication*, Finn, K. E., Sellen, A. J., & Wilbur, S. B. (eds.), New Jersey: Laurence Erlbaum, pp. 459-485.

Holland, P.W., and Leinhardt, S. (eds.) 1979, *Perspectives on social network research*, Academic Press, New York.

Isaacs, E., Walendowski, A., and Ranganathan, D. (2002) Hubbub: A sound-enhanced mobile instant messenger that supports awareness and opportunistic interactions, *Proceedings of the Conference on Computer-Human Interaction 2002*, ACM Press, 179-186.

Lave J. & Wenger, E. (1991) *Situated learning. Legitimate peripheral participation*. Cambridge University Press, Cambridge.

O'Hara, K., Perry, M., Churchill, E. and Russell, D. (2003). *Public and Situated Displays. Social and Interactional Aspects of Shared Display Technologies*, Kluwer Academic Publishers.

Snowdon D. & Grasso A. (2002) Diffusing Information in Organizational Settings: Learning from Experience, *Proceedings of the Conference on Computer-Human Interaction (CHI) '02*, ACM Press, pp. 331-338.

Grasso A. & Mesenzani M. (2002) Supportare comunicazioni informali attraverso comunità locali e distribuite. In Butera F. (Ed.) *Tecnologia E Organizzazione Per L'uomo E L'impresa*, Milano, Franco Angeli.

Albolino, S., Mesenzani, M. & Schael T. (2002) *Proceedings Of Knowledge-Based Intelligent Information Engineering Systems & Allied Technologies - Kes2002*, Italy.

Wellman, B. 1988, Networks as Personal Communities. In Wellman & Berkowitz (Eds.) *Social Structures: A Network Approach*. Cambridge University Press, New York, 130-184.

17. ARTICULATING THE SENSE OF PLACE EXPERIENCED BY VISITORS TO THE JENCKS LANDFORM

INTRODUCTION

Virtual Reality (VR) technology offers the promise of immersion in artificial worlds. Researchers in the area have predicted a new era when users will no longer be limited by their bodies. This contention has highlighted the embodiment/disembodiment debate to the extent that it is now a common theme in films, novels and commentaries on cyberspace (Stone, 1992). For example, Franck (1995) comments that in William Gibson's (1986) novel Neuromancer, Case longs for the 'bodiless exultation of cyberspace'. As the technology matures it is suggested that users will be able to experience a sense of being in places hitherto unknown or unimagined.

If VR technology is successful in its desire to remove the constraints imposed by the physical world, then it raises the question of the nature of the body that will be taken into cyberspace and that which will be left behind and, indeed where will these bodies reside? The desirability, or otherwise, of this duality has been studied by a number of practitioners working in the field of digital art (Stelarc 1996, Vesne, 1995 and Hachiya, 1993), but the question remains how might the illusion of experiencing such places be mediated through technology? One strategy that has been adopted is that of realism (Lombard and Ditton, 1997). If the virtual environment looks like and responds like the real world then, it is contended that the user will experience a sense of 'being there'. A second approach to this problem has been to generate artificial environments that support the user in engagement with specific activities (Jacobson, 1999), the rationale being that the act of undertaking a task or engaging participants' imagination will enable greater engagement with the artificial environment on the part of the user through, for example, the use of multiple media which act on a variety of senses. Critical to the success of this approach is that the synthetic environment is integral to the nature of the task being undertaken. A third factor which it is suggested could impact on the sense of 'being there' experienced by a user is the semantics of the place created in the virtual world (Schubert, Friedman and Usher, 2001). The meanings associated with particular places are highly personal, but so too is the potential for specific places to evoke strong feelings among individuals. The representation of places of historical or cultural significance could evoke a much greater sense of engagement within users than the depiction of a fictitious environment designed by an engineer.

P. Turner and E. Davenport (Eds.), Spaces, Spatiality and Technology, 249-260.

What is clear is that the factors that contribute to the sense of 'being there' in a virtual world are both complex and subtly intertwined. The degree of realism, the nature of the activities supported and the place semantics all contribute to that experience. It is contended that how this will be achieved will eventually determine the success and widespread acceptance of VR technology. Furthermore, that central to this success will be the degree to which the illusion of a sense of place is experienced by the user. In short, how effective is the illusion of 'being there'? The research reported in this chapter will consider the sense of place as experienced in the world and how this can be used to inform both the design and evaluation of virtual worlds. The research was undertaken as part of the BENOGO project which is focussing on the realistic representation of environments as a technique to convey a sense of presence.

The study of the real world reported in this chapter has drawn on the phenomenologist tradition, specifically Merleau-Ponty's emphasises the importance of the body in the experience of the world. He places the body at the centre of our relation to the world and argues that it is only through having bodies that we can truly experience place. In the context of perception Merleau-Ponty (1962) formulated a sense of sight as an embodied vision that is an incarnate part of the flesh of the world: 'our body is both an object among objects and that which sees and touches them'. The body is interpreted as having a central role in how we engage with and learn about the environments we inhabit. A further influence on the work reported was the research of Relph (1976) who adopted a phenomenological approach to the study of place identity. In seeking to characterise place, Relph drew from Wagner's (1972) recognition that 'place, person, time and act form an indivisible unity. To be oneself one has to be somewhere definite, do certain things at appropriate times'. Given such a fusion of meaning, act and context, it has been suggested that generalisations about place cannot be formulated. Relph responded to this by stressing the links between the concepts of 'place, person and act' specifically in the study of place identity. He characterises place identity as more than an address in a gazetteer or a point on a map, identity is considered to be a basic feature of our experience of places which both influences and is influenced by those experiences. Relph suggests that it is not just identity of a place that is important, but also the identity that a person or group has with that place, in particular whether they are experiencing it as an 'insider' or an 'outsider'. In a similar vein to Wagner, Relph has proposed three components of place identity they are as follows: the physical setting; the activities offered by the place and the meanings attributed to the place. Physical setting refers to the relationships between the objects that comprise the place. These could include houses, paths or public areas. Activities are those things which are observed as taking place among the entities that populate the place. Finally meaning is attributed to the place by those that are experiencing it, for example a building may be a work place, a home or a sanctuary and as such will have a particular identity for the individual.

In an attempt to understand how people react to and move around in places, Lynch (1960) in his now classic study, asked residents of three American cities to describe their city in terms of what it was like to live and work in. Based on these responses Lynch proposed that there was indeed some form of collective public image of the city. He proposed three components of an environmental image: identity; structure and meaning. Structure refers to the order and pattern that connects and relates the various parts of a place. In general this takes the form of rules that reduce visual uncertainty. Meaning, like Relph's interpretation, refers to that which the place represents to the individuals that inhabit it. The main focus of Lynch's work was on the identity of a place which is considered to be all those special attributes of a place that make it both recognisable and ultimately unique. Lawson (2001) comments that an overriding theme emerges from the work of Lynch and others, is that architecture and place are human and social concepts just as much as they are physical ones.

The rationale underpinning the work reported in this chapter is that the study of real places, specifically how they are experienced by individuals, will provide a basis for the design of virtual worlds. Such studies, it is suggested, will contribute to the generation of requirements for the creation of more believable, engaging and ultimately satisfying experience of 'being in' a virtual world. In order to provide some context for the research the next section will introduce the BENOGO project.

THE BENOGO PROJECT

BENOGO is a project funded under the European Community's Future and Emerging Technologies 'Presence' initiative (www.benogo.dk). The BENOGO consortium comprises 6 academic institutions from Europe and Israel with expertise in virtual reality, photo-realistic panoramic image acquisition and rendering, the psycho-physics of visual sensing and spatial perception, and the human aspects of new technologies. The project brings together a mixture of novel technologies that will enable real-time visualisation for an observer of recorded real places. The aim of the research is to develop new tools for empirical and theoretical studies of presence based on the concept of the observer's embodiment in the computationally created virtual environment. Furthermore, as real places (possibly known to the observer) with man-made and/or organic objects (like trees, foliage etc.) are otherwise hard to represent in a virtual environment, the objective is to bring about new insight into presence through comparison with the sense of presence experienced in the real world.

The BENOGO experience will be based on true-to-life visual and auditory information presented in real-time. The technology will be designed to support the observer's active exploration of the visual and auditory space, through the addition of a physical dimension to the experience. Through visual and auditory augmentation a sense of life can be added including objects for interaction. Projection technologies will range from Head Mounted Display (HMD) to large screens including a 6-sided CAVE.

The empirical research will exploit the possibilities to investigate the experience of 'being there' in relation to real places and objects The theoretical framework will be based on the concept of embodiment in conjunction with presence and sense of place. This will be investigated in terms of fidelity of experience and presentation as compared to equivalent real-word places, and physiological and neurological aspects like consistency of sensory-motor co-ordination. The framework will be developed in close interaction with, and as a guide for, technical development by focusing on the particular strengths that the technology offers as well as on its weak points. Feedback from empirical studies will form an essential part of the project. The research iterates through 11 demonstrators to achieve these goals. In order to structure the research, four main themes have been identified. These are as follows: the acquisition and real time rendering of places; the augmentation of these rendered images with synthetic virtual reality images and 3D soundscapes; the investigation of the psycho-physiological aspects of presence and finally establishing a sense of place. While it is this last theme that is the focus of this chapter, a more detailed description of the BENOGO project has been previously reported by Arnspang *et al.*, (2002).

The work reported in this chapter forms part of an ongoing 'benchmarking' activity being undertaken as part of the BENOGO project (Turner *et al.*; 2003, Turner and Turner, 2003). The aim of these studies is to better understand how individuals interact with and, as a consequence, make sense of real places. For example, the language they use to describe their sense of being in a place and whether such descriptions reveal common themes. Other factors that have the potential to influence this sense of place include the nature of a task or activity being undertaken or enabled while being in a place. It is contended that the understanding gained by such benchmarking of real places will both inform the design and ground the subsequent evaluation of the synthetic environments created as part of the BENOGO project.

A criticism levelled at the previous benchmarking activities undertaken by the project was expressed by an EU reviewer when they stated that the study of real places placed an unreasonable criteria for success on the synthetic environments. In short, they felt that virtual environments will always be a 'pale shadow' of their real world counterparts. To address this criticism it was decided to study a place that was both natural as it was the stated intent of the project to represent such organic environments, but also exhibited built attributes. The Landform at the Scottish Gallery of Modern Art was chosen as it was felt to fulfil both these requirements in an innovative manner.

LANDFORM UEDA

The Landform is a sculpted landscape that consists of three crescent shaped pools and a serpentine, stepped mound (Figure 1). It forms part of a continuing scheme to develop the grounds around the Scottish National Gallery of Modern Art and the Dean Gallery in Edinburgh. It was created by the landscape architect Charles Jencks

Figure 1. The Landform Ueda, Scottish National Gallery of Modern Art, Edinburgh

and opened to the public in 2002, it took more than two years to plan and construct. It covers more than 3,000 sq m (32,000 sq ft) and rises to a height of 7 m (23 ft). The Landform was chosen for the study as it was felt to deliberately blur the boundary between artificial and natural and as such provided an interesting counterpoint to the environments which typify VR. While the structure is undeniably constructed, it also incorporates natural elements. For example, water and grass have been used to create organic shapes and forms based on Catastrophe Theory. In the Landform it was the architect's intention to use folds to orientate movement, to link the gallery with the surrounding urban environment.

In a newspaper interview (Rudden, 2002) Jencks discussed his thinking during the design of the Landform, he stated that it was his intention to commemorate life, specifically that he was designing to have a 'physical effect'. Jencks went on to say:

> 'When you walk though them, you feel part of them. A lot of landforms, such as the Pyramids (an installation on the M8 between Glasgow and Edinburgh), relate us to nature, and in the city should be enjoyed as a space apart. This is a piece of nature, but a designed piece of nature in praise of grass and water, but when you are here you should feel part of it too'.

He continued by describing the swirls of the Landform as having an almost physical attraction and how he felt that water was central to the experience of the structure as follows:

'While the pathways should be sharp and catch the light, that isn't enough unless the water provides a contrast. It is that pool of flat darkness that ripples into life when there is a breath of air that made me realise if you take away the water the landform lacks energy'.

The architect sought to create a structure with an inherent tension and dynamic, that would connect with people at both a physical and emotional level.

Figure 2. GPS mapping of routes on the Landform Ueda (a) Day 1 – School Children and (b) Day 2 – General Public. Images from the GPS Drawing Project.

To date only one piece of research into the use of the Landform has been reported. The work was conducted as part of an ongoing project into the relationship between places and drawings using GPS technology as a means of creating images while moving through specific places (www.gpsdrawing.com/index.html). In November 2002, at the request of The Lighthouse, a centre for architecture and design in Glasgow, a two day GPS drawing project was conducted on the Landform. On the first day primary school children were equipped with GPS devices which were tracked as they moved around the Landform. On the second day the project was open to the public. The traces from Days 1 and 2 are presented in Figure 2. While the distances covered on both days was similar, 15.55 miles on Day 1 and 16.75 on Day 2, the routes appear to be different. The adults on Day 2 appear to follow more set routes pre-determined by the nature of the structure while the children on Day 1 have adopted a more random approach to exploration of the Landform. Interestingly, the difference in response to the Landform between adults and children was an issue that was to return during the current study.

A STUDY OF PLACE

The study conducted by the author consisted of a series of 10 semi-structured interviews conducted over several days during the summer of 2003 with individuals and couples who had come onto the Landform. The rationale underpinning the decision to use a semi-structured interview technique was that it enabled a flexible approach to data gathering that was deemed appropriate to the nature of the study. The questions asked during each interview were designed to initiate discussions about the experience of being on the Landform and, at a more abstract level, how those feelings were elicited by the nature of the place *per se*. Finally, the questions were informed by the concepts of 'place, person and act' as articulated by Relph (1976). Typically each interview was approximately between 10 and 15 minutes in duration and was recorded throughout. Example questions were as follows:

- How would you describe the Landform as if to a friend?
- Do you feel that the Landform encouraged you to explore?
- Were you aware of others on the Landform?

Permission to report the data gathered during the study was obtained from both the gallery and all participants. The aim of the study was to understand the sense of place experienced by visitors to the Landform. A thematic analysis was conducted on the interview material in order to identify any common themes reported as being felt to contribute to the sense of place

As a technique to reveal sense of place participants were initially asked to describe the Landform as if to a friend. In general two strategies were exhibited. Firstly, those who described it in terms of the shapes and forms which comprised the physical structure and those who characterised it in terms of the emotions that the experience of being there evoked within themselves. Examples of the former included phrases such as: 'hand manipulated'; 'green cream'; 'a twisted flat area, non organic although curved'; 'artificial contouring'; 'two crescent shaped ponds' and a 'sculpted form'. Indeed one participant described the Landform as a 'sexy model, a big version of a model'.

These descriptions raised the dichotomy between the built and natural environment. By utilising naturally occurring elements in the Landform it begins to blur people's sensation of this distinction. Visitors commented on its constructed nature, both in terms of its appearance and their perception of the design process used during its development. The Landform was viewed as an enormous model – the purity of its form echoing the minimalism of traditional architectural models. Indeed findings from previous work have suggested that the material that comprises a physical model can have the potential for impact on the eventual design solution (Smyth, 1999). Porter and Neale (2000) support this position when they argue that a model making fabric can influence the quality of the architecture it replicates. They cite examples of critics who have historically blamed the proliferation of severe Brutalist and bush-hammered concrete architecture of the 1950s and 60s on the widespread use of balsa wood for modelling. Indeed others argue that 'those weaned on a Modernist tradition and who rely on the pristine abstraction of white cardboard models, have helped spread the "International Style" anonymity of a raw concrete built environment stripped of ornamentation'. The level of sophistication of some physical models raises the question of the nature of their relationship with the building that they seek to represent. Indeed, whether the production of the model becomes an end in itself. In the vast majority of cases when physical models are constructed they are done so to articulate particular aspects of a final building. The end is certainly not the model. In certain circumstances this relationship can become blurred.

One of the questions asked of participants sought to tap into the emotions that were experienced when on the Landform. This was developed from Jenck's original intention that the Landform should have both a physical and emotional impact on those who visited it. Descriptions which were grounded in the emotional experience of being in the Landform were illustrated by the following quotations: 'a tranquil place'; 'a place to meditate and get away from the rush of the town'; 'a peaceful place, quiet and relaxing' and 'a place where you can think'. It was clear that the overriding emotion evoked by the Landform was one of serenity and contemplation.

An important indicator of the level of interaction with the Landform was the sense of engagement reported by the participants. While the Landform is undoubtedly atypical and as such is a place that people come to visit, it was considered important to question the level of engagement that its form provoked. More specifically, how that engagement was experienced, for example was it primarily visual or was it felt 'with and through' the body. How successful was the architect in stimulating a physical response to the Landform? In a similar treatment of architecture Pallasmaa (1996) commented that buildings are encountered, they are not merely observed. Their importance lies in their ability to articulate and give significance which can only truly be achieved through physical encounter. He continues by stating that the emphasis on the visual sense in Western culture has resulted in 'designs which housed the intellect and the eye, but that have left the body and the senses, as well as our memories and dreams, homeless'. This imbalance of our sensory system has prompted the suggestion that the increased experience of alienation, detachment and solitude in the world today may be related with a certain pathology of the senses which has in turn lead to isolation, detachment and exteriority (Pallasmaa, 1996). Such a demarcation, it is contended, will impact not only on the nature of the buildings with which we interact but also with the nature of the design process through which they are created. As buildings loose their plasticity and their connection with the language and wisdom of the body, they become isolated in the cool and distant realm of vision. Increasingly architecture is loosing its tactility and measures designed for the body. Indeed the detachment of construction has prompted the view that architecture is rapidly turning into 'stages sets for the eye' (Pallasmaa, 1996). The sense of 'aura', the authority of presence, that Walter Benjamin (1997) regards as a necessary quality of an authentic piece of art has been lost.

This echoes Relph's (1976) idea of the distinction between 'insideness and outsideness' when considering the identity of a place. He contends that to be inside a place is to belong to it and to identify with it, and the more profoundly one is inside the stronger is the identity with the place. The degree to which and the means by which, individuals engage with the Landform will, it is contended, impact on the sense of place experienced by the individual. Indeed the degree to which objects and places can provoke interaction or engagement is an ongoing debate among artists, designers and technologists.

When asked about their experience of engagement while exploring the Landform a number of themes emerged. The Landform was reported as generally encouraging exploration from the outset as it provided a number of approaches. Interestingly the main entrance point was criticised on the grounds of 'the sense of control evoked by such a tiny entrance'. Indeed a recurring theme throughout most of the interviews was whether it was allowed to go on to the Landform at all. One participant described such a conversation in terms of an 'adult negotiation' and commented that adults tend to 'enter the space first with our eyes'. Children, on the other hand, exhibited no such reservations and quickly began to explore the Landform. This observation was echoed by many of the participants when they described the nature of their engagement with the Landform as being akin to the childlike desire to explore.

Walking through the Landform was described as being crucial to the overall experience. Most reported that the Landform encouraged exploration in a 'non-authoritarian' way leaving individuals feeling not 'over directed'. The use of water on the Landform created hard boundaries that clearly limited the choice of routes open to visitors. This was commented on by one person who felt that, while it was essential to enter onto the Landform in order to appreciate its scale, the hard lines created by the water forced particular routes. They suggested that, in their opinion, the water might have been better integrated into the Landform through the use of more faded edges. Beaches were described to illustrate the idea of gradual boundaries that act as an invitation to explore what is beyond. They concluded that the water formed a pattern when viewed from above and that this is not the same experience you have when at ground level in the actual Landform. Interestingly, it was the same participant who described the Landform as a 'sexy model – a big version of a model'. This was discussed as a movement from the visual to the physical in that they described the feeling of being able to walk in particular routes as being experienced through the body. One of the participants commented on the similarity of paths worn on the Landform through people walking in particular patterns with the idea of Desire Lines. These are informal paths that pedestrians prefer to take to get from one location to another rather than using a footpath or an official route. Sometimes they manifest as beaten down paths in grass, these often occur with nearby paths which offer a less direct route. In a similar manner wear on the Landform is indicative of popular routes through its curves and folds, or more often children's preferences for places to slide down its steeply raked surfaces. Furthermore, it was seen as positive that the Landform gradually revealed different viewpoints of itself and the surrounding spaces as part of the exploration process. A number of participants commented on the changing light and shadow as one moved through the Landform and several mentioned that they visited at different times of the year to experience the change of light and its subsequent effect.

Several of the participants commented on the texture of the grass that covered the surface of the Landform, in particular its hardness and the pattern of wear. In general the tactile quality of the Landform was enjoyed and aided its interpretation as an interactive sculpture. One participant commented on the clover and weeds that were growing in the grass that covered the Landform. The observation prompted them to comment that in their opinion the Landform was 'not quite designed for change and that while it was a natural object it was also designed as a fixed object'. It was envisaged that when considering a model of the Landform, little could the architect have known the changes that would occur over time with the finished structure. The wear resulting from visitors and poor drainage and the debris left by the seagulls that congregate every morning before the visitors arrive. All these factors contribute to the dynamic nature of the Landform and in part to the sense of place experienced by the visitor.

CONCLUSIONS

The research reported here reveals two main themes that are pertinent to the design and evaluation of VR environments which strive to convey a sense of place to users. Firstly that a sense of place is experienced through movement of the body not simply by looking with the eyes and secondly that change to a place over time through patterns of usage is an important aspect of place and its identity. Movement is viewed by the architect as being central to the experience of the Landform. This position is echoed by Martin Agis. Agis designs inflatable multi cellular structures that, in a similar vein to Jencks, seek to integrate art and architecture. When discussing his work Agis describes the crucial element as 'the movement of people through the unfolding space'. It is that feeling of connectivity with the self and with others in the space itself that Agis attempts to facilitate with his structures. Indeed to further enhance the sense of engagement Agis has collaborated with the contemporary composer Stephen Montague in the creation of Bright Interiors, a soundtrack of 16 loops that endlessly repeat and interact, as the light and colour interacts in the space. What is critical to Agis's work is the sense of scale, the fact that the structure is experienced from within and the sensory richness that such physical embodiment provides. All the senses are engaged and the result is a rich and intimate experience where the individual is touched at a number of levels both physical and emotional. The result reaffirms the importance of embodiment in terms of presence being a multi sensory experience. This raises the question of how might VR environments be developed that engage the participant on such a multi sensory level? An approach that shows promise is haptic interaction. An example of such work is that reported by Shillito (2002) who describes early attempts to support the work practices of designers and artists through haptic interaction provided via a Phantom force feedback device (Reachin Technologies). The Phantom is a 3 dimensional cursor that enables users to touch, feel and manipulate a virtual environment. In these cases the provision of touch and force feedback appears to be effective in drawing the participant into the situation of the virtual environment and subsequently increasing the sense of presence.

The temporal dimension of a place and how the activities enabled can change supports the contention of Relph (1976) and the contemporary work of Borden

(2001). In his study of urban skateboarders Borden discusses the concept of 'found space', that is space appropriated by skateboarders that is not originally intended for that purpose. For example, the city centre square may provide convenient lunchtime seating for office workers but as night falls it may also provide unforeseen challenges for the cities skateboarders. While the space remains the same it is contended that the sense of place and associate identity is quite different.

The study reported suggests that the body is a key element in terms of how it mediates the comprehension of spaces and the layered meanings that transform them into places. The ability to move through and explore a space and experience it with and through the body is central to this transformation process. A secondary theme highlighted by the study was how the interpretation of place changed over time and the subsequent impact on identity. If VR environments are to successfully capture such attributes of places then it is essential that they are designed to exhibit the necessary multi sensory interaction. Haptic interaction and in particular touch shows some initial promise in this area.

ACKNOWLEDGEMENTS

Thanks are due to the staff at the Scottish National Gallery of Modern Art, in particular Sarah Campbell, and the financial support of the EU Presence programme.

REFERENCES

Arnspang J., Benyon D., Fahle M., W., Granum E., Madsen C., B., Pajdla T., Peleg S,. Smyth M., Turner P., Turner S. and Weinshall (2002) An Investigation into Virtual Representations of Real Places, Proc Presence 2002, Universidade Fernando Pessoa, Porto, Portugal, October 10-11.

Benjamin, W. (1997) *Charles Baudelaire*. Verso, London.

Borden, I. (2001) *Skateboarding, space and the city: Architecture and the Body*. Berg, Oxford and New York.

Franck, K. (1998) It and I: Bodies as Objects, Bodies as Subjects, *Architectural Design*, **68**, **(11/12)**, 16-19.

Franck, K. (1995) When I enter virtual reality, what body will I leave behind, *Architectural Design*, **65(11/12)**, 20-23.

Gibson, W. (1986) *Neuromancer*, Voyager Books, UK.

Hachiya, K. (1993) The Interdiscommunication Machine, www.petworks.co.jp/~hachiya/works

Jacobson, D. (1999) Impression Formation in Cyberspace: Online Expectations and Offline Experiences in Text Based Virtual Commities, *Journal of Computer-Mediated Communication*, **5(1)**, Univ S Calif, USA.

Lawson, B. (2001) *The Language of Space*. Architectural Press, Oxford, UK.

Lombard, M. and Ditton, T. (1997) At the Heart of it all: The Concept of Presence, *Journal of Computer-Mediated Communication*, **3(2)**, Univ. of S. Calif, USA.

Merleau-Ponty, M. (1962) *Phenomenology of Perception*, Smith, C. (trans) Routledge & Kegan Paul Ltd.

Pallasmaa, J (1996) *The Eyes of the Skin, Architecture and the Senses*, Academy Editions.

Porter, T. and Neale, J. (2000) *Architectural Supermodels*. Architectural Press

Rudden, C. (2002) Life Growing in a Fresh Direction, Evening News, 7 Aug, Edinburgh.

Schillito, A. M. (2002) The Tacitus Project, Pixel Raiders, V&A Museum, London, 19 March.

Schubert, T., Friedman, F. and Usher, J. M. (2001) The Experience of Presence: Factor analytic insights, *Presence: Teleoperators and Virtual Environments*, **10**, 266-281.

Smyth, M. (1999) The Activity of Design as Revealed by Tool Usage. *Journal of Design Sciences*, **7(1)**, 11-22.

Stelarc (1996) Ping Body, www.stelarc.va.com.au.

Stone, A. R. (1992) Will the Real Body Please Stand Up?. In M. Benedikt (ed) *Cultures in Cyberspace*, MIT Press.

Turner, P. and Turner, S. (2003) Two Phenomenological Studies of Place, *Proceedings of HCI03 – People and Computers XVII*, Bath UK, 21-35

Turner, S., Turner, P., Caroll, F., O'Neill, S., Benyon, D., McCall, R. and Smyth, M. (2003) Re-creating the Botanics: towards a sense of place in virtual environments. *3rd UK Environmental Psychology Conference*, Aberdeen, June 2003.

Relph, E. (1976) *Place and Placelessness*. Pion Books, UK

Vesna, V. (1995) Bodies Inc, www.bodiesinc.ucla.edu.

Wagner, P., L. (1972) *Environments and Peoples*. Prentice Hall, Englewood Cliffs, NJ.

AFFILIATIONS

Michael Smyth, School of Computing, Napier University, 10 Colinton Road Edinburgh.

XIAOLONG (LUKE) ZHANG AND GEORGE W. FURNAS

18. MULTISCALE SPACE AND PLACE

Supporting User Interactions with Large Structures in Virtual Environments

INTRODUCTION

This chapter is about the exploration of a new design paradigm for virtual space and virtual place. Spatial metaphors have been widely used in support of information access and social interactions. Example designs include Media spaces (Bly *et al.*, 1993) and spatial video conferencing (DeSilve *et al.*, 1995; Sellen and Buxton, 1992). In the design of collaborative virtual environments (CVEs), spatial metaphors are embedded in 3D environments to create shared space for people to work together. Shared space integrates data and users together, and provides an "explicit" and "persistent" spatial context for collaboration (Benford *et al.*, 1996). The sense of space can facilitate social interactions by allowing the partition of available space and permitting users to apply their spatial social skills, and so on (Benford and Greenhalgh, 1997).

Usually, our interests of space in virtual environments lead toward its implications for social interactions. Our understanding, interpretation, and use of virtual space are still largely based on our experience in real space. For example, CVEs are often designed to support activities we see in the real world: meeting (Greenhalgh and Benford, 1995), social gathering (Lea *et al.*, 1997; Waters *et al.*, 1997), product design (Linebarger and Kessler, 2002), etc. While there is nothing wrong to replicate or simulate our real-world experiences in virtual worlds, it is also needed to consider how the unique characteristics of virtual space can benefit our work. This chapter will examine multiscale virtual environments (mVEs), a new design paradigm that exploits the virtuality of virtual environments. In mVEs, a user can choose to work at different interaction scales: being a giant to see the big picture of a structure and manipulate large objects, or being an ant to examine the details of a particular part of the structure and work on small objects. The user's perception and action in mVEs could be very different from what they have in conventional virtual environments. We will study multiscale space and multiscale place separately by emphasizing their different roles in supporting users' actions. Multiscale space refers to the unique spatial aspects of mVEs, and our interests of it lie in its support for user interactions with virtual objects and virtual environments. The notion of

P. Turner and E. Davenport (Eds.), Spaces, Spatiality and Technology, 261-280.

multiscale place emphasizes the social aspects of mVEs, and concerns the impacts of multiscale space on interactions among users.

This new design paradigm could have a great potential to address a challenge we are facing in dealing with structures that cross different scale levels. We are living in a world where things have very different sizes and, as Aristotle argued, remain naturally in their proper places. Objects create different structures at different size-scale levels, and demonstrate important characteristics at different levels. Consequently, the physical world looks differently from scale to scale. The book "Powers of Ten" (Morrison and Morrison, 1982) vividly illustrates the images of the physical world from the *gigantic* galaxy level to the *minuscule* sub-atomic level. Our understanding of such a complex world did not come easily. It took us thousands of years to discover these structures at multiple scale levels and construct a notion of a hierarchical world. Even so, we still do not know the world fully, in particular at those scale levels that are beyond our direct perception scale range. This might be related to our limited cognition and interaction capability.

Compared with the vast scale range of the physical world, the scale range of human beings' cognition and interaction capabilities is limited. In the real world, our naturally born capabilities do not allow us to see atoms with our naked eyes and to reach easily a destination thousands of kilometres away just with our legs. The size scale of matter in this world spans from the level of 10^{-16} m, the size of the smallest elementary particles, to the level of 10^{26} m, the size of the observable universe (Morrison and Morrison, 1982). This range of forty-two orders of magnitude is far beyond the normal interaction scale range of human bodies, which is only about four orders of magnitude from millimetres (10^{-3}) to tens of meter (10^{1}). This mismatch in scale makes it difficult or even impossible for people to observe and manipulate many object structures directly in the real world. People have to rely on instruments to deal with objects at different scales: using microscopes to observe small structures like cells, and using satellites or space shuttles to examine large objects like the Earth. These instruments and people's naked eyes together build a multiple-scale (multiscale) system that helps to deploy our scarce scale resources across the needed scale ranges.

People face similar problems in virtual worlds, where objects like information structures and model structures are becoming increasingly large and across many different levels. The information world has grown and continues to grow rapidly. Billions of web pages are indexed and distributed on the Internet; the hierarchy of a file system on a personal computer may hold tens of thousands of documents; a corporate web site may connect millions of web pages. Model structures people build in virtual environments are also getting larger and larger. A protein structure may have thousands of DNA sequences. A virtual city can hold tens of thousands of buildings. Managing such huge information structures or model structures could be a daunting task. Given our limited cognition resources, we cannot observe all levels of a large structure simultaneously, and we have to focus our attentions on some parts of the structure in interactions. Either local content or global context information has to be hidden. Incomplete information may cause problems in the understanding and management of information structures. Obtaining both detailed contents and sufficient contexts could be a challenge.

One approach to address this issue is to use multiscale technology, which will be introduced soon. In this chapter, we discuss multiscale in 3D virtual environments. It begins with an introduction to multiscale in virtual environments. Then, it forwards to issues concerning user perception and action in multiscale space. Next, we examine emerging issues related to social interactions in multiscale place. Finally, the implications of the notions of space and place for the understanding and design of virtual environments are discussed.

MULTISCALE TECHNOLOGY

Multiscale techniques have been seen in many research projects. The first exploration of multiscale technology was Pad (Perlin and Fox, 1993), and other systems include Pad++ (Bederson and Hollan, 1994) and Jazz (Bederson et al., 2000). These projects largely focused on 2D interfaces.

A 2D multiscale user interface provides users with a ubiquitous zooming capability that allows users to manipulate the rendered size of objects continuously and dynamically, so it is often called zoomable user interface (ZUI) (Perlin and Fox, 1993; Bederson and Hollan, 1994; Bederson et al., 2000). A 2D multiscale environment can be directly understood as one allowing multiple magnifications of display.In such ZUIs, there is another aspect of scale which relates not to perception but to action: zooming also sets users' action domains. For example, manipulating objects through the ZUI window or panning that window is typically constant in the display units (e.g., panning one window width per sec, moving a visible object half a window width by direct manipulation of its image). This means that when users are really zoomed in, they are making very small movements in the virtual world, and when they are zoomed out, they are making huge ones – the display magnification turns into a corresponding magnification of action. We will see that this natural correspondence of perception and action in 2D is not so straightforward in 3D.

Our study explores the understandings and design of multiscale technology in 3D. In a 2D ZUI, displayed size and corresponding action scale are mediated by a simple magnification parameter. In 3D, however, one might argue that no such magnification parameter is needed – all we need to do is to adjust the viewing distance to control the image size of objects we see. If you want to see something small, move in close. If you want to see something big, step back. Imagine the eye as a pinhole camera, and that what we see is the image on the projection plane of the camera. As seen in Figure 1, the projected size can be written as:

$$S_p = \frac{S_0}{D} d_c$$

where: S_p – the projected size
          S_0 – the real size
          D – the distance of the object to pinhole,
          d_c – the distance of projection plane to pinhole

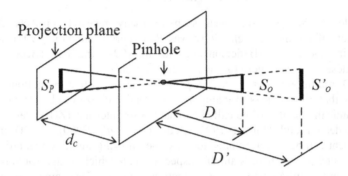

Figure 1. Pinhole Camera

Obviously, the image size, S_p, can be controlled by simply adjusting D. However small an object is, a distance can always be found to make a sizable image projection. For example, to see an object with a size of 1nm, users can set a viewpoint at a distance of 1nm to the object , and get the view angle of the object about 53 degrees, plenty large enough to see good details. It is not necessary to use magnification. In fact, one might argue that the idea of magnifying the world would be fruitless. If the centre of magnification is the pinhole, both the size of the object and its distance to the pinhole will increase proportionally, the projected size will be the same. As seen in the figure, S_0 and S'_0 have the same projected image. So why would there be any sensible notion of scale change for interaction in a 3D virtual environment?

The answer comes from the fact that interaction in a virtual environment involves more than providing a single, static pinhole camera view. There turns out to be many other size-dependent aspects of interaction that bring sense to the notion of a 3D multiscale interface to a 3D multiscale world.

More than just viewing distance, there are other perception parameters, as well as several action parameters that need to be adjusted. If a stereo display is available, for example, the eye separation should be at a scale similar to the viewing distance to generate a correct binocular disparity. If the eye separation and the viewing distance do not match well, say a 1nm viewing distance vs. a 1m eye separation, the left and right images would be totally irrelevant, and stereopsis would be impossible. Similarly, having an action domain comparable with the viewing distance is also critical for interaction. Moving with a step size of 1km under a viewing distance of 1nm would make it hard to keep a consistent view. Any movement will change the view significantly.

In this sense, to work on structures at different sizes, users need a whole coordinated set of interaction size parameters, including viewing distance, eye separation (in stereo views), eye-level (if there is a ground plane), navigation speed, reaching distance, and so on. mVEs, by integrating multiscale technologies into 3D virtual environments, give users the ability to control this set of parameters, which can be mediated by a single measure – *interaction scale*, when they work on objects and structures at various size-scale levels. To work on small objects like atomic lattices or a DNA double-helix, users can be something much smaller than an ant, let's say *a nano-ant* or *nanant*, moving and manipulating very precisely to maintain reasonable action accuracy. Similarly, interacting with a virtual model of the Milky Way Galaxy, the relevant distance scale would be at the level of light years, and users need to work like a super giant, a *giga-giant* or *gigant*, to interact properly in the virtual environment. Although transcending the spatial scale of the space in the real world is impossible, users can have such experience in mVEs.

Some research projects have considered scale as an interaction parameter in 3D virtual environments. The auto-scaling tool (Mine *et al.*, 1997) gave a user an extensible arm length to help reaching object at any distance. The Go-Go technique (Poupyrev *et al.*, 1996) dynamically rescaled a user's arm to increase the reaching distance. The Image-Plane-Interaction (Pierce *et al.*, 1999) allowed a user to manipulate the projection of objects at any distance. However, these tools only considered one particular interaction parameter – arm-reaching distance, and overlooked the need to yoke other perception and action parameters together. Furthermore, these designs, as well as Pad++, focused on single user environments, and gave no consideration to the use of scaling in environments shared by multiple users. The design of mVEs provides users with not just a space, where they can adjust their interaction scale in the work, but also a place, where they and other users can combine their different multiscale capabilities to deal with large structures.

SPACE AND PLACE IN MULTISCALE VIRTUAL ENVIRONMENTS

Philosophical arguments on space and place have had impacts on research in Human-Computer Interaction (HCI). Harrison and Dourish (1996) distinguished these two concepts by their different roles in people's life, and understood space and place distinctively by emphasizing the physical and social aspects respectively. This classification implies a way to understand mVEs: studying the physical properties of space in mVEs to understand how mVEs can support user interactions with objects and virtual environments, and examining the social properties of space to see how mVEs may affect user interactions with others.

In the real world, people usually put more interests in place than space. Architectural design is about to build places embedding social structures, rather than just to create physical structures in space. We can build things in space, but can hardly do anything on the physical properties of space itself. Our philosophical understandings on space have been consistently evolving: from the Greek notion of space as an abstract entity, to the conception of space as supremacy held by Newton and Descartes, to Kant's view of space as *a priori* and being subjective, to the phenomenological view of the critical involvement of human beings in the constructions of the notion of space (see Casey, 1997). The advance of philosophical conceptualization on space may have affected our views on the relationships between human, objects, and space, but our capabilities to manipulate the physical characteristics of space have not improved too much. Thus, in real-world design, all we can do is to build place based on our improved understandings of the relationship between human and space, and to embed social implications in space.

Such a socialized view of space has been reflected in user interface design. In HCI research, new designs often focus on place, rather than space (Fitzpatrick *et al.*, 1996; Gaver, 1992; Bly *et al.*, 1993). This is not a surprise, given the nature of HCI research, which emphasizes human and social issues in the use of technology. While such a social perspective is important, we may also need to think about how to leverage the spatiality of virtual space to enhance user interactions. Virtual space is artificially made, and how we can interact with it is all up to design. New interaction experiences can indeed be created in virtual space to support people's work. Some research projects have explored this direction by going "beyond being real" (Hollan and Stornetta, 1992). For example, distance in virtual environments can be distorted with fisheye views (Furnas, 1986) so that objects of interest can get more space than those of no interest (Robertson and Mackinlay, 1993; Raab and Ruger, 1996); the available space in 2D workspace could be expandable by using zooming tools (Perlin and Fox, 1993; Bederson and Hollan, 1994, Bederson *et al.*, 2000); navigation in 3D could be simplified by using teleportation, which makes spatial separation in virtual environments seemingly diminish. These creative designs not only help users to better work with complicated data and virtual worlds, but also open the doors to new ways for social interactions.

The design of mVEs is such an attempt that overcomes the constraint on spatial scale and allows users to manipulate the scale of virtual environments. mVEs offer a new type of virtual space in which users can observe important characteristics of structures at different scales and act on objects with different sizes easily. Their perception and action in mVEs could be very different from what they have in conventional virtual environments. At the same time, mVEs also provide users with social places different from what they have in real life and in conventional virtual environments. In multiscale places, users will be able to cooperate from different scales and leverage their different capabilities. Hollan and Stornetta (1992) argued that how people communicate with each other is related to what media they use. The introduction of multiscale changes the characteristics of virtual space, which mediates most of collaboration activities in mVEs, and would affect the ways on which users rely in their interactions with others. Thus, our analysis will be at both the individual and collaboration levels. At the individual level, we focus on user interactions with objects and multiscale space in virtual environments. At the collaboration level, we are interested in social interaction among users in multiscale place.

MULTISCALE SPACE

Our interests of multiscale space concern how multiscale may affect users' understandings of and their actions in virtual space. Multiscale technology can visualize the same structure with different representations at different scales and affect users' visual perception and related action. The focus here will be on the impacts of scale on visual perception and action, in particular the integration of interaction parameters, spatial perception, and visually-guided activities. A scale-based information visualization technique will also be briefly introduced.

Integration of Interaction Scale Parameters

A design problem in multiscale space is how to give a user sensible control over the scale, or the suite of various interaction parameters. This has not been a serious problem in traditional virtual environments, where users usually stay at one interaction scale level. In these virtual environments, although there are some circumstances where users need to change a particular interaction parameter, such as quick navigation speed or far reaching distance, situations that require users to alter a whole set of perception and action parameters are rarely seen. In mVEs, however, when users choose to work at different scales, this issue cannot be ignored.

Our approach is to use avatars to integrate interaction parameters together. An avatar is a graphical representation of a user in a virtual environment. In collaborative environments, it provides such information as presence, location, identification and the like about the represented user (Benford et al., 1995), and is widely used in CVE design. An avatar is the virtual body of a user in virtual worlds. In real life, the human body ties our perception and action together, and perception and action parameters are at a scale level similar to the body size – the meter. Our step size is about 1m; arm-reaching distance is at the meter level; the shortest focus distance of our eyes is about 0.1m. The human body can be seen as a measure to define our interaction scale in the physical world. In mVEs, an avatar works as a virtual human body to define the user's perception and action.

In 3D multiscale environments, the avatar metaphor can provide a natural way to tie together the suite of size-based parameters needed for interaction: the size of an avatar is linked to the interaction scale the represented user chooses. By changing this scale, users' avatars will be resized accordingly. Figure 2 shows a user's avatar at two scales, which is sized differently. The left image indicates a larger interaction scale of the user, who has a broader overview range, a faster locomotion speed, and a greater manipulation domain. In comparison, the right image shows that the user, who is at a smaller scale, gets a narrower overview range, a slower speed, and a closer manipulation domain. The avatar metaphor yokes a suite of parameters together by tying interaction scale with the avatar body size.

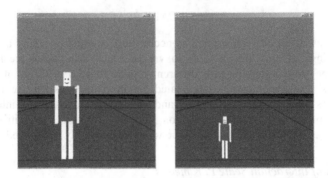

Figure 2. A User's Avatar at Two Different Scales

Interaction scale actually measures the relationship between size parameters of the users and those of the environment. This relationship is relative. Mathematically, to work with a small object, we can either shrink a user's parameters (including observing distance) or grow the world's parameters (maintaining observing distance). Actually these two models would make scant difference for individual users, but when several users work together at different scales, having multiple users independently changing the scale of the world would usually not be desirable. Typically, independent actors would want to change their relation to the world independently, so the implementation of scale control should support the metaphor of each actor changing their own interaction scale parameters. This decision also supports the ant-giant metaphor quite naturally.

The explicit change of interaction scale in 3D relative to the virtual environment will be called generically re-scaling. Scaling-oneself-up, or just scaling-up refers to an increase in the size of a user relative to the virtual environment, and consequently the user's perception and action parameters relative to the virtual environment are increased. Scaling-down decreases the size of the user with respect to the virtual environment, and leads to smaller perception and action parameters.

We notice that other sorts of scaling tools have been used in some research projects. As mentioned previously, the auto-scaling tool (Mine *et al.*, 1997), the Go-Go technique (Poupyrev *et al.*, 1996), and the Image-Plane-Interaction (Pierce *et al.*, 1999) supported scalable arm-reaching distance. However, in order to facilitate the user's interaction with large structures, changing only one specific interaction parameter may not suffice. Other projects, such as the World-In-Miniature(WIM) technique (Stockley *et al.*, 1995) and the CALVIN system (Leight *et al.*, 1996), allowed users to see the virtual world and act on it from different scales. They usually provided users with another view of a scaled-down world at a given scale level, and the dynamic range of scaling is very limited. Also, in these projects, users usually cannot control the scaling process and manipulate interactive parameters. In (Mine *et al.*, 1997), for example, scaling was even designed by choosing a special scaling centre to fool the user's eyes and make the scaling change unnoticeable. Users are passive perceivers of scaling, rather than active controllers.

In mVEs, interaction scale is directly manipulated by users, just as are other spatial parameters, such as location and orientation. This is analogous to the case of 2D ZUIs (Perlin and Fox, 1993; Bederson and Hollan, 1994; Bederson *et al.*, 2000), where interaction scale is treated as a first class spatial parameter, and users can choose any scale by zooming, as directly as they control panning. A working hypothesis of this research is that a fully controllable scaling tool can help users to understand an mVE better by making users active multiscale explorers in their multiscale world.

Changing a user's working scale has several consequences. Here, we focus on the impacts of scaling on spatial perception and such activities as navigation and object manipulation.

Impacts of Multiscale on Spatial Perception

A key issue in re-scaling the world is the choice of scaling centre. When the centre of projection, usually the location where the virtual eye is located in 3D graphics, is the scaling centre, the virtual sizes of objects get larger, but they get correspondingly further away and hence look the same. The user would not experience any change of the views, similar to the phenomenon illustrated in Figure 1. However, if the user is binocular, re-scaling around one eye will lead to movement of, and hence changes to the image in, the other eye. This will change convergence angles on objects and change binocular disparities, affecting the user's depth perception.

Figure 3 presents the views of a three-box configuration viewed at two different binocular scales. For this figure, the eyes' convergence angle has been kept constant, while the eye separation has been increased. One result is that the eyes now converge on a different point. Conversely, to maintain convergence on the middle box, the eyes would have to be substantially crossed. Since humans cannot converge their eyes more than 20-40 degrees comfortably, users cannot look binocularly at objects closer than a few eye-separations away. Examining small details requires getting closer; doing so binocularly requires shrinking eye separations.

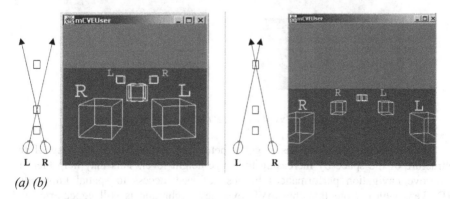

(a) (b)

Figure 3. Different Convergences in Scaling: as a user scales up from (a) to (b), the converged object changes from the middle box to the farthest one

The brain uses the differences in relative positions of objects as seen by the two, differently positioned, eyes to compute depth and construct spatial models of a scene. In real life, disparity cues are effective up to 10m (Cutting and Vishton, 1995), which is about 150 eye separations away. Within that range, people make very subtle discrimination, about 12 arc seconds, which translate the depth difference by 1mm at a distance of 1m and 9cm at 10m. Clearly, if users must engage in subtle depth manipulations at some particular scales, they want to bring interaction scale with the corresponding eye separation into that range. For example, if users need to reposition the middle box right next to the farthest one, they can change their interaction scales so that the views converge on the latter. Then, the depth of the former can be adjusted until it is also converged. Examining large structure requires getting farther from them; doing so with good stereoscopic depth perception requires increasing the eye separation.

For small rescalings, choosing the scaling centre at the midpoint between the eyes can minimize disruptive effects without sacrificing the depth cues (Ware *et al.*, 1998). However, if rescalings are large (e.g., orders of magnitude), the eye changes are still dramatic.

There are also other important candidates for the scaling centre. Observing virtual cities or landscapes, a viewer often has virtual feet planted on a grounding plane, making navigation much easier. In such cases, choosing the standing point as the scaling centre will raise and lower eyes, giving the viewer different overview ranges. Figure 4 shows a user's views of a simple landscape, from the same planar location, but at different eye-heights resulting from changing interaction scale. Occlusion patterns change, exposing potentially different explicit information, and altering depth cues affecting the user's space perception.

 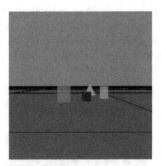

Figure 4. Effects of Eye Level on Spatial Perception

With scaling, users can easily get a better macro-level understanding of the structure of the space by increasing their eye-height level. This may help them to improve navigation performances because of easy access to spatial knowledge (Darken, 1996). Note that this mVE overview technique is still egocentric, and differs from the exocentric one provided by WIM (Stoakley *et al.*, 1995), in which users can see and manipulate their own avatars.

Impacts of Scale on Actions

In the avatar metaphor, intuitively, a user's action should also be proportional to the body size of her avatar. A gigant should have a gigant step and a gigant reach, and a nanant should move with a tiny step and have a much small reach.

Locomotion Speed

It makes sense to have the navigation speed dependent on scale. A nanant with a gigant step would easily get the nanant lost. A gigant with a nanant step would also be a problem, because it would demand tremendous effort to make the view change.

Scale-related speed can help to address a locomotion problem in large space, where a quick speed and an accurate movement near the target need to be balanced. Solutions to this problem include a logarithmic motion function (Mackinlay *et al.*, 1990). In mVEs, this issue can be tackled by the combination of moving and scaling (Furnas and Bederson, 1995), which allows the user to choose a larger speed to approach the target quickly and then to switch to a smaller scale and a slower speed for accurate movement. There is no need to specify the target explicitly as required by logarithmic motions. However, scaling costs time, and could slow down locomotion. Also, users have to be more involved in the control of locomotion.

Scale-dependent speed could have an impact on perception. Motion parallax cues are from moving. A proper motion parallax cue which is consistent with other visual cues, such as elevation and stereopsis, can help users to understand the virtual space better. However, a very fast motion may hurt animation quality, increasing cognitive load in interaction. In addition, scaling will change a user's view of the world, so maintaining a consistent understanding of the locomotion direction at different scales could be a challenge for the user.

Manipulation

Manipulation could also be designed to be scale-dependent, giving a gigant user a larger action domain than a nanant user, just as a taller person can reach farther than a shorter one in real life. However, mimicking reality can miss special opportunities of virtual environments. While some actions may need to be tied with scale, other actions may benefit from the independence of scale. Tools like the auto-scaling tool (Mine *et al.*, 1997), the Go-Go technique (Poupyrev *et al.*, 1996), and Image-Plane-Interaction (Pierce *et al.*, 1997) all ignore the constraint of the distance, and make it easy for the user to grab any object in sight without considering distance.

While these tools allow the user to select and move any visible object, handling a small and distant object with a small image is still difficult for them. In mVEs, the combination of scale-dependent navigation and scale-independent selection can give some help. Knowing where a distant object is, users can first choose a fast moving speed to approach it quickly. As soon as it is becomes visible, they can select it. Thus, multiscale tools improve the dynamic range of selection (Guiard, 1999).

Scale-Based "Semantic" Representation

We mentioned earlier that our limited visual perception does not allow us to see very big or small objects. Therefore, we have to use various tools to change the sizes of objects in observation. In virtual worlds, we might aspire to do more. That is, in order to be maximally semantically informative, the representation of a structure might change in a non-geometric way with the change of interaction scale. In 2D ZUIs this technique is called "semantic zooming" (Perlin and Fox, 1993; Bederson and Hollan, 1994) and has been used successfully to provide users with scale-based context-sensitive information. In mVEs, a similar tool called scale-based "semantic" representations is provided to help users observe important characteristics of a structure at different scale levels. For example, working on a model structure of a new type of materials, users can see its molecular structures at one scale, and atomic structures at another. With the dynamic and continuous control of interaction scale, users can also know how these two models are related to each other. Applying such techniques in modelling a virtual city, users will easily see the images and features of the city at the levels of city, district, neighbourhood, and street. The smooth transition between these images can help users better understand how issues at different scales relate. The detailed design and implementations of this scale-based "semantic" representation can be found in (Zhang and Furnas, 2005).

So far, we have discussed several aspects of multiscale space, including what interaction scale means to the user, what impacts it may have on user perception and action, and how information is visualized across different scale levels. All these issues concern interactions between individual users and multiscale space. When users work together, multiscale space becomes multiscale places, and concerned issues are turned to interactions among users.

MULTISCALE PLACE

When users gather in a multiscale place and collaborate synchronously, they can choose different interaction scales. This raises many cross-scale collaboration issues, such as spatial relationship, action coordination, awareness, and information sharing. In this section, our focuses will be on cross-scale spatial relationship and cross-scale actions. Cross-scale awareness and cross-scale information sharing issues, which have been discussed in great details in our other papers (Zhang and Furnas, 2002; Zhang, 2004), will be introduced very briefly.

Spatial Relationship

When users choose different scale in a multiscale place, their avatars will be sized differently, and so occupy different volumes of space and have different influence scopes. Consequently, users' understandings of the same space may vary from scale to scale. Their space-mediated interactions could be affected by the discrepancy in the perception of space.

Using space to mediate social interactions is common in real life and CVEs. Under the spatial model proposed by Benford *et al.* (1994), interactions are mediated by aura, nimbus, and focus, which are all sub-spaces around a user's avatar and move with it. Aura delimits the enabled interaction space of a user. The collision of two auras will trigger social interactions between users. Focus and nimbus control the level of awareness between users. Focus determines the attention range. Nimbus sets the boundaries of the presence of a user, and decides the availability of the user to others.

In traditional CVEs, a user's aura, focus, and nimbus are usually fixed in shape and size. In multiscale places, however, the size of these functional spaces might logically be proportional to the user's avatar size so that her awareness ranges change when she becomes larger or smaller. As the user works as a giant, she will have a larger aura, focus, and nimbus that enable her to interact with more distant users. Similarly, as the user works as an ant, the scope for her interaction and awareness is shrunk so that she can concentrate her work with in a relatively small space. As seen in Figure 5, sphere-shaped auras of two users at two different scales have different diameters, indicating their scale-dependent awareness scopes.

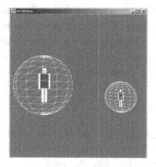

Figure 5. Scale Dependent Auras

Certainly, it is possible to give the user a fixed-size aura, focus, and nimbus, making these subspaces consistent and scale-independent. If so, no matter at what scale she is working, the user will have the same interaction space and awareness range. It could be useful in situations where the user shrinks herself but still hopes to maintain a larger interaction space. However, it could be a problem when the user scales up. Keeping a consistent interaction space will give the user an interaction space smaller than her avatar body size. This means she can only interact with and be aware of those users inside her body, and only those users inside her body will be able to be aware of her. The interaction domain of the user is severely limited. With scalable social interaction spaces, the user will not have such problems. Scalable interaction spaces can help to adapt her actions to her observation scale so that her social interactions (or action domains) can be consistent with the range of perception.

Scalable interaction and awareness ranges could affect users' interactions both positively and negatively. On the positive side, users can modify their interaction distances by simply changing interaction scale. To interact with distant users, a user can increase the aura size by scaling up; to reduce her availability, the user can simply scale down to shrink the nimbus. However, due to the size change of these interaction spaces, a distance which can trigger social interactions at one scale may not do anything at all at another. This may confuse users. Also, when these spaces are re-scaled, users may find some unexpected events. For example, when a user scales up, her aura is increased and touches other users who were outside the interaction ranges previously, triggering new interaction events. This kind of interactions may not be wanted. Similarly, when the user scales down, she may lose the focus of those users who were previously focused. Another problem of scalable aura, focus, and nimbus is that the awareness ranges of users will become asymmetric. In traditional CVEs, users are usually at the same scale level, and their interaction ranges are similar, giving them symmetric awareness ranges. For example, when a user's avatar falls inside another user's focus, it is very likely that the focus of the former can also catch the avatar of the latter. In multiscale places, different sized focuses will give users different attention ranges. Separated by the same distance, a user with a smaller focus may not be aware of other users, whose larger focuses provide full awareness of her. This asymmetric awareness may seriously affect the collaboration if the user does not realize the existence of this problem. Such scale-related spatial issues are not seen in real life and conventional virtual environments, and may distract users from their primary tasks or even interrupt their work. Therefore, these issues have to be addressed in future research.

Cross-Scale Manipulation on Object

Users need to coordinate their activities on objects at different scale. We considered two issues here: how a user's activities may affect others, and how they can work on the same object at different scales. For the first issue, it becomes important when two users are working on the same object at the same time. The deletion of a structure by a user may remove some objects that are important to the other. To avoid this problem, we adopted a design option to use a locking mechanism to check whether two different people's activities may interfere. Although the locking mechanism is not new in collaboration systems (Singhal and Zyda, 1999), what makes this design differ from others is the consideration of the scale factor in locking. When a user begins to work on an object at a particular scale level, the object and related objects at other levels would be locked. For example, when a user is moving an object inside a hierarchy, all its parent objects will have a locking flag, preventing them from being deleted. It should be noticed that what objects should be locked is highly task-dependent. While the above example requires locking all nodes above the interesting objects, tasks like moving a node and all its children to a distant place may need to lock all objects below the interesting node. Therefore, the locking tool allows users to specify which nodes to lock in their work.

For the issues concerning the synchronous collaboration on the same object at different scale, one challenge is to get the object with an appropriate size for users' actions. If two users are at different scales, a target object that is at a right size to one user could be huge or tiny to the other. Without a proper size of the target object, manipulating the object collaboratively could be a problem. One way to address this issue is to provide shared subjective views of the target object to different users by scaling the object temporarily. If it is too small for a user, a scaled-up model can be given. If an object is too large, it can be scaled down. As seen in Figure 6-a, the object of interest, a box, is too small in the view. As the box is selected, it is automatically scaled up (Figure 6-b). Similarly, if an object is too large, it can be scaled down.

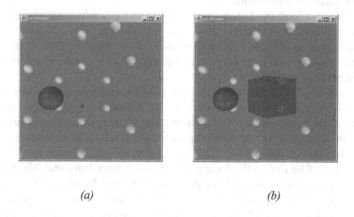

(a)   (b)

Figure 6. Auto-Scaling in Cross-Scale Object Manipulation

Another design option we provided is to render the shared object with fixed-size representations so that its size does not change with the scale. Users will always be able to see it with the same appearance at different scales. The drawback of these approaches is that if the size of the object somehow becomes important in collaboration (e.g., moving it into a box), having a view with a distorted size could be a problem. To address this, a toggle tool is provided so that users can change the object back to its actual size. Such automatic re-scaling techniques can also be applied in other collaboration actions, such as passing an object across scales.

Cross-Scale Avatar Manipulation

When each participant is aware of others' working contexts at different scales, they can combine their knowledge from different scales and their different action capabilities to complete some difficult or time-consuming work easily and quickly. To achieve this goal, users should be allowed to be involved in others' work directly. One design choice is to make a user's avatar controllable by others. Imagine a situation where an ant-like user needs to take an object to a very distant place. Certainly, she can change her scale back and forth to get this work done. If she could get help from a giant-like partner, they together can do the work in an innovative way: the giant can simply move the ant to the destination approximately, and then the ant fine-tunes her position by herself. Such collaboration will be valuable to actions that require both fast speed and high precision.

The implications of such a direct manipulation of avatars for HCI deserve more attentions. In CVEs, a user's avatar can provide important awareness information, but usually cannot be controlled by others. That is to say, an avatar in general only *affords* providing awareness information in social interactions in CVEs. In other words, the affordance of an avatar object in virtual environments is to support obtaining awareness information.

Affordance, coined by J. J. Gibson (1979) and extended by Norman (1990), refers to perceivable physical properties of objects that suggest activities. Affordances provide people with information about what can be done. A good affordance design should help users to know what objects can be acted on and how to act on them (Norman, 1990).

Some properties of an artefact can also afford social interactions among users. Bradner (2001) called such properties social affordances. Although the social affordance of an avatar primarily lies in its support of collaboration awareness, an avatar, as an object in a virtual environment, can also afford manipulation activities, just like other non-avatar objects. The reason that an avatar is not usually used in such a way might be due to the legacy that people inherit from real life, where it is not often seen that adult people have their bodies moved by others (except in some extreme cases, such as public protests, where people are moved by the police).

Designs to support social interactions in multiscale places do not have to follow real-life experiences. Multiscale virtual worlds are not replications of the real world. Instead, multiscale, as a new technology, provides users with new experiences, and should not be interpreted with old metaphors. Allowing the direct manipulation of avatars by others is an effort to break down the metaphor of "reality", and to help people work on things they would not be able to do in real life. Of course, this direct interference with other users should be regulated. The user should be aware of the action of her avatar being moved by others and have a control over whether this action can be done. Therefore, before any avatar manipulation activity happens, the avatar owner is warned, and informed of who is going to move her avatar. Her responses determine whether such coordinated activity will go on.

Cross-Scale Awareness and Cross-Scale Information Sharing

In collaboration, a user needs to be aware of other users and their activities. In CVEs, avatars carry awareness information. In multiscale places, however, scalable avatars post new challenges for awareness. A nanant user could be too small to be visible, and a gigant user could be too big to be fully comprehensible. Social interactions could be hurt because of the lack or incompletion of awareness information.

We address this issue by setting a maximum and a minimum limit for avatar size. When an avatar reaches a size limit, it is rendered with a nominal size, and stops growing or shrinking. At the same time, a visual cue appears above the avatar, indicating the actual avatar size is different from what is presented. Toggle tools are provided to allow users to check the actual size of an avatar.

Cross-scale context sharing is another issue for cross-scale collaboration. To collaborate, users need to know their working contexts. In conventional CVEs, sharing information is relative easy, because users are usually interacting with the same set of objects. In multiscale places, however, users may work on different structures and objects at different scales. Their individual views may be very different, and context sharing could be difficult. Imagine a scenario in which two users are working on the same model structure, but one at the molecular level and the other at the atomic level. Seeing different things, how could they share information across scales?

We address this issue by animating the connections between two users' seemingly irrelevant views. The animation is created by interpolating users' view positions, view orientations, and interaction scales. The animated dynamic view transition could help users understand how their views and their work are related to each other.

Cross-scale awareness and cross-scale information sharing have been discussed in our other papers. For detailed theoretical analyses and technical implementations, please see Zhang and Furnas (2002) and Zhang (2004) respectively.

Our understandings and analysis of multiscale space and multiscale place led to the design and implementation of a Java-based prototype system that support multiscale interactions (Zhang, 2004). Several experiments have been conducted in the prototype system. It has been found that in multiscale places, collaboration between two users allows them to better accomplish search-based tasks in a vast area (Zhang and Furnas, 2003). Another preliminary result shows that multiscale can improve user performances in navigation. A negative consequence of multiscale technology has also been discovered: social distance negotiation in multiscale places could be a big challenge for users at different scales (Zhang and Furnas, 2002).

CONCLUSION

In this chapter, we have presented a novel interactive environment, mVE, and discussed issues concerning multiscale space and multiscale place. We have examined the meanings of scale and multiscale for user interaction in terms of size parameters of perception and action. mVEs give users the freedom to manipulate a suite interaction parameters in their work, determining the spatial relationship between users and virtual space. In mVEs, user collaboration across different interaction scales raises many new issues. Our discussions have been focused on the impact of multiscale on spatial relationship among users and cross-scale manipulation.

In our research, virtual space and virtual place issues have been studied separately. For multiscale space, we have focused on the physical properties of virtual environments, and investigated how the unique spatial features may benefit people's work. Our interests of multiscale place are in the implications of multiscale technology for space-mediated social interactions. Treating space and place separately can help us understand what mVEs can do best to support collaboration. Clearly, 3D space gives virtual environments some edges over 2D space in visualizing and managing complicated objects and data, and multiscale space further enhances this advantage. However, it should be remembered that in support of collaboration activities that focus on message exchange, 3D places may not offer users more benefits than other virtual places like chatting rooms can do, due to extra costs required to deal with activities that are not directly related to communications, such as 3D navigation. Thus, introducing multiscale into virtual environments may actually make this matter even worse, because users have to pay more attentions to scale control, object representations, and spatial relationship in mVEs. This may further impede people's work if the primary goal of collaboration is to exchange information rather than to manage complicated structures.

Dix has discussed the distinctions between communication-oriented and artefact-oriented collaboration and argued that design practices should focus on suiting technologies with the nature of collaboration (Dix, 1994). However, many CVE projects focused on supporting conferencing and social gathering, in which communications, rather than the management of data structures, is the key. By treating space and place differently, we will have no difficulty in understanding that the potentials of 3D virtual environments in support of collaboration may lie more in artefact-oriented collaboration than in communication-cantered collaboration, and deliver designs that can better exploit the spatiality of virtual environments to facilitate people's work. This is also true for mVEs.

In the future, we will continue our research on multiscale space and multiscale place. For space, we are interested in two issues: how multiscale technology may affect users' access of spatial information at different levels and whether this technology can help users better integrate spatial information across different levels. Another direction we will pursue is to put multiscale places under practical lenses. We would like to see how people like materials scientists and architects would use multiscale places in the construction of cross-scale model structures in their work.

ACKNOWLEDGEMENT

This research was supported, in part, by Microsoft Research. We would also thank the anonymous reviewers for their helpful comments and suggestions

REFERENCES

Bederson, B.B., and Hollan, J. (1994). "Pad++: A Zooming Graphical Interface for Exploring Alternate Interface Physics", *Proceedings of the ACM 1994 Symposium on User Interface and Software Technology (UIST '94)*, 17-26.

Bederson, B. B., Meyer, J., and Good, L. (2000). "Jazz: An Extensible Zoomable User Interface Graphics Toolkit in Java", *Proceedings of the ACM 2000 Conference on User Interface and Software Technology (UIST 2000)*, 171-180.

Benford, S. (1996). "Tutorial on Collaborative Virtual Environments", Retrieved August 3, 2003 from the World Wide Web http://www.crg.cs.nott.ac.uk/people/Steve.Benford/CVEs.html

Benford, S., Bowers, J., Fahlén, L., Greenhalgh, C., and Snowdon, D. (1995). "User Embodiment in Collaborative Virtual Environments Papers: Advanced Media for Collaboration", *Proceedings of the ACM 1995 Conference on Human Factors in Computing Systems (CHI '95)*, 242-249.

Benford, S., Fahlén, L., Greenhalgh, C., and Bowers, J. (1994). "Managing Mutual Awareness in Collaborative Virtual Environments", *Virtual Reality Software and Technology: Proceedings of the VRST '94 Conference*, 223-236.

Benford, S., and Greenhalgh, C. (1997). "Introducing Third Party Objects into the Spatial Model of Interaction", *Proceedings of the Fifth European Conference on Computer Supported Cooperative Work (ECSCW '97)*, 189-204.

Bly, S., Harrison, S. and Irwin, S. (1993). "Media Spaces: Bringing People Together in a Video, Audio and Computing Environment", *Communications of the ACM*, **36(1)**, 28-47

Bradner, E. (2001). "Social Affordances of Computer-Mediated Communication Technology for Geographically Distributed Work", *Extended Abstracts of the ACM 2001 Conference on Human Factors in Computing Systems (CHI 2001)*, 67-68.

Casey, E. (1997). *The Fate of Place*, University of California press, Berkley, California.

Cutting, J. E. and Vishton, P. M. (1995). Perceiving layout and knowing distances: The integration, relative potency, and contextual use of different information about depth, in: Epstein, W. and Rogers, S. (Eds) *Perception of Space and Motion*, Academic Press, San Diego, 69-117.

Darken, R.P. (1996). "Navigating Large Virtual Space", *International Journal of Human-Computer Interactions*, **8**, 49-71.

DeSilve, L., Tahara, M., Aizawa, K., and Hatori, A. (1995). "A Teleconferencing System Capable of Multiple Person Eye Contact (MPEC) Using Half Mirrors and Cameras Placed at Common Points of Extended Lines of Gaze", *IEEE Transactions on Circuits and Systems for Video Technology*, **5(4)**, 268-277.

Dix, A. J. (1994). Computer-Supported Cooperative Work - A Framework, in: Rosenburg D. and Hutchison, C. (Eds,) *Design Issues in CSCW*, Springer-Verlag, London, 23-37.

Fitzpatrick, G., Kaplan, S. and Mansfield, T. (1996). "Physical Spaces, Virtual Places and Social Worlds: A Study of Work in the Virtual", *Proceedings of the ACM 1996 Conference on Computer Supported Work (CSCW '96)*, 334-343.

Furnas, G. W. (1986). "Generalized Fisheye Views", *Proceedings of the ACM 1986 Conference on Human Factors in Computing Systems (CHI '86)*, 16-23.

Furnas, G. W., and Bederson B. B. (1995). "Space-Scale Diagrams: Understanding Multiscale Interfaces Papers: Navigating and Scaling in 2D Space", *Proceedings of the ACM 1995 Conference on Human Factors in Computing Systems (CHI '95)*, 234-241.

Gaver, W. (1992). "The Affordances of Media Spaces for Collaboration", *Proceedings of the ACM 1992 Conference on Computer-Supported Collaborative Work (CSCW '92)*, 17-24.

Gibson, J. J. (1997). *The Ecological Approach to Visual Perception*, Houghton Mifflin, Boston, MA.

Greenhalgh, C., and Benford, S. (1995). "MASSIVE: A Collaborative Virtual Environment for Teleconferencing", *ACM Transactions on Computer-Human Interaction*, **2(3)**, 239-261.

Guiard, Y., Beaudouin-Lafon, M., and Mottet, D. (1999). "Navigation As Multiscale Pointing: Extending Fitts' Model to Very High Precision Tasks", *Proceedings of the ACM 1999 Conference on Human Factors in Computing Systems (CHI '99)*, 450-457.

Harrison, S. and Dourish, P. (1996). "Re-Place-ing Space: The Roles of Place and Space in Collaborative Systems", *Proceedings of the ACM 1996 Conference on Computer Supported Cooperative Work (CSCW '96)*, 67-76.

Hollan, J., and Stornetta S. (1992). "Beyond Being There", *Proceedings of the ACM 1992 Conference on Human Factors in Computing Systems (CHI '92)*, 119-125.

Linebarger, J. M. and Kessler, G. D. (2002). "GroupMorph: A Group Collaboration Mode Approach to Shared Virtual Environments for Product Design," *Proceedings of the ACM 2002 Conference on Collaborative Virtual Environments (CVE 2002)*, 145-126.

Lea, R., Honda, Y., and Matsuda, K. (1997). "Virtual Society: Collaboration in 3D Spaces on the Internet", *Computer Supported Collaborative Work*, **6(2/3)**, 227-250.

Leigh, J., Johnson, A., and DeFanti, T. (1996). "CALVIN: An Immersimedia Design Environment Utilizing Heterogeneous Perspectives", *Proceedings of IEEE International Conference on Multimedia Computing and Systems '96*, 20-23.

Mackinlay, J., Card, S., and Robertson, G. (1990). "Rapid Controlled Movement through a Virtual 3D Workspace", *Proceedings of the ACM 1990 Conference on Computer Graphics and Interactive Techniques (SIGGRAPH '90)*, 171-176.

Mine, M., Brooks, F., Sequin, C. (1997). "Moving Objects In Space: Exploiting Proprioception in Virtual-Environment Interaction", *Proceedings of the ACM 1997 Conference on Computer Graphics and Interactive Techniques (SIGGRAPH '97)*, 19-26.

Morrison, P, and Morrison P. (1982). *Powers of Ten: About the Relative Size of Things in the Universe*, Scientific American Books, Inc., New York.

Norman, D. A. (1990). *The Design of Everyday Things*, Doubleday, New York.

Perlin, K., and Fox D. (1993). "Pad: An Alternative Approach to the Computer Interface", *Proceedings of the ACM 1993 Conference on Computer Graphics and Interactive Techniques (SIGGRAPH '93)*, 57-64.

Pierce, J., Forsberg, A., Conway, M., Hong, S., Zeleznik, R., and Mine, M. (1997). "Image Plane Interaction Techniques in 3D Immersive Environments", *Proceedings of the 1997 Symposium on Interactive 3D Graphics*, 39-43.

Poupyrev, I., Billinghurst, M., Weghorst, S., and Ichikawa, T. (1996). "The Go-Go Interaction Technique: Non-Linear Mapping for Direct manipulation in VR", *Proceedings of the ACM 1996 Symposium on User Interface Software and Technology (UIST '96)*, 79-80.

Raab, A., and Ruger, M. (1996). "3D-Zoom: Interactive Visualization of Structures and Relations in Complex Graphics", *3D Image Analysis and Synthesis*, 125-132.

Robertson, G., and Mackinlay, J. (1993). "The Document Lens", *Proceedings of the ACM 1993 Symposium on User Interface Software and Technology (UIST '93)*, 101-110.

Sellen, A., and Buxton, B. (1992). "Using Spatial Cues to Improve Videoconferencing", *Proceedings of the ACM 1992 Conference on Human Factors in Computing Systems (CHI '92)*, 651-652.

Singhal, S., and Zyda, M. (1999). *Networked Virtual Environments: Design and Implementation*, ACM Press, New York.

Snowdon, D., and Jää-Aro, K. (1997). "A Subjective Virtual Environment for Collaborative Information Visualization", *Virtual Reality Universe '97*.

Stoakley, R., Conway, M., and Pausch, R. (1995). "Virtual Reality on a WIM: Interactive Worlds in Miniature", *Proceedings of the ACM 1995 Conference on Human Factors in Computing Systems (CHI '95)*, 265-272.

Ware, C., Gobrecht, C., and Paton, M. (1998). "Dynamic Adjustment of Stereo Display Parameters", *IEEE Transactions on Systems, Man and Cybernetics*, **28(1)**, 56-65.

Waters, R., Anderson, D., Barrus, J., Brogan, D., Casey, M., McKeown, S., Nitta, T., Sterns, I., and Yerazunis, W. (1997). "Diamond Park and SPLINE: Social Virtual Reality with 3D Animation, Spoken Interaction, and Runtime Extendibility", *Presence: Teleoperators and Virtual Environments*, **6(4)**, 461-481.

Zhang, X., and Furnas, G. (2002). "Social Interactions in Multiscale CVEs", *Proceedings of the ACM 2002 Conference on Collaborative Virtual Environments (CVE 2002)*, 31-38.

Zhang, X., and Furnas, G. (2003). "The Effectiveness of Multiscale Collaboration in Virtual Environments", *Extended Abstracts of the ACM 2003 Conference on Human Factors in Computing Systems (CHI 2003)*, 790-791.

Zhang, X., and Furnas, G (2005). "mCVEs: Using Cross-Scale Collaboration To Support User Interaction With Multiscale Structures", *Presence: Teleoperators and Virtual Environments*, **14(1)**, Special issues on Collaborative Information Visualization Environments.

PHIL TURNER, SUSAN TURNER AND FIONA CARROLL

19. THE TOURIST GAZE: TOWARDS CONTEXTUALISED VIRTUAL ENVIRONMENTS

INTRODUCTION

"To be at all - to exist in any way - is to be somewhere, and to be somewhere is to be in some kind of place. Place is as requisite as the air we breathe, the ground on which we stand, the bodies we have. We are surrounded by places. We walk over them and through them. We live in places, relate to others in them, die in them...."

Casey, 1997:ix

This chapter argues that our bodily experience of place may provide a key to achieving a contextualised sense of presence in virtual environments. We begin by briefly reviewing current practice in evaluating virtual environments. The evaluation of these environments hinges on measuring our sense of being there. This is treated as our sense of presence but as we will show this is a curious decontextualised sense of being there. From there we turn to the question of contextualised presence – what it is and why it is becoming important for current and emerging virtual reality (VR) applications. We draw upon the philosophical, empirical and phenomenological treatments of body, place and the conjunction of the two to inform this discussion. We conclude by proposing a new paradigm for designing and evaluating contextualised virtual environments, based on the metaphor of tourism and the tourist gaze (Urry, 2002).

Understanding Presence

Understanding and measuring presence is a key aim of virtual reality research. Presence has numerous and frequently conflicting definitions. Lombard and Ditton's (1997) review of the usage of the term revealed six different explications in the VR literature: these include social richness, realism, transportation, immersion, social actor within medium and medium as social actor. Despite this diversity they concluded that in the context of immersive VR (as opposed to desktop or non-immersive VR) that presence was most usually characterised as transportation. (Terms such as co-presence and social presence are also used to denote the sense of being together with others in such environments). In contrast to these rather loose, qualitative descriptions of presence, Schloerb (1995) has proposed a quantitative approach to the problem, comprising two categories of presence, subjective and objective. Subjective presence relates to judgements an individual might make of

P. Turner and E. Davenport (Eds.), Spaces, Spatiality and Technology, 281-297.
© 2005 *Springer. Printed in the Netherlands.*

their sense of 'being there' while the objective variety is measured by an individual carrying out a task in the virtual environment. This interest in the objective, empirical and task-orientation may reflect the origins of presence research revealed by the full title of the premier VR journal - Presence: tele-operators and virtual environments.

Underpinning these variations in defining this key concept (and perhaps being a contributory factor to this variation) is the range of theoretical bases for the study of presence. In a recent review of presence research, Schuemie *et al.* (2001) identify a number of 'theories' (the term is used very loosely) cited in the VR literature. Unsurprisingly, psychology figures strongly, for example, Alcañiz *et al.* note that, "There is no doubt that it [Presence] is formed through an interplay of raw sensory data and various cognitive structures." (2002:202). Variants on involvement (e.g. Witmer and Singer, 1998; Ryan, 2000) are also frequently cited and more recently the role of the body, affect and the importance of narrative are beginning to appear (e.g. Slater *et al.*, 1998, Alcañiz *et al.*, *ibid.* and Ryan, 2000 respectively).

The problem of context in virtual environments

One perspective which is conspicuous by its absence is any consideration of context. VR / presence research is wholly decontextualised. VR researchers are interested, in both a general and highly specific sense, as to whether the users of their systems perceive themselves to be present or immersed in that particular virtual world. There is a concentration on the fidelity of representation of Euclidian space and its properties (collision detection, perspective, depth perception); a case of computer science / mathematics meets cognitive psychology. Furthermore these representations are very frequently generic situations – they are placeless, for example, buildings are represented on endless Euclidean planes. To date VR technology has allowed us to create virtual spaces and environments which can be defined by means of coordinate geometry, not virtual places. As Casey puts it, "The triumph of space over place is the triumph of space in its endless extensiveness, its coordinated and dimensional spread-outness, over the intensive magnitude and qualitative multiplicity of concrete places." Casey, 1997: 201. However these spaces are nowhere: places in contrast are always somewhere. At their simplest, and as we shall see there are numerous descriptions and definitions, places are lived spaces. Places are contextualised, existential spaces.

The role and importance of the body has largely been ignored by designers of VR systems, human-computer interaction designers, psychologists and most philosophers – until quite recently. Perhaps part of the problem is that bodies are a given and everyday and as such not particularly worthy of note. The philosopher Maurice Merleau-Ponty (1945) is usually credited with bringing our attention to our bodies; while ecological psychology – largely initiated by Gibson (1986) has investigated the role of the body in our dealings with the world. The place of the body in the design of interactive systems has largely been confined, (Dourish, 2000 is a notable exception), to the discipline of ergonomics (Murrell, 1965).

As virtual reality continues to develop meaningful applications, it will become necessary to grasp the nettle of understanding how we experience and understand these contextualised virtual spaces, these virtual places. The key research question being, "how do create lived, embodied virtual spaces?"

OF BODIES AND PLACES

The literature on place research helps us to understand, reason about and express what it means to be somewhere specific (i.e. a place). This section briefly reviews three overlapping perspectives on place. The first of these is the philosophical; we then consider the empirical (embracing psychological and sociological perspectives) and the first-person or phenomenological. Each is necessarily a brief sketch. Perhaps the most substantial strands of twentieth-century writings on place are the crucial notion of place as *interaction*, vide Derrida's "denial that place... place is an event, a matter of taking place." (Casey, 1997: 339) The strong emphasis on place as a fundamentally *embodied* phenomenon.

Philosophical perspectives

The scant attention paid to the contextualisation of virtual space has parallels in the philosophical treatment of the nature of being, space and place. The short account which now follows draws heavily on Edward Casey's monograph *The Fate of Place* (Casey, 1997). Interestingly, the earliest writers were clear about the fundamental association between being and place. In the fourth century B.C., for example, we find Archytas of Tarentum observing that: "to be (at all) is to be in (some) place" Casey, *ibid*, p.4.

And half a century or so later, Aristotle includes *where* as one of the ten essential characteristics of every substance. Aristotle's concept of place is as a container or boundary for an object, as in the sense of being held in place – an intriguing pre-figuring of the physical restrictions of some forms of virtual reality. However, from Plato until almost the present, this archaic primacy of place is submerged in Euclidean *space*, in concepts of the relationship between space and time, and in the dominance of the positivist scientific paradigm directed at uncovering universally applicable laws. Place disappears as a fundamental aspect of being and becomes a mere site or specific instance of universal Euclidean space, until the concept is reclaimed by modern and post-modern authors.

Place and Bodies: Intertwined Perspectives

As Casey so ably shows, Kant, Whitehead, Husserl and Merleau-Ponty were all active in re-introducing place to philosophical discourse and were instrumental in demonstrating the importance of the body when thinking about place. Kant speaks of '... this body is *my body*; and the place of that body is at the same time *my place*' (Dreams of a Spirit-Seer). Kant goes on to argue that positions in space are relational, that is, should be understood in reference to the sides of the body, to the moving body and so forth. These ideas were neither fully developed or widely adopted and lay dormant until Whitehead's critique which appeared in *Science and the Modern World* (Whitehead, 1925/ 1997).

> "We have to admit that the body is the organism whose states regulate our cognition of the world. The unity of the perceptual field therefore must be a unity of bodily experience".

Science and the Modern World (Whitehead, 1925: 91)

We begin this review of the body, place and being-in-the-world with a brief treatment of the work of Husserl, Merleau-Ponty and Heidegger.

Husserl

Husserl noted the 'privileged position' of the human body: in one respect it is merely an unremarkable physical thing, but it is also the *Leib* – a lived body. The lived body is the bearer of the 'I'. However for Husserl, the body not only gives rise to the three dimensions but "everything that appears belongs to its environs" – everything which is encountered is around the body.

Merleau-Ponty

In his *Phenomenology of Perception* (1945), Merleau-Ponty argues that it is only though our lived bodies do we have access to what he describes as the *primary world*. Without our bodies there could be no world. The lived body is central as it his *corporeal intentionality*, this concept replaces the Cartesian mind-body distinction. The world and the lived body together form what Merleau-Ponty calls an *intentional arc* which binds the body to the world. This arc anchors us in and to the world. More than this Merleau-Ponty argues that the movement of the lived body actually creates (produces) existential space (this is of particular interest as places are existential space). It is not, however, the 'objective' movement of the body as such, instead it is the experience of this movement, "Far from my body's being for me no more than a fragment of space, there would be no space at all for me if I had no body". To feel our body (kinaesthesia) feeling its surroundings is not merely an exercise in self-reflection but the means by which we 'prehend' the world. This kinaesthetic feedback is the means by which we both objectify the world and orient ourselves within it. To orientate ourselves is to adopt an external point or frame of reference. Thus we need bodies to both create the world and to orientate ourselves within it. Merleau-Ponty's position (and other closely related thought) is reflected in Tuan's work in humanistic geography, particularly his account of how the growing child learns to comprehend his place in the world (Tuan, 1977, ch. 3)

Heidegger: being-in-the-world

Of Heidegger's complex and labyrinthine body of work, we have chosen to highlight two aspects only for the purposes of this discussion. In deciding to consider Heidegger's treatment of being-in-the-world as dwelling and his discussion of the nature of 'in' we will not consider Heidegger's explicit writings on space and spatiality or his discussion of readiness-to-hand or whether something is present-at-hand. Disregarding the role of the human body, Heidegger identifies the existential character of being-in-the-world with human beings propensity of inhabiting and dwelling.

> 'In' is derived from 'innan' – 'to reside', "habitare", "to dwell". 'An' signifies 'I am accustomed', 'I am familiar with', 'I look after something' ... The expression 'bin' is connected with 'bei', and so 'ich bin' ['I am'] means in its turn 'I reside' or 'dwell alongside' the world which is familiar to me in such and such a way. "Being" [Sein], as the infinitive of 'ich bin' (that is to say, when it is understood as an existentiale), signifies 'to reside alongside ...' 'to be familiar with ... ' 'Being-in is thus the formal existential expression for the Being of Dasein, which has Being-in-the-world as it essential state.'

Dasein's way of being-in consists in dwelling or residing, that is, being 'alongside' the world as if it were *at home* there. The ideas of the phenomenological geographer Relph, discussed later in this chapter, draw heavily on these concepts. Heidegger holds that human beings (which he refers to as *Dasein*) and world are not two distinct entities but only one which results from Dasein's involvement in the world. Thus the *in* of being-in-the-world is unrelated to ideas of Aristotlean containment, instead *in* is better understood in terms of *in*volvement. Heidegger characterises everyday life as being an engaged, absorbed involvement in an undifferentiated world. Coyne develops this idea in his *Technoromanticism* (1999) when he writes,

> "This is an experience with which everyone can identify: we are often most absorbed while working in the garden, driving, jogging, watching television, typing at a computer, or just engaged in the day-to-day routine of work. (In this respect, "immersion" is not a special feature of VR. A text editor, CAD system, computer game, or spreadsheet can be just as much an *immersive environment.*"

As this very brief discussion has shown, it is meaningless to reason about place without considering the central role of the body or our being-there.

Empirical treatments of place

Recent literature in environmental psychology is rich in empirically derived models of the lived experience of place. (The concept under study is variously labelled - with slightly different if overlapping definitions - as sense of place, place identity, place attachment and place dependence.) We have reviewed this material in more detail elsewhere (Turner and Turner, to appear), but in brief, the approach is generally one of interview and questionnaire surveys of perceived feelings towards, and conceptualisations of, places significant to individuals. Not infrequently, sense of place scales are derived from the results. In some studies, the places concerned are selected by the researchers, in others by the participants themselves, but in almost all the participants have long-term involvement with the location. There are scattered accounts of shorter-term experience, but these are confined to place attachment, the reasons for fondness for place.

Actions, Conceptions And Physical Attributes

Canter's work (1977) is among the landmarks in this genre of place literature, proposing a threefold model comprising relationships between actions, conceptions and physical attributes. Similarly, Sixsmith (1986) identifies personal, social and physical dimensions in a study of the meanings of 'home'. Canter's original structure is extended some two decades later in the application of facet theory (a mean of dealing with complex multidimensional data) to place research (Canter, 1997). The facets in this case are activities belonging to the place (the facet of functional differentiation), physical characteristics (aspects of design), individual, social and cultural goals (place objectives) and the scale of the place – e.g. whether an individual room or an entire city (scale of interaction). Canter's approach is robustly positivist, refuting the usefulness of 'personal value judgements... being treated as if they were technical definitions for the existence of common experiences' (Canter, 1997:117). Typical of more recent work in this vein, Gustafson (2001) proposes a highly detailed model of meanings of place organised around the three poles of 'self, 'environment' and 'others', integrating his own empirical work with concepts from the literature. A rather different approach to rationalising sense of place is provided by Jorgensen and Stedman (2002), who draw on classical psychological attitude theory to define sense of place as beliefs about the relationship between self and place (the cognitive component of the attitude), feelings towards the place (the affective component) and the behaviours afforded by the place (the conative or behavioural component).

Many other examples could be cited, but in summary, the experience of place is characterised by empiricists as (i) grounded in the physical characteristics of the environment, and interaction with it, but also (ii) bound up with the individual's previous experience and expectations, while in many models it is (iii) a social phenomenon, and almost always (iv) a property of long-term engagement with the environment in question.

While the first two aspects are crucial for any attempt to create a contextualised presence in virtual environments, the latter two are significant constraints to basing this work on current empirical models of place and exploiting existing sense of place scales. For the present at least, interacting with others in immersive HMD or even CAVE-mediated environments is cumbersome or impossible except through the restricted medium of avatars. Moreover, technical limitations in current photo-realistic environments such as BENOGO prevent the similarly photo-realistic representation of other human beings (or any other moving objects) in the space created. And while these technological obstacles will certainly be overcome in the future, it is difficult to conceive of long-term engagement with a particular virtual environment over a period of months or years. (MUDS and similar environments are well-acknowledged exceptions to this, but here we are concerned with endeavours to re-create real-world places.)

First-person, embodied perspectives on place

First person, embodied and phenomenological accounts of place are more interesting for the VR context. In contrast to generalised empirically-based accounts of place, there is a stimulating body of work which is unapologetically individual and deeply phenomenological in character. It is significant for the consideration of virtual places, since these – at least when mediated by head-mounted display or CAVEs – are intrinsically individual experiences. This literature commonly manifests as direct first-person accounts of relationships with particular places, or hermeneutic readings of physical environments. The approach is best explained by illustration from representative examples. In this pair of extracts from Stefanovic (1998), the author explores how two radically different urban environments both succeed in creating a sense of place. The first piece relates to the town of Cavtat on the Adriatic coast, the second to Mississauga, a suburb of Toronto. Both are deeply familiar to the Stefanovic: the paper "…reflects a personal journey to two, particularly special places of being-at-home."

> "… the three spiritual landmarks invoking the centrality of place testify to a depth of tradition and an awareness of the belonging together of finitude, dwelling and human destiny. The Mausoleum, with its cemetery of rows of pure, white headstones, is approached gradually at the end of a lengthy climb uphill along stone steps, and the reward is a panoramic treasure-view of sky, water and sun."

> "Overall, the image of the settlement as a whole is of the non-threatening: the homogeneity from one identical garage to the next seems to signify that nothing is unexpected. No risks are implied by virtue of enigmatic spatial patterns to disrupt the notion of a perfectly ordered, and safe community. The message, indeed, is of a secure environment, of shelter, of refuge, of insideness and a cradling against any threats from the outside world."

Stefanovic, 1998: 34 & 41

Note in the first extract how the environment is experienced through bodily movement. Physical sensation is very much part of these phenomenological accounts of place, as can be seen in this extract from Downing (2003), a meditative discussion of how designers' memories of significant places are pivotal to the creation of meaningful environments.

> [The kitchen] was also a place of sensuous delights, a place of fragrances: mouth-watering roasts, mashed potatoes, homemade breads, and pies that were to-die-for. The aroma of food wove through the intimate dramas of our gatherings and makes this 'place' one my nose and mouth can re-create before my mind's eye can conjure it visually… It was also a place of family history. By being small and quiet, I gained admission to confidences concerning other people's lives. If I stayed under the table long enough, I would eventually hear of heartbreak, love, hate…

Downing, 2003:215

Downing's material, in identifying recurring patterns in designers' relationships with place – secret places, gregarious places, places of comfort, among others – also demonstrates how individual accounts may be brought together without losing their intensely personal qualities.

The distillation of patterns or themes is a common element in the phenomenologically-informed place literature, retaining elements of the richness of individual sources while allowing authors to move beyond the particular. Indeed, environmental themes engendering place and its antithesis, placelessness, are central to Relph's 1976 monograph; the prototypical (and still much-cited), instance of the phenomenological approach to place. He characterises place identity thus:

> "...the static physical setting, the activities and the meanings – constitute the three basic elements of the identity of places. A moment's reflection suggests that this division, although obvious, is a fundamental one. For example, it is possible to visualise a town as consisting of buildings and physical objects, as is represented in air photographs. A strictly objective observer of the activities of people within this physical context would observe their movements much as an entomologist observes ants, some moving in regular patterns, some consuming objects and so on. But a person experiencing these buildings and activities sees them as far more than this – they are beautiful or ugly, useful or hindrances, home, factory, enjoyable, alienating; in short, they are meaningful."

Relph, 1997:47

Relph's discussion of 'insideness' and 'outsideness' offers a compelling insight for contextualising the VR experience. For an individual to feel inside a place is to feel safe, at-home and attached to the place. To experience outsideness is to experience the reverse of these states. (The dialectic insideness-outsideness is closely related to Heidegger's concepts of 'in' and 'dwelling discussed above). The modes of insideness and outsideness offer a valuable classification and vocabulary for describing and understanding people's response to virtual re-creation of place. They are briefly described below. The description draws on the commentary on Relph's work by Seamon (n.d.) who is also a prominent phenomenological geographer; his review of methodology in this domain (*ibid*) is an extremely useful survey (although his discussion of some techniques may not be entirely in accord with other phenomenologists).

Existential insideness	The feeling of attachment and being at home. Place is "experienced without deliberate and self-conscious reflection yet is full of significances".
Existential outsideness	Feeling separate from or out of place. Place may feel alienating, unreal, or unpleasant. Examples include feelings of homelessness and homesickness.
Objective outsideness	A deliberate dispassionate separation from place. Place is a thing to be studied and manipulated.

Incidental outsideness	Place is experienced as the mere background for activities. For example, the experience of the landscape streaming past as one drives somewhere, or the cityscape visible from an anonymous conference suite.
Behavioural insideness	This type of insideness involves deliberate attention to the qualities of a place. Place is perceived as a set of entities, views and/or activities.
Empathetic insideness	Here a person is trying to be open to a place and to understand it better. The necessary pre-conditions are a genuine interest or care / concern for the place.
Vicarious insideness	Deeply-felt second-hand involvement with place. One is transported through imagination – through paintings, novels, music, film and other creative media.

This subtle, nuanced range of relationships with place appears to have far greater potential as a means of discussing and evaluating contextualised presence than variants on the simple question "How far did you feel present in the environment you have experienced?" It also affords a means of considering place experiences distinct from those arising from long-term engagement. As such, it allows for considering the some relationships to places – or virtual places - as a form of tourism, a paradigm which we consider further in the final section.

CONTEXT, PRESENCE AND MEASUREMENT IN VR

In contextualising presence we move the locus of attention from trying to assess an individual's sense of 'being there' to ask the question of the participant in a VR experiment, 'Where are you?" and of ourselves, 'Where am I?". A recovering patient or accident victim's first words on regaining consciousness are, almost always, 'Where am I?". It is not a matter of debate that they are present - unless the accident has been remarkably destructive. This primordial focus on place is not confined to adult, experimentally-inclined or accident-prone members of our species. Children are often deeply attached to special places. An animal perceives his territory as, in some sense 'his' which he defends against intruders of the same species. It would be easy to speculate phylogenetically that a sense of place or belonging to a place might have given rise to a sense of identity, a self of self, of self-awareness or being somewhere and then later in the decontextualised laboratory, a disembodied sense of being-there. Indeed, there is much research in personal and developmental psychology in this vein, but as interesting as this discussion is, it must wait from another day. The problem in hand is a practical one: what do we do about asking the right questions about peoples' experiences of contextualised virtual reality?

Present where?

We have suggested that there is an increasing focus on grounding VR applications in real purposes: examples of these are realistic, grounded training environments and the ever present virtual tourism. Before discussing these in a little detail, we also recognise that this a nascent application area and other examples might include virtual archaeology, for example, recreating a fragile site such as Lascaux. A virtual Lascaux would permit the experience of being there - not just viewing the pictures on the walls – but feeling the claustrophobia of the cave.

Training environments

There is considerable interest in creating realistic virtual environments – low cost simulators – for use in a range of different training setting. Of these, safety-critical and emergency management applications are of particular industrial importance. The recent DISCOVER project aimed to create a pair of real, virtual environments, namely, an oil platform (the offshore application) and a commercial ship (the maritime application) – the "SS Oxymoron'. See Turner and Turner, 2000 for a discussion of the project. The project aimed to create a pair of collaborative virtual environments (CVE) to supplement and perhaps even replace physical simulators.

Conventional physical simulators are expensive and can be physically enormous (see figure 1 below). Their clear strength as a training environment lies with a simple observation made by one of the trainers to us, "After thirty minutes, the trainees refers to the simulator as my ship'. Not only do the trainees experience a sense of presence but of involvement, identity and a relationship with the simulator which approaches the real thing.

A physical simulator can create a sense of contextualised presence, a sense of place by looking, behaving, smelling and moving like the real ship it is simulating. More than this, some of the time it is used in ways indistinguishable from a real ship (this points at the importance of the reality, fidelity and truth of the training scenario). One of the physical simulators used at a DISCOVER partner site was exploited to help determine which trainees should be promoted. We (as part of the project team) were told of one instance where a trainee was involved in a (virtual) collision between his (virtual) ship and a (virtual) dock which resulted in his (real) dismissal.

As we have already noted, the aim of the maritime-aspect DISCOVER project was to create a real–virtual ship which could be used to deliver credible safety-critical training to senior mariners. The challenge was to create that sense of 'my ship' when engaged with the CVE maritime simulator.

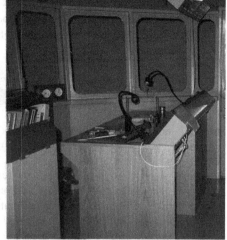

Figure 1. A physical simulator (exterior view). The large grey structure houses a ship simulator at the Danish Maritime Institute (DMI). The large floors of the structure house the array of computers which are required to drive the virtual reality displays near the top of the simulator.

Figure 2. This is a view of the interior of a smaller physical simulator located at DMI. The control panel is an accurate recreation of the instruments on a real ship's bridge. The presence of books and charts is authentic. The 'greyed-out' panels are 'windows' out of which can be seen the virtual scene.

While it would be stretching the truth to say that we succeeded in creating a *sense of ship*, we did learn that the most important factor was the realism of the narrative used to engage / train the mariners (see Turner and Turner, 2002). We return to the role of narrative in creating virtual places later in this chapter.

Virtual tourism

The BENOGO project is part of the Future and Emerging Technology (FET) programme funded by the European Union (2002-2005), intended to identify key VR research areas. BENOGO is developing novel technology while in parallel defining an application for that technology. The technology is concerned with real-time image based rendering (e.g. Bakstein and Pajdla 2003; Feldman *et al.*, 2003) while the application area is 'being there without going' – to quote the project's by-line. Rather than visiting a place in person, individuals will be able to experience a specific place, say, the interior of Notre Dame in Paris by donning a head mounted display (HMD) through which photorealistic images will be experienced. Early experiments with the BENOGO technology have hinted at what might be achieved but also highlight the very real challenges of trying to recreate real places convincingly. In the first of these studies a photo-realistic virtual representation of a glasshouse in the Prague botanical gardens was recreated (figure 3 is an image taken in the botanical gardens). Participants experienced a 360 panorama of the interior of the tropical glasshouse via a head-mounted display.

Figure 3. An image captured in the Botanical Gardens in Prague and used in the first of the BENOGO experiments.

A second study used a photo-realistic representation of a spacious stairway and landing at the Technical University of Prague, again presented by a head-mounted display. This was augmented by a computer-generated table on the landing behind which participants sat on at real table and chair. The audio environment was silent save for the augmented sound of breaking glass. The major difference in this study was the introduction of a contextualising narrative in the form of a scenario. Participants were asked to imagine themselves as a security guard on the stairs and to report any untoward events to security control room staff (played by a member of the project team). The sound of breaking glass part way through the ten minutes exploration was designed to fit this scenario.

Figure 4. Sitting at the top of the stairs as a security guard

Though the two experimental studies were very broadly similar in terms of their technical aspects, the experiences they afforded differed significantly. People were much more engaged in the security guard study and even found a rationale for sounds and movements which were not intentionally introduced into the environment but which were consistent with the scenario. As one participant said, while playing the role of the security guard,

> "I think it took a lot of my attention just looking down, if anybody were coming in or going and then of course I was listening to all these... these voices around ..."

The voices were overheard from unrelated activity in the surrounding laboratory. This highlights (at least) two important issues: firstly, the use of a meaningful narrative significantly adds to engagement and sense of being in that place. Secondly, tools and instruments used in the evaluation of virtual environments are too decontextualised to be of any great value in situations such as this.

DISCUSSION AND FURTHER WORK

At present, the users of virtual reality systems are (broadly) either researchers, experimental subjects, games players, members of the military or trainees learning their way around something like the ISS. Collectively they are all (not only those participants in explicit virtual being-in-another-place applications such as BENOGO) virtual reality *tourists*. A tourist is someone who has travelled to another place for a brief sojourn, an experience that necessarily entails a distinct period of transition and discontinuity from the everyday world. In Relph's terms, the successful tourist experience, depending on individual disposition, is one of behavioural or empathetic insideness, or in unsympathetic conditions one of incidental or even existential outsideness. The concept of virtual reality as *tourism* brings together a fair representation of the actual process of donning an HMD and being transported to another world and the first-person experience of being elsewhere. This leaves the vexed question as to the role of the body. While a convincing case for the importance of the body in the creation and experience of place has been made by Merleau-Ponty and others, the state of current VR technology is not up to the task. Instead we argue that the role of the body in virtual environments can be attenuated by recognising that a tourist's corporeality may be less important than their visual sense.

Virtual environments visited by the tourist are subject to what Urry (2002) describes as the *tourist gaze*. Recalling Foucault's medical gaze, Urry notes that the tourist gaze is 'directed to features of the landscape, which separate them off from everyday experience. Such aspects are viewed because they are taken to be in some sense out of the ordinary." Often the gaze is static, from a vantage point such as a balcony or 'official' viewpoint, or if mobile, insulated from the world by the windows of a train or the route of a sign-posted walk. The gaze is directed by anticipation and imagination, by the promotional narratives of the tourism industry, by cultural stereotypes and expectations. Both tourists and prime tourist sites are manipulated so that the gaze falls upon what the gazer expects to see – untidy aspects of real life are tidied away or outlawed, (houses in the English Lake District must be built to traditional styles and of traditional materials) and the 'typical' features brought to prominence (for example by routing the tourist on scenic walks or populating historic sites with artisans in traditional costume.) Some places – French towns are particularly good at this – prime the tourist gaze by announcing the attractions on the place-name sign marking the town boundary "ses églises, son marché, ses fromages..." As Culler notes, tourists act as semioticians, reading the landscape for signifiers of certain pre-established notions or signs derived from various discourses of travel and tourism (Culler: 1981:128).

Returning to the tourist gaze, Urry details nine different aspects (his numbering is preserved) of which we present a sample of the more relevant to the current discussion:

> [2.] Tourist relationships arise from a movement of people to, and their stay in, various destinations. This necessarily involves some movement through space, that is the journeys, and periods of stay in a new place or places.
>
> [3.] ... there is a clear intention to return 'home' within a relatively short period of time.
>
> [4.] The places gazed upon for purposes not directly connected with [...] work and [...] offer some distinct contrast with work
>
> [6.] Places are chosen to be gazed upon because there is anticipation, especially through daydreaming and fantasy [...] Such anticipation is constructed and sustained through a variety of non-tourist practices, such as film, TV [...] which construct and reinforce that gaze.
>
> [8.] The gaze is constructed through signs and tourism involves collections of signs. When tourists see two people kissing in Paris what they capture in the gaze is 'timeless romantic Paris'

The adoption of the metaphor of the tourist and his or her accompanying selective gaze discloses a new way to reason about, design and evaluate both traditional and contextualised virtual environments.

FURTHER WORK

We have highlighted aspects from the philosophical treatments of place, the body and being-in-the-world which suggested how such approaches may contribute to creating contextualised presence and have led us to propose the metaphor of the virtual tourist. We have also seen how the phenomenological approach have been used to great effect in the understanding of the experience of place. We conclude by identifying further work which might be undertaken in pursuit of the aim of contextualising virtual environments. The three main research lines are:

1.   Making 'reality' more tractable and ...
2.   Designing for the tourist gaze
3.   Employing chiaroscuro rather than photorealism.

While the first two of these research questions are logically separate, they are more naturally treated as two aspects of the same issue.

Restricted Reality And The Tourist Gaze

Recreating real places using virtual reality is the stuff of science fiction. The computational demands of recreating a place which would satisfy for all of our senses are astronomical (there are also telling *in principle* objections too). One way of dealing with this problem is to, in some sense, restrict reality. This is already true of real world tourism. Urry has demonstrated that being a tourist is to be managed; is being exposed to a cut-down (inauthentic) version of the place being visited; is to be whisked along the tourist trail in an air-conditioned coach. Elsewhere, we have suggested that the recreation of real places might be restricted to viewpoints - where we are encouraged to gaze at a feature from the comfort of a public car park. Alternately we might recreate places which can only be viewed from a particular range of orientations and elevations (Turner and Turner, in press). This is the stuff of stage design from which we can learn.

Having constrained reality we now turn our attention to the question of priming the tourist. Without wishing to overstretch the metaphor, we must prepare the VR participant for their 'trip'. Real world tourists read guide books, watch travel programmes and generally *invest* in their trip, constructing a narrative of the journey long before closing the front door. It is, after all supposed to be pleasurable or interesting. We need, then to investigate managing the transition from the real to the virtual world. Once there, the tourist orients themselves, heads for the key attractions; follows the signage; display canonical behaviour. We need to establish, develop the equivalents in virtual environments. In short, we need to find ways to prime or direct our VR tourists so that the essential elements which convey a sense of place attract the gaze.

Chiaroscuro Rather Than Photorealism

The third line of research we have identified would remove the focus on the fidelity of recreation of a real place, and instead draw inspiration from the use of chiaroscuro by artists, the practice of stage and set designers, the reinforcing role of narrative and the research of place and tourism researchers. Artists such as JMW Turner, for example, deconstructed the traditional water colour technique further in his fine gradations of colour and light. His portrayals of Venice are a compelling instance of the creation of a sense of place through a 2-dimensional canvas. In many of his works, Turner's Venice is conveyed through impressionistic sketches, details are absent or vague, the edges of the space ill-defined. Yet the spectator is transported to the Rialto or St. Mark's Square. Chiaroscuro is a technique which employs light and shade in pictorial representation to achieve a heightened illusion of depth – to model body and form more clearly and to create an emotional response to the scene.

In raising the possibilities of adopting such an approach with one our colleagues on the BENOGO project, she commented, "[having worked] as a scenographer mean to arrange space by using different effects (movement, time, space, light, sound, texture, colour, smell and temperature) to generate the desired feelings. Working with the physical environment as VR, means to transport the sensed data from the physical world to the virtual environment. The problem by finding the essence of a place is that it may become very subjective because the person who tries to find the essence reads his or her own feelings being in that place".

ACKNOWLEDGEMENTS

We gratefully acknowledge the support of the EU for the BENOGO project, the contribution of our other BENOGO partners and in particular the work of Rod McCall and Shaleph O'Neill at Napier with the third author on the collection and preliminary analysis of the data. Thanks also to Lisbeth Wittendorff Lorentzen of the University of Ejsberg for her comments on scenography.

AFFILIATIONS

Phil Turner, Susan Turner and Fiona Carroll, School of Computing, Napier University, Edinburgh.

REFERENCES

Alcañiz, M., Baños, R., Botella, C., Cottone, P., Freeman, J., Gaggioli. A, Keogh, E., Mantovani, F., Mantovani, G., Montesa, J., Peripiña, C., Rey, B. Riva, G. and Waterworth, J. (2002) The EMMA Project: Engaging Media for Mental Health Applications. *Proc. Fifth Annual International Workshop Presence 2002*, Porto, Portugal, 201-212.
Bakstein, H. and Pajdla, T. (2003) Rendering novel views from a set of omni-directional mosaic images. In *Proceedings of Omnivis 2003*. Los Alamitos: IEEE Press.
Canter, D. (1977) *The Psychology of Place*. London: Architectural Press.
Canter, D. (1997) The Facets Of Place. In G. T. Moore and R. W. Marans, (Eds.), *Advances in Environment, Behavior, and Design, Vol. 4: Toward the Integration of Theory, Methods, Research, and Utilization*. New York: Plenum, 109-147.
Casey, E.S. (1997). *The Fate of Place*. Univ. of California Press, Berkeley & Los Angeles
Culler, J. (1981) Semiotics of Tourism, *American Journal of Semiotics*, **1(1-2)**, 127-140
Dourish, P. (2000) *Where the action is*. MIT Press.
Downing, F. (2003) Transcending memory: remembrance and the design of place, *Design Studies*, **24(3)**, 213-235.
Feldman, D., Assaf, Z., Weinshall, D. and Peleg, S. (2003) New View Synthesis with Non-Stationary Mosaicing. In *Proceedings of Mirage 2003*, INRIA, France.
Gibson, J.J. (1986) *The Ecological Approach To Visual Perception*, Lawrence Erlbaum Associates, Hillsdale, NJ.
Gustafson, P. (2001) Meanings of place: Everyday experience and theoretical conceptualizations, *Journal of Environmental Psychology*, **21**, 5-16.
Jorgensen, B. S. and Stedman, R. C. (2001) Sense of place as an attitude: Lakeshore owners attitudes towards their properties. *Journal of Environmental Psychology*, **21**, 233-248.
Lessiter, J., Freeman, J., Keogh, E., and Davidoff, J. D. (2001). A Cross-Media Presence Questionnaire: The ITC Sense of Presence Inventory. *Presence: Tele-operators and Virtual Environments*, **10(3)**, 282-297.

Lombard, M. and Ditton, T. (1997) At the heart of it all: The concept of Presence. *Journal of Computer-Mediated Communication*, **3(2)**. Published electronically.

Merleau-Ponty, M. (1945) *The Phenomenology Of Perception*. London: Routlege

Murrell, K.F.H. (1965) *Ergonomics – Man in his working environment*, London: Chapman and Hall.

Relph, E. (1976) *Place and Placelessness*, London: Pion Books

Ryan, M.-L. (2000) *Narrative As Virtual Reality: Immersion And Interactivity In Literature and Electronic Media*. Baltimore: Johns Hopkins University Press.

Seamon D. (no date) http://www.arch.ksu.edu/seamon/index.htm

Schloerb, D. W. (1995) A Quantitive Measure Of Telepresence. *Presence: Tele-operators and Virtual Environments*, **4(1)**, 64-80.

Sixsmith, J. (1986). The meaning of home: An exploratory study of environmental experience. *Journal of Environmental Psychology*, **6**, 281-298.

Slater M., Usoh M. & Steed A. (1994). Depth of presence in virtual environments. *Presence, Tele-operators and Virtual Environments*, **3**, 130-144

Slater, M., Steed, A., McCarthy, J. and Marinelli, F. (1998) The influence of body movement on presence in virtual environments, *Human Factors*, **40,** 469-477.

Stefanovic, I.L. (1998) Phenomenological encounters with place: Cavtat to Square One, *Journal of Environmental Psychology*, **18**, 31–44

Tuan, Y.-F. (1997) *Space and Place: the Perspective of Experience*. Minneapolis: University of Minnesota Press.

Turner, P. and Turner, S. (2000) Cui Bono?, *Proceedings of the 1st French-British Virtual Reality International Workshop*, Brest, July 2000.

Turner, P. and Turner, S. (2002) Embedding context of use in CVE design. *Presence: Tele-operators and virtual environments*, **11(6)**, 665-676.

Turner, P. and Turner, S. (to appear) Place and Sense of Place. *Presence: Tele-operators and virtual environments*.

Urry, J. (2002) *The Tourist Gaze* (second edition). London: Sage.

Whitehead, A.N.(1925/ 1997) *Science and the Modern World*. Free Press.

Witmer, B.G. and Singer, M.J. (1998) Measuring Presence in Virtual Environments: A Presence Questionnaire. *Presence: Teleoperators and Virtual Environments*, **7(3)**, 225-240.

INDEX